THE CHRISTIAN HERITAGE OF THE 50 UNITED STATES OF AMERICA

D1534016

Catherine Millard
Eph. 2:8-10
6:10-18
Phil 4:8,13
Psalm 106:35

THE CHRISTIAN HERITAGE OF THE 50 UNITED STATES OF AMERICA

Catherine Millard, D. Min.

Illustrator: Maxwell Edgar

Christian Heritage Ministries
6597 Forest Dew Court
Springfield, VA 22152
(703) 455-0333

www.christianheritagetours.com

ISBN: 0-9658616-5-1

Library of Congress Catalog Card No: 00-091176

© 1999 by Catherine Millard

Published by: Christian Heritage Ministries
Distributed by: Christian Heritage Tours, Inc.

Illustrator: Maxwell Edgar

DEDICATION

To our valiant, prayerful State Coordinators in each of the 50 United States of America, who have worked diligently to establish "Christian Heritage Week" for the youth of their State — America's future leaders — on a State-by-State basis.

*Seals of the 50 United States of America — Genealogical
Tree Tapestry.* National Cathedral, Washington, D.C.

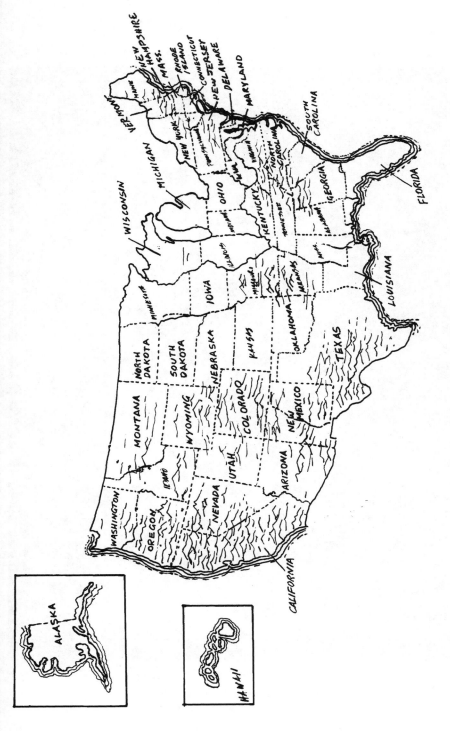

Map of the 50 United States of America.

DEFINITIONS OF HERALDIC TERMS USED IN THE DESCRIPTION OF STATES' COATS OF ARMS

Azure – blue in color

Charge – that which is depicted on the shield

Cincture – a belt or girdle

Crest – figure above the shield (usually an animal or bird resting on a wreath)

Dejected – thrown down or overturned

Dexter – right-hand side of shield

Embowed – bent

Ensigned – having something placed above, as a staff ensigned with a flag

Fillet – ribbon or band

Gules – red in color

In fess – placed like a fesse, that is, horizontal bar across the shield, occupying one-third part between center and base, supposed to represent a knight's belt or girdle

Or – gold

Phrygian cap – liberty cap

Proper – in natural color

Quasi – seeming

Sable – black

Sinister – left-hand side of shield

Supporters – the figures placed on each side of the shield to support it

Table of Contents

Overview of the States

The United States of America: Wonder of wonders among nations! Never in the history of the world had a nation been born like that of the United States. Never had such high and noble principles been incorporated within the legal framework and founding documents of a nation. Never before had small ragtag armies from 13 independent, weak colonies united themselves with a resolve that enabled them to fight and win a war against the world power of that day. Never before had a young nation so quickly gained recognition and respect among all the nations of the world. Never before had a people so submitted themselves to God and His government, thus reaping the fruit of liberty for themselves, their families, their cities, states and nation. That liberty which originated from God Himself, included God's mighty hand of protection, guidance and favor.

But the war against Great Britain having been won in 1781, and the 13 colonies transformed into states, this nation faced a new challenge: Could it govern itself as one united body and yet maintain the individuality of each independent state? John Quincy Adams, sixth president of the United States, delivered an address entitled *The Jubilee of the Constitution** on April 30, 1839, for the 50th anniversary of the inaugural of George Washington as President of the United States. Referring to the Revolutionary War, he stated:

> Six long years it raged with unabated fury, and the Union was yet
> no more than a mutual pledge of faith, and mutual participation of
> common sufferings and common dangers. The omnipotence of the
> British Parliament was vanquished. The independence of the United
> States of America was not granted, but recognized. The nation had
> 'assumed among the powers of the earth, the separate and equal
> station, to which the laws of nature and nature's God, entitled it,' -
> but the one, united people had yet NO GOVERNMENT...there still
> remained the last and crowning act, which the people of the Union,
> alone were competent to perform - the institution of civil government,
> for that compound nation, the United States of America...

A Faulty Foundation

The Articles of Confederation, adopted by Congress in 1777, served as the governing structure for the new nation for eight years. However, it was a weak document and faulty at its very foundation. It was inconsistent with the *Declaration of Independence,* that brilliant document adopted on July 4, 1776, which expressed to the world the new nation's grievances against Great Britain and the principles upon which she declared war as her only recourse. At the heart of the document was the acknowledgement of God Himself - basing their rights to become an independent nation upon "the laws of nature and of nature's God," enumerating the rights of man "*endowed* upon them by their Creator . . . appealing to the Supreme Judge of the world" and relying on the "protection of Divine Providence." In addition, it declared that "governments are instituted among men, deriving their just powers from the *consent* of the governed, and in conclusion, stating that the Declaration was adopted by the representatives "in the name and by the authority of the good people of these colonies," and that they acted as one body, "the United States of America."

* See Appendix I of this book for longer excerpts of John Quincy Adams' Address.

The *Articles of Confederation,* on the other hand, were of a different nature. Adams pointed out that the Declaration was based upon the foundation of God's law, written upon the heart of man, whereas the *Articles of Confederation* was based on "human institutions, and prescriptive law and colonial charters." He said, "the cornerstone of the one was right, that of the other was power." While the Declaration had been issued by the authority of the people of the *united* colonies, the *Articles of Confederation* maintained the sovereignty of each state - contrary to, and at odds with, the principle of a united nation.

For years the Continental Congress and state legislatures struggled to refine the faulty document. It was George Washington who first suggested a complete revising of the *Articles of Confederation.* A convention of delegates from the state legislatures, apart from the Congress itself, met for the first time in September of 1786. A second convention was held in Philadelphia in May 1787 in the same room in which the Declaration of Independence had been signed. Concerning it, Adams wrote:

> The Constitution of the United States was the work of this Convention. But in its construction the Convention immediately perceived that they must retrace their steps, and fall back from a league of friendship between the sovereign states, to the constituent sovereignty of the people; from power to right - from the irresponsible despotism of state sovereignty, to the self-evident truths of the *Declaration of Independence.* In that instrument, the right to institute and to alter governments among men was ascribed exclusively to the people - the ends of government were declared to be to secure the natural rights of man; and that when the government degenerates from the promotion to the destruction of that end, the right and the duty accrues to the people, to dissolve this degenerate government and to institute another...A Constitution for the people, and the distribution of the legislative, executive and judicial powers, was prepared. It announced itself as the work of the people themselves...

The Constitution

Adopted by Congress on September 17, 1787, the Constitution was sent to the legislatures of the states, each calling a convention to consider whether or not to ratify the document. When nine states approved, it would become the supreme law of the land. Months of debate and fiery discussion resulted. Often by narrow majorities, the states gave their approval. Delaware, Pennsylvania and New Jersey were the first states to ratify, all in December of 1787. By August of 1788, a total of 11 states had ratified, and Congress decided that the Constitution would go into effect on March 4, 1789. George Washington was unanimously elected President by the electoral college, and Congress made New York City its temporary capital. The two remaining states finally ratified - North Carolina in November of 1789 and Rhode Island in May of 1790.

At that time, the people of each state were largely isolated from the other states, and even from those within their own state. The entire population of the United States in 1790 was only about four million people, who mainly lived along the Atlantic seacoast. Most lived by farming or fishing with no machinery to save on labor. Only about 100,000 had ventured beyond the Allegheny Mountains. Bad roads kept people isolated. Stagecoaches took a week to go from Boston to New York. Both of these cities were unpaved, unlighted towns with animals roaming the streets. There was little manufacturing, and communication was poor. It had taken nearly a month for the Declaration of Independence to travel from Philadelphia to Charleston, South Carolina. There were few newspapers, and books were rare.

But the bond of unity having been established through the years of struggle for independence, and a firm Biblical foundation having been finally established to govern the nation, it grew rapidly.

The Northwest Ordinance

While the Continental Congress under the *Articles of Confederation* had been weak, it did succeed in passing one of the most profound pieces of legislation in the history of nations. A vast wilderness of land, west of the Alleghenies and northwest of the Ohio River, called the Northwest Territory, had been won in the war with the British. Through the efforts of men like Thomas Jefferson, the established states agreed to relinquish any claims to this land. The *Northwest Ordinance of 1787* provided that the inhabitants of new states in the territory would be admitted to the United States "on an equal footing with the original states in all respects whatever, and shall be at liberty to form a permanent constitution and state government." In addition, it prohibited slavery in the new states.

The significance of this legislation is that throughout history most nations that had acquired new territories made them colonies that were subjects and subordinates. But one of the first pieces of legislation of the new nation was a revolutionary move in that the new states, once they had grown sufficiently, could take their place as equals among the already established states. It was indeed evidence of the Christian character of the new nation and a reflection of the generous nature of God Himself.

Once established, it became the guiding principle as other territories were acquired, and more states added. Thus began the great westward migration. The result was that within 125 years, the nation had grown to 48 states stretching from the Atlantic to the Pacific, with two more added in 1959.

In 1791, Vermont having played an important role in the Revolution, became the 14th state, the first to be added to the original 13. Kentucky, originally part of Virginia, had grown dissatisfied with the distant political authority of Virginia, the latter eventually consenting to a separation in 1789, and Kentucky became the 15th state in 1792. Tennessee, once part of North Carolina, was admitted to the Union in 1796. Maine gained separation from Massachusetts in 1819, and admission to statehood in 1820. Mississippi was admitted in 1817, and Alabama in 1819.

In 1803, Ohio became the first of five states admitted to the Union from the Northwest Territory. The others were admitted as follows: Indiana in 1816, Illinois in 1818, Michigan in 1837 and Wisconsin in 1848. By 1850, the once wilderness of the Northwest Territory had become a thriving and important part of the nation, with two major metropolitan centers, Chicago and Cincinnati.

The Louisiana Purchase

God's favor and provision for the nation was again evident in 1803 with the purchase of the Louisiana Territory, which doubled the size of the country. Proverbs 21:1 states that, "The king's heart is in the hand of the Lord, as the rivers of water: He turneth it whithersoever He will."

When President Thomas Jefferson sent James Monroe to France to assist Robert R. Livingston in negotiations for the purchase of the Port of New Orleans and its immediate area, his sole purpose was to secure free navigation of the Mississippi River for the United States. It was not expected that the mission to purchase the land for $10,000,000 or less would be successful.

To the astonishment of the American ambassadors, the negotiations which had been going nowhere, suddenly took a complete turn-around. Napoleon and his ministers offered to sell the whole Louisiana Territory for $15,000,000. Thomas Jefferson wisely accepted it.

The vast area, though not clearly defined, extended from the Mississippi to the Rocky Mountains. The Lewis and Clark Expedition was sent to explore the territory all the way to the Pacific. Much opposition followed with many prominent leaders predicting it would take hundreds of years to inhabit the vast wilderness. However, only nine years later, Louisiana became the first state of the territory to be admitted to the Union. In all, 13 states or parts of states were made out of the territory:

> Missouri, 1821; Arkansas, 1836; Iowa, 1846; Minnesota, 1858; Kansas, 1861;
> Nebraska, 1867; Colorado, 1876; North and South Dakota, 1889; Montana, 1889;
> Wyoming, 1890 and Oklahoma, 1907.

Florida

As with the Louisiana Territory, there were often no clear definitions of boundaries in the wilderness areas, and much uncertainty as to what country owned a particular portion of land. Such was the case with Florida. After years of conflicting claims, the United States purchased the region from Spain for $5,000,000 in 1821. Florida became a state in 1845.

Texas and States West

Texas had first been explored by Spanish adventurers from Mexico. After the Louisiana Purchase in 1803, many Americans, including slave-holders, began to settle in the area. In 1822, Mexico won its independence from Spain. Conflicts arose between the settlers and the Mexican government, resulting in war. In 1836 Texas declared independence from Mexico, and shortly after, offered to join herself to the United States, which was at first declined, due to opposition to the extension of the slave territory. It became a key issue in the presidential election of 1844, and the following year Texas was annexed as the 28th state.

A dispute over whether the Rio Grande River was the boundary between Mexico and the United States led to war. In a Peace Treaty signed in 1848, Mexico was paid $15,000,000 and ceded a vast territory stretching from Texas to the Pacific. The area was further expanded by the Gadsden Purchase of 1853 (Southern New Mexico and Arizona).

The Gold Rush in 1848 vastly increased the population of California, which gained statehood in 1850. Likewise, the discovery of gold in Nevada in 1859 marked her increase in population, and she became a state in 1864, even though she lacked the required number of residents for statehood. Other states that had been part of the territory ceded by Mexico were Utah, admitted in 1896; New Mexico and Arizona in 1912 and portions of Kansas, Colorado and Wyoming.

West Virginia was originally part of Virginia, but separated by the Allegheny Mountains. The two were vastly different from one another. In 1861, when Virginia withdrew from the Union, the northwestern counties declared their independence from the mother state. West Virginia was admitted to statehood in 1863.

Oregon Region

The arrival of missionaries marked the first permanent American settlements in the Oregon Region, which included the three states west of the Rocky Mountains and north of California. It was claimed by the United States and Great Britain. Missionary Marcus Whitman personally led a caravan of 200 wagons across the treacherous land, civilization following Christianity. In 1846, England gave up her claim to the territory. Oregon became a state in 1859, Washington in 1889 and Idaho in 1890.

Alaska and Hawaii

The last two states, both admitted to the Union in 1959, are vastly different from one another. Alaska, the northernmost and largest state, had been controlled and exploited for years by trading monopolies. The United States purchased Alaska from Russia in 1867 for $7.2 million. American missionaries introduced Christianity to Hawaii in 1820, and brought great advancements to the Hawaiian people. In 1893 the native queen was deposed, and Hawaii asked to be joined to the United States. Annexation took place in 1898, and Hawaii became the 50th state on August 21, 1959.

Introduction

At the dawn of a new century, it is time for the 50 states of these United States of America to rediscover and retrieve the Christian heritage that rightfully belongs to them. May this book, *The Christian Heritage of the 50 United States of America,* serve as a source of information, inspiration and commitment from the citizens of each state as they reflect upon the noble words, deeds and sacrifices of their forefathers.

The cause is timely, because an insidious agenda is underway at the very heart of the nation and her 50 states. In the last 10 to 15 years, persons seeking to rewrite America's history have launched attacks on states, towns, counties, cities and precincts. In much the same way, these same agents previously attacked our national history. Atheists, modernists promoting a one-world government, and groups such as the American Civil Liberties Union are often backed by unlimited funds, and the liberal media, library and education establishments. In attempts to foist their politically-oriented version of history upon the American people, they further their cause through tactics that include lies, deceit, censorship and removal of historic records and documents, the rewriting of history, and attempts to intimidate those who would oppose them. Education has been targeted, beginning with the youngest of children and continuing through college and university-age students. They carry their influence into government at all levels.

Following are just a few brief summaries of some of these attacks.

Kentucky: On May 5, 2000 in a preliminary injunction, the U.S. District Court ordered the removal of the Ten Commandments, along with key historic documents, from two courthouses and a mountain school district. The documents included: The Mayflower Compact; Abraham Lincoln's statement, "The Bible is the best gift God has ever given to man;" the national motto, "In God we Trust;" the first sentence of the Preamble of the Declaration of Independence; and the Preamble of the Kentucky Constitution.

State of Ohio: The state motto, "With God all Things are Possible," was declared unuseable by the U.S. Sixth Circuit Court of Appeals on April 25, 2000.

Stow, Ohio: This city was forced in February, 1999 by the American Civil Liberties Union, to remove the cross of Christ from its historic seal, which dates back to the 1600's.

Edmond, Oklahoma: The American Civil Liberties Union won a court ruling over the citizens of this city in June, 1996 that required them to remove the cross of Christ from their historic seal, dating back to the 1880's.

San Diego County, California: In 1993, the citizens of the city of La Mesa were taken to court by the American Civil Liberties Union, and forced to remove the cross of Christ from their historic seal dating back to the 1700's.

Zion, Illinois: In 1992, the City of Zion was forced by the American Atheists group to remove the cross of Christ and "God Reigns" from their historic seal.

These attacks have been all too successful. Our founding fathers never would have permitted such atrocities. But today's citizens are often ignorant of the truth and uninformed, thus allowing their irreplaceable history to be removed. My prayer for this book is that we become educated and equipped to stand up and preserve the liberties for which our forefathers pledged their lives, their fortunes and their sacred honor.

My Own Fascination With American History

Having grown up on the continent of Africa, I first became fascinated with the heroes of early American history while studying in France as a young woman. Years later, and then living in the United States, I became a Christian as well as a U.S. citizen, and thus began the exciting unfolding to me of the connection between America's rich history and the Bible itself. I learned that her unique history was due to a carefully and prayerfully laid foundation by men and women who had put God first in both their lives and their nation.

My own life took a dramatic turn-around when I lost control of my car in a blinding snowstorm in 1979, but was miraculously saved as I cried out to God. From that time, my passion became the study of God's Word. I withdrew from the master's degree program I had nearly completed and spent the next three years in seminary.

Having taken a part-time job as a multi-lingual interpreter/tour guide in our nation's capital, I became familiar with the historic landmarks, and discovered more and more evidences of our Christian heritage in buildings, monuments, sculpture, art and artifacts. The more people asked questions, the more I researched to find the answers, spending many hours studying original documents in the Library of Congress.

I became increasingly aware that the Christian element of our history - though so prominently engraved upon landmarks and buildings - was blatantly absent from the guide books and presentations, and even the exhibits themselves. The Lord directed me to write my first book, *God's Signature Over Our Nation's Capital*.

In 1984, I founded and incorporated Christian Heritage Tours to provide tours that tell the truth about the history of this nation in our capital city, which soon expanded to include other key historic sites such as Pennsylvania's Philadelphia, Gettysburg, and Valley Forge, and Jamestown, Yorktown and Williamsburg, Virginia.

In time, I became more aware that this deliberate rewriting of America's history was prevalent in our children's textbooks in the schools. Courses in history and geography have been replaced with global studies. Today a generation of public school students can complete 12 years of elementary and high school training with virtually no understanding of the Christian heritage upon which the nation was founded and developed. Sadly, most college and university students are no better informed.

As I became aware of this great loss, I continued to research America's original history, resuming post-graduate studies for my D.Min. in Christian Education. I found it necessary to write more books, including: *The Rewriting of America's History, A Children's Companion Guide to America's History, Great American Statesmen and Heroes, The Christian Heritage of Our Nation - History Curricula - National Landmarks; National Memorials;* and *U.S. Presidents and Their Churches*.

In 1991, I launched a new outreach, Christian Heritage Ministries, to institute observances of "Christian Heritage Week" in each state. New Mexico was the first state to celebrate her Christian heritage with a proclamation by the governor, November 10-16, 1991. To date, all 50 States in the Union have observed "Christian Heritage Week" during the academic school year.

While the wonders of this nation founded in 1776 have been sung around the world, not many are aware of the 50 stories that were written as each state became a part of the Union.

But may the turn of the century mark a new period in America's Christian history - one in which both adults and children learn once again the great stories of this nation and her 50 states. May it inspire us to rededicate our lives to the Lord Jesus Christ, to study and know the Word of God and how to apply it to every area of our lives - from personal, to governmental levels. May we become faithful in our praying for this nation, and may the pastors of America preach the mighty revival sermons common in the founding era of this country. May we not only become remembrancers of our history, but may we, the U. S. citizens of today, walk in the footsteps of our founding fathers, reestablishing the Biblical foundation which they so carefully laid, and following the illustrious examples of our American forebears.

– Catherine Millard

LAUS DEO

GEORGE WASHINGTON MEMORIAL WINDOW

*After the Original in the U.S. Capitol. General Washington
is pictured in Conference with General Lafayette and Baron
von Steuben in a Revolutionary War Scene of 1780.*

After the Original Marble Statue in the Hall of Fame, U.S. Capitol, Washington D.C.

ALABAMA
(name of an Indian tribe)

The Preamble to the Constitution of the State of Alabama states that, *We the people of the State of Alabama, in order to establish justice, insure domestic tranquility, and secure the blessings of liberty to ourselves and our posterity, invoking the favor and guidance of Almighty God, do ordain and establish the following Constitution and form of government for the State of Alabama.*

Alabama joined the Union on December 14, 1819 as the 22nd State.

State Capital: Montgomery.

State Motto:
"Audemus Jura Nostra Defendere," translated from Latin to mean, "We Dare Defend Our Rights."

State Creed:
> *"I believe in Alabama, a state dedicated to a faith in God and the enlightenment of mankind; to a democracy that safeguards the liberties of each citizen and to the conservation of her youth, her ideals, and her soil. I believe it is my duty to obey her laws, to respect her flag and to be alert to her needs and generous in my efforts to foster her advancement within the statehood of the world."*[1]

State Seal:
The seal of Alabama consists of a map of the territory showing its rivers; with surrounding States. It originated with William Wyatt Bibb, Governor of Alabama Territory in 1817.[2]

State Coat of Arms:
The shield is supported on either side by bald eagles, symbolic of courage. The crest is a model of the ship, the Baldine, that Iberville and Bienville sailed from France to settle a colony near present-day Mobile (1699). The motto beneath the shield is "Audemus Jura Nostra Defendere," translated from Latin to read, "We Dare Defend Our Rights." Beneath the motto is the state name.[3]

State Bible:
The State Bible was purchased for use by the Executive Department in 1853. It has been used continuously by the state for the inauguration of Alabama governors since that time. On the flyleaf of the Bible is an inscription: "Executive Office, Alabama, 1853."

In 1861 when Jefferson Davis took the oath of office as President of the provisional government of the Confederate States of America, he also used the State Bible. Inside the front cover is a notation by Judge John Phelan who served as Clerk of the Alabama Supreme Court, attesting to the fact that this was the Bible used by Davis. An affidavit was added to the flyleaf in 1884 by Judge Phelan's son, Ellis, who served as Secretary of State. This affidavit states that the handwriting on the note is that of Judge Phelan, who did in fact witness the inauguration of Davis.

After Davis' inaugural address, the oath was administered by Howell Cobb, President of the Provisional Congress. A newspaper reported President Davis kissed the Bible, and then, turning to the vast assemblage, said with deep and solemn emphasis, "So help me God."[4]

State Flag:
According to the *Acts of Alabama, 1895*, the state flag is a crimson cross of St. Andrew on a field of white. The bars forming the cross are not less than six inches broad and extend diagonally across the flag from side to side.[5]

Display:
The Alabama flag should be flown on the dome of the Capitol when the two houses of the legislature are in session and is to be used by the state on all occasions when it is necessary or customary to display a flag.

The flag of the State, as well as the flag of the United States, is required to be displayed every day on which school is in session, at all schools in the State which are supported, even in part, by public funds.

Salute to the Flag:
"Flag of Alabama, I salute thee. To thee I pledge my allegiance, my service, and my life."

State Song:
"ALABAMA"[6]

First "Christian Heritage Week:" March 14-20, 1993, proclaimed by the Governor.

Of Historic Interest:
Jabez Lamar Monroe Curry (1825-1903) was chosen by the citizens of Alabama to represent them in the U.S. Capitol's Hall of Fame. While at Harvard University, he met Rutherford B. Hayes, a fellow-student, whose friendship he maintained throughout life. At the age of 21, he was a volunteer in the Mexican War. During the Civil War, he rendered invaluable service to the Confederacy, as a member of the Confederate House of Representatives in Richmond, and later, as Lieutenant-Colonel of Cavalry under General Joseph Wheeler.[7]

So deeply was this Alabama son affected by the war, that he studied for the ministry, becoming a Baptist Minister of the Gospel. He loyally fulfilled his position as president of a Baptist College in Alabama for three years; subsequently teaching at Richmond College and distinguishing himself as a leader in Southern education.[8]

At his election to the presidency, Rutherford B. Hayes offered Curry a position in his Cabinet, which the latter declined in favor of his career in education.

Curry became a noted preacher, stating that he "loved to preach." He was invited to serve as pastor in seventeen Baptist churches; to include churches in St. Louis, New Orleans and San Francisco. Three invitations to serve as College President - at *Georgetown College,* Kentucky; *Mercer University,* Georgia and *The University of Alabama,* respectively, were declined in favor of Southern education. Among numerous honors and degrees conferred upon him was the Decoration of the Royal Order of Charles III by the Spanish Government for his service as Envoy Extraordinary and Minister Plenipotentiary to Spain.[9]

Jabez Curry is remembered and honored as a selfless Christian educator, preacher, leader and orator.

Other Heroes

World-renowned Helen Keller was born at "Ivy Green," in historic Tuscumbia. "Ivy Green" was built in 1820 by David Keller, grandfather of Helen Keller. The original well-pump where Helen first understood the word "water" remains in the backyard.

A 1915 Library of Congress book issued by the Department of Education is entitled, *Washington's Birthday, Programs and Selections for their Celebration, for Use in the Schools of Alabama.* In it, an exhortation is made to the Teachers of Alabama, as follows:

> The importance of the observance of special days as an essential part of schoolwork cannot be overestimated. In recognition of this idea, a majority of the States in the Union require on the part of the schools the celebration of special days.

> A change in the ordinary routine of school work is demanded for the good of the pupils. Unless accompanied by an inculcation of moral truths and patriotic sentiments the daily schoolwork becomes uninteresting...It has come to be considered a necessity that special attention should, by the observance of the anniversary of great and good men and women, be given to the teaching of the great principles of morality and patriotism...There never was a time in the history of the Union when so much is being written and spoken about the origin of American Institutions and the men who have performed a conspicuous part in establishing and maintaining the government. George Washington was the great central force of the Revolutionary period. We cannot too often direct the attention of the children to his great character. His memory should be treasured and the anniversary of his birth should be celebrated as long as there is a voice among men to shout the praise of freedom.

> I therefore request earnestly that in your school you will set apart the 22nd day of February as a time for the celebration, and that you will join me in an earnest endeavor to have the pupils in every public school in Alabama render a suitable program.
> — Superintendent of Education

Program
— Words of Wisdom of The First American —
— Sayings of Washington —

1st Child — To be prepared for war is one of the most effectual means for preserving peace.

2nd Child — Citizens, by birth or choice, of a common country, that country has a right to concentrate your affections.

3rd Child — The name of an American must always exalt the just pride of patriotism.

4th Child — From the gallantry and fortitude of her citizens, under the auspices of Heaven, America has derived her independence.

5th Child — Observe good faith and justice toward all nations; cultivate peace and harmony with all.

6th Child — The ever favorite object of my heart is, the benign

4

influence of good laws under a free government.

The Original Thirteen
(To be spoken by thirteen children, representing the thirteen original colonies.)

First Child — I am Virginia. I have given my noble sons to my country, but today I wish to speak only of one, the fairest, the most illustrious — Washington.

Second Child — I am New Jersey, and the elms at Princeton still whisper of his fame.

Third Child — I am Massachusetts, and his name is still as powerful among my people as when his cannon frowned upon Boston from Dorchester Heights.

Fourth Child — I am New York, and in my noblest city the first president took his oath of office.

Fifth Child — I am New Hampshire, and I bring granite from my mountains, that his deeds may be written on imperishable tablets.

Sixth Child — I am Maryland, and my Potomac's stream murmurs ever of love as it glides past his tomb.

Seventh Child — I am Connecticut, the land of steady habits, and as a model for our children we hold him up whose title was "An Honest Man."

Eighth Child — I am Rhode Island, and the name of Roger Williams is not more dear to me than the memory of Washington.

Ninth Child — I am Delaware, and when the ice cracks and booms on my noble river it seems to thunder the story of that Christmas night so long ago.

Tenth Child — I am North Carolina, and the shade of Francis Marion bids me join in reverence to his valiant leader.

Eleventh Child — I am South Carolina, and through the storm of war I have kept his memory sacred.

Twelfth Child — I am Pennsylvania, and the old State House at Philadelphia seems to be filled with his invisible presence.

Thirteenth Child — I am Georgia, youngest of all, and I bring palms to celebrate his victories.

Virginia — Let us speak of his truthfulness.

New Jersey — Let us admire his modesty.

Massachusetts — Let us praise his courage.

New York — Let us remember his deeds.

New Hampshire — Let us emulate his piety.

Maryland — Honor the statesman!

Connecticut — The general!

Rhode Island — The truth-teller.

Delaware — The hero!

North Carolina — The Cincinnatus of the west.

South Carolina — The Father of his Country!

Pennsylvania — "Providence left him childless that his country might call him father."

Georgia — Then let us speak of him still as (all joining in) "First in War, First in Peace, First in the Hearts of his Countrymen."

— Lucia M. Mooney

The Banner Betsy Made

(To be recited by a girl dressed in Quaker
costume and carrying a large flag.)

We have nicknamed it "Old Glory"
As it floats upon the breeze.
Rich in legend, song and story
On the land and on the seas;
Far above the shining river,
Over mountain glen and glade
With a fame that lives forever
Streams the banner Betsy made.

Once it went from her, its maker,
To the glory of the wars,
Once the modest little Quaker
Deftly studded it with stars
And her fingers swiftly flying
Through the sunshine and the shade
Welded colors bright, undying,
In the banner Betsy made.

When at last her needle rested
And her cherished work was done,
Went the banner, love-invested,
To the camps of Washington;
And the glorious Continentals
In the morning light arrayed
Stood in rugged regimentals
'Neath the banner Betsy made.

How they cheered it and its maker,
They the gallant sons of wars.
How they blessed the little Quaker
And her flag of stripes and stars;
'Neath its folds, the foemen scorning,
Glinted bayonets and blade,
And the breezes of the morning
Kissed the banner Betsy made.

Years have passed, but still in glory
With a pride we love to see,
Laureled with a nation's glory
Waves the emblem of the free;
From the rugged pines of Northland
To the deep'ning everglade,
In the sunny heart of Southland
Floats the banner Betsy made.

Now she sleeps whose fingers flying
With a heart to freedom true,
Mingled colors bright, undying —
Fashioned stars and field of blue;
It will lack for no defenders
When the nation's foes invade,
For our country close to splendor
'Neath the banner Betsy made.

EDWARD LEWIS "BOB" BARTLETT, 1904-1968, ALASKA

After the Original Bronze Statue in the Hall of Fame, U.S. Capitol,
Washington D.C.

7

ALASKA
(the great land)

The Preamble to the Constitution of the State of Alaska
states that, *We the people of Alaska, grateful to God and to*
those who founded our nation and pioneered this great land...

Alaska joined the Union on January 3, 1959 as the 49th State.

State Capital: Juneau.

State Motto:
"North to the Future."

State Seal:
The rays beyond the mountains portray the famous Alaskan northern lights. The smelter denotes mining; the train depicts Alaska's railroads and the ships her ocean transportation. The trees represent Alaska's timber, while the farmer, his horse and the three bundles of wheat denote agriculture. The fish and seal on the outer borders emphasize the importance of Alaska's fishing and seal industry.

State Flag:
The winning design for Alaska's flag was created by a 13-year-old student, Benny Benson in 1926. It depicts eight gold stars on a field of blue, symbolizing the Big Dipper and the North Star.[1]

State Song:
"Alaska's Flag"[2]

First "Christian Heritage Week:" April 4-10, 1999, proclaimed by the Governor.

Of Historic Interest:
The United States of America paid $7.2 million dollars to Russia for Alaska; negotiated in March, 1867 by William Seward, U.S. Secretary of State and Edward de Stoeckel of Russia.

Alaska's greatest hero in the U.S. Capitol's Hall of Fame is **Senator E.L. "Bob" Bartlett**. An article which appeared in *The Washington Daily News* and *The Evening Star* of December 2, 1970 elaborated upon the subject as follows:

> **Bartlett is Honored**
> The Senate has passed legislation to permit Alaska to place a statue
> of the late Senator E.L. "Bob" Bartlett in the Capitol, where each
> state is allowed to display two statues. His statue would be the first
> for Alaska. Senator Bartlett, who died in 1968, played a key role in
> winning Alaska's statehood.

The Congressional Record of the U.S. Senate dated December 1, 1970 gives an explanation of Senate Concurrent Resolution 2:

> Mr. Mansfield. Mr. President, I am delighted that this signal honor is being accorded to a former colleague of ours, a man who was more responsible than any other person for achieving statehood for Alaska, a man who is deserving of this honor. May I say, speaking personally, that I am delighted my long time friend and former colleague, the late Senator E.L. "Bob" Bartlett, will have a statue placed in Statuary Hall among the other great pioneers and achievers of this nation.

On April 27, 1971, at the *Unveiling Ceremonies* in the U.S. Capitol's Main Rotunda, **Bob Bartlett's** moving words were printed upon the Program Brochure. He stated,

> The Alaska star, the star that makes the 49th in our flag, is fixed in place, secure. It has a magnetic, challenging light which you and I, in our own ways, in love of God, in love of humanity, must keep shining bright.
> — Bob Bartlett, 1959.

American Patriotism

An article entitled, ***American Patriotism and What It Means*** was published in the May, 1917 edition of the magazine, **Alaska**:

> American patriotism consists of being loyal to the spirit of American institutions. This is a land of liberty and law — liberty regulated by law — not license depending on caprice.
>
> It is a land whose cardinal principle is that the people should own and conduct the Government — not a land where the Government owns the people.
>
> It is a land which favors the development of the individual and seeks to accord to him all the freedom of thought and action consistent with the welfare of others — a land where neither life, liberty nor property can be taken without "due process of law" — a land where every man's home is his castle.
>
> This Government, being a Government of the people, is in this war in order that these things may not perish from the face of the earth — that they may not be made to yield to the "divine right of kings."
>
> If one is attached to these things he is an American in spirit. If he does all he can to forward these ends, he is a loyal and patriotic American. — Robert W. Jennings

Of further interest is *President Harding's Tribute*, printed in a 1926 Library of Congress book, ***Glimpses of Alaska from 1728 to the Present Date.*** It is hereunder reprinted:

> The late President Warren G. Harding, upon returning from his memorable trip through Alaska said, in his address in Seattle, July 27, 1923:
>
> "There can be none to dispute to Alaska's preeminence as the empire of scenic wonders. Since the water journey by the inside route is very little less wonderful and impressive than the vast domain of

9

Alaska itself, it would seem that we need only to have our people understand its fascinations and compensations..."

Praise was bestowed on the people of Alaska by the President "as the finest and most hospitable people in all the world."

"There is no finer citizenship in the United States, no more promising a childhood anywhere," he added. "Indeed, in this citizenship and in this vigorous childhood, both devoted to Alaska as the land of their homes, lies the solution of the Alaska problem. In them is the assurance of Alaska's ultimate and adequate development..."

Author Scott C. Bone, in his 1926 volume, *Alaska, Its Past, Present and Future,* records, after President Harding's untimely death:

Tribute at Memorial Meeting in Juneau
"A good name is better than precious ointment; and the day of death than the day of one's birth."

"Sorrow is better than laughter; for by the sadness of the countenance the heart is made better."

So speaketh the Holy Writ.

Warren G. Harding was a godly, God-fearing man. He kept the commandments.

Two short weeks ago, on a beautiful Sabbath Day, he worshipped God in a little native church at Sitka. He joined in the singing of old hymns and was devout and reverent. The simple service rested him. His journey was ending. It was his last day in Alaska.

And now the good God who shapes our destinies has called him Beyond and the entire nation mourns. Alaska mourns him deeply.

Warren G. Harding loved his fellowmen. He loved the beautiful world in which he lived. He loved children. He loved nature. He loved dogs. His great soul was attuned to everything created by his Maker. The beauties of this Northland, its waters and mountains, inspired and overwhelmed him. He loved Alaska. He had implicit faith in Alaska. His tribute to this Territory in the speech which closed his public career was the climax of his memorable journey. It becomes a sacred utterance — a benediction — preceding a longer and final journey.

He was a just man. He dealt justly with mankind. Never by word or act did he knowingly wrong a fellowman. His high office did not put him out of touch with humanity or make of him less of a human being. His heart ever throbbed with affection for all humanity.

He loved his country passionately and served it with unswerving devotion and fidelity. The history of this Republic will give him rank with the very great Presidents of the United States.

10

The key to Warren G. Harding's character is found in the creed he promulgated many years ago for the guidance of his then little newspaper in his home town. He thus enjoined his co-workers:

"Remember there are two sides to every question. Get both.

"Be truthful. Get the facts. I would rather have one story exactly right than a hundred half wrong.

"Be decent. Be fair. Be generous. Boost; don't knock.

"Remember there is good in everybody. Bring out the good and never needlessly hurt the feelings of anyone.

"In reporting a political gathering, get the facts. Tell the story as it is — not as you would like to have it. Treat all parties alike.

"Treat all religious matters reverently.

"If it can possibly be avoided, never bring ignominy to an innocent woman or child in telling of the misdeeds or misfortunes of a relative."

If newspaperdom of this twentieth century would uniformly observe and adhere to such a creed, what a brighter and better world this would be! If in our everyday lives, if in our relations with one another, such a creed were scrupulously practiced, how much happier we should be! There is a sermon in that creed.

A fine, true-hearted, Christian gentleman — a steadfast, helpful friend of Alaska — has gone to his reward. Peace be unto him — peace and rest.

JOHN CAMPBELL GREENWAY 1872-1926

After the Original Bronze Statue of John Campbell
Greenway in the Hall of Fame, U.S. Capitol,
Washington, D.C.

ARIZONA
(from the Indian, "little spring")

The Preamble to the Constitution of the State of Arizona states that, *We the people of the State of Arizona, grateful to Almighty God for our liberties, do ordain this Constitution.*

Arizona joined the Union on February 14, 1912 as the 48th State.

State Capital: Phoenix.

State Motto:
 "Ditat Deus" translated from Latin to mean, "God Enriches."

State Seal:
 In the background of the seal is a range of mountains with the sun rising behind the peaks. At the right side of the range of mountains there is a storage reservoir and a dam. Below this, in the middle distance, are irrigated fields, and orchards reaching into the foreground, at the right of which are cattle grazing. To the left, in the middle distance on a mountain, is a quartz mill in front of which is a miner with a pick and shovel. Above this is the motto "Ditat Deus," meaning, "God Enriches." In a circular band surrounding the whole seal is inscribed: "Great Seal of the State of Arizona" and the year of admission to the Union - 1912.

State Flag:
 The State Flag represents the setting sun, consisting of 13 rays, alternate red and yellow, the upper half. The lower half is a plain blue field. Superimposed on the center of the flag, in the face of the setting sun, is a copper-colored star. The copper color represents one of the State's major industries.[1]

State Song:
 The Arizona State Song (Anthem) was adopted by the Fourth State Legislature. The words were written by Margaret Rowe Clifford and the music by Maurice Blumenthal. The title of the anthem is "Arizona March Song."[2]

ARIZONA MARCH SONG
Come to this land of sunshine
To this land where life is young.
Where the wide, wide world is waiting,
The songs that will now be sung.
Where the golden sun is flaming
Into warm, white, shining day,
And the sons of men are blazing
Their priceless right of way.

Come stand beside the rivers
Within our valleys broad.
Stand here with heads uncovered,
In the presence of our God!
While all around, about us

The brave, unconquered band,
As guardians and landmarks
The giant mountains stand.

Not alone for gold and silver
Is Arizona great.
But with graves of heroes sleeping,
All the land is consecrate!
O, come and live beside us
However far ye roam
Come and help us build up temples
And name those temples "home."

First "Christian Heritage Week:" September 13-19, 1998, proclaimed by the Governor.

Of Historic Interest:

Arizona's hero in the Hall of Fame is **John Campbell Greenway (1872-1926).** It is recorded that whatever Greenway did, he did well, spending two years at the *University of Virginia,* followed by further academic work at *Phillips Andover Academy* in Massachusetts. He entered Yale University's *Sheffield Scientific School,* graduating at age 24. Elected to honor societies, he was also President of his Senior Class.[3]

As a student at Yale University, he met Theodore Roosevelt, a fellow-student, whose friendship he maintained throughout life. In the Spanish War, he became one of Roosevelt's Rough Riders, receiving a Silver Star Citation for bravery. Upon completing his term of office in the White House, Roosevelt received the following telegram from Greenway:

Well done, my good and faithful servant.[4]

Senator Ashurst of Arizona commended this hero with the words,

The superb romance in his career; laborer, captain of industry, athlete, soldier, idealist, philosopher, philanthropist — are attributes stronger than wealth, office or power could bestow, for he was a man of inflexible integrity and unsullied character; a true and pure modesty.[5]

ARKANSAS
(people of the south wind)

> The Preamble to the Constitution of the State of Arkansas states that,
> *We the people of the State of Arkansas, grateful to Almighty God for the
> privilege of choosing our own form of government, for our civil and re-
> ligious liberty, and desiring to perpetuate its blessings and secure the same
> to ourselves and posterity, do ordain and establish this Constitution.*

Arkansas joined the Union on June 15, 1836 as the 25th State.

State Capital: Little Rock.

State Motto:
"Regnat Populus," translated from Latin to mean, "The People Rule."

State Seal:
The shield shows the Angel of Mercy to the viewer's left, and the Sword of Justice to the
viewer's right, while the figure of Liberty is depicted above, encircled by 13 stars representing the 13 original states, surrounded by sunbeams. A central bald eagle, emblem of the
United States, holds in its beak a scroll bearing Arkansas' motto, "Regnat Populus" in Latin,
translated to mean, "The People Rule." The Angel of Mercy holds the shield, denoting a
steamboat, a plow, a beehive and a sheaf of wheat, symbolizing Arkansas' agricultural and
industrial blessings.[1]

State Flag:
The 25 stars represent Arkansas' position as the 25th State in the Union. The three stars
below "ARKANSAS" depict the State's status as the third State formed from the Louisiana
Purchase. The single star above "Arkansas" symbolizes the Confederacy of which the State
was a part from 1861-1865. The diamond-shaped exterior border with its 25 stars portrays
Arkansas' uniqueness, as the only diamond-producing State in the Union.[2]

State Song:
"Arkansas (You Run Deep in Me)"[3]

First "Christian Heritage Week:" February 27 - March 5, 1994, proclaimed by the
Governor.

Of Historic Interest:
  Arkansas' greatest hero in the U.S. Capitol's Hall of Fame is **Uriah Milton Rose (1834-
1913)**, chosen by the people of Arkansas to represent them. The *Arkansas Gazette* of May
30, 1965 published the following article:

> ...In an address given to the Bar Association in 1911, Judge Rose
> gave the following account of the early days of his legal career. It is
> hereunder excerpted:
>
> "I came to be a lawyer seemingly in a purely casual or accidental

15

way. My parents having both died when I was about fourteen years old, I was thrown on my own resources without any very brilliant prospects.

About three years later, one of the best-known men in the county, by the name of Rutherford Harrison Roundtree, called and stayed all night at the home where I was sojourning. He had been clerk of one of the higher courts of the county for many years, and no man in the community had a more enviable reputation for good sense and incorruptible integrity. My surprise was very great when next morning he offered me a place as deputy clerk in his office; an office which I gladly accepted.

It is to this man — practical, well-balanced and wisely considerate in all his conduct, a man of large mind and a warm heart —— that I owe a debt of gratitude.

Judge Rose's **Memoirs** reveal his early childhood. His father had a notion that education should begin in the cradle; and a passion for teaching his children. Hence, Uriah could not remember when he did not read. At age five he began studying Latin. A private family tutor, a Scottish man of the Presbyterian faith named James Martin, instructed him until 1847, at which time he attended an academic school in the country.[4]

Uriah Rose's son, George B. Rose, relates that his grandfather was a devout Christian and member of his church. His love of the Old Testament Scriptures led him to name his son Uriah. The latter had a singular charm which always won for him the regard of everyone with whom he came in contact.[5]

Early in 1907, President Theodore Roosevelt passed through Little Rock. At a luncheon given to him, Judge Rose responded to a toast in his honor. This made so favorable an impression upon Mr. Roosevelt that he appointed him as ambassador to the *Hague Peace Conference* of that year...

The President's letter is hereunder excerpted:

My dear Mr. Rose:

...There are very few...about whom it is possible immediately to say...they can be trusted to do any work. After I had seen you and listened to you, it was perfectly evident that you came in (this) class...We should be represented by our strongest men, and I think you, Porter and Choate are in that category. I want men who...with entire sincerity will work for peace, but who do not forget that at present in this world the only nations fit to have peace are those who are willing to fight if need arises...

Sincerely yours,
Theodore Roosevelt[6]

United States President: William Jefferson Clinton (42nd).

16

CALIFORNIA
(name of island in
16th century book,
"Las Sergas de Esplandian")

The Preamble to the Constitution of the State of California states that, *We the people of the State of California, grateful to Almighty God for our freedom, in order to secure and perpetuate its blessings, do establish this Constitution.*

California joined the Union on September 9, 1850 as the 31st State.

State Capital: Sacramento.

State Motto:
"Eureka," translated from Greek to mean "I Have Found It."

State Seal:
The design for the Great Seal of the State of California was adopted at the Constitutional Convention of 1849. Thirty-one stars are displayed, one for each state which joined the Union, including the admission of California in 1850. Beneath them appears the motto, EUREKA! The awesome peaks of the Sierra Nevada stand for the grandeur of God's creation. The ships in San Francisco Bay signify commerce. A miner laboring with pick, rocker and pan represents industry. Agricultural bounty is seen in a sheaf of wheat and clusters of grapes. Keeping watch over this tableau is the armored figure of Minerva, typifying peace and war. At her feet a grizzly bear symbolizes the State of California.

State Flag:
The Bear Flag was first raised in 1846 by American settlers during an uprising against rule from Mexico. The white background of the flag represents purity, while the red in the star and bar denotes courage. The grizzly bear, (now extinct) and regarded as an animal of great strength, portrays this quality on the banner. The star symbolizes sovereignty, after the Lone Star of Texas.[1]

State Song:
"I Love You, California."[2]

First "Christian Heritage Week:" April 26 - May 2, 1992, proclaimed by the Governor.

Of Historic Interest:
In 1921 the War History Department of the California Historical Survey Commission issued a book entitled, *California in the War — War Addresses, Proclamations and Patriotic Messages* of Governor William D. Stephens. Reprinted below are but a few, reflecting California's identity:

Flag Day Proclamation
June 14, 1918
Ever since the day Betsy Ross stitched together the Stars and Stripes,
our flag has stood for the freedom of mankind. Not once has it been

17

borne into battle for a cause other than the establishment and protection of human liberties. Until the beginning of this war, we have fought only that our own freedom or that of peoples dependent upon us might not be swept aside.

Today, however, the forces of the United States fight on foreign soil as an ally of foreign nations for the freedom of the world and at their head flies the Stars and Stripes twined with the Union Jack, the Tricolor and the flags of our other noble allies.

Under such circumstances the celebration of Flag Day, June 14th, should enlist the enthusiastic interest and support of us all. I urge that assemblages be held in all communities; that the Star Spangled Banner be sung and the pledge of allegiance to our flag renewed.

Thanksgiving Day Proclamation
November 22, 1918

By proclamation of the President of the United States, Thursday, the 28th day of November, has been designated a day of thanksgiving and prayer.

Never before in the history of our country has there been such occasion for praise to Almighty God. The most cruel war of the centuries has come to an end. America has done a proud part in the great cause for right and justice, and the generations to come will honor the memory of the brave men who gave their lives in order that the peoples on this earth might be free.

Those who have suffered loss of loved ones find a measure of solace in contemplation of what the sacrifice means for human liberty. The world's freedom is now secure. Peace — we hope enduring peace — is now at hand. Our men sent overseas have helped to establish a new Christian fraternity among the nations. Justice has triumphed over the heartlessness of might. The women and children of all lands are safe.

It has been our privilege in California to give a generous measure of aid in the conflict. We have provided in full measure from our abundant production of food; we have rallied to the call of the national government in its financial needs; and we have supplied more than our quota of men for the armies. We are grateful that we have been able thus to serve the nation.

Now, therefore, I, William D. Stephens, Governor of California, do hereby declare the said 28th day of November, 1918, to be a legal holiday for thanksgiving and prayer.

Community Day Proclamation
December 27, 1918

In order to preserve to the State of California the social and moral asset which it has acquired through the development of the cooperative spirit during the war, and in order to weld our people into a more perfect democracy, I hereby appoint Friday, December 27, 1918, as *Community Day*, and call upon all leaders of war activities, all state, county, and city officials, as well as all other public-spirited citizens to join in the movement, and to urge their friends and neighbors to join in the movement inaugurated by the State Council of Defense, to the end that on that day a community council will be organized in every community district in California. The idea of community organization has already been endorsed by the President and other national authorities.

During the Christmas season let us thus put the spirit of peace and good will into practical application.

— William D. Stephens

Officially Recorded Presidential Inaugural Scriptures:
Richard Milhous Nixon was sworn into office on January 20, 1969. A *Washington Post* article of the same date gives us these details:

> Mrs. Nixon will hold two family Bibles opened to Isaiah 2, verse 4, for her husband's oath-taking. The verse expresses the new President's hope that 'nations will beat their swords into plowshares, and their spears into pruning hooks' that 'nation shall not lift up sword against nation, neither shall they learn war anymore.'

January 20, 1973, marked **Richard Nixon's** Second Inauguration as first officer of the Executive Branch of our government. A *Washington Evening Star* article, dated January 21, 1973, covered the event as follows:

> As he did four years ago, President Nixon spoke the oath with his left hand resting on two Nixon family Bibles, 100 and 145 years old. His wife Pat held them. Each was open to Isaiah 2:4, which speaks of nations that 'shall beat their swords into plowshares and their spears into pruning hooks, neither shall they learn war anymore.'

On January 20, 1981 and January 20, 1985, **Ronald Reagan**, our 40th president, made his pledge of allegiance to the Constitution of the United States with his left hand upon his mother's Bible, the New Indexed Bible, King James Version, having selected her favorite Scripture verse:

> If my people, which are called by My name, shall humble themselves, and pray, and seek my face, and turn from their wicked ways; then will I hear from heaven, and will forgive their sin, and will heal their land. (II Chronicles 7:14)

United States Presidents: Richard Milhous Nixon (37th), Ronald Reagan (40th).

DENVER IN 1858

After a photograph of Denver in 1858. Library of Congress Collection.

20

COLORADO
(red)

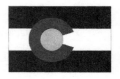

The Preamble to the Constitution of the State of Colorado states that, *We the people of Colorado, with profound reverence for the Supreme Ruler of the Universe, in order to form a more independent and perfect government; establish justice; insure tranquility; provide for the common defense; promote the general welfare and secure the blessings of liberty to ourselves and our posterity, do ordain and establish this Constitution for the State of Colorado.*

Colorado joined the Union on August 1, 1876 as the 38th State.

State Capital: Denver.

State Motto:
"Nil Sine Numine," translated from Latin to mean "Nothing Without Providence."

State Seal:
The Great Seal of Colorado contains the watchfulness of God, Roman fasces and a band of red, white and blue, upon which appears "Union and Constitution." The state motto, "Nil Sine Numine" is Latin for "Nothing Without Providence." The date 1876 indicates the year Colorado became a state, that is, 100 years after the signing of the Declaration of Independence, hence her name, "The Centennial State."[1]

The official colors of the seal, fixed by a 1876 Executive Order, are as follows:

Red:
The sky behind the mountains, the single band with the word "UNION" and the ring containing the words "STATE OF COLORADO, 1876";

Dark Blue:
The mountains, the background behind the shield, the single band with the word "CONSTITUTION," and the six stars dividing the year of statehood from the lettering "STATE OF COLORADO," the two dots separating the words "STATE OF COLORADO";

White:
The snowcaps of the three mountains, the clouds surrounding the mountains, the band with the word "AND," the banner containing the words "Nil Sine Numine," the triangle with an eye, symbolic of the watchfulness of God, the fasces, and innermost ring;

Gold:
The rays emanating from the watchfulness of God, the background in the lower shield, the small decorative circles on the innermost white ring, and the ring situated between the red ring and outer silver ring of the seal;

Silver:
The outside ring of the seal, the lettering "State of Colorado" and "1876," the ax head, the heads of both miners' tools, the two bands binding the fasces behind the two bands entitled "UNION" "CONSTITUTION," the outline of the shield, and the dividing line between the upper and lower portions of the shield;

Brown:
The handles of the miner's tools, the handle of the ax;

Black:
The lettering of the words "UNION," "AND," "CONSTITUTION," the words "NIL SINE NUMINE," the outline tracing the cascade of the banner containing the words "NIL SINE NUMINE," the outlines encircling the small decorative circles on the innermost white circle, and the outlines of the single band "AND."

State Flag:
Embodied in the flag are the colors of the national flag, the blue of Colorado skies, the gold of her metal, the white of mountain snows and the red of her soil.[2]

State Song:
"Where the Columbines Grow" by Arthur J. Flynn.

First "Christian Heritage Week:" April 24-30, 1994, proclaimed by the Governor.

Of Historic Interest:
Housed in the Library of Congress collection, is an interesting book by Alice Polk Hill entitled *Colorado Pioneers in Picture and Story.* Written in 1915, it vividly portrays Colorado's Christian foundations under the subtitle, *The Development of Pioneer Enterprises — Establishing Forces of Civilization: Churches.* The following historic facts are recorded:

> The influence of the Christian religion was present in Denver from the beginning. In the fall of 1858, the Rev. G.W. Fisher preached in the open, under cottonwood trees, and in the homes of the pioneers.
>
> The directors of the two town companies encouraged church building by donating lots. The Auraria Town Company, January 17, 1859, unanimously adopted the following resolution:
>
> "Resolved. That there be and there is hereby donated to the first four religious societies that will build a church or house of worship in the city of Auraria, one lot to each, to be selected by anyone appointed by the societies for that purpose."
>
> The Rev. Mr. Fisher preached faithfully to the isolated community during the winter of '58-'59, but there were no churches built.
>
> Albert D. Richardson, in June, 1859, wrote: "When I asked a miner if there was any church, he replied, 'No, but we are going to build one before next Sunday.'" This clearly illustrates the pioneer spirit.

Richardson vividly describes a "Sunday morning."

"One Sunday morning, while walking through the diggings, revealed nearly all the miners disguised in clean clothing. Some were reading and writing, some ministering to the sick, and some enacting the part of every-man-his-own-washer-woman, rubbing valiantly away at the tub. Several hundred men in the open air were attending public religious worship, perhaps the first ever held in the Rocky Mountains. They were roughly clad, displaying weapons at their belts, and represented every section of the Union and almost every nation of the earth. They sat upon logs and stumps, a most attentive congregation, while the clergyman, upon a rude log platform, preached from the text: 'Behold, I bring you good tidings of great joy.' It was an impressive spectacle — that motley gathering of goldseekers among the mountains, a thousand miles from home and civilization, to hear the good tidings forever old and yet forever new."

When spring opened, the prospects were dismal: it was doubtful whether the infant city would live to see another winter. And, when the gold excitement broke out in May, there was no time for churchbuilding. However, the Rev. Mr. Fisher kept on talking of the "gold that was sure and pure."

Mr. Goode, a Methodist minister, organized the first church in Denver, August, 1859, with Jacob Adriance as secretary, which was the beginning of the **Trinity Methodist Episcopal Church**.

The first **Methodist Episcopal Church Society** was incorporated July 22, 1863. The Lawrence Street church was the first building owned by the society.

On the first day of April, 1888, the first services were held in the basement of the present Trinity church, and $60,000 was raised in less than one hour towards the cost of completing the church building.

Mr. Peter Winne, who is a man of splendid character and sterling worth, has been a member of this church for fifty-two years. He was a potential factor in the building of the church, and, at the age of seventy-five years, he is still an active member.

From the choir in this church, Mrs. Wilberforce Whiteman has lifted her rich contralto voice in God's praise for nineteen years.

Rev. J.H. Kehler, an Episcopalian, who was familiarly called Father Kehler, came to Denver, January 1860, with his four daughters. Immediately upon Mr. Kehler's arrival, he inaugurated regular services at Goldrick's school house. One stormy Sunday morning there were only two persons in the church, Mr. Amos Steck and Colonel J.H. Dudley. They thought, of course, they would be dismissed without a sermon, but Father Kehler, equal to the situation, selected the

23

text: "Where two or three are gathered together in My name, there will I be, in the midst of them," and thereupon preached an excellent sermon.

John M. Chivington of the **Methodist Episcopal Church** came in May, 1860. In that same year, W.M. Bradford of the **Methodist Episcopal Church South** put up the first building that was erected for church purposes in Denver, but the Civil War scattered many of the members, including Preacher Bradford, who hastened away to the South. The church was closed for awhile, and it was sold later to the Episcopalians, when it became **St. John's Church in the Wilderness**.

Following Father Kehler came Rev. H.B. Hitchings, who preached six years and was succeeded by Rev. George M. Randall, a learned, eloquent man, greatly beloved by his congregation. Later, he became bishop.

Rev. Walter Moore followed, and was in turn succeeded by E.V. Finch.

While on a trip around the world, Rev. H. Martyn Hart of England stopped in Denver and preached a sermon in that little church, which was followed by a call to the parish. A man of honest purpose, untiring energy and unlimited faith is this dean of **St. John's Cathedral**. His daughter, Miss Hart, is an earnest worker in the church.

November 3, 1859, the following notice appeared in the "News:"

Union Sunday School
A Union Sunday School for the children of Auraria and Denver will be held every Sunday at 3 o'clock p.m. at the house of preachers Fisher and Adriance. The school will be not only a union school, but a union of all denominations.

At the appointed time came twelve pupils. Mr. Tappan wrote to the Baptist Sunday School of Lawrence, Kansas, soliciting a supply of books. They were freighted across the plains by Jones & Cartwright, free of charge. Upon examination, Mr. Tappan discovered, to his surprise, that they were the same books which he had solicited from his old Bible class in the Rev. Dr. Stowe's church in Boston for the Kansas Sunday school. This box of books had an eventful history. After serving its time in Denver, it was sent to the first anti-Mormon Sunday school in Salt Lake City.

D.C. Collier was elected superintendent of the Union Sunday school, and Goldrick became a teacher. The second Sunday, fifteen children took their seats on the rough wooden benches, and the school, keeping pace with the wonderful advance of the country, continued to grow, until it taxed the capacity of the two rooms. By that time, denominational schools were formed, and, having passed the period of usefulness, it was discontinued, leaving only pleasant memories of the men who founded and guided it.

24

Goldrick took part in every movement for improving the environment of the pioneer. He was an educated man, with a sincere love for his fellowman, and his name was a household word from the day of his arrival to the day of his death...

Under the leadership of Governor John Evans, in 1863, the Denver Methodists laid the foundations of the **Colorado Seminary**. This was the first school for advanced learning in the Territory of Colorado. The school was opened November, 1864, and maintained until 1867, when, in consequence of accumulated indebtedness, it was closed. The property was sold, and bought by Governor Evans. In 1879, the **Colorado Seminary** was reorganized under the original charter. A new board was appointed and Governor Evans returned, as a gift, the seminary property he had bought twelve years before to save it. To this he added $3,000 for laboratory apparatus. Vice President Bailey gave $13,000, and the businessmen generally contributed liberally to reinstate the seminary. In 1880, a second and coordinate corporation was formed, under the name, "University of Denver." All the property is owned and the material affairs managed by the seminary corporation, while the university corporation controls and directs the higher departments of university training.

Rev. David H. Moore was elected chancellor of the new university and president of **Colorado Seminary**...

— Alice Polk Hill
— 1915

Colorado's Heroine:
A *Times Herald* article dated February 23, 1959, gave the following headlines:

Colorado's First in Statuary Hall
Statue of Woman Doctor to be Unveiled in Capitol

Colorado's Dr. Florence Rena Sabin will be the third woman to be honored with a place in the Capitol's Statuary Hall, when her bronze likeness is unveiled during ceremonies in the Capitol Rotunda at 2 p.m. on Thursday...

Dr. Sabin was the first woman to become a full professor (in 1917) at Johns Hopkins University, the first woman elected to life membership in the National Academy of Sciences, the first woman member of the Rockerfeller Institute for Medical Research and the first woman to serve as president of the National Association of Anatomists.

JONATHAN TRUMBULL, 1710-1785, CONNECTICUT

After the Original Marble Sculpture in the Hall of Fame,
U.S. Capitol, Washington, D.C.

CONNECTICUT
(long river place)

The Preamble to the Constitution of the State of Connecticut states that, *The people of Connecticut, acknowledging with gratitude, the good providence of God, in having permitted them to enjoy a free government; do, in order more effectually to define, secure and perpetuate the liberties, rights and privileges which they have derived from their ancestors; hereby ordain and establish this Constitution and form of civil government.*

Connecticut joined the Union on January 9, 1788 as the 5th State.

State Capital: Hartford.

State Motto:
"Qui Transtulit Sustinet," translated from Latin to mean, "He Who Transplanted Still Sustains." The late Charles J. Hesally, former State Librarian, wrote in an article entitled, "The Public Seal of Connecticut," which was published in the 1889 edition of the *Connecticut State Register and Manual,* that one should look to the 80th Psalm as the source for the motto: "Thou hast brought a vine out of Egypt, Thou has cast out the heathen and planted it." (Psalm 80, verse 8).

State Insignia:
"The Constitution State," from *The Fundamental Orders of Connecticut*, written in 1638-1639 by Thomas Hooker, founder of Connecticut. This document was the first free Constitution in the world.

State Seal:
Three grape vines, supported and bearing fruit, under which a banner has inscribed upon it the Latin phrase, "Qui Transtulit Sustinet," translated to mean, "He Who Transplanted Still Sustains." The outer border contains, in Latin, the words, Siglium Republicae Connecticutensis, meaning, Seal of the Republic of Connecticut.[1]

State Flag:
The General Assembly of 1897 provided an official description of the flag, setting the dimensions at five feet, six inches in length, and four feet, four inches in width, of azure blue silk, with the armorial bearings in argent white silk, with the design in natural colors and bordure of the shield embroidered in gold and browns, the streamer bearing in dark blue the motto, "Qui Transtulit Sustinet." (He Who Transplanted Still Sustains).[2]

State Hero:
Nathan Hale (1755-1776), "The Martyred Spy," has officially been designated Connecticut's State Hero.[3] Born in Coventry and educated at Yale University, Hale served as a schoolmaster and was commissioned as a Captain in the Continental Army in 1775. In September, 1776, at General George Washington's request for a volunteer, Nathan Hale crossed enemy lines to gather information as to the strength and plans of the British. Upon returning, he

was betrayed by his Tory cousin, Samuel, and hanged as a spy on September 22, 1776, without the benefit of a trial. Nathan Hale's immortalized last words were, "I only regret that I have but one life to lose for my country." Connecticut's State Hero is memorialized at the Hale Homestead in Coventry.

First "Christian Heritage Week:" September 24-30, 2000.

Of Historic Interest:
  Jonathan Trumbull (1710-1785), was chosen as Connecticut's greatest hero in the U.S. Capitol's Hall of Fame. A close friend of George Washington, he was Governor of Connecticut during the Revolutionary War. After the signing of the Declaration of Independence, he alone, of the 13 colonial governors, remained in office. Jonathan Trumbull excelled in dispatching needed supplies speedily; also enlisting more soldiers than any other State, with the exception of Massachusetts. He was thus a significant factor in America's independence.[4]

At the age of thirteen Trumbull entered Harvard College, a Divinity School in those days. His studies comprised Greek, Hebrew and Latin; later extending to physics, ethics, geography, geometry, and forensics. He greatly promoted the practice of Christian virtues, values and morals on campus. Graduating from Harvard at 17, Jonathan pursued studies in Theology with a minister/tutor for two and a half years, in order to become a Minister of the Gospel. Trumbull was a member of the Congregational Church in Colchester and preached sermons.[5]

However, upon the untimely death of his older brother, he was obliged to leave the full-time ministry in order to assist his father in his business; and eventually succeeded him.

Trumbull was elected to the Colonial Assembly at 23. He also served as Governor's Assistant for 22 years, opposing the Stamp Act passed by Parliament, which he deemed unconstitutional. In the years preceding the American Revolution, he founded an academy and a public library, as well as helping to found an Indian School. Later this school was moved to Hanover, New Hampshire, becoming *Dartmouth College.*[6]

Jonathan Trumbull was elected to Chief Justice of the Colony and then Governor at age 59, holding this position during the Revolutionary War. Connecticut financed the expedition against Ticonderoga, the northern fort captured by Ethan Allen. Half of the powder used at Bunker Hill came from Connecticut; George Washington using the cannon, powder and shot from Ticonderoga to drive the British out of Boston.

Washington wrote to Trumbull from Army Headquarters in Valley Forge, that the American Army would cease to exist if food did not arrive speedily. Within five days, Trumbull dispatched 300 beef cattle to Washington in Valley Forge. Twenty-one regiments of soldiers were sent, and 252 ships fitted out from Connecticut, which Washington called "The Supply State."[7]

In one of Trumbull's letters we read that there was a price put on his head by the British. In fact, his home, which still stands in Lebanon, had a secret room above the attic stairs for escape if needed.

Throughout his life Jonathan Trumbull maintained a personal relationship with his Redeemer, Jesus Christ. "The Lord Reigneth!" was his oft-repeated response in times of crisis. After the Revolutionary War had been won, George Washington wrote to his friend Trumbull,

"It is my wish that the mutual friendship . . . which has been fostered in the tumult of public life, may not wither in the serenity of retirement."[8]

Roger Sherman (1721-1793) is the second of Connecticut's great heroes in the U.S. Capitol's Hall of Fame. The only member of the Continental Congress to sign the Declaration of 1774, the Declaration of Independence, the Articles of Confederation and the U.S. Constitution, he served in the Connecticut legislature, the Continental Congress, the Constitutional Convention, the U.S. House of Representatives (1789-91) and the U.S. Senate (1791-93).

Thomas Hooker, the founder of Connecticut, and one of New England's greatest men of God, was born in 1586 in Markfield, Leicestershire, England. He died at Hartford, Connecticut, in 1647.[9]

Hooker was a fellow of *Emmanuel College*, Cambridge, after which he became the assistant to a minister in Chelmsford. Archbishop Laud ordered him to refrain from preaching the Gospel of Christ, his preaching being considered outside the format of the established Church of England. He then taught school in Little Braddon; John Eliot, missionary to the Indians, becoming his assistant. Under intense persecution, Hooker left for Holland, embarking on a ship bound for New England in 1633.[10]

After arriving in America, he was appointed as pastor of the church at Newtown, (Cambridge), his spiritual influence in the colony being immeasurable. In 1636, Thomas Hooker founded Connecticut, the new colony encompassing the towns of Hartford, Windsor and Weathersfield.[11]

The Fundamental Orders of Connecticut — the first written Constitution — made by the people and for the people in the history of civilization, limiting the powers of government, was drawn up by Hooker and adopted by the assembly of planters of the three towns of Connecticut, on January 14, 1638.[12]

THE PILGRIMAGE TO THE CONNECTICUT VALLEY
In the Summer of 1636 Thomas Hooker Led one Hundred people into the Valley and Founded Hartford.

29

The preface to what is considered to be his greatest work, *A Survey of the Summe of Church Discipline (wherein the Way of the Churches of New England is warranted out of the Word, and all Exceptions of Weight, which are Made against it, Answered . . .)*, gives insight into this great American statesman's understanding of the church and how it strayed away from the true gospel; but was finally brought to deliverance by the Reformation.

...Sometimes God makes an eclipse of the Truth at midday, that so He might express his wrath from heaven, against the unthankfulness, prophaneness and atheism of a malignant world. Hence it was he let loose those hellish delusions, immediately after the Ascension of our Saviour; that though His life and conversation gave in evidence beyond gainsaying, that He was true man: though the miracles and wonders He wrought in His life and death, resurrection and ascension, were witnesses undeniable, that He was true God: yet there arose a wretched generation of heretics, in the first, second and third hundred years, who adventured not only against the express verdict of the Scripture, but against sense and experience, fresh in the observation and tradition of living men, with more than satanical impudency to deny both the natures of our blessed Saviour. Some denied the Deity of our Saviour, and would have Him mere man...First, they began to encroach upon the Priestly Office of our Saviour, and not only to pray for the dead, and to attribute too much to the martyrs and their worth; and to derogate from the merits, and that plentiful and perfect redemption wrought alone by the Lord Jesus. The Spouse of Christ thus like the unwise virgins, was taken aside with the slumber of idolatry, till at last she fell fast asleep as the following times give in abundant testimony. Not long after, these sleeps were attended with suitable dreams, for not being content with the simplicity of the Gospel, and the purity of the worship appointed therein: They set forth a new and large edition of devised and instituted ceremonies, coined merely out of the vanity of men's carnal minds, which as so many blinds, were set up by the subtlety of satan, merely to delude men, and mislead them from the Truth of God's worship, under a pretense of directing them more easily in the way of grace: and under a colour of kindling, they quenched all true zeal for, and love of the Truth...When God had revenged the contempt of the authority of His Son, by delivering up such condemners to the tyranny and slavery of Antichrist...They then began to sigh for some deliverance from this spiritual, more than Egyptian bondage; and being thus prepared to lend a listening ear unto the truth, God sent them some little reviving in their extremities, a daystar arising in this their darkness...

— Thomas Hooker[13]

CAESAR RODNEY, DELAWARE

After the Marble Statue of Caesar Rodney in the Hall of Fame, U.S. Capitol, Washington, D.C.

DELAWARE
(After Lord De la Warr)

The Constitution of the State of Delaware states that, *Through Divine goodness, all men have by nature the rights of worshipping and serving their Creator according to the dictates of their consciences...*and, *It is the duty of all men frequently to assemble together for the public worship of Almighty God; and piety and morality, on which the prosperity of communities depends, are hereby promoted;...*

Delaware joined the Union as the First State to ratify the U.S. Constitution on December 7, 1787.

State Capital: Dover.

State Motto:
"Liberty and Independence," derived from the Order of Cincinnati, and approved in 1847.[1]

State Seal:
While attempting to get the great seal engraved, Thomas McKean "consulted an ingenious gentleman in the art of Heraldry" who suggested that the design selected would be more suitable for a medal than the seal of a state. During the time a new design was being considered, it was agreed that the ancient seal of New Castle County, devised by William Penn in 1683, should be used pro tempore as the Great Seal of Delaware until the new seal was made. Meanwhile the British invaded New Castle County, captured numerous State records, and carried away with them the Great Seal pro tempore. The Legislature then resolved that the 1683 seal of Kent County should be used pro tempore as the Great Seal and in the event it became lost the ancient seal of Sussex County should be used.

On January 17, 1777, the Committee appointed to design a Great Seal brought in their report which was accepted and adopted. It was resolved that the committee "employ a skillful workman to make a Silver Seal of the diameter of three inches, and of a circular form, and that there be engraven thereon a Sheaf of Wheat, an Ear of Maize, and an Ox in full stature, in a shield, with a river dividing the Wheat Sheaf and Ear of Maize from the Ox, which is to be cut in the nether part of the shield below the River; that the Supporters be an American soldier under arms on the right, and a Husbandman with a hoe in his hand on the left, and that a Ship be the Crest; and that there shall be an inscription around the same near the edge or extremity thereof in the words following, in capital letters, "THE GREAT SEAL OF DELAWARE STATE," with the figure "1777." The American soldier represents maintenance of liberty; the Husbandman portrays the importance of farming in Delaware; the Sheaf of Wheat has been adapted from the Sussex County Seal and signifies Delaware's agricultural bounty; the Ship is the symbol for New Castle County's ship-building industry and the coastal seaboard of the state; the Corn comes from the Kent County Seal, and symbolizes the basis for Delaware's economy; the Water (stripes) reflects the Delaware River, facilitating the State's transportation of products; the Ox stands for the role of animal husbandry in Delaware's economy; the dates depict major changes to the State Seal, as follows: In 1793 the American soldier and the Husbandman were omitted; in 1847 both were reinstated and Delaware's State Motto was adopted; 1907 represents the 1777 Seal, with the words "State of Delaware" added.[2]

32

State Flag:
The State Flag of Delaware was adopted on July 24, 1913. In accordance with the design authorized at that time, the State Flag has a background of colonial blue, surrounding a diamond of buff color in which is placed the Coat of Arms of the State of Delaware. Below the diamond are the words, "December 7, 1787," indicating the day on which Delaware was the first State to ratify the United States Constitution. Delaware thus became the first state in the Union, and is therefore given the honor of first place in great national events, such as Presidential Inaugurations.

State Song:
"Our Delaware." Written by George B. Hynson and put to music by Will M.S. Brown.

First "Christian Heritage Week:" December 6-12, 1992, proclaimed by the Governor.

Of Historic Interest:
Delaware is the first State to have celebrated her 8th annual "Christian Heritage Week," December 5-11, 1999.

Caesar Rodney (1728-1784), was chosen by the citizens of Delaware as their greatest hero. On June 26, 1934, at the unveiling of Caesar Rodney's statue in the Hall of Fame of the U.S. Capitol, Dr. George H. Ryden of the University of Delaware stated of him:

> ...Caesar Rodney was one of Delaware's greatest sons, the principal founder of our State as a political entity, independent of Pennsylvania, and one of a galaxy of distinguished men who in a time of great stress and danger were not afraid to think nobly and to act courageously when they severed the tie of the mother country with her colonies.[3]

Rodney, Thomas McKean and George Read were Delaware's appointees to the First Continental Congress.[4] Rodney had the dramatic distinction of casting the vote which made the colonies unanimous in voting for independence.

As the day of the vote drew near, Caesar had returned to Dover to fulfill other responsibilities as speaker of the Delaware Assembly.[5] While McKean was an enthusiastic supporter of independence, Read would not vote in favor of it, thus cancelling one another's votes.

McKean hired a messenger to make the 80-mile trip to Dover on horseback, in order to alert Rodney to the problem.[6] He quickly responded, making the ride in sultry weather, a thunderstorm and a change of horse in mid-course. He arrived at the State House in Philadelphia muddied and weary, but just in time to cast his vote on that historic day. In answer to the roll call vote, he said:

> As I believe the voice of my constituents and of all sensible and honest men, is in favor of independence, my own judgment concurs with them. I vote for independence.[7]

It has been said that had even one of the colonies not voted in favor of independence, the Declaration of Independence may have never been signed.[8] **Caesar Rodney** has been designated as Delaware's "Heroic rider of the American Revolution," on the back of the U.S. 25 cent coins, portraying Delaware as the first State to ratify the U.S. Constitution.

GENERAL KIRBY-SMITH

After the Original Bronze Statue in the Hall of Fame, U.S. Capitol, Washington D.C.

FLORIDA
(flowery)

The Preamble to the Constitution of the State of Florida states that, *We the people of the State of Florida, being grateful to Almighty God for our Constitutional liberty, in order to secure its benefits, do ordain and establish this Constitution.*

Florida joined the Union on March 3, 1845 as the 27th State.

State Capital: Tallahassee.

State Motto:
"In God We Trust," (from inscription on Great Seal).

State Seal:
The Legislature of 1868 adopted a joint Resolution as follows: "That a Seal of the size of an American silver dollar, having in the center thereof a view of the sun's rays over a highland in the distance, a cocoa tree, a steamboat on water, and an Indian female scattering flowers in the foreground, encircled by the words "Great Seal of the State of Florida: In God We Trust," be and the same is hereby adopted as the Great Seal of the State of Florida.[1]

State Flag:
The flag is described in these words: "the Seal of the State, of diameter one-half the hoist, in the center of a white ground. Red bars in width one-fifth of the hoist, in the center of a white ground. Red bars in width one-fifth the hoist, extending from each corner toward the center, to the outer rim of the seal."[2]

State Song:

OLD FOLKS AT HOME
Way down upon de Swanee Ribber,
Far, far away,
Dere's wha my heart is turning ebber,
Dere's wha de old folks stay.
All up and down de whole creation
Sadly I roam,
Still longing for de old plantation,
And for de old folks at home.

Chorus
All de world am sad and dreary,
Ebrywhere I roam;
Oh, darkeys, how my heart grows weary,
Far from de old folks at home!

Second Verse
All round de little farm I wandered
When I was young,
Den many happy days I squandered,
Many de songs I sung.
When I was playing wid my brudder

Happy was I;
Oh, take me to my kind old mudder!
Dere let me live and die.

Third Verse
One little hut among de bushes,
One dat I love
Still sadly to my memory rushes,
No matter where I rove.
When will I see de bees a-humming
All round de comb?
When will I hear de banjo strumming,
Down in my good old home?[3]

First "Christian Heritage Week:" May 16-22, 1999, proclaimed by the Governor.

Of Historic Interest:
   General Edmund Kirby Smith (1824-1893) was selected by the citizens of Florida as their greatest hero in the U.S. Capitol's Hall of Fame.

   An address given by Thomas J. Wood of the Class of 1845 - *Twenty-fourth Annual Reunion of the Association of the Graduates of the United States Military Academy, West Point, New York, June 9, 1893,* states:

> E. Kirby Smith
> No. 1255 Class of 1845
> Died at Sewanee, Tennessee
> March 28, 1893, aged 69.
>
> In the month of June, 1841, 112 youths representing nearly every state in the Union, were admitted to the U.S. Military Academy. In the month of June, 1845, 38 of that number passed their final examinations, and dating from July 1, following, were attached to the various arms of service in the Army as Brevet Second Lieutenants. Seventy-four of the original 112 had fallen by the wayside in the trying Olympiad between June, 1841 and June, 1845.
>
> Among those who entered the Academy in June, 1841 and who reached the coveted goal in June, 1845 was a bright, cheery, genial, cordial, frank youth from Florida. He was borne on the Academic rolls as Edmund K. Smith; and under that name was commissioned in the Army.
>
> He was born in St. Augustine, Florida, May 16, 1824. His ancestors, of both branches of his family, had been connected with the Military service...
>
> Edmund K. Smith, of the class of 1845, early became a favorite with his classmates. His genial temperment, and frank, cordial manners opened all hearts to him. I cannot recall having ever heard an unkind remark made about him. He soon became known as "Ned Smith;" but later on, the sobriquet "Seminole" was applied to him. This appellation was due to his nativity in Florida, and that Florida, not long previous, had been the seat of the Seminole War. "Seminole's" intellectual capacity was of the highest order, especially in Mathematics and the associated sciences...

On May 8, 1846, was fought the Battle of Palo Alto. The Mexican Army, numbering between six and seven thousand combatants, was commanded by General Arista. The American Army, commanded by General Taylor, numbered about two thousand two hundred men of all arms. In this battle, Lieutenant Edmund K. Smith received "the baptism of blood..."

During the night, the Mexican Army retreated and occupied a very strong position at Reseca de la Palma, about six miles from Palo Alto, athwart the line of march of the American Army from Point Isabel to Fort Brown. During the afternoon of the 9th of May, the American Army forced the Mexican Army from its strong position, drove it into a precipitous retreat, and compelled it to recross the Rio Grande. The Fifth Infantry, to which E.K. Smith was attached, rendered very distinguished service in the Battle of Reseca...

He was with his regiment in the battle of Contreras, August 20, 1847. Again his gallant conduct deserved and received the marked recognition of the government. He was brevetted Captain, to date from August 20, 1847, "for gallant and meritorious conduct in the battle of Contreras, Mexico..."

From November, 1852, to the breaking out of the great sectional war in the Spring of 1861, he was on frontier duty. March 3, 1855, he was promoted Captain in the Second Cavalry. His regiment was stationed on the frontier of Texas. In an action with the Comanche Indians, May 13, 1859, in Nestunga Valley, Texas, he was severely wounded. He was promoted Major, Second Cavalry, January 31, 1861.

April 6, 1861, Major E. Kirby Smith resigned his commission in the Army of the United States, and cast in his fortunes with the Confederate States...

That his services during the war were brilliant and distinguished was at the time, and remains to this day, a matter of common fame. That his services were eminently satisfactory to the authorities of the Confederate Government, and to the people of the Confederate States is attested by the fact that he passed through all the grades from Brigadier-General to General.

At the close of the war General Smith was, financially, a wreck, with a family, consisting of his wife and a number of children, to support. Without repining or weakness, with high resolve, with exalted integrity, and with firm self-confidence, he betook himself, without previous training or experience, to civil pursuits...

He was connected with a Military School in Kentucky; then with the University of Nashville; and finally, with the University of the South at Sewanee, Tennessee. He passed the last seventeen years of his eventful life as Professor of Mathematics in that seat of learning...

The swift-winged telegraph has informed the people of the United States that General E. Kirby Smith died March 28, 1893. His remains repose in the little cemetery near Sewanee, on the crest of the Cumberland Mountains.[4]

In a letter from Harper's Ferry, dated June 2, 1861, General Kirby-Smith writes:

> My good friend McClelland is Major-General, second in command to Scott, and is moving down from Wheeling, by the Baltimore and Ohio road, with 20,000 men; General Patterson from Pennsylvania is some twenty miles north of us at Chambersburg, with 13,000 men, whilst General McDowell operates from Alexandria by Leesburg and Manassas Gap with a column of ten or fifteen thousand, bringing upon our rear forty or fifty thousand men, commanded by able generals...
>
> What will become of us, God only knows. We are in the hands of that Providence who knows the justice of our cause.[5]

Hernando de Soto (1500-1542), the discoverer of Florida, arrived in Florida on May 25, 1539. *A Narrative of the Expedition of Hernando de Soto into Florida by a Gentleman of Elvas,* published at Evora in 1557, gives an account of the Gospel being preached to the Indians on the Isle of Cuba. The governor was besought by two blind men who asked him to restore their sight. The governor replied that:

> ...in the high heavens was He that had power to give them health, and whatsoever they could ask of Him; whose servant he was; and that this Lord made the heavens and the earth, and man after his own likeness, and that He suffered upon the cross to save mankind, and rose again the third day, and that he died as he was man, and as touching His divinity, He was, and is immortal; and that He ascended into heaven, where He standeth with His arms open to receive all such as turn unto Him: and straightway he commanded him to make a very high cross of wood, which was set up in the highest place of the town; declaring unto him, that the Christians worshipped the same in resemblance and the memory of that whereon Christ suffered. The Governor and his men kneeled down before it, and the Indians did the like. The Governor willed him, that from thenceforth, he should ask whatever they stood in need of, of that Lord that he told him was in heaven...[6]

AFTER "DISCOVERY OF THE MISSISSIPPI by DE SOTO A.D. 1541" by WILLIAM H. POWELL
MAIN ROTUNDA, U.S. CAPITOL

CRAWFORD LONG. M.D. GEORGIA'S TRIBUTE

After the Original Marble Sculpture of Crawford W. Long,
M.D. in the Hall of Fame, Washington, D.C.

GEORGIA
(After George II of England)

The Preamble to the Constitution of the State of Georgia states that, *To perpetuate the principles of free government, insure justice to all, preserve peace, promote the interest and happiness of the citizen and of the family and transmit to posterity the enjoyment of liberty, we the people of Georgia, relying upon the protection and guidance of Almighty God, do ordain and establish this Constitution.*

Georgia joined the Union on January 2, 1788 as the 4th State.

State Capital: Atlanta.

State Motto:
  "Wisdom, Justice, Moderation."

State Seal:
  The current Great Seal of Georgia was adopted by the State Constitution of 1798. On its front side appear three pillars supporting an arch, emblematic of the three branches of Government—the legislative, judicial, and executive. A man stands with a drawn sword defending the principles of wisdom, justice and moderation inherent in its Constitution. The reverse of the seal shows a ship with cotton and tobacco, and a man plowing, representing Georgia's agriculture and commerce.

State Flag:
  At the Constitutional Convention of 1787, it was agreed that each state, while loyal to the United States flag, should also have its own flag. After the Georgia Seal was adopted in 1799, the first state flag was designed with the Coat of Arms centered on a field of blue. In 1879, the General Assembly of Georgia passed an act changing the flag to a vertical band of blue next to the staff occupying one-third of the flag: the remainder was divided into three horizontal bands with the upper and lower in red and the middle in white. In 1905, the State Seal was added to the vertical blue band. The present state flag was designed by John Sammons Bell, an Atlanta Attorney and was adopted as the official flag of Georgia in 1956. The Secretary of State is designated by law as the custodian of the state flag.[1]

State Pledge of Allegiance:
  "I pledge allegiance to the Georgia flag and to the principles for which it stands: Wisdom, Justice and Moderation."

State Song:
  "Georgia on my Mind."

First "Christian Heritage Week:" May 7-13, 1995, proclaimed by the Governor.

Of Historic Interest:
  Crawford W. Long , M.D. (1815-1878) was chosen by the citizens of Georgia as

their greatest hero in the U.S. Capitol's Hall of Fame. The inscription on the base of his marble statue reads:

GEORGIA'S TRIBUTE

Crawford W. Long, M.D.
Discoverer of the use of
Sulphuric Ether as an anaesthetic in surgery
on March 30, 1842 at
Jefferson, Jackson county,
Georgia U.S.A.

"My profession is to me a Ministry from God."

James Edward Oglethorpe was an Englishman. At an early age he went to Oxford to study, but was drawn away from college by the clash of arms. Oglethorpe was a soldier for many years; later he became a member of Parliament.[2]

Oglethorpe, like many other noble men before him, thought of America as a "haven for persecuted Christians." King George II gave him a Charter for the land between the Savannah and the Altamaha, and made his heart glad by declaring that all Protestants should be tolerated there.[3] This occurred in 1732.

In the next year after Oglethorpe planted the settlement, a band of sturdy German Protestants arrived. These Protestants built their homes above Savannah, and called the Colony "Ebenezer," which means "the Lord hath helped us." Between these two settlements, a band of pious Moravian immigrants founded a colony. Then followed the settlement of Augusta, far up the Savannah River and well out among the Indians, which served as a sort of outpost.[4] John and Charles Wesley, great leaders of the Protestant Revival in England, accompanied more immigrants to settle in Georgia.

Officially Recorded Presidential Inaugural Scripture:
At his inaugural oath-taking ceremony, which took place on January 20, 1977, **James Earl Carter** made this observation:

> Here before me is the Bible used in the inauguration of our first President in 1789, and I have just taken the Oath of Office on the Bible my mother gave me just a few years ago, opened to a timeless admonition from the ancient prophet Micah: 'He hath showed thee O man, what is good, and what doth the Lord require of thee, but to do justly, and to love mercy, and to walk humbly with thy God.' (Micah 6:8) (Excerpted from a *Washington Post* article dated January 21, 1977.)

U.S. President: James Earl Carter (39th).

HENRY OPUKAHAIA FIRST HAWAIIAN CHRISTIAN

Henry Opukahaia — First Hawaiian Christian. After the Original Drawing in the "Memoirs of Henry Obookiah, a Native of Owyhee, and a Member of the Foreign Mission School, who died at Cornwall, Connecticut, February 17, 1818, aged 26 years."

HAWAII
(homeland)

**The Preamble to the Constitution of the State of Hawaii states
that,** *We the people of Hawaii, grateful for Divine Guidance...*

Hawaii joined the Union on August 21, 1959 as the 50th State.

State Capital: Honolulu.

State Motto:
"Ua Mau Ke Ea O Ka Aina I Ka Pono," meaning, "The Life of the Land is Perpetuated in Righteousness." This motto was given to the kingdom by King Kamehameha III who reiterated his mother's dying words as he gave thanks to Almighty God at Kawaiah'o Church for the return of his kingdom in 1843. It was made the official motto of the State of Hawaii in 1959.[1]

State Seal:
The Great Seal is based on the Territorial Seal. It is circular and between the outer lines are the words: "State of Hawaii Ua Mau Ke Ea O Ka Aina I Ka Pono." The year 1959 just with the circle signifies the date the State government was organized. The heraldic shield in the center has a figure of King Kamehameha I on the dexter side and Liberty, holding the Hawaiian flag, on the sinister. Below the shield is the phoenix surrounded by taro leaves, banana foliage and sprays of maidenhair fern. With color added, the seal becomes the State Coat of Arms.[2]

State Flag:
Adopted in 1816, it was modified in 1845. The British Union Jack recalls the one presented to King Kamehameha I in 1793 by Captain George Vancouver. The eight stripes are for the principal islands of Hawaii.

State Song:
"Hawaii Ponoi" was the national song of the Kingdom of Hawaii. It was composed by King Kalakaua and set to music by Captain Henri Berger, bandmaster of the Royal Hawaiian Band. It was made Hawaii's National Anthem in 1876, and adopted as the State Anthem in 1967.[3]

First "Christian Heritage Week:" February 12-22, 1994, proclaimed by the Governor.

Of Historic Interest:
Sandwich Islands. Captain Cook named the islands he discovered after the Earl of Sandwich, then First Lord of the Admiralty. However, as early as 1818, King Kamehameha I is reported to have protested, stating that each island should be called by its own name, and the entire group the "Islands of the King of Hawaii." The name *Sandwich Islands* continued to be used unofficially for many years, but its use in official communications gradually became obsolete after 1844.

The Memoirs of Henry Opukahaia, first Hawaiian Christian, were reprinted six times in their first year of publication. Following are excerpts:

43

God will carry through his work for us. I do not know what will God do for my poor soul. I shall go before God and also before Christ. I hope the Lord will send the Gospel to the heathen land, where the words of the Savior never yet had been. Poor people! Worship the wood and stone, and shark and almost everything their god. The Bible is not there, and heaven and hell, they do not know about it... O what a wonderful thing is that the hand of the Divine Providence has brought me from the heathenish darkness where the light of Divine truth had never been. And here I have found the name of the Lord Jesus in the Holy Scriptures, and have read that His blood was shed for many. O what a happy time I have now, while my poor friends and relations at home, are perishing with hunger and thirsty, wanting of the Divine mercy and water out of the wells of salvation. My poor countrymen who are yet living in the region and shadow of death, without knowledge of the true God, and ignorant of the future world, have no Bible to read, no Sabbath. I often feel for them in the night season, concerning the loss of their souls. May the Lord Jesus dwell in my heart, and prepare me to go and spend the remaining part of my life with them. But not my will, O Lord, but thy will be done.[4]

His life and prayers for the salvation of his own people motivated the first missionaries — 18 persons in all — to bring the Gospel of Jesus Christ to Hawaii in 1826. They left from Cornwall, Connecticut, on the ship, "The Thaddeus." Included in the group were John Honoree, Thomas Hopoo and William Tennooe of Hawaii and George Tamoree, Son of Tamoree, King of Atooi and Oneeheow.

The openness of the monarchy in allowing the people to be instructed in reading and Christian education was a direct result of the confidence and respect they maintained for the missionaries. That summer, King Kaumualii wrote this simple letter in his limited English to the Secretary of the American Board, expressing his belief in the value of Christianity and its educational impact upon his people:

July 28th, 1820

Dear Friend:

I wish to write a few lines to you to thank you for the good book you was so kind as to send my son. I think it is a good book, one that God gave us to read. I hope all my people will soon read this, and all other good books. I believe that my idols are good for nothing, and that your God is the only true God - the one that made all things. My idols I have hove away - they are no good - they fool me - they do me no good. I gave them coconuts, plantains, hogs, and good many things, and they fool me at last. Now I throw them all away. I have done now. When your good people learn me, I worship your God. I feel glad your good people come here to help us. We know nothing. I thank you for giving my son learning. I thank all America people.

Accept this from your friend,

King Tamoree
Kaumualii[5]

44

WILLIAM EDGAR BORAH·1865·1940

After the Bronze Statue of Senator William Borah in the
Hall of Fame, U.S. Capitol, Washington, D.C.

IDAHO
(sun coming
down mountains)

The Preamble to the Constitution of the State of Idaho states that, *We the people of the State of Idaho, grateful to Almighty God for our freedom, to secure its blessings and promote our common welfare, do establish this Constitution.*

Idaho joined the Union on July 3, 1890 as the 43rd State.

State Capital: Boise.

State Motto:
"Esto Perpetua," translated from Latin to mean "It is Perpetuated."

State Seal:
The Idaho State Seal was designed by Emma Edwards Green, who became the first and only woman to design the Great Seal of a State, and to achieve such distinction in the United States.[1]

Description of the Great Seal, *by Emma Edwards Green:*
"I made the figure of the man most prominent in the design, while that of the woman, signifying justice, as noted by the scales; liberty, as denoted by the liberty cap on the end of the spear, and equality with man as denoted by her position at his side, also signifies freedom. The pick and shovel held by the miner, and the ledge of rock beside which he stands, as well as the pieces of ore scattered about his feet, all indicate the chief occupation of the State. The stamp mill in the distance, which you can see by using a magnifying glass, is also typical of the mining interest of Idaho. The shield between the man and woman is emblematic of the protection they unite in giving the State. The large fir or pine tree in the foreground in the shield refers to Idaho's immense timber interests. The husbandman plowing on the left side of the shield, together with the sheaf of grain beneath the shield, are emblematic of Idaho's agricultural resources, while the cornucopias, or horns of plenty, refer to the horticultural. Idaho has a game law, which protects elk and moose. The elk's head, therefore, rises

46

above the shield. The state flower, the wild Syringa or Mock Orange, grows at the woman's feet, while the ripened wheat grows as high as her shoulder. The star signifies a new light in the galaxy of states...The river depicted in the shield is our mighty Snake or Shoshone River, a stream of great majesty."

State Flag:
A silk flag, with a blue field, 5 feet 6 inches fly, 4 feet 4 inches on pike is bordered by gilt fringe 2 1/2 inches wide, with the State Seal of Idaho in the center. The words "State of Idaho" are embroidered in gold block letters two inches high on a red band below the Great Seal.[2]

State Song:
"Here We Have Idaho"[3]

First "Christian Heritage Week:" October 16-22, 1994, proclaimed by the Governor.

Of Historic Interest:
Senator William E. Borah (1865-1940) is Idaho's greatest hero in the Hall of Fame. A *Washington Post* article dated June 7, 1947, states that a eulogy termed Senator Borah "greater" than any of the seven men who were President during his 33 years in the Senate. The article goes on to elaborate:

> ...The speaker was Senate President Arthur Vandenberg (R. Mich.), who now uses the same desk, chair and office once occupied by Borah. The Idaho Senator died in 1940 - "an implacable defender of the Constitution" and the people's advocate in the finest sense of the word..." Borah was in the Senate during the Administrations of Theodore Roosevelt, Taft, Wilson, Harding, Coolidge, Hoover and Franklin D. Roosevelt. "I again thank Idaho for bringing William Edgar Borah back to us," Vandenberg concluded, "and I thank God for having given his living genius to our blessed land."

READING THE BIBLE WITH HIS FAVORITE BOY, "TAD"

After a Photograph in a 1923 Guidebook of the Lincoln Memorial.

ILLINOIS
(man)

The Preamble to the Constitution of the State of Illinois states that, *We the people of the State of Illinois, grateful to Almighty God for the civil, political and religious liberty which He has permitted us to enjoy and seeking His blessing upon our endeavors...and secure the blessings of freedom and liberty to ourselves and our posterity, do ordain and establish this Constitution for the State of Illinois.*

Illinois joined the Union on December 3, 1818 as the 21st State.

State Capital: Springfield.

State Motto:
"State Sovereignty, National Union"

State Seal:
After Illinois gained statehood, State officials decided to choose a duplicate of the Great Seal of the United States for their Illinois Seal, on February 19, 1819. Secretary of State, Sharon Tyndale was responsible for creating the present seal. In 1867, he asked Senator Allen C. Fuller to sponsor a bill authorizing a new seal. But a controversy arose when the Senate discovered that Tyndale planned to use Fuller's bill to change the wording, "State Sovereignty, National Union" to "National Union, State Sovereignty" in light of the Civil War.

The Senate disagreed with Tyndale and amended and passed the bill on March 7, 1867, restoring the original wording. Though Tyndale followed the General Assembly's Motto, he changed the banner's placement on the seal so that, though "National Union " followed "State Sovereignty," it was much more prominent. Moreover, the word "Sovereignty" was upside down, further decreasing its readability.[1]

State Flag:
Illinois' first State Flag was adopted in 1915. More than 50 years later, Chief Petty Officer Bruce McDaniel of Waverly, then serving in Vietnam, urged that a new flag be designed to include the word "Illinois." Without his state's name on it, the identity of the Illinois flag hanging in his mess hall was often questioned. On July 1, 1970, a white field, carrying the word "Illinois" and the emblem portion of the State Seal became the state's official Flag.[2]

State Insignia:
"Land of Lincoln."

State Song:
"Illinois."

First "Christian Heritage Week:" September 15-21,1996, proclaimed by the Governor.

Of Historic Interest:

Illinois' greatest hero is **Abraham Lincoln.** On his way from Springfield, Illinois to Washington to take his place as 16th U.S. President, Lincoln stopped in Philadelphia, where he delivered a moving address:

Independence Hall, February 22, 1861

I am filled with deep emotion at finding myself standing in this place, where were collected together the wisdom, the patriotism, the devotion to principal, from which sprang the institutions under which we live.

You have kindly suggested to me that in my hands is the task of restoring peace to our distracted country. I can say in return, sir, that all the political sentiments I entertain have been drawn, so far as I have been able to draw them, from the sentiments which originated in and were given to the world from this hall. I have never had a feeling, politically, that did not spring from the sentiments embodied in the **Declaration of Independence.**

I have often pioneered over the dangers which were incurred by the men who assembled here and framed and adopted that Declaration. I have pondered over the toils that were endured by the officers and soldiers of the army who achieved that independence. I have often inquired of myself what great principle or idea it was that kept this Confederacy so long together. It was not the mere matter of the separation of the colonies from the motherland, but that sentiment in the Declaration of Independence which gave liberty, not alone to the people of this country, but hope to all the world, for all future time. It was that which gave promise that in due time the weights would be lifted from the shoulders of all men, and that all should have an equal chance. This is the sentiment embodied in the Declaration of Independence.

Now, my friend, can this country be saved on this basis? If it can, I will consider myself one of the happiest men in the world if I can help to save it. If it cannot be saved upon that principle, it will be truly awful. But if this country cannot be saved without giving up that principle, I was about to say I would rather be assassinated on this spot than surrender it.

Now, in my view of the present aspect of affairs there is no need of bloodshed and war. There is no necessity for it. I am not in favor of such a course and I may say in advance that there will be no bloodshed unless it is forced upon the government. The government will not use force, unless force is used against it.

My friends, this is wholly an unprepared speech. I did not expect to be called on to say a word when I came here. I supposed I was merely to do something toward raising a flag. I may, therefore, have said something indiscreet. But I have said nothing but what I am willing to live by, and, if it be the pleasure of Almighty God, to die by.

A. Lincoln[3]

Lincoln's pastor, Dr. Phineas D. Gurley, of the *New York Avenue Presbyterian Church* (two blocks from the White House), said:

> I have had frequent and intimate conversations with him on the subject of the Bible and the Christian religion, when he could have no motive for deceiving me, and I consider him sound, not only on the truth of the Christian religion, but on also its fundamental doctrines and teachings. And more than that, in the latter days of his chastened and weary life, after the death of his son Willie and his visit to the battlefield at Gettysburg, he said to me with tears in his eyes, that he had lost confidence in everything but God and that he loved the Savior...[4]

Illinois' Heroine:

Illinois' second illustrious person in the Hall of Fame is **Frances E. Willard (1839-1898)**, "Crusader for Temperance," who was the first woman chosen for the honor of representing her State in Statuary Hall. She was the founder of the ***Women's Christian Temperance Union.*** At a national convention of that organization she delivered a beautiful message which can be summed up as the essence of her life:

> One vital organic thought, one absorbing purpose, one undying ambition. It is that Christ shall be the world's King...King of its courts, its camps, its commerce; King of its colleges and cloisters; King of its customs and constitutions...Christ and His law, the true basis of government and the Supreme authority in national and individual life.[5]

In the February 17, 1905 Joint Resolution of both the U.S. House of Representatives and the Senate, Frances Willard is called "one of the most eminent women of the United States" . . . She served as president of *Evanston College for Ladies,* later to become part of *Northwestern University.*

The poet, John Greenleaf Whittier, wrote of her:

> She knew the power of banded ill,
> But felt that love was stronger still,
> And organized for doing good,
> The world's united womanhood ...

Another moving tribute delivered to the United States Senate on the centennial of her birth, gives insight into her distinguished life and accomplishments for God's glory and the good of mankind:

> ...We consider her life as a woman of culture, an educator, and the fountainhead of one of the greatest movements in all history, we realize that there really is no method by which we can measure all the good Frances Willard did. The hundreds of thousands of women organized in the cause of temperance are but a suggestion of the real results of her activities. No one dares to argue but that she made purer the moral atmosphere of the United States and the world. She made people cleaner-minded and saner; millions of wives and children bless her name...

At the acceptance of her statue in the U.S. Capitol's Hall of Fame, Congressman Littlefield of Maine declared:

> The home is the basic unit of our Christian civilization. It is the foundation upon which our free institutions rest. Upon its integrity, purity and character the quality of our civilization depends. It is a holy shrine. Whatever profanes it pollutes the sacred temple of liberty itself. Whoever defends and enobles it insures to our children and our children's children the blessings of freedom and the enduring of the government of the people, for the people, and by the people. A civilization based upon a lecherous and debauched home is rotten to the core.
>
> Statesmen, warriors and patriots may strive and build and achieve, but all their striving, building and achieving is in vain, even as "sounding brass or a tinkling cymbal" is. It disregards the eternal moral verities and does not conserve the true happiness and the highest welfare of mankind. This divinely gifted woman bent every energy, shaped every purpose, and devoted every aspiration of a godly life to the consummation of this happiness and welfare. It is fitting that her work should be thus recognized.
>
> When Illinois decided to place another statue in the Capitol Hall of Fame, many outstanding names came to mind. Probably no state in the Union has been more fortunate in this respect than Illinois. There were Lincoln, Douglas, Grant, Logan and a host of others...I repeat that it is not surprising that the people of Illinois should choose Frances Willard for a distinction like this...In every land, women rise and call her blessed...

FRANCES E. WILLARD, 1839-1898, ILLINOIS

After the Marble Statue of Frances Willard in the Hall of Fame, U.S. Capitol, Washington, D.C.

Officially Recorded Presidential Inaugural Scriptures:
On March 4th, 1865, **Abraham Lincoln** was sworn into office for a second term as President of the United States. *The New York Times* describes the ceremony as follows:

> The oath to protect and maintain the Constitution of the United States was administered to Mr. Lincoln by Chief Justice Chase, in the presence of thousands, who witnessed the interesting ceremony while standing in mud almost knee-deep. *The New York Times*, New York, Sunday, March 5, 1865.

In his inaugural address which immediately followed the oath-taking, the 16th President of the United States incorporated biblical quotations from Matthew 7:1 and 18:7 respectively:

> "...But let us judge not that we not be judged..." and "...Woe unto the world because of its offenses, for it must needs be that offenses come, but woe to that man by whom the offense cometh."

Lincoln's only known inaugural Bible is a King James Version of the Holy Bible, published by the Oxford University Press in London. Written on its flyleaf are the following words:

> To Mrs. Sally Carroll from her devoted husband Wm. Thos. Carroll
> 4 March 1861.

U.S. President: Abraham Lincoln (16th).

GENERAL LEW WALLACE
1827 – 1905

*After the Marble Statue of Lew Wallace in the Hall of Fame, U.S.
Capitol, Washington, D.C.*

INDIANA
(land of the Indians)

The Preamble to the Constitution of the State of Indiana states that, We the people of the State of Indiana, grateful to Almighty God for the free exercise of the right to choose our own form of government, do ordain this Constitution.

Indiana joined the Union on December 11, 1816 as the 19th State.

State Capital: Indianapolis.

State Motto:
"The Crossroads of America."

State Seal:
"A perfect circle, two and five eighths (2 $5/8$) inches in diameter, enclosed by a plain line. Another circle within the first, two and three eighths (2 $3/8$) inches in diameter enclosed by a beaded line, leaving a margin of one quarter ($1/4$) of an inch. In the top half of this margin are the words 'Seal of the State of Indiana.'"

"At the bottom center, 1816, flanked on either side by a diamond, with two (2) dots and a leaf of the tulip tree (liriodendron tulipifera), at both ends of the diamond. The inner circle has two (2) trees in the left background, three (3) hills in the center background with nearly a full sun setting behind and between the first and second hill from the left.

"There are fourteen (14) rays from the sun, starting with two (2) short ones to the left, the third being longer and then alternating, short and long. There are two (2) sycamore trees on the right, the larger one being nearer the center and having a notch cut nearly half way through, from the left side, a short distance above the ground. The woodsman is wearing a hat and holding his ax nearly perpendicular on his right. The ax blade is turned away from him and is even with his hat.

"The buffalo is in the foreground, facing to the left of front. His tail is up, front feet on the ground with back feet in the air - as he jumps over a log.

"The ground has shoots of blue grass, in the area of the buffalo and woodsman."[1]

State Flag:
The torch in the center stands for liberty and enlightenment; the rays represent their far-reaching influence. "The field of the flag shall be blue with nineteen (19) stars and a flaming torch in gold or buff. Thirteen (13) stars shall be arranged in an outer circle, representing the original thirteen (13) states; five (5) stars shall be arranged in a half circle below the torch and inside the outer circle of stars, representing the States admitted prior to Indiana; and the nineteenth star, appreciably larger than the others and representing Indiana shall be placed above the flame of the torch. The outer circle of stars shall be so arranged so that one (1) star shall appear directly in the middle at the top of the circle, and the word 'Indiana'

shall be placed in a half circle over and above the star representing Indiana and midway between it and the star in the center above it. Rays shall be shown radiating from the torch to the three (3) stars on each side of the star in the upper center of the circle."[2]

State Song:
  "On the Banks of the Wabash, Far Away."[3] Words and music by Paul Dresser.

State Poem:

INDIANA
God crowned her hills with beauty,
Gave her lakes and winding streams,
Then He edged them all with woodlands
As the settings for our dreams.
Lovely are her moonlit rivers,
Shadowed by the sycamores,
Where the fragrant winds of summer
Play along the willowed shores...[4]

State Banner:
  The state banner was adopted by the 1917 General Assembly as part of the commemoration of the State's 1916 Centennial celebration, after a competition sponsored by the Daughters of the American Revolution. The prize-winning design was submitted by Paul Hadley of Mooresville, Indiana.

First "Christian Heritage Week:" February 26-March 4, 1995, proclaimed by the Governor.

Of Historic Interest:
  At the Unveiling and Reception of the statue of **General Lew Wallace (1827-1905),** Indiana's greatest hero in the Hall of Fame, Mr. Beveridge of Indiana gave this Address:

> ...He became a healer of wounds which misguided heroism had made on the Nation's breast. He went back to his law office at Crawfordsville, but it could not contain or retain the genius whom God had appointed for a more notable purpose. He served his clients faithfully; but his brain was busy with splendid dreams.
>
> And so Lew Wallace chafed under the duties of his country law office in Crawfordsville. And Grant made him governor of New Mexico. In the slumberous atmosphere of that curious Territory, with the European and almost oriental conditions about him, with the desert sands reminding him of deserted Palestine, Lew Wallace conceived and partly wrote *Ben Hur*.
>
> This book has been translated into every modern tongue and even into the Japanese. It is the best appreciation of Jesus that ever has been penned by merely mortal and uninspired fingers. Only the all-seeing and all-wise One knows how many millions it has lifted closer to an understanding of and an affection for the Savior of the world.
>
> Thus it was that Lew Wallace, the soldier of a Nation, become Lew Wallace, the author for a world.

We plan our little schemes of life, but a higher Designer than we thwarts those plans; and after all is done we see how much wiser than our device is that larger wisdom which shapes our destinies. God always knows what He is about. There is no man here who has not found that some of his cleverest calculations have been frustrated by events to his own well-being and usefulness...[5]

In the *Preface* to his book, ***The First Christmas,*** published by Harper & Bros., New York, in 1899, Lew Wallace explains how and why he came to write ***Ben Hur:***

I heard the story of the Wise Men when a small boy. My mother read it to me; and of all the tales of the Bible and the New Testament none took such a lasting hold upon my imagination, none so filled me with wonder. Who were they? Whence did they come? Were they all from the same country? Did they come singly or together? Above all, what led them to Jerusalem, asking of all they met the strange question, "Where is he that is born King of the Jews? For we have seen his star in the east, and are come to worship him."

Finally I concluded to write of them. By carrying the story on to the birth of Christ in the cave by Bethlehem, it was possible, I thought, to compose a brochure that might be acceptable to the Harper Brothers. Seeing the opportunities it afforded for rich illustration, they might be pleased to publish it as a serial in their Magazine.

When the writing was done, I laid it away in a drawer of my desk, waiting for courage to send it forward: and there it might be still lying had it not been for a fortuitous circumstance.

There was a great mass Convention of Republicans at Indianapolis in '76. I resolved to attend it, and took a sleeper from Crawfordsville the evening before the meeting. Moving slowly down the aisle of the car, talking with some friends, I passed the state-room. There was a knock on the door from the inside, and some one called my name. Upon answer, the door opened, and I saw Colonel Robert G. Ingersoll looking comfortable as might be considering the sultry weather.

"Was it you called me, Colonel?"

"Yes," he said. "Come in. I feel like talking."

I leaned against the cheek of the door, and said, "Well, if you will let me dictate the subject, I will come in."

"Certainly. That's exactly what I want."

I took seat by him, and began:

"Is there a God?"

Quick as a flash, he replied, "I don't know: do you?"

And then I — "Is there a Devil?"

And he — "I don't know: do you?"

"Is there a Heaven?"

"I don't know: do you?"

"Is there a Hell?"

"I don't know: do you?

"Is there a Hereafter?"

"I don't know: do you?"

I finished, saying, "There, Colonel, you have the texts. Now, go."

And he did. He was in prime mood; and beginning, his ideas turned to speech, flowing like a heated river. His manner of putting things was marvellous; and as the Wedding Guest was held by the glittering eye of the Ancient Mariner, I sat spellbound, listening to a medley of argument, eloquence, wit, satire, audacity, irreverence, poetry, brilliant antitheses, and pungent excoriation of believers in God, Christ, and Heaven, the like of which I had never heard. He surpassed himself, and that is saying a great deal.

The speech was brought to an end by our arrival at the Indianapolis Central Station nearly two hours after its commencement. Upon alighting from the car, we separated: he to go to a hotel, and I to my brother's a long way up northeast of town. The street-cars were at my service, but I preferred to walk, for I was in a confusion of mind not unlike dazement.

To explain this, it is necessary now to confess that my attitude with respect to religion had been one of absolute indifference. I had heard it argued times innumerable, always without interest. So, too, I had read the sermons of great preachers — Bossuet, Chalmers, Robert Hall, and Henry Ward Beecher — but always for the surpassing charm of their rhetoric. But — how strange! To lift me out of my indifference, one would think only strong affirmations of things regarded holiest would do. Yet here was I now moved as never before, and by what? The most outright denials of all human knowledge of God, Christ, Heaven, and the Hereafter which figures so in the hope and faith of the believing everywhere. Was the Colonel right? What had I on which to answer yes or no? He had made me ashamed of my ignorance: and then — here is the unexpected of the affair — as I walked on in the cool darkness, I was aroused for the first time in my life to the importance of religion. To write all my reflections would require many pages. I pass them to say simply that I resolved to study the subject. And while casting round how to set about the study to the best advantage, I thought of the manuscript in my desk. Its closing scene was the child Christ in the cave by Bethlehem:

why not go on with the story down to the crucifixion? That would make a book, and compel me to study everything of pertinency; after which, possibly, I would be possessed of opinions of real value.

It only remains to say that I did as resolved, with results — *first,* the book **"Ben-Hur,"** and, *second,* a conviction amounting to absolute belief in God and the divinity of Christ.

In his *Autobiography,* published by Harper & Bros. in 1906, Wallace adds the following:

...I believe in the Divinity of Jesus Christ; and that there may be no suspicion of haggling over the word "divinity," permission is besought to quote the preface of a little volume of mine, *The Boyhood of Christ:* "Should one ask of another, or wonder in himself, why I, who am neither minister of the Gospel, nor theologian, nor churchman, have presumed to write this book, it pleases me to answer him, respectfully — I wrote it to fix an impression distinctly in my mind. Asks he for the impression thus sought to be fixed in my mind, then I would be twice happy did he content himself with this answer — The Jesus Christ in whom I believe was, in all the stages of his life, a human being. His divinity was the Spirit within him, 'and the Spirit was God.'"

— Lew Wallace

JAMES HARLAN, 1820-1899

After the Bronze Sculpture of James Harlan in the Hall of Fame, U.S. Capitol, Washington, D.C.

IOWA
(beautiful land)

The Constitution of the State of Iowa states that, *We the people of the State of Iowa, grateful to the Supreme Being for the blessings hitherto enjoyed, and feeling our dependence on Him for a continuation of those blessings, do ordain and establish a free and independent government...*

Iowa joined the Union on December 28, 1846 as the 29th State.

State Capital: Des Moines.

State Motto:
"Our Liberties we Prize; and our Rights we will Maintain."[1]

State Seal:
One of the initial acts of the first Iowa Legislature in 1847 was to create the Great Seal of Iowa. The two-inch diameter seal pictures a citizen soldier standing in a wheat field, surrounded by farming and industrial tools, with the Mississippi River in the background. An eagle is overhead, holding in its beak a scroll bearing the state motto, "Our Liberties we Prize, and our Rights we will Maintain." The motto was the work of a three-man Senate committee and was incorporated into the design of the seal at their suggestion.[2]

State Flag:
The state flag, designed by Mrs. Dixie Cornell Gebhardt of Knoxville and a member of D.A.R., consists of three vertical stripes of blue, white and red. **Blue** stands for loyalty, justice and truth; **white** for purity; and **red** for courage. On a white center stripe is an eagle carrying in its beak blue streamers inscribed with the state motto, "Our Liberties we Prize, and our Rights we will Maintain. The word Iowa is in red letters just below the streamers.[3]

All schools must fly the state flag on school days. The flag may be flown on the sites of public buildings. When displayed with the United States flag, the state flag must be flown below the national emblem.

State Song:
"Song of Iowa."

First "Christian Heritage Week:" September 20-26, 1998, proclaimed by the Governor.

Of Historic Interest:
James Harlan (1820-1899) was chosen by the citizens of Iowa as their greatest hero in the U.S. Capitol's Hall of Fame. Harlan was a U.S. Senator and friend of Abraham Lincoln, who appointed him Secretary of the Interior in his second Cabinet. Following the death of Lincoln, his son, Robert Lincoln, married Harlan's daughter, Mary.[4]

Harlan's family lived in a log cabin constructed with wooden pegs. The family's only books were a Bible, Harvey's Evening Meditations and an Almanac. His upbringing being similar to that of Lincoln, he used to read at night by the light of a wood fire. It is recorded that Harlan's home was "a preaching place" for itinerant ministers, which formed and fashioned the boy's Christian foundations and way of life.[5]

Throughout his life, Harlan was active in the Methodist church, being an elder who sometimes preached from the pulpit. At the age of twenty, he attended a seminary for a short space of time, speaking frequently at temperance and Sunday School gatherings.

James Harlan attended *Asbury Methodist College* (now De Pauw University), subsequently marrying a resident in the college town, Ann Eliza Peck. He strongly opposed slavery. At the age of thirty-five, he took his place in the United States Senate. He also studied law and became the President of *Iowa Wesleyan College.*[6]

During the Civil War, Senator Harlan enthusiastically supported Lincoln's policies. Not only did he introduce the bill that gave war powers to the President and to Congress, but he voted for its appropriations.

Robert and Mary Lincoln hastened to see Harlan at his home in Mount Pleasant, Iowa, at the end of his life. His will designated that his mansion be given to Wesleyan University. Upon its door are marks and the ages of his grandchildren, who were Abraham Lincoln's grandchildren as well.[7]

Officially Recorded Presidential Inaugural Scriptures:
No Inaugural Bible for **Herbert C. Hoover** has as yet been found. Of the several Bibles in his possession, an American Standard Version comes with the following inscribed card:

Presented by the International Council of Religious Education representing the Educational Boards of the Protestant Christian Churches of the United States and Canada. March 4, 1929.

Proverbs 29:18 was the choice made by this President as he took the oath of office:

> Where there is no vision, the people cast off restraint. But he that
> keepeth the law, happy is he.
>   (Proverbs 29:18) American Standard Version

United States President: Herbert Clark Hoover (31st).

GEORGE WASHINGTON GLICK, 1827-1911, KANSAS

*After the Original Marble Sculpture, Hall of Fame, U.S.
Capitol, Washington, D.C.*

KANSAS
(people of the south wind)

KANSAS

The Preamble to the Constitution of the State of Kansas states that, *We the people of Kansas, grateful to Almighty God for our civil and religious privileges...*

Kansas joined the Union on January 29, 1861 as the 34th State.

State Capital: Topeka.

State Motto:
"Ad Astra Per Aspera," translated from Latin to mean "To the Stars through Difficulties."

State Seal:
The Great Seal of the State of Kansas is described as follows: "The east is represented by a rising sun, in the right-hand corner of the seal; to the left of it, commerce is represented by a river and a steamboat; in the foreground, agriculture is represented as the basis of the future prosperity of the state, by a settler's cabin and a man plowing with a pair of horses; beyond this is a train of ox-wagons, going west; in the background is seen a herd of buffalo, retreating, pursued by two Indians, on horseback; around the top is the motto, "Ad Astra Per Aspera," and beneath is a cluster of thirty-four stars, representing Kansas' admittance as the 34th State in the Union. The circle is surrounded by the words, "Great Seal of the State of Kansas, January 29, 1861."[1]

The motto, "Ad Astra Per Aspera," - "To the Stars through Difficulties," was adopted as part of the Great Seal of the State of Kansas.

State Flag:
In 1927, the State Legislature determined that the State flag should consist of a sunflower (the State flower) atop the State seal on a blue background. Directly beneath the sunflower is a blue and gold bar signifying Kansas as part of the Louisiana Purchase.[2] The word "Kansas" in gold block letters was added to the flag in 1961.

State Song:
"Home on the Range," adopted in 1947.[3]

HOME ON THE RANGE
Oh, give me a home where the buffalo roam,
Where the deer and the antelope play,
Where seldom is heard a discouraging word,
And the sky is not clouded all day...

First "Christian Heritage Week": April 23-29, 1995, proclaimed by the Governor.

Of Historic Interest:
George Washington Glick (1827-1911) was chosen by Kansan citizens as their hero in the U.S. Capitol's Hall of Fame. The *Topeka Journal* newspaper, in its April 13, 1912 article, describes his eventful life as follows:

64

George W. Glick, the ninth Governor of Kansas, was born at Greencastle, Ohio, July 4, 1827. His great-grandfather came from Germany and settled in Pennsylvania shortly before the Revolution and with his four brothers, took an active part in the (American Revolutionary) War. His grandfather was a soldier in the War of 1812, and his father, Isaac Glick, was a politician of considerable note in Ohio. George W. Glick was reared on his father's Ohio farm and had the common school education of the time. When 21 years of age he entered the law office of Buckland & Hayes (Rutherford B. Hayes — later to become U.S. President) at Fremont, and two years later was admitted to practice law. He practiced law at Fremont until the Spring of 1859, when he moved to Achison, Kansas, and Achison has been his home ever since...In 1868, Glick was sent to the Kansas legislature and was reelected for four successive terms and again in 1874, 1876 and 1882. In 1873 he was elected to the State Senate and when he returned to the House in 1876, was Speaker pro tempore...In 1882, he was again nominated for Governor and elected...He was an advocate of important laws...

Governor Glick has long owned a valuable heirloom. It is a Bible of the German Lutheran Church, printed in 1819 by subscription, each subscriber contributing one hundred dollars. The Bible has been in the family for three generations.

Officially Recorded Presidential Inaugural Scriptures:
Dwight D. Eisenhower was sworn into office on January 21, 1953, on two inaugural Bibles, his own West Point (American Standard Version) Bible and Washington's Inaugural Bible. Eisenhower's Bible contains the following lines:

> Presented to Dwight David Eisenhower upon his graduation from USMA, June, 1915.

II Chronicles 7:14, Eisenhower's choice of inaugural Scripture for his swearing in, is marked with a blue pencil:

> If my people, who are called by my name, shall humble themselves and pray and seek my face, and turn from their wicked ways, then will I hear from heaven, and will forgive their sin, and will heal their land. (II Chronicles 7:14)
> American Standard Version

George Washington's inaugural Bible was simultaneously opened to Psalm 127 on this occasion:

> Except the Lord build the house, they labor in vain that build it; except the Lord keep the city, the watchman waketh but in vain. It is vain for you to rise up early, to sit up late, to eat the bread of sorrows; for so he giveth his beloved sleep. (Psalm 127:1-2)

Eisenhower's second inauguration took place on January 21, 1957. At this time, the President's West Point Bible lay under his hand, his choice being the twelfth verse of the thirty-third Psalm:

> Blessed is the nation whose God is Jehovah. The people whom he
> hath chosen for his own inheritance. (Psalm 33:12)

United States President: Dwight D. Eisenhower (34th).

McDOWELL

1771 – 1830

After the Bronze Statue of Dr. Ephraim McDowell in the Hall of Fame, U.S. Capitol, Washington, D.C.

KENTUCKY
(from the Indian,
"land of tomorrow")

The Preamble to the Constitution of the Commonwealth of Kentucky states that, *We the people of the Commonwealth of Kentucky, grateful to Almighty God for the civil, political and religious liberties we enjoy, and invoking the continuance of these blessings, do ordain and establish this Constitution.*

Kentucky joined the Union on June 1, 1792 as the 15th State.

State Capital: Frankfort.

State Motto:
"United We Stand, Divided We Fall."[1] The motto is taken from "Liberty Song," a popular composition that was written in 1768 by John Dickinson of Pennsylvania. One of the verses of the "Liberty Song" states: "Then join hand in hand, brave Americans all, By uniting we stand, by dividing we fall." The song was popular during the Revolutionary War.

State Seal:
On December 20, 1792, the General Assembly approved an act to create the State Seal. The act states:

> Be it enacted by the General Assembly, that the Governor be empowered and is hereby required to provide at the public charge a seal for this Commonwealth; and procure the same to be engraved with the following device, viz: 'Two friends embracing, with the name of the State over their heads and around about the following motto: United we stand, divided we fall.'

In 1962 the General Assembly passed an act making the Seal of Kentucky depict a frontiersman clasping the shoulder and shaking the hand of a statesman. The frontiersman represents the spirit of the Kentucky frontier settlers. The statesman represents the Kentuckians who served their State and nation in the halls of government.

State Flag:
The Kentucky State Flag is navy blue silk or bunting, with the seal of the Commonwealth encircled by a wreath of goldenrod, embroidered, printed, or stamped on the center. The dimension of the flag may vary. Jessie Cox, an art teacher in Frankfort, designed the flag according to the specifications of the act. She and her sister made several of the early flags.[2]

State Song:
"My Old Kentucky Home" by Stephen Collins Foster, 1853.

First "Christian Heritage Week:" June 16-22, 1996, proclaimed by the Governor.

Of Historic Interest:
Ephraim McDowell (1771-1830) was chosen by the citizens of Kentucky as their hero

in the U.S. Capitol's Hall of Fame.

McDowell was a talented surgeon displaying the character traits of gentleness, humility, skillful insight, imagination and boldness far beyond the era he lived in. McDowell was the first surgeon in the world to conduct abdominal surgery, removing from the ovary of Jane Crawford a tumor weighing twenty pounds. Both surgeon and patient exemplified the highest courage. McDowell rode sixty miles through the wilderness to visit Mrs. Crawford, a forty-seven-year-old woman of character and intelligence; mother of five. He told her that unless the tumor were removed, she would die within two years. However, if she agreed to this operation, never before performed, it might mean instant death. Mrs. Crawford rode sixty miles to Dr. McDowell's office in Danville, being aware of the acute pain accompanying this operation. (Dr. Crawford Long of Georgia discovered the use of sulfuric acid as an anaesthetic in surgery only thirty years later).[3]

McDowell performed this operation on a clean table, using clean instruments, as modern sterilization had not as yet been discovered. During the entire twenty-five minute operation, Mrs. Crawford was perfectly conscious, singing psalms to the glory of God. She lived thirty-one fruitful years after her successful operation. It is recorded that a group of Kentuckians gathered outside his office, prepared to arrest him for murder, should Mrs. Crawford have died. Dr. McDowell, however, left us this account, that before the operation, he had written and placed in his pocket the simple prayer: "Almighty God, be with me, I humbly beseech Thee, in attendance in Thy holy hour. Give me becoming awe of Thy presence . . . Direct me, O God, in performing this operation, for I am but an instrument in Thy hands . . . upon this poor afflicted woman."[4]

DR. EPHRAIM McDOWELL'S HOME AND APOTHECARY
IN DANVILLE, KY., AS THEY APPEARED ABOUT 1795.

Another successful operation was that performed on Mrs. Overton at **The Hermitage**, home of President Andrew Jackson, in Nashville. She was the wife of one of Mrs. Jackson's nephews, adopted by General Jackson. Dr. McDowell rode a hundred and fifty miles to Tennessee to perform this operation. General Jackson, it is reported, heated the water and passed the doctor his instruments, as needed. General Jackson then had McDowell remove a tumor from the neck and shoulder of one of his black servants. Upon the completion of the successful operation on his wife, Mr. Overton sent Dr. McDowell a check in the amount of $1,500.00, which was promptly returned by the doctor with a note that an error had probably been made, his bill being for $500.00. Mr. Overton again sent his original check to McDowell, stating, with gratitude, that it did not cover the services received.[5]

More than thirty operations for the removal of stones from the bladder were performed by McDowell. Among these was one performed on fourteen-year-old James K. Polk, who later became President of the United States. Philadelphia then being the medical center of the nation, Ephraim McDowell gained the reputation of being the greatest physician and surgeon west of that city. He was thrice called upon to perform Caesarian operations. Two were successful for both mother and baby.[6]

McDowell pioneered the termination of blood-letting, which he stated was a deterrent to recovery; as well as being wary of drugs, declaring that "they were often more a curse than a blessing to the human race."

This brilliant Kentuckian surgeon was immune to public opinion, treating all who sought his aid, rich and poor, black and white; accepting only what they could afford. His happiness was in serving others, quoting the following Scripture as his modus operandi: "I have learned in whatever state I am, therewith to be content." (Philippians 4:11)[7]

McDowell received many criticisms from the medical profession, to include that of Dr. James Johnson, editor of the *London Medical and Chirurgical Review.* After McDowell's death, however, when the facts of abdominal surgery became irrefutable, Dr. Johnson wrote that he "asked pardon of God and Dr. McDowell of Danville."[8]

Kentuckians can justly be proud of Ephraim McDowell, who, with Henry Clay, represents Kentucky in the Hall of Fame.

United States President: Abraham Lincoln, born in Kentucky (16th).

THE THOMAS JEFFERSON READING ROOM MURAL PAINTING. LIBRARY of CONGRESS WASHINGTON, D.C.

THIS ROOM IS DEDICATED TO THOMAS JEFFERSON

A Tribute to Thomas Jefferson, third U.S. President, who acquired Louisiana for the Union.

LOUISIANA
(After Louis XIV of France)

The Preamble to the Constitution of the State of Louisiana states that, *We, the people of Louisiana, grateful to Almighty God for the civil, political, economic and religious liberties we enjoy...and secure the blessings of freedom and justice to ourselves and our posterity, do ordain and establish this Constitution.*

Louisiana joined the Union on April 30, 1812 as the 18th State.

State Capital: Baton Rouge.

State Motto:
Union, Justice, Confidence (on seal).

State Seal:
In 1902, Governor William Wright Heart directed the Secretary of State to use a seal of this description: "A Pelican, with its head turned to the left, in a nest with three young; the Pelican, following the tradition in act of tearing its breast to feed its young; around the edge of the seal to be inscribed "State of Louisiana." Over the head of the Pelican to be inscribed "Union, Justice," and under the Pelican to be inscribed "Confidence."

State Flag:
The official State Flag, which consists of a field of solid blue with the pelican group from the State Seal in white and gold.[1]

State Song:
"Give me Louisiana." Words and music by Doralice Fontane. Arrangement by John W. Schaum.

First "Christian Heritage Week:" May 29 - June 1, 1996, proclaimed by the Governor.

Of Historic Interest:
In 1803, **Thomas Jefferson**, third president of the United States, purchased the territory of Louisiana from Napoleon for $15,000,000.

Another worthy tribute to **Thomas Jefferson (1743-1826),** together with other significant persons in the founding period era, is prominently engraved on a wall plaque adjacent to his inscribed pew, in Williamsburg's famed Bruton Parish Episcopal Church (c.1713):

> **To the Glory of God and in Memory of the Members of the Committee** which, in 1777, Drafted the "Act Establishing Religious Freedom" in Virginia:
>
> **Thomas Jefferson,** Vestryman of St. Anne's Parish
> Edmund Pendleton, Vestryman of Drysdale Parish
> George Wythe, Vestryman of Bruton Parish

George Mason, Vestryman of Truro Parish
Thomas Ludwell Lee, Vestryman of Overwharton Parish
Being all Members of the Committee.

Of further interest, is a description of The Battle of New Orleans:

The Battle of New Orleans

During the War of 1812, the loyalty to the United States of the population of the Louisiana Purchase was doubted by the British, and an expedition against New Orleans was organized. In October, 1814, the news of a secret expedition, which was to be joined at Jamaica by the Chesapeake force under Admiral Cochrane, and then proceed against Mobile and New Orleans, was received from American envoys in Europe. President Madison urged Georgia, Kentucky, and Tennessee to send militia to the defense of the Gulf. Andrew Jackson, who was in command of the Department of the South, arrived in New Orleans on December 2, and began energetic preparations for resistance.[2]

The British fleet of more than 50 vessels, carrying about 7,500 soldiers, reached Lake Borgne in December, and on December 13 captured five American gunboats. On December 22 a part of the British force advanced up Bayou Bienvenu, purposely left unguarded by Jackson, and was attacked the next day both by the schooner *Carolina* and by American troops; but the approach of British reinforcements caused Jackson to fall back. He was attacked on December 28, but his lines could not be broken, though the *Carolina* was destroyed by hot shot and the cotton bales which formed part of his entrenchments were set on fire. Another attack (Jan. 1, 1815) was also unsuccessful.[3]

Jackson, whose army amounted to scarcely 5,000 men, chiefly militia, was now reinforced by about 2,000 Kentucky militia; and Sir Edward Pakenham, brother-in-law of the Duke of Wellington, arrived with troops sufficient to raise the British forces to more than 10,000 veterans. Meanwhile, Jackson had drawn crude, though effective, earthworks across the plain of Chalmette, south of the city. These were defended by about 5,000 men; while General Morgan, with 2,500 men, held the opposite side of the river.[4] Pakenham sent a part of his forces to attack Morgan; and thinking that raw militia could not withstand his veterans, Pakenham made a direct frontal assault upon the entrenchments (Jan. 8). His troops disregarded the artillery fire, and approached within 200 yards of the American lines. The militia, many armed with their own squirrel rifles, then opened fire with such deadly accuracy that in half an hour the attacking force was shattered. Pakenham was killed, and the British loss reached over 2,000 men; while on the American side only 13 were killed and 58 wounded...[5]

WILLIAM KING, 1768-1852, MAINE

After the Original Sculpture of William King in the Hall of Fame,
U.S. Capitol, Washington, D.C.

MAINE
(After the ancient French province, "Mayne")

The Preamble to the Constitution of the State of Maine states that, *We the people of Maine, in order to establish justice, insure tranquility, provide for our mutual defense, promote our common welfare, and secure to ourselves and our posterity the blessings of liberty, acknowledging with grateful hearts the goodness of the Sovereign Ruler of the Universe in affording us an opportunity, so favorable to the design; and imploring God's aid and direction in its accomplishment, do agree to form ourselves into a free and independent State, by the style and title of the State of Maine and do ordain and establish the following Constitution for government of the same.*

Maine joined the Union on March 15, 1820 as the 23rd State.

State Capital: Augusta.

State Motto:
"Dirigo," translated from Latin to read, "I direct or I lead."[1]

State Seal:
The Coat of Arms is described in the Laws of 1820 as follows: "A shield, argent, charged with a Pine Tree; a Moose Deer, at the foot of it, recumbent. Supporters: on the dexter side a Husbandman, resting on a scythe; on the sinister side, a Seaman, resting on an anchor. In the foreground, representing sea and land, and under the shield, the name of the State in large Roman Capitals. The whole surmounted by a Crest, the North Star."[2] (Maine has over 17 million forested acres.)

State Flag:
Maine's Coat of Arms is featured on a blue field matching the shade of blue in the flag of the United States. The state flag was adopted by the Maine Legislature in 1909.[3]

State Song:
"State of Maine Song."[4] Chosen by the people of Maine and dedicated to them.

First "Christian Heritage Week:" October 15-21, 1995.

Of Historic Interest:
William King (1768-1852) represents Maine as their greatest hero in the U.S. Capitol's Hall of Fame. For seven long years this able statesman worked tirelessly to effectuate the separation of Maine from Massachusetts, which occurred in 1820, when Maine gained statehood. Prior to this event, King had been sent by Maine (then part of Massachusetts) as their representative to both the House and Senate of Massachusetts.[5]

For his exceptional services in securing Maine's independence from Massachusetts as a State, William King was elected Maine's first governor. He espoused education for all children, serving as an overseer of ***Bowdoin College,*** and then a Trustee of ***Waterville (Colby) College.***[6]

King possessed a unique personality, a forceful mind and depth of thought, commanding the respect and admiration of the people of Maine.

After the vote of separation from Massachusetts, but just prior to the establishment of Maine's Constitutional Convention, King visited Thomas Jefferson at Monticello, discussing the new State's Constitution. He reported later, that the exact contents of Jefferson's advice to him are found in Article VIII of Maine's Constitution, the part on education.[7]

A marble monument to William King's memory was erected in Bath by the State of Maine; after which his statue was dispatched to the U.S. Capitol, to accompany permanently the illustrious heroes chosen by each State in the nation's Hall of Fame.

Popham Colony:

The first **Thanksgiving Day** service in what was to become the United States of America was held on August 9, 1607, by colonists en route to found the short-lived **Popham Colony** at what is now Phippsburg, Maine. After the two ships reached one of the Georges Islands off the Maine Coast, the Reverend Richard Seymour led a group in "gyvinge God thanks for our happy metinge and saffe aryval into the country."

The Memorial Volume of the Popham Celebration, August 19, 1862: Commemorative of the Planting of the Popham Colony on the Peninsula of Sabino, August 19, A.D. 1607, Establishing the Title of England to the Continent (Published under the Direction of the Rev. Edward Ballard, Secretary of the Executive Committee of the Celebration) appeared in print in 1863. This important celebration commenced with the following Address:

Address of the Hon. C. J. Gilman

Two hundred and fifty-five years ago this day, under the auspices of a Royal charter granted by King James, there assembled on the Peninsula of Sabino, and near to this spot, a party of Englishmen, who formed the first civil and Protestant government of the New World, and by formal occupation and possession, established the title of England to the continent. In the year 1607, in the month of August, on the 19th day of the month, the Commission of George Popham for the Presidency of the new Government was read. Captain Raleigh Gilbert, James Davies, Richard Seymour, the preacher, Capt. Richard Davies, and Capt. Harlow, were all sworn assistants.

In commemoration of this event, the Historical Society of this State, in correspondence with citizens in different parts of the State, have concurred in this celebration; and it is proposed from time to time, in the valley of the Sagadahoc, on the Peninsula of Sabino, to recall and to illustrate the events of the past, and by this and future celebrations to assign to Maine her true historic position...

In order that the record of events, which here transpired, may be made still more vivid and impressive, it has been thought fit and proper to insert in the wall of the Fort a "Memorial Stone." The President of the Historical Society, the President of Bowdoin College, the representative of the government of the State and the representative of the government of the United States, in the disposition and adjustment of this stone, will participate. Before the commencement of these interesting exercises, let us imitate the example of those who stood here two hundred and fifty-five years ago this day. As the Rev. Richard Seymour, Chaplain of the Colony was invited to perform acts of religious worship then, so now do I invite the Right Rev. George Burgess, Bishop of the Diocese of Maine, to perform acts of religious worship according to the ceremonial of the Episcopal Church of that day.

In accordance with this request, the Bishop proceeded to the religious duties of the occasion, using, as nearly as the changed circumstances of the case would allow, the same services, taken from the *Prayer Book* of the time of King James, as were employed by the colonists in their solemnities on the day commemorated, under the guidance of their Chaplain, the Rev. Richard Seymour. They were as follows:

An Order for Morning Prayer

At what time soever a sinner doth repent him of his sin from the bottom of his heart, I will put all his wickedness out of my remembrance, saith the Lord. Ezekiel XVIII.

I will go to my Father, and say to him, Father, I have sinned against heaven: and against thee, and am no more worthy to be called thy son. Luke XV.

Dearly beloved brethren, the Scripture moveth us in sundry places to acknowledge, and confess our manifold sins and wickedness, and that we should not dissemble nor cloke them before the face of Almighty God our heavenly Father, but confess them with an humble, lowly, penitent, and obedient heart to the end, that we may obtain forgiveness of the same by his infinite goodness and mercy. And although we ought at all times humbly to acknowledge our sins before God, yet ought we most chiefly so to do, when we assemble and meet together, to render thanks for the great benefits that we have received at his hands, to set forth his most worthy praise, to hear his most holy word, and to ask those things which are requisite and necessary, as well for the body as the soul. Wherefore I pray and beseech you, as many as are here present, to accompany me with a pure heart and humble voice, unto the throne of the heavenly grace, saying after me.

[A general confession to be made of the whole congregation after the minister, kneeling.]

Almighty and most merciful Father: We have erred and strayed from thy ways like lost sheep. We have followed too much the devices and desires of our own hearts. We have offended against thy holy laws. We have left undone those things which we ought to have done; and we have done those things which we ought not to have done; and there is no health in us. But thou, O Lord, have mercy upon us, miserable offenders. Spare thou them, O God, which confess their faults. Restore thou them that are penitent; according to thy promises declared unto mankind in Christ Jesus our Lord.

And grant, O most merciful Father, for his sake, that we may hereafter live a godly, righteous, and sober life, to the glory of thy holy Name. Amen.

Almighty God, the Father of our Lord Jesus Christ, who desireth not the death of a sinner, but rather, that he may turn from his wickedness, and live: and hath given power and commandment to his Ministers to declare and pronounce to his people, being penitent, the absolution and remission of their sins: He pardoneth and absolveth all them that truly repent and unfeignedly believe his holy Gospel. Wherefore let us beseech him to grant us true repentance, by his Holy Spirit, that those things may please him, which we do at this present and the rest of our life hereafter, may be pure, and holy, so that at the last, we may come to his eternal joy, through Jesus Christ our Lord.

[The people shall answer:]

Amen.

[Then shall the minister begin the Lord's Prayer with a loud voice.]

Our Father, which art in Heaven, Hallowed be thy Name, Thy Kingdom come. Thy will be done in earth as it is in Heaven. Give us this day our daily bread and forgive us our trespasses, as we forgive them that trespass against us. And lead us not into temptation; But deliver us from evil. Amen.

[Then likewise he shall say,]

O Lord, open thou our lips.

Answer. And our mouth shall show forth thy praise.

Pastor. O God, make speed to save us.

Answer. O Lord, make haste to help us.

[Then all of them standing up, the Presbyter shall say or sing.]

Pastor. Glory be to the Father, and to the Son, and to the Holy Ghost. As it was in the beginning, is now, and ever shall be, world without end. Amen

Praise ye the Lord.

Answer. The Lord's name be praised.

[Then shall follow certain Psalms in order, as they are appointed in a table made for that purpose.]...

JOHN HANSON, 1715-1783

After the Original Bronze Sculpture of John Hanson in the Hall of Fame, U.S. Capitol, Washington, D.C.

MARYLAND
(After Queen Henrietta Maria,
wife of King Charles I
of England and daughter of
Henry IV of France)

The Constitution of the State of Maryland states that, *We the people of the State of Maryland, grateful to Almighty God for our civil and religious liberty...and, Nothing shall prohibit...the making reference to, belief in, reliance upon, or invoking the aid of God or a Supreme Being in any governmental or public document, proceeding, activity, ceremony, school, institution or place.*

Maryland joined the Union on April 28, 1788 as the 7th State.

State Capital: Annapolis.

State Motto:
"With Favor wilt Thou Compass us as With a Shield."

State Seal:
The Great Seal of Maryland is used by the Governor and Secretary of State to authenticate official documents. The original, like the present one, was brought to this country in early colonial days. Its design stems from the time of the American Revolution.[1] Only the Reverse has ever been cut, although the Obverse is used, as for decoration on public buildings.

The Obverse of the State Seal:
Lord Baltimore is shown armed and mounted. The Latin inscription translated is, "Cecilius, Absolute Lord of Maryland and Avalon, Baron of Baltimore."

The Reverse of the State Seal:
Lord Baltimore's Coat of Arms, with figures of a farmer and fisherman, are shown. The wording on the scroll, translated from Italian, reads: "Manly Deeds, Womanly Words." The wording around the border translated from Latin reads: "With Favor wilt Thou Compass us as With a Shield."

State Flag:
Maryland's flag bears the arms of the Calvert and Mynne families (the latter wrongly identified as the Crossland family in the act of creating the State Flag). Calvert was the family name of the Lords of Baltimore who founded Maryland, and their colors of gold and black appear in the first and fourth quarters of the flag. Mynne was the family of Anne Calvert, the wife of George Calvert, first Lord Baltimore. The red and white Mynne colors, with a cross, appear in the second and third quarters. This flag was first flown on October 11, 1880, in Baltimore at a parade marking the 150th anniversary of the founding of Baltimore. It also was flown on October 25th, 1888, at Gettysburg Battlefield for ceremonies dedicating monuments to Maryland's regiments of the Army of Potomac. Officially, it was adopted as the State Flag in 1904.[2]

Maryland law requires that if any ornament is affixed to the top of a flagstaff carrying the Maryland flag, the ornament must be a gold cross.

State Song:
  "Maryland, My Maryland!"

  The nine stanza poem, "Maryland, My Maryland," was written by James Ryder Randall in 1861. A native of Maryland, Randall was teaching in Louisiana in the early days of the Civil War, and he was outraged at the news of Union troops being marched through Baltimore. The poem articulated Randall's love of the Confederacy. Set to the traditional tune of "Lauriger Horatius" ("O, Tannenbaum"), the song achieved wide popularity in Maryland and throughout the South.

  "Maryland, My Maryland" was adopted as the State Song in 1939.[3]

MARYLAND, MY MARYLAND
by James Ryder Randall

I

The despot's heel is on thy shore, Maryland!
His torch is at thy temple door, Maryland!
Avenge the patriotic gore, That flecked the streets of Baltimore,
And be the battle queen of yore, Maryland! My Maryland!

II

Hark to an exiled son's appeal, Maryland!
My mother State! to thee I kneel, Maryland!
For life and death, for woe and weal, Thy peerless chivalry reveal,
And gird thy beauteous limbs with steel, Maryland! My Maryland!

III

Thou wilt not cower in the dust, Maryland!
Thy beaming sword shall never rust, Maryland!
Remember Carroll's sacred trust, Remember Howard's warlike thrust,
And all thy slumberers with the just, Maryland! My Maryland!

IV

Come! 'tis the red dawn of day, Maryland!
Come with panoplied array, Maryland!
With Ringgold's spirit for the fray, With Watson's blood at Monterey,
With fearless Lowe and dashing May, Maryland! My Maryland!

V

Come! for thy shield is bright and strong, Maryland!
Come! for thy dalliance does thee wrong, Maryland!
Come to thine own heroic throng, Stalking with Liberty along,
And chant thy dauntless slogan song, Maryland! My Maryland!

VI

Dear Mother! burst the tyrant's chain, Maryland!
Virginia should not call in vain, Maryland!
She meets her sisters on the plain- "Sic semper!" 'tis the proud refrain
That baffles minions back again, Maryland! My Maryland!

VII

I see the blush upon thy cheek, Maryland!
For thou wast ever bravely meek, Maryland!

But lo! there surges forth a shriek, From hill to hill, from creek to creek-
Potomac calls to Chesapeake, Maryland! My Maryland!

VIII
Thou wilt not yield the vandal toll, Maryland!
Thou wilt not crook to his control, Maryland!
Better the fire upon thee roll, Better the blade, the shot, the bowl,
Than crucifixion of the soul, Maryland! My Maryland!

IX
I hear the distant thunder-hum, Maryland!
The Old Line's bugle, fife, and drum, Maryland!
She is not dead, nor deaf, nor dumb- Huzza! she spurns the Northern scum!
She breathes! she burns! she'll come! she'll come! Maryland!

First "Christian Heritage Week:" February 23 - March 1, 1997, proclaimed by the Governor.

Of Historic Interest:
The "Star Spangled Banner," our National Anthem, was written by **Francis Scott Key** during the Battle of Baltimore, in the 1812-1814 War. A gigantic 42 feet by 30 feet flag flying through the night, over the embattled Fort McHenry, had been made by Baltimore citizens to express their outrage and defiance of the British. For Francis Scott Key, the banner symbolized a profound patriotism to which he responded with words testifying to God's protection and saving power, later to become the National Anthem. The last stanza reads:

> ...Blest with victory and peace may the Heaven-rescued land, Praise the power that hath made and preserved us a nation! Then conquer we must when our cause it is just, And this be our motto, "In God is our trust." And the Star-Spangled Banner in triumph shall wave, O'er the land of the free and the home of the brave.

John Hanson (1715-1783) served as the First President of the United States in Congress Assembled under the ratified Articles of Confederation at Philadelphia (1781-1782).

The following article appeared in Baltimore's *Evening News*, July 19, 1897:

> ...An Act of Congress of July 2nd, 1864 authorizes the President to "invite each and all the States to provide and furnish statues in marble or bronze, not exceeding two in number from each State, of deceased persons who have been citizens thereof and illustrious for their historic renown or for distinguished civil or military services, such as each State shall determine to be worthy of that national commemoration...

> Without wishing to detract from the other distinguished names mentioned, I sincerely hope that the Commission will imitate Massachusetts and Rhode Island and choose two persons to represent Maryland, one to typify the Colonial period and the other the Revolutionary...

> John Hanson (is) one of the most brilliant statesmen of the Revolution, who helped to plant the tree of liberty, and who upheld it, with strong arm and unwavering heart, when shaken rudest by the storms

of war...In the political discussions against the oppressions of Great Britain, John Hanson entered with an ardent soul into the defense of Colonial freedom...It is only in times of peril that the worth of men can be truly valued. At such periods, courage has all its honor — wisdom all its loveliness...Hanson served in the Continental Congress...He had witnessed the struggles of his country's birth. He had aided to strengthen its infancy and to advance its growth, and, now that the liberties of his country had been established, full of years, fuller of honors, blessed in his life, more blessed in the happiness of his country, this great statesman yielded his last breath...

John Hanson was chosen by Marylanders to represent them as their hero in the U.S. Capitol's Hall of Fame. A silver plaque on the side of his family pew, in the 1695 *Gloria Dei* (The Olde Swede's) *Church* in Philadelphia, states the following:

John Hanson
President of the United States
in Congress Assembled
Elected 1781
Attended Gloria Dei Church
While in office
He is attributed
with having proclaimed
the first National Thanksgiving
Day.

MARYLAND STATE HOUSE
ANNAPOLIS

SAMUEL ADAMS

MASSACHUSETTS

*After the Original Marble Statue of Samuel Adams in the Hall of
Fame, U.S. Capitol, Washington, D.C.*

MASSACHUSETTS
(great mountain place)

The Constitution of the Commonwealth of Massachusetts states that, *As the happiness of a people, and the good order and preservation of civil government, essentially depend upon piety, religion and morality; and as these cannot be generally diffused through a Community, but by the institution of the public worship of God, and of public instructions in piety, religion and morality: Therefore, to promote their happiness and to secure the good order and preservation of their government, the people of this Commonwealth have a right to invest their legislature with power to authorize and require, and the Legislature shall, from time to time, authorize and require the several towns, parishes, precincts, and other bodies politic, or religious societies, to make suitable provision, at their own expense, for the institution of the public worship of God, and for the support and maintenance of public protestant teachers of piety, religion and morality.*

Massachusetts joined the Union on February 6, 1788 as the 6th State.

Capital of the Commonwealth: Boston.

Motto of the Commonwealth:
"By the Sword we Seek Peace, but Peace only Under Liberty."[1]

Seal of the Commonwealth:
The final form of the seal was determined by a state-wide contest. The arms, according to legislative enactment, consist of "a shield having a blue field or surface with an Indian thereon, dressed in a shirt and moccasins, holding in his right hand a bow, and in his left hand an arrow, point downward, all of gold; and, in the upper corner of the field, above his right arm, a silver star with five points. The crest is a wreath of blue and gold, on which in gold is a right arm, bent at the elbow, clothed and ruffled, with the hand grasping a broadsword." The shield's shape is called "Plantagenet;" the Indian model used was of the Algonquin Indians; the arrow points downward to indicate that the Indian is peaceful. The star indicates that Massachusetts was one of the original thirteen states, being the sixth to join the Union. The sword illustrates the Latin motto, written in gold on a blue ribbon around the bottom of the shield: "Ense petit placidam sub libertate quietem." This is the second of two lines written around 1659 by Algernon Sydney, an English soldier and politician, in the book of Mottos in the Kings Library in Copenhagen, Denmark. Translated it means: "By the Sword we Seek Peace, but Peace only Under Liberty."[2]

Flag of the Commonwealth:
The State Flag is white, bearing on both sides a representation of the Coat of Arms (except that the five-pointed star is white instead of silver).

Song of the Commonwealth:
"All Hail to Massachusetts," words and music by Arthur Marsh.[3]

ALL HAIL TO MASSACHUSETTS
All hail to Massachusetts, the land of the free and the brave!
For Bunker Hill and Charlestown, and flag we love to wave;
For Lexington and Concord, and the shot heard 'round the world;
All hail to Massachusetts, we'll keep her flag unfurled.
She stands upright for freedom's light that shines from sea to sea;
All hail to Massachusetts! Our country 'tis of Thee!

All hail to grand old Bay State, the home of the bean and the cod,
Where pilgrims found a landing and gave their thanks to God.
A land of opportunity in the good old U.S.A.
Where men live long and prosper, and people come to stay.
Don't sell her short but learn to court her industry and stride;
All hail to grand old Bay State! The land of pilgrim's pride!

All hail to Massachusetts, renowned in the Hall of Fame!
How proudly wave her banners emblazoned with her name!
In unity and brotherhood, sons and daughters go hand in hand;
All hail to Massachusetts, there is no finer land!
It's M-A-S-S-A-C-H-U-S-E-T-T-S.
All hail to Massachusetts! All hail! All hail! All hail!

First "Christian Heritage Week:" May 10-16, 1992.

Of Historic Interest:
  The Preamble to the Constitution of the Commonwealth, 1780, written by John Adams, Samuel Adams, and James Bowdoin, states:

> WE, therefore the people of Massachusetts, acknowledging, with grateful hearts, the goodness of the Great Legislator of the Universe, in affording us, in the course of His Providence, an opportunity, deliberately and peaceably, without fraud, violence or surprise, on entering into an Original, explicit, and Solemn Compact with each other; and of forming a new Constitution of Civil Government, for Ourselves and Posterity, and devoutly imploring His direction in so interesting a design, DO agree upon, ordain and establish, the following Declaration of Rights, and Frame of Government, as the CONSTITUTION OF THE COMMONWEALTH OF MASSACHUSETTS.

In 1830, **Daniel Webster** wrote: "I shall enter on no encomium upon Massachusetts; she needs none. There she is. Behold her, and judge for yourselves. There is her history; the world knows it by heart. The past, at least, is secure. There is Boston and Concord and Lexington and Bunker Hill; and they will remain forever."

John Adams' famous speech given to Congress on July 2, 1776, on the proclamation of the Declaration of Independence reads:

> The second day of July, 1776, will be the most memorable epoch in the history of America, to be celebrated by succeeding generations

86

as the great anniversary festival, commemorated as the day of deliverance by solemn acts of devotion to God Almighty from one end of the Continent to the other, from this time forward forevermore. You will think me transported with enthusiasm, but I am not. I am well aware of the toil, the blood, and treasure that it will cost us to maintain this Declaration and support these States; yet, through all the gloom, I can see the rays of light and glory; that the end is worth all the means; that posterity will triumph in that day's transaction, even though we shall rue it, which I trust in God we shall not.

Samuel Adams was the organizer of the American Revolution. An inscription on the base of his famed statue in Boston, reads as follows:

Samuel Adams, 1722-1803, A Patriot.
He organized the Revolution and
signed the Declaration of Independence.
Governor, A true Leader of the People.
A Statesman, Incorruptible and Fearless.
Erected A.D. 1880
bequeathed to the City of Boston
by Jonathan Phillips

Sam Adams (1722-1803) was chosen by Massachusetts as their greatest hero in the Hall of Fame. His oration, given in Independence Hall on August 1, 1776, gives credence to the fact that the Bible is the basis for America's freedoms and liberties:

Countrymen and Brethren,
...Our forefathers threw off the yoke of popery in religion; for you is reserved the honor of leveling the popery of politics. They opened the Bible to all, and maintained the capacity of every man to judge for himself in religion...Our glorious Reformers, when they broke through the fetters of superstition, effected more than could be expected from an age so darkened: But they left much to be done by their posterity. They lopped off indeed some of the branches of popery, but they left the root and stock when they left us under the domination of human systems...and decisions, usurping the infallibility which can be attributed to Revelation alone. They dethroned one usurper only to raise up another. They refused allegiance to the pope, only to place the civil Magistrate on the throne of Christ, vested with authority to enact laws, and inflict penalties in His Kingdom. And if we now cast our eyes over the nations of the earth, we shall find, that instead of possessing *the pure Religion of the Gospel,* they may be divided either into infidels, who deny the truth; or politicians, who make religion a stalking horse for their ambition; or professors who walk in the trammels of authodoxy, and are more attentive to traditions and ordinances of men, than to oracles of Truth. The Civil Magistrate has everywhere contaminated Religion, by making it an engine of policy;...

Benjamin Franklin's Boyhood in Boston,
from his Autobiography

Dear Son:

I have ever had the pleasure in obtaining any little anecdotes of my

87

ancestors. You may remember the enquiries I made among the remains of my relations when you were with me in England, and the journey I undertook for that purpose. Imagining it may be equally agreeable to you to know the circumstances of my life, many of which you are yet unacquainted with, and expecting the enjoyment of a week's uninterrupted leisure in my present country retirement, I sit down to write them for you...

And now I speak of thanking God, I desire with all humility to acknowledge that I owe the mentioned happiness of my past life to His kind Providence, which led me to the means I used and gave them success...This obscure family of ours was early in the Reformation, and continued Protestants through the reign of Queen Mary, when they were sometimes in danger of trouble on account of their zeal against popery. They got an English Bible, and to conceal and secure it, it was fastened open with tapes under and within the cover of a joint-stool. When my great-great-grandfather read it to his family, he turned up the joint-stool upon his knees, turning over the leaves then under the tapes. One of the children stood at the door to give notice if he saw the apparitor coming, who was an officer of the Spiritual Court. In that case, the stool was turned down again upon its feet, when the Bible remained concealed under it as before. This anecdote I had from my uncle Benjamin...

Josiah, my father, married young, and carried his wife with three children to New England, about 1682...I was the youngest son, and the youngest child but two (of seventeen children), and was born in Boston, New England...My mother, the second wife, was Abiah Folger, daughter of Peter Folger, one of the first settlers of New England, of whom honorable mention is made by Cotton Mather, in his church history of the country entitled, *Magnolia Christi Americana*, as "a godly, learned Englishman," if I remember the words rightly...

I was put to the grammar-school at eight years of age, my father intending to devote me, as the tithe of his sons, to the service of the Church. My early readiness in learning to read (which must have been very early, as I do not remember when I could not read), and the opinion of all his friends, that I should certainly make a good scholar, encouraged him in this purpose of his. My uncle Benjamin, too, approved of it, and proposed to give me all his short-hand volumes of sermons, I suppose as stock to set up with, if I would learn his character. I continued, however, at the grammar-school not quite one year, though in that time I had risen gradually from the middle of the class of that year to be the head of it, and farther was removed into the next class above it, in order to go with that into the third at the end of the year. But my father, in the meantime, from a view of the expense of a college education, which having so large a family, he could not well afford, and the mean living many so educated were afterwards able to obtain, — reasons that he gave to his friends in my hearing, — altered his first intention, took me from the grammar-school, and sent me to a school for writing and arithmetic, kept by a then famous man, Mr. George Brownell, very successful in his profession generally, and that by mild, encouraging methods. Under him I acquired fair writing pretty soon, but I failed in the arithmetic, and made no progress in it. At ten years old I was taken home to assist my father in his business, which was that of a tallow-chandler and sope-boiler; a business he was not bred to, but had assumed on his arrival in New England, and on finding his dying trade would not maintain his family, being in little request. Accordingly, I was employed in cutting wick for the candles, filling the dipping mold and the molds for cast candles, attending the shop, going on errands, etc. I disliked the trade...

There was a salt-marsh that bounded part of the mill-pond, on the edge of which, at high water, we used to stand to fish for minnows. By much trampling, we had made it a mere quagmire. My proposal was to build a wharf there fit for us to stand upon, and I showed my comrades a large heap of stones, which were intended for a new house near the marsh, and which would very well suit our purpose. Accordingly, in the evening, when the workmen were gone, I assembled a number of my play-fellows, and working with them, diligently like so many emmets, sometimes two or three to a stone, we brought them all away and built our little wharf. The next morning the workmen were surprised at missing the stones, which were found in our wharf. Inquiry was made after the removers; we were discovered and complained of; several of us were corrected by our fathers; and, though I pleaded the usefulness of the work, mine convinced me that nothing was useful which was not honest.

I think you may like to know something of his person and character. He had an excellent constitution of body, was of middle stature, but well set, and very strong; he was ingenious, could draw prettily, was skilled a little in music, and had a clear, pleasing voice, so that when he played psalm tunes on his violin and sung withal, as he sometimes did in an evening after the business of the day was over, it was extremely agreeable to hear. He had a mechanical genious too, and, on occasion was very handy in the use of other tradesmen's tools; but his great excellence lay in a sound understanding and solid judgment in prudential matters, both in private and publick affairs...

My mother had likewise an excellent constitution: she suckled all her ten children. I never knew either my father or mother to have any sickness but that of which they dy'd, he at eighty-nine, and she at eighty-five years of age. They lie buried together at Boston, where I some years since placed a marble over their grave, with this inscription:

> Josiah Franklin,
> And Abiah his wife,
> Lie here interred.
> They lived lovingly together in wedlock
> Fifty-five years.
> Without an estate, or any gainful employment,

By constant labor and industry
With God's blessing,
They maintained a large family
Comfortably,
And brought up thirteen children
And seven grandchildren
Reputably.
From this instance, reader,
Be encouraged to diligence in thy calling,
And distrust not Providence.
He was a pious and prudent man;
She, a discreet and virtuous woman.
Their youngest son,
In filial regard to their memory,
Places this stone.
J.F. born 1655, died 1744, AEtat 89.
A.F. born 1667, died 1752, — 85...

From a child I was fond of reading, and all the little money that came into my hands was ever laid out in books. Pleased with the *Pilgrim's Progress,* my first collection was of John Bunyan's works in separate little volumes...

...My brother had, in 1720 or 1721, begun to print a newspaper. It was the second that appeared in America, and was called the *New England Courant.* The only one before it was the *Boston News Letter.** I remember his being dissuaded by some of his friends from the undertaking, as not likely to succeed, one newspaper being, in their judgment, enough for America. At this time [1771] there are not less than five and twenty. He went on, however, with the undertaking, and after having worked in composing the types and printing off the sheets, I was employed to carry the papers thro' the streets to the customers.

He had some ingenious men among his friends, who amus'd themselves by writing little pieces for this paper, which gain'd it credit and made it more in demand, and these gentlemen often visited us. Hearing their conversations, and their accounts of the approbation their papers were received with, I was excited to try my hand among them; but, being still a boy, and suspecting that my brother would object to printing anything of mine in his paper if he knew it to be mine, I contrived to disguise my hand, and, writing an anonymous paper, I put it in at night, under the door of the printing-house. It was found in the morning, and communicated to his writing friends when they called in as usual. They read it, commented on it in my hearing, and I had the exquisite pleasure of finding it met with their approbation, and that, in their different guesses at the author, none were named but men of some character among us for learning and ingenuity. I

---

* The *New England Courant* was really the fourth newspaper that appeared in America; but Franklin's brother had been the printer of the second, the *Boston Gazette.* — Ed.

suppose now that I was rather lucky in my judges, and that perhaps they were not really so very good ones as I then esteemed them.

Encourag'd, however, by this, I wrote and convey'd in the same way to the press several more papers, which were equally approv'd;...

My friend Collins undertook to manage a little for me. He agreed with the captain of a New York sloop for my passage, under the notion of my being a young acquaintance of his that ... could not appear or come away publicly. So I sold some of my books to raise a little money, was taken on board privately, and as we had a fair wind, in three days I found myself in New York, near 300 miles from home, a boy of but 17, without the least recommendation to or knowledge of, any person in the place, and with very little money in my pocket.

My inclinations for the sea were by this time worn out, or I might now have gratify'd them. But, having a trade, and supposing myself a pretty good workman, I offer'd my service to the printer in the place, old Mr. William Bradford, who had been the first printer in Pennsylvania, but removed from thence upon the quarrel of George Keith. He could give me no employment, having little to do, and help enough already; but says he: "My son at Philadelphia has lately lost his principal hand, Aquila Rose, by death; if you go thither, I believe he may employ you." Philadelphia was 100 miles farther; I set out, however, in a boat for Amboy, leaving my chest and things to follow me round by sea...

— Benjamin Franklin[4]

Of further interest to history-loving Americans, is Christ Church, Philadelphia; Benjamin Franklin being a pew-holder and regular attendant at this church — now named "the nation's church."

A **1920 Christ Church Handbook** states the following regarding its inception and Franklin's involvement in his church:

Christ Church was the first Church of England congregation gathered in Pennsylvania, and dates from 1695. By deed of November 15th of that year the lot on which most of the present edifice stands, including the yard on the south, was conveyed to Joshua Carpenter, the trustee chosen to hold it for that pious use.

At the instance of Henry Compton, the Bishop of London, Penn's Charter provided that that Bishop should have power to appoint a chaplain for the service of any congregation consisting of not less than twenty residents who might desire such a minister...

In speaking of the influence of the members of this congregation on public affairs during the provincial era, Provost Stille said: "I must not forget to claim for some of them the great honor of having been the founders and the early guardians of the College and Academy of Philadelphia. Doctor Franklin, who first conceived the plan of this establishment, was a pewholder in this Church. When he looked around for those who would appreciate and support his project, he took from this congregation, mainly, the men of education and of means who would aid him. His first choice for Headmaster of the Academy was the Reverend Richard Peters, for nearly ten years the Rector of Christ Church. Finding it impossible to induce Mr. Peters to accept the place, he made the final choice of Rev. William Smith, a member of this congregation. In a short time the College, thus founded by two members of this Parish, was possibly unrivalled, and certainly not surpassed, by any seminary at that time existing in the Province. Of the trustees previous to the Revolution, nearly four-fifths were members here. And Mr. Peters was for many years the President of the Board."[5]

Benjamin Franklin also founded the Pennsylvania Hospital in 1751, for which he composed the cornerstone inscription. It reads:

In the year of Christ, 1755: George the second happily reigning, (for he sought the happiness of the people); Philadelphia flourishing, for its inhabitants were publick-spirited. This building, by the bounty of the Government and of many private persons, was piously founded, for the relief of the sick and miserable. May the God of mercies bless the undertaking!

United States Presidents: John Adams (2nd); John Quincy Adams (6th); John F. Kennedy (35th); George Bush, born in Massachusetts (41st).

MICHIGAN
(great lake)

The Preamble to the Constitution of the State of Michigan states that, *We, the people of the State of Michigan, grateful to Almighty God for the blessings of freedom and earnestly desiring to secure these blessings undiminished to ourselves and our posterity, do ordain and establish this Constitution.*

Michigan joined the Union on January 26, 1837 as the 26th State.

State Motto:
"Si Quaeris Peninsulam Amoenam Circumspice," translated from Latin to mean, "If you Seek a Pleasant Peninsula, Look About You."[1]

State Seal:
Michigan's Great Seal was designed by Lewis Cass from the pattern of the Seal of the Hudson Bay Fur Company. It was presented to the Constitutional Convention of 1835.[2]

At the top of the seal are the words, "E Pluribus Unum." These words come from our National Motto meaning, "Out of Many, One" — the formation of one nation from many states.

Below is the American Eagle, our national emblem. This symbolizes the superior authority and jurisdiction of the United States. In his talons he holds three arrows and an olive branch with 13 olives. The arrows emphasize that our nation is ready to defend its principles. The olive branch signifies our desire for peace. The olives represent the first 13 original states.

"Tuebor," meaning, "I will Defend," refers to Michigan's frontier position.

The shield is supported by two animals representing Michigan . . . the elk on the left and the moose on the right.

Michigan is on an international boundary, and the figure of the man shows his right hand upraised symbolizing peace. The left hand holds a gunstock to indicate that although Michigan loves peace, she is ready to defend her State and nation.

"Si Quaeris Peninsulam Amoenam Circumspice" means, "If you seek a Pleasant Peninsula, Look about You." Evidently this refers to the Lower Peninsula. The Upper Peninsula was added in 1837, in compensation for the loss of a strip of land on the southern border obtained by Ohio when Congress recognized Michigan as a State.

The words, "The Great Seal of the State of Michigan, A.D. MDCCCXXXV" complete the State Seal. Omitting this legend, it was adopted as the Coat of Arms of the State of Michigan.

State Flag:
Michigan's State flag was adopted by the legislature in 1911 with a simple phrase: "The

93

State Flag shall be blue, charged with the arms of the State."

Pledge of Allegiance to the Michigan Flag:
I pledge allegiance to the flag of Michigan and the State for which it stands, two beautiful peninsulas united by a bridge of steel, where equal opportunity and justice to all is our ideal.

First "Christian Heritage Week:" September 10-16, 1995, proclaimed by the Governor.

Of Historic Interest:
Lewis Cass (1782-1866) was chosen by the citizens of Michigan as their hero in the Hall of Fame. He was Governor of Michigan Territory for eighteen years. This Territory comprised the unmapped area of Michigan, Iowa, Wisconsin and Minnesota, stretching out to the Mississippi River.[3]

President James Madison had appointed Cass at age 31 to this task. The population at the time is estimated at 3,000 pioneers. Indians of the Sioux, Winnebago, Ottawa and Chippewa Tribes were present.[4]

During his long and able leadership, there were no Indian wars. Similar to William Penn in Pennsylvania, Roger Williams in Rhode Island and the Calverts in Maryland, Cass shared the reputation of fair dealing with the Indians, but on a wider scale. He studied their character and maintained fair and honest dealings with them. He kept his promises and ensured their understanding and upholding of their contracts, winning respect and confidence.[5]

Cass was known by the Indians as "the Great White Father" in Detroit, being more significant to them than the U.S. President in Washington. Twenty-one solemn treaties were made by Cass with the Indians, by which most of them migrated beyond the Mississippi River, leaving the greater part of the domain — the great Northwest — to the pioneers, without conflict.[6]

Lewis Cass was elected to the U.S. Senate, a post which he maintained for twelve years. He believed that a good education, extended to all the people, was the primary safeguard of a democratic republic.

HENRY MOWER RICE
1817–1894
UNITED STATES SENATOR
MINNESOTA

*After the Original Marble Statue in the Hall of Fame, U.S. Capitol,
Washington, D.C.*

MINNESOTA
(sky-colored waters)

The Preamble to the Constitution of the State of Minnesota states that, *We, the people of the State of Minnesota, grateful to God for our civil and religious liberty, and desiring to perpetuate its blessings and secure the same to ourselves and our posterity, do ordain and establish this Constitution.*

Minnesota joined the Union on May 11, 1858 as the 32nd State.

Capital: St. Paul.

State Motto::
"L'Etoile du Nord." (Star of the North)

State Seal:
The official seal shows a barefoot farmer plowing a field near St. Anthony Falls on the Mississippi River. The farmer's axe, gun and powderhorn rest on a nearby tree stump, as he looks at an Indian riding a horse. Minnesota's State motto, "L'Etoile du Nord," French for "Star of the North," also appears on the seal.

State Flag:
Minnesota's State flag was redesigned in 1957, just before the State's 100th birthday. It is royal blue, bordered with gold fringe. In the center on one side is the State Seal, and around the seal is a wreath of six "lady slippers," the State flower. Around the wreath is a ring of 19 stars, because Minnesota was the 19th State admitted to the Union after the original thirteen. The largest star is for Minnesota, the "North Star State."

Minnesota has 10,000 lakes.

State Song:
"Hail! Minnesota."

Written by two students at the University of Minnesota in 1904 and 1905, it was the official University song until 1945, when it became the State song.[1]

First "Christian Heritage Week:" September 21-27, 1997, proclaimed by the Governor.

Of Historic Interest:
Henry Mower Rice (1817-1894) represents Minnesota in the U.S. Capitol's Hall of Fame. After his father's death, when Henry was quite young, he lived with friends, studying law, after the completion of his primary education. When he was 18, he moved to Detroit and participated in the surveying of the canal route around the rapids of Sault Ste. Marie, between Lake Superior and Lake Huron. In 1839 he secured a position at Fort Snelling, near what is now the city of Minneapolis.[2]

Rice won the trust and admiration of the Indians, being instrumental in negotiating the

United States Treaty with the Ojibway Indians in 1847. He was a key figure in the bill passed to establish Minnesota Territory, and subsequently served as its delegate to the U.S. Congress from 1853-1857. His efforts to bring about the Minnesota Enabling Act facilitated Minnesota's statehood.[3]

In 1858 Henry Rice was elected one of Minnesota's first Senators, serving faithfully his State and nation until 1863. Rice also served on the Board of Regents of the University of Minnesota from 1851-1859 and as president of the Minnesota Historical Society. As a United States commissioner during the period 1887-1888, this Minnesotan hero continued to render valuable service in negotiating treaties with the Indians.[4]

Minnesota Explorers and Missionaries

An 1881 Library of Congress book entitled, *Minnesota Explorers and Pioneers from A.D. 1659 to A.D. 1858,* by the Rev. Edward Duffield Neill (President of Macalester College; Member of the Massachusetts Historical Society and author of *History of Minnesota, Founders of Maryland*, etc.), gives the following account:

Early Missions among the Ojibways
and Dahkotahs of Minnesota
...In the month of June, 1820, the Rev. Dr. Morse, father of the distinguished inventor of the telegraph, visited and preached at Mackinaw, and in consequence of statements published by him, upon his return, a Presbyterian Missionary Society in the state of New York sent a graduate of Union College, the Rev. W.M. Ferry, father of the present United States Senator from Michigan, to explore the field. In 1823 he had established a large boarding school composed of children of various tribes, and here some were educated who became wives of men of intelligence and influence at the capital of Minnesota. After a few years, it was determined by the Mission Board to modify its plans, and in the place of a great central station, to send missionaries among the several tribes to teach and to preach...

Missions among the Sioux A.D. 1835
About this period, a native of South Carolina, a graduate of Jefferson College, Pennsylvania, the Rev. T.S. Williamson, M.D., who previous to his ordination had been a respectable physician in Ohio, was appointed by the American Board of Foreign Missions to visit the Dahkotahs with the view of ascertaining what could be done to introduce Christian instruction. Having made inquiries at Prairie du Chien and Fort Snelling, he reported the field was favorable.

The Presbyterian and Congregational Churches, through their joint Missionary Society, appointed the following persons to labor in Minnesota: Rev. Thomas S. Williamson, M.D., missionary and physician; Rev. J.D. Stevens, missionary; Alexander Huggins, farmer; and their wives; Miss Sarah Poage, and Lucy Stevens, teachers; who were prevented during the year 1834, by the state of navigation, from entering upon their work.

During the winter of 1834-35, a pious officer of the army exercised a good influence on his fellow officers and soldiers under his command. In the absence of a chaplain or ordained minister, he, like

General Havelock of the British army in India, was accustomed not only to drill the soldiers, but to meet them in his own quarters, and reason with them "of righteousness, temperance, and judgment to come."

As there had never been a chaplain at Fort Snelling, the Rev. J.D. Stevens, the missionary at Lake Harriet, preached on Sundays to the Presbyterian church, there, recently organized.

Writing on January twenty-seventh, 1836, he says, in relation to his field of labor:

"Yesterday a portion of this band of Indians, who had been some time absent from this village, returned. One of the number (a woman) was informed that a brother of hers had died during her absence. He was not at this village, but with another band, and the information had just reached here. In the evening they set up a most piteous crying, or rather wailing, which continued, with some little cessations, during the night. The sister of the deceased brother would repeat, times without number, words which may be thus translated into English: 'Come, my brother, I shall see you no more for ever.' The night was extremely cold, the thermometer standing from ten to twenty below zero. About sunrise, next morning, preparation was made for performing the ceremony of cutting their flesh, in order to give relief to their grief of mind. The snow was removed from the frozen ground over about as large a space as would be required to place a small Indian lodge or wigwam. In the centre a very small fire was kindled up, not to give warmth, apparently, but to cause a smoke. The sister of the deceased, who was the chief mourner, came out of her lodge followed by three other women, who repaired to the place prepared. They were all barefooted, and nearly naked. Here they set up a most bitter lamentation and crying, mingling their wailings with the words mentioned. The principal mourner commenced gashing or cutting her ankles and legs up to the knees with a sharp stone, until her legs were covered with gore and flowing blood; then in like manner her arms, shoulders, and breast. The others cut themselves in the same way, but not so severely. On this poor infatuated woman I presume there were more than a hundred long deep gashes in the flesh. I saw the operation, and the blood instantly followed the instrument, and flowed down upon the flesh. She appeared frantic with grief. Through the pain of her wounds, the loss of blood, exhaustion of strength by fasting, loud and long-continued and bitter groans, or the extreme cold upon her almost naked and lacerated body, she soon sank upon the frozen ground, shaking as with a violent fit of the ague, and writhing in apparent agony. 'Surely,' I exclaimed, as I beheld the bloody scene, 'the tender mercies of the heathen are cruelty!'

The little church at the fort begins to manifest something of a missionary spirit. Their contributions are considerable for so small a number. I hope they will not only be willing to contribute liberally

RESCUE   HORATIO GREENOUGH

After the Marble Masterpiece, "Rescue," by Horatio Greenough.
U.S. Capitol, Washington, D.C.

of their substance, but will give themselves, at least some of them, to the missionary work.

The surgeon of the military post, Dr. Jarvis, has been very assiduous in his attentions to us in our sickness, and has very generously made a donation to our board of twenty-five dollars, being the amount of his medical services in our family..."

Chippeway Missions at Pokeguma

Pokeguma is one of the "Mille Lacs," or thousand beautiful lakes for which Minnesota is remarkable. It is about four or five miles in extent, and a mile or more in width.

This lake is situated on Snake River, about twenty miles above the junction of that stream with the St. Croix.

In the year 1836, missionaries came to reside among the Ojibways and Pokeguma, to promote their temporal and spiritual welfare. Their mission house was built on the east side of the lake; but the Indian village was on an island not far from the shore.

In a letter written in 1837, we find the following results of the missions: "The young women and girls now make, mend, wash, and iron after our manner. The men have learned to build log houses, drive team, plough, hoe, and handle an American axe with some skill in cutting large trees, the size of which, two years ago, would have afforded them a sufficient reason why they should not meddle with them..."

JEFFERSON DAVIS, 1808-1889, MISSISSIPPI

After the Original Bronze Statue in the Hall of Fame, U.S. Capitol,
Washington, D.C.

MISSISSIPPI
(father of waters)

The Constitution of the State of Mississippi states that, *We the people of Mississippi, in convention assembled, grateful to Almighty God, and invoking His blessing on our work do ordain and establish this Constitution...no preference shall be given by law to any religious sect or mode of worship; but the free enjoyment of all religious sentiments and the different modes of worship shall be held sacred. The rights hereby secured shall not be construed to justify acts of licentiousness injurious to morals or dangerous to the peace and safety of the State, or to exclude the Holy Bible from use in any public school of this State.*

Mississippi joined the Union on December 10, 1817 as the 20th State.

State Motto:
"Virtute et Armis," translated from Latin to mean, "By Valor and Arms." This was suggested by the Honorable James Rhea Preston, who was at the time Superintendent of Education in the State of Mississippi.

State Seal:
The present State Seal has been in use since Mississippi became a State in 1817. It is described as follows: "The Great Seal of the State of Mississippi" around the margin, and in the center an eagle with an olive branch and a quiver of arrows in its claws.[1]

State Coat of Arms:
The Coat of Arms is a "Shield in color blue, with an eagle upon it with extended pinions, holding in the right talon a palm branch, and a bundle of arrows in the left talon, with the word "Mississippi" above the eagle; the lettering on the shield and the eagle to be in gold; below the shield two branches of the cotton stalk, saltierwise, as in submitted design, and a scroll below extending upward and one each side three-fourths of the length of the shield; upon the scroll, which is to be red, the motto be printed in gold letters upon white spaces, as in design accompanying, the motto to be — "Virtute et Armis."[2]

State Flag:
The flag of Mississippi comprises "one with width two-thirds of its length; with the union square, in width two-thirds of the width of the flag; the ground of the union to be red and a broad blue saltier thereon, bordered with white and emblazoned with thirteen (13) mullets or five-pointed stars, corresponding with the original States of the Union; the field to be divided into three bars of equal width, the upper one blue, the center one white, and the lower one extending the whole length of the flag, red — the national colors; the staff surmounted with a spear-head and a battle-axe below; the flag to be fringed with gold, and the staff gilded with gold." The Canton Corner is a replica of the Confederate Battle Flag.[3]

Pledge to the Flag:
"I salute the flag of Mississippi and the sovereign State for which it stands, with pride in her history and achievements and with confidence in her future under the guidance of Almighty God."[4]

State Song:
  "Go Mississippi."[5]

First "Christian Heritage Week:" September 18-24, 1994, proclaimed by the Governor.

Of Historic Interest:
  Jefferson Davis (1808-1889), President of the Confederacy, was chosen by the citizens of Mississippi as their greatest hero in the U.S. Capitol's Hall of Fame. On August 21, 1863, Davis proclaimed a Day of Fasting, Humiliation and Prayer, which was heralded by Robert E. Lee in his General Order No. 83. Chaplain Jones of the Confederate Army reported that there were "at least fifteen thousand professions of faith in Jesus Christ as personal Savior," and that "a precious revival was already in progress in many of the commands."[6]

An historic plaque on the *Natchez Trace* (the old road between Jackson and Tupelo) states the following concerning the missions to the Indians:

Bethel Mission

Bethel, meaning House of God, was opened in 1822 as one of thirteen Choctaw mission stations.

Indians and squaws labored hard during four weeks, "frequently till 10 o'clock at night, by the light of the moon or large fires" to clear the forest and erect buildings. The missionaries who took the Gospel to the wilderness also taught farming, carpentry, weaving and housekeeping as well as reading, writing and arithmetic to Choctaw and half-breed children. In 1826, people moved from the Trace to new roads and Bethel was closed.

BLAIR

After the Original Marble Statue of Francis Preston Blair in the Hall of Fame, U.S. Capitol, Washington, D.C.

MISSOURI
(from the Indian, "canoe haver")

The Preamble to the Constitution of the State of Missouri states that, *We the people of Missouri, with profound reverence for the Supreme Ruler of the Universe, and grateful for His goodness, do establish this Constitution for the better government of the State.*

Missouri joined the Union on August 10, 1821 as the 24th State.

State Capital: Jefferson City.

State Motto:
"Salus Populi Suprema Lex Esto," translated from Latin to mean, "Let the Welfare of the People be the Supreme Law."

State Seal:
The Great Seal of the State of Missouri, the basis of the Coat of Arms, has many special meanings of its own. Robert Wells, a lawyer, state legislator and judge, designed the seal. The State Seal portrays, by its helmet and buckled belt, that although Missouri is a strong state, she wishes to be free to handle her own matters. The grizzly bears signify the size and strength of the state and the courage of her people. The new crescent moon is there to remind us that we can make our future better; it is also a special heraldic symbol, indicating that Missouri was the second state formed out of the Louisiana Purchase. The larger star, rising into a group of 23 stars, was to remind people that Missouri became the 24th state only after solving many difficulties. The helmet shows the power of the people of the state. There are two mottos: "United We Stand, Divided We Fall," which tells us how important it is to support the whole United States. "Salus Populi Suprema Lex Esto" translated from Latin, means "Let the Welfare of the People be the Supreme Law." That reminds Missourans that the state government functions to help better their lives.[1]

State Flag:
After achieving statehood, Missouri adopted an official flag on March 22, 1913. The flag was designed by the late Mrs. Marie Elizabeth Watkins Oliver, wife of former State Senator R.B. Oliver. The flag consists of three horizontal stripes of red, white and blue. The Missouri flag embraces national pride, and at the same time expresses the characteristics of Missouri and Missourans. The three large stripes are symbolic of the people of the state: the **blue** stripe represents vigilance, permanency and justice; the **red** stripe represents valor, and the **white** stripe symbolizes purity. The Missouri Coat of Arms is in the center of the flag, signifying both Missouri's independence as a state, and her place as a part of the whole United States. Having the Coat of Arms in the center of the national colors represents Missouri, as she is the geographical center of the nation. By mingling the state Coat of Arms with the national colors of red, white and blue, the flag signifies the harmony existing between the two. Twenty-four stars surround the Coat of Arms, representing Missouri as the 24th state to join the Union.[2]

State Song:
"Missouri Waltz." The song came from a melody by John V. Eppel and was arranged by Frederic Knight Logan, using lyrics written by J.R. Shannon.[3] First published in 1914, the

105

song did not sell well and was considered a failure. By 1939, the song had gained popularity and six million copies had been sold. Sales increased substantially after Missouran Harry S. Truman became U.S. President, and it was reported that the "Missouri Waltz" was his favorite song.

First "Christian Heritage Week:" October 31 - November 6, 1993, proclaimed by the Governor.

Of Historic Interest:
Harry S. Truman was born in Lamar, Missouri, in 1884. He became a Jackson County Judge , a United States Senator, and Vice President prior to becoming U.S. President (1945-1953). Truman is called "the man from Independence." His boyhood homes, the summer White House, his first courtroom, the Truman Library and Museum and his gravesite are all in Independence, Missouri.

The dream of many Presbyterians nationwide was to build a national church at the seat of government. This dream was finally realized when in October, 1947, **President Harry S. Truman** publicly proclaimed the reality of a *National Presbyterian Church* in the nation's capital. In keeping with Truman's proclamation, President Dwight D. Eisenhower laid the cornerstone to the handsome, neo-gothic edifice constructed on October 14, 1967, the first service being held on September 7, 1969.

Francis Preston Blair (1821-1875), is one of Missouri's greatest heroes represented in the U.S. Capitol's Hall of Fame. In a speech he delivered at Memphis, Tennessee on Thursday, September 20, 1866, this American Christian statesman returned to the Biblical principles of the Declaration of Independence, and our founding fathers' abhorrence of slavery. It is hereunder excerpted:

> ...Shakespeare, who peopled a world of his own with individuals not less natural than those around us, but of higher faculties and profounder philosophies, says: "Sure He that made us with such large discourse, looking before and after, gave us not that capability and God-like reason to rust in us unused."

> ...The principles that loom up in the *Declaration of Independence* gave a broad daylight that presented the dangers in bold relief to our eyes, and pointed the way to shun them. Our northern kinsmen heard the warning voice of the southern statesman, who spoke aloud of the whole country and they quietly discarded the victims of slavery whom they had brought from Africa. The South as quietly adapted its subjects as all their own. What infatuation was this, with the wise example of the North before them, inculcated by its venerable philosopher, Franklin, its deep-read jurist, Jay, and its highly gifted patriot, soldier and statesman, Hamilton, involving the utter blotting out of slavery from our institutions? But if the voice of these less interested in the matter could not prevail, how could the voice of the Old Dominion (the mother, it may be said, not only of our 'dead empires' in the South, but also of our great free and living empires of the Northwest) remain unheeded as if unheard? She was the first to proclaim abhorrence of slavery, revolting at the importation of Africans, forced on her by the monarchs associated in the mercantile Assiento treaty with Spain, in which the royal and aristocratic cupid-

ity of two kingdoms stooped to the infamy of becoming slave-traders, in partnership with those who hunted down the unhappy race on their own shores, and the black bloodhounds who carried on the chase in their own regal right; that made their own subjects a prey to task masters beyond the ocean. Virginia was the first to announce the purpose of Independence, on the ground of opposition to this revolting policy of the Imperial Government, and the clause of the *Declaration of Independence* places it in a more abhorrent light than any other classes of separation from that government. Her son, Richard Henry Lee, was the first to propose that Declaration. Jefferson was its author; and the greatest of all her sons, Washington vindicated it in arms, and established it by his administration. But these were not the only representatives of Virginia who urged the necessity of the deliverance of the whole country from slavery and the removal of its subjects from the midst of our people. Patrick Henry, the orator, who, in advance, and more potently than any other, proclaimed and animated the revolution. James Madison who was the Father of the Constitution; George Mason, who was the compeer of these illustrious men, in the efforts to remove from our soil even the footsteps of a slave; and Lafayette, the comrade, who considered himself, by the adoption of Washington, a son of Virginia, united in invocation to redeem the whole country from the dark shadow of death which must forever cloud the light of freedom among us, as long as the victims remained in a land where they had suffered bondage.

One great step has been taken towards the relief of the enslaved and the enslaver, in emancipation; but it is not effectual, and must be merely partial for the time, and to be followed by a heavier calamity that the slavery custom had made tolerable...Mr. Jefferson, in one of his prophecies in regard to the black race, said: "Nothing is more certainly written in the book of fate than that these people are to be free, nor is it less certain that the two races, equally free, cannot live in the same government. Nature, habits, opinion had drawn indelible lines of distinction between them. It is still in our power to direct the process of emancipation and deportation peaceably and in such slow degree as that the evil will wear off insensibly and their place be pari passu (slowly but surely) filled up with free white laborers. If on the contrary it is left to force itself on, human nature must shudder at the prospect held up..."

Here is prophecy, confirmed in part already by fact; that part yet to come is inevitable, but offers an alternative - it is deportation, or the destruction of one race or the other...

The Honorable Thomas Hart Benton (1782-1858), is another Missouran statesman, chosen by its citizens to represent them in the U.S. Capitol's Hall of Fame. In a famous speech by **Benton**, delivered at the Capitol at Jefferson City, on May 26, 1849, this American hero leaves the following historic record for posterity:

...When I came this day to office, I found there a note requesting me to call at 1 o'clock at the President's House. It was then one and I immediately went over. He expected that the two Bills for the admission of Maine and to enable Missouri to make a Constitution would have been brought to him for his signature; and he had summoned all the members of the administration to ask their opinions in writing, to be deposited in the Department of State, upon two questions, whether Congress had a constitutional right to prohibit slavery in a territory? and 2) whether the 8th section of the Missouri Bill (which interdicts slavery forever in the territory north of 26 1/2 latitude) was applicable only to the territorial state or would extend to it after it should become a state? As to the first question, it was unanimously agreed that Congress have the power to prohibit slavery in the territories...

This great Missouran son reverts to the Biblical authority of our founding fathers on their abhorrence and abolition of slavery:

...Never has there appeared upon earth a body of men who left a richer inheritance, or a nobler example to their posterity. Wisdom, modesty, decorum, forbearance, dignity, moderation, pervaded all their works and characterized all their conduct...They founded a new government with the wisdom of the sages; they administered it in their day with temperance and judgment. They left us the admiration and envy of the friends of freedom throughout the world...Taught to admire the founders of our government in my early youth, I reverence them now; taught to value their work then, I worship it now...

Other Notable Missourans:

Samuel Clemens, alias Mark Twain, grew up in Hannibal, Missouri. He watched riverboats on the Mississippi River. It was thus that he took the pseudonym, Mark Twain. His attachment to the river and his boyhood years in Missouri are portrayed in his world-renowned novels about Tom Sawyer and Huckleberry Finn. Monuments to this author and the two above-cited characters are in Hannibal, Missouri. The Mark Twain birthplace is in Florida, Missouri.

General John J. Pershing was born in 1860 in the vicinity of Laclede, Missouri. He became one of America's most distinguished military leaders. Graduating from West Point, he served in the Spanish-American War and in the campaign against Mexican bandit Pancho Villa. Pershing commanded the American Forces in Europe in World War I. Pershing's boyhood home is in Laclede, Missouri.

Officially Recorded Presidential Inaugural Scriptures:

Harry S. Truman's Second Inaugural Bible was presented to him by the citizens of Jackson County, Missouri as a memorial to his mother. One of two volumes, this magnificent Gutenberg facsimile is a Latin Vulgate translation of Scripture, being one of two volumes. Truman has penned in ink, at the bottom of the page containing Exodus 20:

I placed my hand on this 20th Chapter of Exodus, January 20, 1949 when I took the oath of office.

The New York Times elaborates upon this event in its January 20, 1949 issue:

Truman and Barkley Take Oaths in Capitol at Noon — Record Inauguration Seen. President Truman asserted tonight that his su-

108

preme interest was to see the United States assume the world leadership that God has intended. He said that he would try to achieve this goal for the benefit of the people of the whole world and not for the selfish benefit of this or any other country...President Truman announced today that when he takes the oath of office tomorrow, his hand will rest on two Bibles, one opened at the Sermon on the Mount and the other opened at the 10 Commandments. He especially recommended the 10th Commandment for observance in the Capital City...

Texts make a good program: Mr. Truman turned familiarly to the Sermon on the Mount in his plain, favorite White House Bible, and to Exodus in the Gothic Latin he could not read in the Gutenberg facsimile, a 2-volume treasure altogether about eight inches thick. Yesterday, Charles G. Ross, the President's Secretary, was telling correspondents in confidence about the President's selection of the two Biblical texts. A Chicago newspaperman remarked that they made a mighty good program for a President. Today another reporter told the President about this. "It is a good program," replied Mr. Truman with emphasis. "Especially the 10th Commandment. If you read the 10th it will do you a lot of good, especially in Washington."

In the White House texts issued today, the 10th Commandment was rendered as follows:

"Thou shalt not covet thy neighbor's house, thou shalt not covet thy neighbor's wife, nor his manservant, nor his ox, nor his ass, nor anything that is thy neighbor's."

United States President: Harry S. Truman (33rd).

Sub Hoc Signo Vinces.

NOVEMBER 8, 1889, 10:40 A. M.

···HISTORY···

OF THE

SOCIETY

OF THE

FRAMERS OF THE CONSTITUTION

OF THE

STATE OF MONTANA.

1890.

JULY 4, 1889.   AUGUST 17, 1889.

MONTANA
(Latin for "mountainous")

The Preamble to the Constitution of the State of Montana states that, *We the people of Montana, grateful to God for the quiet beauty of our state, the grandeur of our mountains, the vastness of our rolling plains, and desiring to improve the quality of life, equality of opportunity and to secure the blessings of liberty for this and future generations do ordain and establish this Constitution.*

Montana joined the Union on November 8, 1889 as the 41st State.

State Capital: Helena.

State Motto:
"Oro y Plata," translated from Spanish to mean "Gold and Silver."

State Seal:
The Great Seal of the State of Montana is as follows: A central group representing a plow, a miner's pick and shovel; upon the right, representation of the great falls of the Missouri River; upon the left, mountain scenery, and underneath the words "Oro y Plata." The seal must be two and one-half inches in diameter, and surrounded by these words: "The Great Seal of the State of Montana."[1]

State Flag:
The official Montana state flag bears the state seal on a blue field and carries gold fringe on the top and bottom borders. Inscribed on the colorful seal is the state motto, "Oro y Plata," translated to mean "Gold and Silver." In the seal are shown mining equipment, a gold pan and a plow, while the background is formed of mountains, from which the state derives its name. Flags similar to the official state flag, but bearing the inscriptions "First Montana Volunteers" and "Second Montana Volunteers" have been carried into battle by Montana forces as their official colors.

State Song:
"Montana"[2]

First "Christian Heritage Week:" October 15-21, 2000.

Of Historic Interest:
A 1903 Library of Congress book entitled, ***History of the Society of the Framers of the Constitution of the State of Montana — July 4, 1889 to August 17, 1889*** (Written and Arranged by Henry Knippenberg, Member from Beaverhead County, Glendale), gives the following address:

Address
by H. Knippenberg

Gentlemen — Will you not let me say, my brethren and friends.
I wish to thank you, one and all, for the kind words that you have
uttered here. I wish to thank you for the uniform and cordial coop-

eration which you have so generously extended to me the past year in my work of organization. I do not wish to act under any false modesty. I realize the fact that, in a large degree, I have been the creative power in this work of social organization. It has cost me time, labor, and some money; but this time, labor and money combined has been a willing sacrifice of love; love for the present, love for the future. Ours has been indeed an exalted privilege. Few men in this world ever enjoy one as great. Called and chosen by the greatest power in the State, the people, to hew out of the quarry a stone — a foundation stone; a corner stone — upon which the people themselves might erect a Temple — a Temple of Liberty, Truth, Justice and Mercy. Wisely and well the work was done. For when the people saw it they accepted it with glad acclaim, saying, "Grace, grace unto it."

But great as was our privilege, so great is the work yet to be done. When the children of Israel took possession of the promised land, and supposed they had it all, there came to them this message: "There remains yet much land to be possessed." And so this same message comes to us Montanians; there remains great possibilities yet for us to accomplish.

Where is the prophet that will dare tell us of the future greatness of this temple; of its culture; of its Christian influence, of its wealth; of its moral power, of its political power. I fear were such a prophet found, and could we return even one hundred years from now we would have to declare, as did the Queen of Sheba of old, "The half was not told me."

But bear this in mind, true greatness comes not from without, but from within. Our greatness will be only what our homes are. Happy, secure and great will our future be, if the future men and women shall come from homes trained and reared at the family altar of purity, and regenerated by the spirit of loyalty and patriotism.

Gentlemen, let us not deceive ourselves. Theorize and speculate as you will, nevertheless the history of the ages passed, and the experience of all the nations of the centuries, bear witness to the eternal truth: "Righteousness exalteth a nation, but sin is a reproach to any people," found to be true in the past, we shall find it true in the future. Truth is never false. Do not take the right from me in saying let our lives and our examples be such in this our beloved State, in this our beloved country, that our loyalty to the flag, our love for our country, our devotion to our State shall be akin to that of the "sweet singers" of old, "If I forget thee, O Jerusalem, let my right hand forget her cunning. If I remember not thee, let my tongue cleave to the roof of my mouth. If I prefer not thee, O Jerusalem, above my chief joy."

One by one, we shall pass away. Our work shall then have been done, but our influence will remain, for good or for ill. My prayer is now that for each of us there may be erected and remain a monument not of crumbling stone or granite, but a monument erected in the hearts of a loving people bearing this inscription: Here lies a man — a man while living that was *true to God, true to his home, true to his country, true to humanity.*

My friends, again I thank you.

The President announced that we had no further business to transact, and that the Society would meet again this evening at...9 o'clock, at the "Hotel Helena," in the banquet hall.

Wm. Muth, Chairman of the Committee of Arrangements asked that the members meet at 8:30 o'clock in the parlors of the "Hotel Helena."

Adjourned.

WILLIAM·JENNINGS·BRYAN
1860 - 1925

*After the Bronze Statue of William Jennings Bryan in the Hall of
Fame, U.S. Capitol, Washington, D.C.*

NEBRASKA
(flat river)

The Preamble to the Constitution of the State of Nebraska states that, *We, the people, grateful to Almighty God for our freedom, do ordain and establish the following declaration of rights and frame of government.*

Nebraska joined the Union on March 1, 1867 as the 37th State.

State Capital: Lincoln.

State Motto:
"Equality before the Law."[1]

State Seal:
Nebraska's State Seal originated as follows: "Be it enacted by the Legislature of the State of Nebraska: Sec. 1. That the Secretary of State shall be, and he is hereby authorized and required to procure, at the cost and expense of the state, and as soon after the passage of this act as practicable, a seal for the state, to be designed and known as the great seal of the State of Nebraska, and of the design and device following, that is to say: The eastern part of the circle to be represented by a steamboat ascending the Missouri river; the mechanic arts to be represented by a smith with a hammer and anvil; in the foreground, agriculture to be represented by a settler's cabin, sheaves of wheat, and stalks of growing corn; in the background a train of cars heading toward the Rocky Mountains, and on the extreme west, the Rocky Mountains to be plainly in view; around the top of this circle, to be in capital letters, the motto: "Equality before the Law," and the circle to be surrounded with the words, "Great Seal of the State of Nebraska, March 1st, 1867."[2]

State Flag:
Nebraska's Flag is described thus: "There is hereby designated a banner for the State of Nebraska which shall consist of a reproduction of the great seal of the state, charged on the center in gold and silver on a field of national blue."[3]

State Song:
BEAUTIFUL NEBRASKA
Beautiful Nebraska, peaceful prairie land.
Laced with many rivers and the hills of sand:
Dark green valleys cradled in the earth.
Rain and sunshine bring abundant birth.
Beautiful Nebraska, as you look around,
You will find a rainbow reaching to the ground:
All these wonders by the Master's hand:
Beautiful Nebraska land.
We are so proud of this state where we live...[4]

First "Christian Heritage Week:" August 29 - September 4, 1999, proclaimed by the Governor.

Of Historic Interest:

Thomas Jefferson Memorial Day is celebrated annually on April 13.[5]

Nebraskan sculptor John Gutzon Borglum, (1867-1941) designed the ***Mount Rushmore National Monument.***

William Jennings Bryan (1860-1925) takes his place as Nebraska's greatest hero in the U.S. Capitol's Hall of Fame. His bronze statue was executed by great master sculptor, Rudulph Evans. Bryan's father being gravely ill as a young man, he made a vow to the Lord that if he recovered, he would worship three times daily, keeping his vow in his family throughout his life. The boy was adept at expounding upon the Scriptures in Sunday School and church gatherings.[6]

A member of the Presbyterian Church, he continued to preach and lecture throughout his life, maintaining his stance upon the Divine inspiration and infallibility of the Scriptures. At college, Bryan was the President of the debating society, led prayer meetings and was valedictorian of his graduating class.[7]

Bryan became a lawyer, and was elected to the Nebraska State Legislature at age 29. The following year he took his seat as a delegate in the U.S. House of Representatives, later becoming Editor-in-Chief of the ***Omaha World Herald*** newspaper. This statesman mastered penmanship.

In 1896, Bryan defended the laborer and farmer against all who would exploit them, by delivering one of the most brilliant speeches in the history of American politics – his "Cross of Gold" speech. It concluded thus:

> ...You shall not press down upon the brow of labor this crown of thorns, you shall not crucify mankind upon a cross of gold.[8]

Bryan was thrice chosen by his party for U.S. President, failing each time by narrow margins. He was appointed to the State Department, however, negotiating 30 treaties with leading world nations. After this two-year appointment, Bryan returned to full-time Christian work, spec-ifically taking a stand against the theory of evolution, which was being forcibly introduced into the United States educational system, and which, he maintained, was leading America's youth away from God. Bryan was successful in securing laws in Florida and Tennessee forbidding the teaching of this godless Darwinian theory in schools.

The matter came to a head in the Scopes Trial in Dayton, Tennessee, in which a High School principal admitted he had taught the theory of evolution, and a fourteen-year-old student, that he had been taught. Attracting nationwide attention, crowds of people forced the court in Dayton into the courtyard. The defense spoke for freedom to teach. However, Bryan heroically won the case, the teacher being fined $100.00. William Jennings Bryan died shortly thereafter, leaving a magnificent legacy to his State and the nation.[9]

Missionaries:

The Reverend Moses Merrill and his wife, Eliza Wilcox Merrill, were the first resident missionaries to the Nebraska Indians. They arrived in Bellevue in 1833 and continued their work until Reverend Merrill's death in 1840. Samuel Allis and the Reverend John Dunbar, who arrived in Bellevue in 1834, served as missionaries to the Pawnee tribe for 12 years.

Heroes:
Nebraska's Hall of Fame, officially recognizing prominent Nebraskans, includes **John J. Pershing**, General, Armies of the United States (1919) and Army Chief of Staff (1921-24).

Officially Recorded Presidential Inaugural Scripture:
Gerald R. Ford was inaugurated as 38th President of the United States on August 9, 1974. Raising his right hand, Mr. Ford rested his left hand on a Bible held by his wife and opened to one of his favorite passages, the 5th and 6th verses of the 3rd Chapter of Proverbs:

> Trust in the Lord with all thine heart; and lean not unto thine own understanding. In all thy ways acknowledge Him and He shall direct thy paths.

Then, in a firm voice, he took the oath of office:

> I, Gerald Ford, do solemnly swear that I will faithfully execute the office of President of the United States and will to the best of my ability preserve, protect and defend the Constitution of the United States.

United States President: Gerald R. Ford, born in Nebraska (38th).

NEVADA
(snow-capped)

The Preamble to the Constitution of the State of Nevada states that, *We the people of the State of Nevada, grateful to Almighty God for our freedom, in order to secure its blessings, insure domestic tranquility, and form a more perfect Government do establish this Constitution.*

Nevada joined the Union on October 31, 1864 as the 36th State.

State Capital: Carson City.

State Motto:
 "All for our Country."[1]

State Seal:
 The seal of the Territory of Nevada, United States of America, was approved on November 29, 1861 and specified the following design: "Mountains, with a stream of water coursing down their sides, and falling on the over-shot wheel of a quartz-mill at their base; a miner leaning on his pick, and upholding a United States flag, with a motto expressing the two ideas of loyalty to the Union, and the wealth to sustain it." "Volens et Potens."[2]

 In 1864 after the State Constitution had been adopted, the Constitutional Convention authorized the Secretary of the Territory to procure a State Seal. Although the seal was used officially, it was not legally enacted into law until 1866.

 The State Seal is embossed with the words "The Great Seal of the State of Nevada" around the outer edge. Within this is a composite picture showing the mining, agriculture, industry and scenery of Nevada, under which is a scroll with the State Motto, "All for our Country."

State Flag:
 Nevada's State flag has a cobalt blue background; in the upper left quarter is a five-pointed silver star between two sprays of sagebrush, crossed to form a half wreath; across the top of the wreath is a golden scroll with the words, "Battle Born," meaning that Nevada joined the Union during the Civil War. The name "Nevada" is below the star and above the sprays in golden letters.[3]

State Song:
 "Home means Nevada."[4]

First "Christian Heritage Week:" August 30 - September 6, 1997, proclaimed by the Governor.

Of Historic Interest:
 Patrick McCarran (1876-1954) was selected by the citizens of Nevada as their greatest hero in the U.S. Capitol's Hall of Fame.
 The Senator McCarran Memorial Statue Committee (created under authority of Ch. 312, Nevada Compiled Laws, 1955 Session, Nevada State Legislature) presided over the

Unveiling Ceremonies of his statue in the Main Rotunda of the U.S. Capitol, March 23, 1960. The following appeared in the program:

Patrick Anthony McCarran - champion of the American way of life - won acclaim as a U.S. Senator who authored or sponsored as much constructive legislation for the benefit of his country and his State as any single man in American history.

Rancher, State legislator, lawyer, district attorney, associate and Chief Justice of the Nevada Supreme Court, U.S. Senator, he was born in Reno, Nevada, August 8, 1876, the son of rancher parents. He was a University of Nevada graduate, where he excelled as an athlete, debater and orator. He studied law while herding sheep, and was admitted to the Nevada Bar in 1905.

A State legislator in 1903, he sponsored and fought through to passage in Nevada the country's first law limiting a man's hours of work to an eight-hour day – an act whose Constitutionality was challenged through to the U.S. Supreme Court, and there upheld.

Senator McCarran was a lawyer and district attorney in one of the West's best known mining camps, Tonopah, before opening law offices in Reno, from where he was elected to the Supreme Court of Nevada in 1912, serving as Chief Justice in 1917-1918. His opinions remain as prized legal text material, one in fingerprinting still required reading for Scotland Yard, and others dealing with minerals, water, and community property still standing as legal landmarks.

Elected to the U.S. Senate in 1932 and re-elected in 1938, 1944, and 1950, Patrick McCarran lived in a whirlwind of controversy as he helped shape the times of his era. His name is on as much diversified and vital legislation with national and international impact as any person who ever sat in the Senate of the United States. His illustrious roll call of laws of tremendous importance to the Nation's well-being and security include his authorship and sponsorship of the Civil Aeronautics Act of 1938, Federal Airport Act of 1945, Administrative Procedures Act of 1946, Internal Security Act of 1951, Immigration and Nationality Act of 1952. He was the first advocate of a separate U.S. Air Force.

His record was one of boldness and courage in the Halls of Congress where he was a great defender of the Constitution of the United States, a heroic figure dedicated to protecting his Country from enemies without and subversives within.

His devotion to the duties of his office of U.S. Senator, his enduring love of his Country and his native State, his willingness to shoulder to solution the largest or smallest problems of his fellow man in low and high places...these character trademarks stamped him as a man whose influence will remain indelibly engraved upon the destinies of the Nation he did so much to help guide in times of stress to its present eminence among the nations of the world.

The Statue

Through the official act of the State Legislature, 1955 Session, the "people of Nevada, represented in Senate and Assembly," approved Senate Bill No. 230, directing that a bronze statue of the late Senator Patrick A. McCarran should be placed in Statuary Hall in recognition of his service to the State of Nevada and the nation at large, as a "distinguished statesman and courageous patriot." Subsequently, the 1957 Legislature of Nevada appropriated the necessary funds, "to be matched equally by public contributions," to provide the statue and make the necessary arrangements for its placement in Statuary Hall of the United States Capitol.

The Senator McCarran Memorial Statue Committee proceeded to carry out the directives of the Nevada State Legislature, and more than matched the State appropriation through donations from the many friends of the late Senator. After careful consideration, the Committee selected Yolande Jacobson (Mrs. J. Craig Sheppard) of Reno, Nevada, to execute the statue.

The bronze figure, standing on its marble base, is seven feet high and meets the specifications as prescribed by the Architect of the Capitol, under the direction of the Joint Committee on the Library, authorized in 1872 to exercise proper jurisdiction over all works of art in the United States Capitol. The Joint Committee has the final determination as to where the statue will be permanently located in the Capitol. The preliminary work on the statue was done in Senator McCarran's home town of Reno, Nevada, and completed in New York City.

"Glendale School" in Reno (circa 1858). Earliest Existing Schoolhouse in Nevada. Patrick McCarran Attended this School.

120

The foundations of Nevada were laid, when preacher of the Gospel, **"Bible-Totin' "** **Jedediah Smith** led an expedition through present-day Nevada, travelling east to west in 1826, and returning through central Nevada in 1827.

Constitution of the State of Nevada
Article I, Section 1 of the *Constitution of the State of Nevada* states that,

> All men are, by nature, free and equal, and have certain inalienable rights, among which are those of enjoying and defending life and liberty; acquiring, possessing and protecting property, and pursuing and obtaining safety and happiness.

Article I, Section 4 states,

> The free exercise and enjoyment of religious profession and worship, without discrimination or preference, shall forever be allowed in this state: and no person shall be rendered incompetent to be a witness on account of his opinions on matters of his religious belief; but the liberty of conscience hereby secured shall not be so construed as to excuse acts of licentiousness, or justify practices inconsistent with the peace or safety of this state.

Article XI, Section 1 further decrees that,

> The legislature shall encourage, by all suitable means, the promotion of intellectual, literary, scientific, mining, mechanical, agricultural and moral improvements, and also provide for the election by the people, at the general election, of a superintendent of public instruction, whose term of office shall be two years from the first Monday of January, A.D. [Anno Domini — The Year of our Lord (Jesus Christ)]* eighteen hundred and sixty-five, and until the election and the qualification of his successor, and whose duties shall be prescribed by law.

* Author's translation from Latin, in parentheses.

DANIEL WEBSTER, 1782-1852, NEW HAMPSHIRE

After the Original Marble Sculpture in the Hall of Fame, U.S.
Capitol, Washington, D.C.

NEW HAMPSHIRE
(Named after Hampshire County, England)

The Constitution of the State of New Hampshire states that, *As morality and piety, rightly grounded on high principles, will give the best and greatest security to government, and will lay, in the hearts of men, the strongest obligations to due subjection; and as the knowledge of these is most likely to be propagated through a society, therefore, the several parishes, bodies, corporate or religious societies shall at all times have the right of electing their own teachers, and of contracting with them for their support or maintenance or both...*

New Hampshire joined the Union on June 21, 1788 as the 9th State.

State Capital: Concord.

State Motto:

"Live Free or Die," which was spoken by General John Stark, New Hampshire's most distinguished hero of the Revolutionary War.[1]

State Seal:

The focal point of New Hampshire's Great Seal features the frigate "Raleigh," which was constructed at Portsmouth in 1776, being one of the first 13 warships commissioned by the Continental Congress for America's new navy. Bordering the Raleigh, is a laurel wreath. The Seal was signed into Legislature in 1931. The outer circumference of the Seal reads: SEAL OF THE STATE OF NEW HAMPSHIRE 1776. The rising sun in the background represents the birth of liberty in 1776, as follows:

> The Seal of the State shall be two inches in diameter, circular, with the following detail and no other: A field crossed by a straight horizon line of the sea, above the center of the field; concentric with the field the rising sun, exposed above the horizon about one third of its diameter; the field encompassed with laurel; across the field for the full width within the laurel, a broadside view of the frigate Raleigh, on the stocks; the ship's bow dexter and higher than the stern; the three lower masts shown in place, together with the fore, main and mizzen tops, shrouds and mainstays; an ensign staff at the stern flies the United States flag authorized by Act of Congress on June 14, 1777; a jury staff on the mainmast and another in the foremast each flies a pennant; flags and pennants are streaming to the dexter side; the hull is shown without a rudder; below the ship the field is divided into land and water by a double diagonal line whose highest point is sinister; no detail is shown anywhere on the water nor any on the land between the water and the stocks except a granite boulder on the dexter side; encircling the field is the inscription, SEAL . OF . THE . STATE . OF . NEW HAMPSHIRE, the words separated by round periods, except between the parts of New Hampshire; at the lowest point of the in-

scription is the date 1776, flanked on either side by a five-pointed star, which group separates the beginning and end of the inscription;...[2]

State Emblem:

"The State Emblem shall be of the following design: Within an elliptical panel, the longest dimension of which shall be vertical, there shall appear an appropriate replica of the 'Old Man of the Mountains,' surrounding the inner panel, and enclosed within another ellipse, there shall be at the bottom of the design the words of the state motto . . . ; and at the top of the design between the inner and outer elliptical panels, the words, New Hampshire, appropriately separated from the motto, if adopted, by one star on each side. Said emblem may be placed on all printed or related material issued by the state and its subdivisions relative to the development of recreational, industrial, and agricultural resources of the state."[3]

State Flag:

"The State Flag shall be of the following color and design: The field shall be blue and shall bear upon its center in suitable proportion and colors a representation of the State Seal. The Seal shall be surrounded by a wreath of laurel leaves with nine stars interspersed. When used for military purposes, the flag shall conform to the regulations of the United States."[4]

State Song:

"The song 'Old New Hampshire' with words by Dr. John F. Holmes and music by Maurice Hoffman is hereby declared to be the State Song of New Hampshire."[5]

OLD NEW HAMPSHIRE

With a skill that knows no measure,
From the golden store of fate
God, in His great love and wisdom;
Made the rugged Granite State;
Made the lakes, the fields, the forests;
Made the rivers and the rills;
Made the bubbling crystal fountains
Of New Hampshire's Granite Hills.

Refrain

Old New Hampshire, Old New Hampshire,
Old New Hampshire, grand and great,
We will sing of Old New Hampshire,
Of the dear old Granite State.

Builded He New Hampshire glorious
From the borders to the sea;
And with matchless charm and splendor
Blessed her for eternity.
Hers, the majesty of mountain;
Hers, the grandeur of the lake;
Hers, the truth as from the hillside
Whence her crystal waters break.

Refrain
Old New Hampshire, Old New Hampshire,
Old New Hampshire, grand and great,
We will sing of Old New Hampshire,
Of the dear old Granite State.

First "Christian Heritage Week:" October 22-28, 2000.

Of Historic Interest:
Daniel Webster (1782-1852) orator and senator, was chosen by the citizens of New Hampshire to represent them as their greatest hero in the U.S. Capitol's Hall of Fame. Webster wrote:

> I do not remember when or by whom I was taught to read, because I cannot, and never could recollect a time when I could not read the Bible. I suppose I was taught by my mother, or by my elder sisters. My father seemed to have no higher object in the world than to educate his children to the full extent of his very limited ability...[6]

> I have read through the entire Bible many times. I now make it a practice to go through it once a year. It is the book of all others for lawyers as well as for divines; and I pity the man that cannot find in it a rich supply of thought, and of rules for his conduct. It fits man for life —it prepares him for death![7]

Franklin Pierce (1804-1869):
On December 3, 1865, in his later years, Franklin Pierce was baptized by Dr. Eames of *St. Paul's Episcopal Church* in Concord, at which time he promised to "renounce the devil and all his works, the vain pomp and glory of the world, with all covetous desires of the same and the sinful desires of the flesh, to no longer follow nor be led by them, and to obediently keep God's holy will and commandments and to walk in the same all the days of his life."[8]

United States President: Franklin Pierce (14th).

RICHARD STOCKTON 1730-1781 NEW JERSEY

After the Original Marble Statue in the Hall of Fame, U.S. Capitol, Washington, D.C.

126

NEW JERSEY
(after the island of Jersey)

The Preamble to the Constitution of the State of New Jersey states that, *We the people of the State of New Jersey, grateful to Almighty God for the civil and religious liberty which He hath so long permitted us to enjoy, and looking to Him for a blessing upon our endeavors to secure and transmit the same unimpaired to succeeding generations, do ordain and establish this Constitution.*

New Jersey joined the Union on December 18, 1787 as the 3rd State.

State Capital: Trenton.

State Seal:

New Jersey's State Seal was designed by Pierre Eugene du Simitiere and presented in May, 1777, to the Legislature.

The three plows in the shield honor the state's agricultural tradition. The helmet above the shield faces forward, an attitude denoting sovereignty and thus particularly fitting for one of the first governments created under the notion that the state itself is sovereign. The crest above the helmet is a horse's head.

The supporting female figures are Liberty, symbolizing the freedoms established with the Declaration of Independence; and Ceres, representing abundance. Liberty, on the viewer's left, carries the liberty cap on her staff. Ceres holds a cornucopia filled with harvested crops. Inscribed upon a banner: "Liberty and Prosperity - 1776."

State Flag:

The following memorandum appears in the Minutes of the New Jersey General Assembly for March 11, 1896:

> The minutes of the last meeting were read and approved.
>
> Mr. (Charles F.) Hopkins (of Morris County) offered the following memorandum, which was read:
>
> On March 23rd, 1779, during the War of the Revolution, the Continental Congress, by resolution, authorized and directed the Commander-in-Chief to prescribe the uniform, both as to color and facings, for the regiments of the New Jersey Continental Line.
>
> In accordance with this resolution, General Washington, in General Orders dated Army Headquarters, New Windsor, New York, October 2nd 1779, directed that the coats for such regiments should be dark blue, faced with buff.
>
> On February 28th, 1780, the Continental War Officers in Philadelphia directed that each of said regiments should have two flags, one the United States flag and the other a State flag, the ground to be of the color of the facing. Thus, the State flag of New Jersey became

the beautiful and historic buff, as selected for it by the Father of his Country, and it was displayed in view of the combined French and American armies in the culminating event of the War of the Revolution, the capitulation of a British army under Lieutenant General Earl Cornwallis at Yorktown, in 1781.

The same color has been prescribed for the state flag of New York, where law requires it to be displayed with the United States flag over the Capitol when the legislature is in session.[1]

First "Christian Heritage Week:" September 1-7, 1996, proclaimed by the Governor.

Of Historic Interest:

Richard Stockton (1730-1781) was selected by the citizens of New Jersey as their greatest hero in the U.S. Capitol's Hall of Fame. At 18 he graduated from the College of New Jersey (now Princeton University). He studied law, becoming a noted lawyer. As a Trustee of Princeton College, Stockton travelled to Scotland, pursuading the great revivalist and preacher of the Gospel, John Witherspoon, D.D., a Presbyterian Minister, to become president of Princeton.[2]

Stockton served eight years in the New Jersey Executive Council prior to the Revolutionary War. He was also an Associate Justice of the Supreme Court. In June of 1776, Richard Stockton, Elias Boudinot (his brother-in-law), Dr. Benjamin Rush and Rev. John Witherspoon, were all elected to the Continental Congress.[3]

Stockton was commissioned to make an official report on the state of the Army at Ticonderoga. He writes that the New Jersey soldiers were "marching with cheerfulness, but a great part of the men are bare-footed and bare-legged. There is not a single shoe or stocking to be had in this part of the world, or I would ride a hundred miles through the wilderness and purchase them with my own money."[4]

This Revolutionary War hero was obliged to move his family from Princeton, as the British Army followed Washington's retreat to Philadelphia. Stockton was, however, discovered by the Tories, who confined him to a New York jail, where he was badly treated and without adequate food or heat. After Congress' appeal and Washington's warning, he was finally freed. His physical condition, however, having deteriorated, he never recovered vigor.[5]

His home, "Morven," had been invaded by the British, his library, documents and furnishings burned, his portrait disfigured and his farm destroyed. Unable to regain strength, his friends provided for the bare necessities of his family. Broken health prevented his attending the Continental Congress to which he had been re-elected. He died prior to the surrender of the British in 1781, and was interred in a Quaker cemetery, in an unmarked tomb.[6]

Richard Stockton stands out as the embodiment of our Declaration of Independence: ". . . and for the support of this Declaration, with a firm reliance upon the protection of Divine Providence, we mutually pledge to each other our lives, our fortunes and our sacred honor" - New Jersey's noblest son in the Revolutionary War.

John Witherspoon (1723-1794) was president of Princeton University, and is considered Princeton's greatest educator to this day. Preacher of the Gospel, Witherspoon was the only minister-signer of the Declaration of Independence. His historic speech, given to the Continental Congress on July 4, 1776 motivated members to sign the document:

There is a tide in the affairs of men, a nick of time we now perceive before us. To hesitate is to consent to slavery. That noble instrument on your table, which insures immortality to its authors, should be subscribed this very morning by every pen in this House. For my part, of property I have some, of reputation more. That reputation is staked upon the issue of this contest, that property pledged, and although these gray hairs must soon descend into the sepulchre, I had infinitely rather they should descend thither by the hands of the public executioner than desert at this crisis the sacred cause of my country.[7]

Officially Recorded Presidential Inaugural Scriptures:

Grover Cleveland's Inaugural Bible was published by the American Bible Society in 1851. He was the only President to hold office for two non-consecutive terms. In the front of the Bible is inscribed:

S.G. Cleveland from his affectionate mother, July, 1852

On the next page is inscribed:

On this Bible the Oath of Office was administered to Grover Cleveland 22nd President of the United States by Hon. Morrison R. Waite, Chief Justice of the United States, March 4, 1885, Test: James H. McKenney (L.S.) Clerk Supreme Court of the United States.

The Bible upon which **Cleveland** took his oath of office was a small, well-worn Morocco-covered, gilt-edged Bible. It was a gift from the President's mother, when, as a youth, he first left home to seek his fortune.

An interesting article by Alexander R. George entitled "Inaugural Pageant" gives us a vivid description of the first Cleveland Inauguration:

Cheers 'like the roaring of Niagara' greeted President-elect Cleveland as he rode from the White House to the Capitol in an open barouche drawn by President Arthur's spanking bays. The presidential carriage was lined with black and white robes. Vice-President-elect Hendricks rode in another open barouche, lined with crimson satin and pulled by four white horses, two famous Arabians in the lead.

After taking the oath of office, President Cleveland kissed the small, worn Bible his mother had given him as a boy when he left home. Phil Sheridan, still vigorous and ruddy, stood nearby.

The 'cameramen' hurriedly spread black mantles over their machines and 'shot' the scene while hundreds of men and boys looked on from the roof of the Capitol. It was estimated there were 150,000 people massed on the grounds and nearby streets...

G. Hazelton, in his book entitled, *The National Capitol*, writes:

By the President's special request, it (his Bible) was used for the ceremony. It was opened by the Chief Justice without any intention of selecting a particular place and the place that was kissed by the President was, therefore, the result purely of chance. As the type used in the Bible is small, the lips of the President touched six verses of 112th Psalm, from verse 5 to 10 inclusive...'A good man showeth favor, and lendeth: he will guide his affairs with discretion. Surely he shall not be moved forever; the righteous shall be in everlasting remembrance. He shall not be afraid of evil tidings; his heart is fixed, trusting the Lord. His heart is established; he shall not be afraid, until he sees his desire upon his enemies. He hath dispersed, he hath given to the poor; his righteousness endureth forever; his horn shall be exalted with honor. The wicked shall see it, and be grieved; he shall gnash with his teeth, and melt away; the desire of the wicked shall perish." Psalm 112:5-10

At his second inauguration in 1893, Cleveland's hand rested upon Psalm 91:12-16:

They shall bear thee upon their hands, lest thou dash thy foot against a stone. Thou shalt tread upon the lion and adder. The young lion and the dragon shalt thou trample under feet. Because he hath set his love upon me, therefore will I deliver him: I will set him on high, because he hath known my name. He shall call upon me, and I will answer him: I will be with him in trouble; I will deliver him, and honor him. With long life will I satisfy him, and show him my salvation.

— Psalm 91:12-16

United States President: Grover Cleveland, born in New Jersey (22nd; 24th).

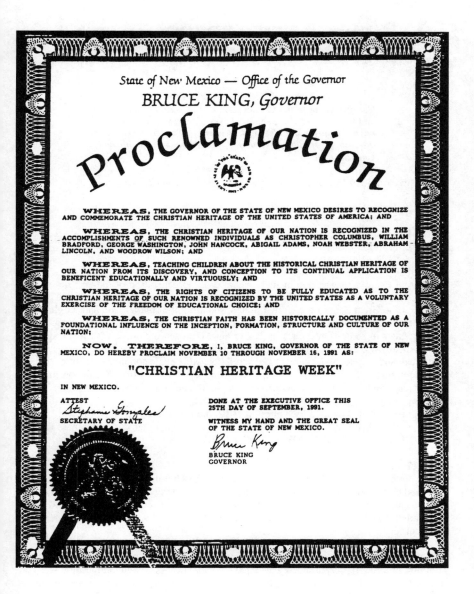

State of New Mexico — Office of the Governor

BRUCE KING, *Governor*

Proclamation

WHEREAS, THE GOVERNOR OF THE STATE OF NEW MEXICO DESIRES TO RECOGNIZE AND COMMEMORATE THE CHRISTIAN HERITAGE OF THE UNITED STATES OF AMERICA; AND

WHEREAS, THE CHRISTIAN HERITAGE OF OUR NATION IS RECOGNIZED IN THE ACCOMPLISHMENTS OF SUCH RENOWNED INDIVIDUALS AS CHRISTOPHER COLUMBUS, WILLIAM BRADFORD, GEORGE WASHINGTON, JOHN HANCOCK, ABIGAIL ADAMS, NOAH WEBSTER, ABRAHAM LINCOLN, AND WOODROW WILSON; AND

WHEREAS, TEACHING CHILDREN ABOUT THE HISTORICAL CHRISTIAN HERITAGE OF OUR NATION FROM ITS DISCOVERY, AND CONCEPTION TO ITS CONTINUAL APPLICATION IS BENEFICENT EDUCATIONALLY AND VIRTUOUSLY; AND

WHEREAS, THE RIGHTS OF CITIZENS TO BE FULLY EDUCATED AS TO THE CHRISTIAN HERITAGE OF OUR NATION IS RECOGNIZED BY THE UNITED STATES AS A VOLUNTARY EXERCISE OF THE FREEDOM OF EDUCATIONAL CHOICE; AND

WHEREAS, THE CHRISTIAN FAITH HAS BEEN HISTORICALLY DOCUMENTED AS A FOUNDATIONAL INFLUENCE ON THE INCEPTION, FORMATION, STRUCTURE AND CULTURE OF OUR NATION;

NOW, THEREFORE, I, BRUCE KING, GOVERNOR OF THE STATE OF NEW MEXICO, DO HEREBY PROCLAIM NOVEMBER 10 THROUGH NOVEMBER 16, 1991 AS:

"CHRISTIAN HERITAGE WEEK"

IN NEW MEXICO.

ATTEST

Stephanie Gonzales
SECRETARY OF STATE

DONE AT THE EXECUTIVE OFFICE THIS 25TH DAY OF SEPTEMBER, 1991.

WITNESS MY HAND AND THE GREAT SEAL OF THE STATE OF NEW MEXICO.

Bruce King
BRUCE KING
GOVERNOR

New Mexico was the first State in the Union to have celebrated "Christian Heritage Week" during the academic school year, with a governor's signed Proclamation, November 10-16, 1991.

NEW MEXICO
(Spain's name for the area)

The Preamble to the Constitution of the State of New Mexico states that, *We the people of New Mexico, grateful to Almighty God for the blessings of liberty, in order to secure the advantages of state government, do ordain and establish this Constitution.*

New Mexico joined the Union on January 6, 1912 as the 47th State.

State Capital: Sante Fe.

State Motto:
"Crescit Eundo," translated from Latin to mean, "It grows as it goes."

State Seal:
The first Great Seal was designed shortly after the organization of the territory of New Mexico in 1851. It consisted of the American Bald Eagle, our national emblem, as portrayed on the Great Seal of the United States; shielding the smaller Mexican Eagle within its outstretched wings. This is symbolic of the change of government from Mexico to the United States in 1846. The American Bald Eagle, representing bravery, skill and strength, clasps six arrows, three in either talon. The smaller, Mexican Brown Eagle, grasps a snake in its beak and a cactus in its talons. The scroll below the eagle contains the motto, "Crescit Eundo," translated from Latin to mean, "It Grows as it Goes." In 1887, the original seal was officially adopted with the addition of the 1850 date at the bottom.[1]

When New Mexico joined the Union in 1912, the Legislature changed the word "Territory" to "State" and the 1850 date to 1912, to read on its outer circumference, GREAT SEAL OF THE STATE OF NEW MEXICO - 1912.[2]

State Flag:
The first flag of New Mexico as 47th State in the Union was authorized in 1915 and designed by historian Ralph Emerson Twitchell of New Mexico. It portrayed a field of blue with a small United States flag in the upper right-hand corner and "New Mexico" embroidered diagonally across the flag from the lower left-hand-side to the upper right-hand corner.

In 1920, the Daughters of the American Revolution, New Mexico Chapter, advocated the adoption of a flag representing New Mexico's personality. A design competition was conducted in 1923, which was won by a Sante Fe physician. It consists of a red, setting sun, on a field of gold.[3]

State Song:
"O Fair New Mexico." The State Song was written by Elizabeth Garrett, blind daughter of New Mexico sheriff, Pat Garrett. In 1917, it became the official State Song.[4] The song was put into music in 1928 by John Phillip Sousa, America's famed and beloved March composer.

First "Christian Heritage Week:" November 10-16, 1991, proclaimed by Governor Bruce King. New Mexico was the first State in the Union to have an official "Christian Heritage Week."

Of Historic Interest:
  Dennis Chavez (1888-1962) was selected by the people of New Mexico to represent them in the U.S. Capitol's Hall of Fame.

  Senate Document No. 128, 89th Congress, 2nd Session, on the *Acceptance of the Statue of Dennis Chavez,* presented by the State of New Mexico, describes in detail the proceedings in the Rotunda of the U.S. Capitol, on March 31, 1966. Among the numerous commendatory speeches given by distinguished leaders and statesmen, the following are quoted:

> **Remarks by the Honorable Robert L. Bennett**
> **Acting Commissioner of Indian Affairs:**
> It is an honor for me to represent the Indian people of this Nation here today as we honor the memory of Senator Dennis Chavez. Most of us who were on the Navajo Reservation when he was in the Senate know of his devotion to the service of the Indian people. The mark of this man was in the fact that notwithstanding his grandfather's death at the hands of the Navajo and Apache Indians, he extended the hand of friendship to them. They, in turn, grasped it and came to love him as he loved them. It is no wonder then that at his passing they cried out the words inscribed in Navajo on his statue, "We have lost our voice."

> and

> **Remarks by His Excellency Dr. Guillermo Sevilla-Sacasa**
> **Ambassador from Nicaragua**
> Mr. Vice President, Mr. Speaker, Mr. Chief Justice, Senator Anderson, ladies and gentlemen: I am honored and deeply gratified to be present this afternoon at the solemn ceremony of unveiling the bronze statue of the eminent statesman and parliamentarian, Dennis Chavez.

> Dennis Chavez loved his country, he served it with fervent devotion and with unswerving faith in its glorious destiny. Therefore, in his own right, he joins the assembly of illustrious Americans whose lives were an example and who, upon their death, had earned the everlasting gratitude of their compatriots and friends.

> In these hallowed halls of the most highly respected monument of the Nation, the Capitol, which reflects the history of the United States of America, bronze and marble have a soul. Bronze and marble speak, impress, inspire, and guide the ever-victorious march of this great Nation, which is a bastion of peace, liberty and justice throughout the world - a generous and powerful nation, proud of its people and of the prestige of its institutions.

> All those who met and knew Dennis Chavez can never forget him. When Dennis Chavez died, he was one of the patriarchs of the U.S. Senate, where so many eminent personalities share responsibility under the aegis of a common land. Dennis Chavez was admired as a

politician, a gentleman, and a friend.

Dennis Chavez was very devoted to the sister nations of Latin America. He believed, and rightly so, that the best friends of the United States are in Latin America, and in this belief he always tried to help them. Dennis Chavez was aware of our faults, but he tried generously to overlook them. Dennis Chavez was aware of our virtues, and he gallantly took pleasure in making them known.

Dennis Chavez visited many of our countries, and he won the affection of our peoples. I might say that Dennis Chavez has monuments of affection erected in the heart of Latin America.

Dennis Chavez honored me with his friendship. We passed through this rotunda and these halls many times together, talking about inter-American matters, the problems which afflict us, the dangers that threaten our democracy and our freedom, and the manner in which those dangers can be averted. On many occasions we paused to contemplate the statues in this rotunda which consecrate the exalted human values which the United States of America presents to the world.

I salute Dennis Chavez, restored in bronze, and I say to him, in the presence of his esteemed widow and beloved children, that the peoples of Latin America whom he so dearly loved, join in this tribute of rightful recognition to his excellent qualities as an eminent statesman, a true gentleman, and a loyal friend.

ROBERT R. LIVINGSTON - NEW YORK

After the Original Bronze Statue in the Hall of Fame, U.S. Capitol,
Washington, D.C.

NEW YORK
(After the Duke of York, who became James II)

The Preamble to the Constitution of the State of New York states that, *We, the people of the State of New York, grateful to Almighty God for our freedom, in order to secure its blessings, do establish this Constitution.*

New York joined the Union on July 26, 1788 as the 11th State.

State Capital: Albany.

State Motto:
"Excelsior," translated from Latin to mean: "Ever Upward."

State Seal:
The Great Seal of 1777 was designed by a committee including founding fathers Robert Morris (financier of the American Revolution) and John Jay (first U.S. Supreme Court Chief Justice and Governor of New York).

State Coat of Arms:
Shield. A clear blue sky with the golden rays of the sun centered behind a range of three mountains, the middle one being the highest; below, a ship and sloop under sail, facing each other and about to meet on a river, bordered by a grassy shore fringed with shrubs, in natural colors.

Crest (above the shield). On a wreath of blue and gold, an American eagle in its natural colors, facing toward the right, above a two-thirds globe of the world, showing the north Atlantic Ocean with outlines of its shores.

Supporters. The two figures on the outside of the shield appear to be joined with the shield as a unit formed by the extension of the scroll:

On the dexter side of the Shield. The figure of Liberty in natural colors, her unbound hair decorated with pearls. She is clothed in blue with red sandals, a loose robe of red hanging down from her shoulders to her feet. In her right hand, she holds a staff topped with a gold liberty cap; her left arm is bent at the elbow, the hand supporting the shield at its top right. A royal crown lies at her left foot, thrown down to illustrate victory over the British monarchy's power.

On the sinister side of the Shield. The figure of Justice in natural colors, her unbound hair decorated with pearls. She is clothed in gold with a blue belt, fringed in red, wearing sandals and robe as Liberty, and bound about the eyes with a narrow band of cloth. In her right hand she holds a gold-handled sword, held erect, and resting on the top left point of the shield; her left arm is also bent at the elbow, holding scales.[1]

State Flag:

"The State Flag is hereby declared to be blue, charged with the arms of the State in the colors as described in the blazon of this section."

Chapter 229 of the Laws of 1896 read: "State Flag. The State flag is hereby declared to be buff, charged with the arms of the State in the colors as described in the blason of this section." However, a letter from the first State Historian, Hugh Hastings, dated March 27, 1901 and addressed to Governor B.B. Odell, relates the following:

> Hon. B.B. Odell, Jr.
> Executive Chamber,
> Albany, New York
>
> Sir:
>
> The bill of Senator Ellsworth to change the color of the State flag from buff to blue, is now awaiting your action. The objections to buff are these:
>
> First: It is not a primary color;
> Second: Buff fades easily under strong sunlight, or after two or three days' exposure to rain;
> Third: Buff is the recognized quarantine color of the world;
> Fourth: In Russia, the yellow flag indicates sorrow and death;
> Fifth: On the quarantine boat which meets incoming Steamers, the present buff flag cannot be distinguished from the quarantine flag.
>
> The buff flag was adopted by the Legislature in 1896, mainly on the representations of Major Asa Bird Gardiner, who contended that Washington had selected buff as the color for the State flag of New York.
>
> During the Revolutionary War, all the New York State battle-flags were blue, as the records will demonstrate, and as the colors on the second floor of the Capitol at the eastern approach, will prove. A few weeks ago when the Chinese Minister, Wu Ting Fang, was given a review by the Twenty-third Regiment in Brooklyn, he imagined that in honor of the occasion, our State flag was a Chinese flag, improvised for his particular benefit, and out of compliment to him.
>
> We should also remember that yellow is the Spanish color as well as the Chinese; and that our flag should consist of one of the standard colors of the National emblem, red, white and blue.
>
> Some criticism has been raised as to what particular class of blue should be used for the State color. That proposition was very carefully considered before the bill was introduced in the Senate. It was found that the regulations of the United States army prescribe simply the word "blue" to designate the color or uniform; and that the United States statutes provide that the color used in the National emblem shall be "blue" – "of the color of the clear sky; of the color of the spectrum between wave lengths .505 and .415 micron, and more especially .487 to .460, but of such light mixed with white."
>
> Trusting that you may see your way clear to eliminate from the State service what is generally designated as a "colorless rag," and establish for our State flag a primary color, durable and substantial, beautiful to the eye, capable of arousing an enthusiasm that buff never could, I have the honor to remain with assurances of the highest esteem, Sir.
>
> Yours very respectfully,
>
> Hugh Hastings,
> State Historian

It was thus that the color of the New York State flag was changed to blue, as described in Chapter 229 of the Laws of 1901.[2]

First "Christian Heritage Week:" May 12-18, 1996, proclaimed by the Governor.

Of Historic Interest:
   Robert R. Livingston (1746-1813) was chosen by the citizens of New York to represent them as their greatest hero in the U.S. Capitol's Hall of Fame. Livingston was the heir to 13,000 acres east of the Hudson River.

At the age of 15 he entered *King's College,* of which his uncle Phillip was one of the founders, and became a close friend of John Jay. *King's College* later became *Columbia University.* Both Livingston and Jay graduated together. Both spoke at their commencement, which took place at *Trinity Church* on Wall Street. Livingston's Address was *Liberty,* while Jay spoke on *Peace.* Livingston won the honors. Both became lawyers.[3]

At the close of the Continental Congress, Livingston served two years as Secretary of Foreign Affairs. He kept Congress and other significant persons apprised of European affairs, thus uniting the New States in a closer bond.

On April 30, 1789, Chancellor Robert Livingston administered the oath of office to George Washington, as first United States President. This occured on the balcony of Federal Hall in New York City. After Washington had kissed the Bible, opened between the 49th and 50th chapters of Genesis, Livingston, turning to the crowd assembled, paid tribute to Washington with the words, "Long Live George Washington, President of the United States!"[4]

An Inaugural Worship Service ensued at *St. Paul's Chapel - Trinity Church,* where George Washington and members of his government worshipped the Lord, some of whom were wardens and vestrymen of this church. Washington's pew is still to be seen at *St. Paul's Chapel.*

Fisher Ames was one of the Committee of Congress and sat in the pew with Washington. In a letter to George Richards Minot from New York, dated May 3rd, 1789, he writes the following:

> ...I was present in the pew with the President, and must assure you that, after making all deductions for the delusion of one's fancy in regard to characters, I still think of him with more veneration than for any other person. Time has made havoc upon his face. That, and many other circumstances not to be reasoned about, conspire to keep up the awe which I brought with me. He addressed the two Houses in the Senate Chamber; it was a very touching scene, and quite of the solemn kind. His aspect grave, almost to sadness; his modesty; his voice deep, and so low as to call for close attention; added to the series of objects presented to the mind, and overwhelming it, produced emotions of the most effecting kind upon the members. I sat entranced. It seemed to me an allegory in which virtue was personified, and addressing those whom she would make her votaries. Her power over the heart was never greater, and the illustration of her doctrine by her own example was never more perfect...[5]

Robert Livingston was appointed Chairman of the New York State Convention on the ratification of the U.S. Constitution.

He possessed a brilliant mind, demonstrating geniality in all his dealings. He was appointed by President Thomas Jefferson to the Ministry to France and was directed to purchase the port of New Orleans from the French government. Napoleon made him the astounding offer of the Louisiana Purchase, consisting of 1,171,931 square miles (more than double the total area of the United States) for a mere $15,000,000. This acquisition of vast western territory made the United States a world power.[6]

Livingston was the founder and first president of the *American Academy of Fine Arts* as well as being a trustee of the *New York Society Library*.[7] He is remembered in history as a Christian statesman, lawyer and diplomat of the highest order.

John Jay (1745-1829) served as governor of New York and first Chief Justice of the U.S. Supreme Court. This distinguished founding father was elected president of the American Bible Society. After his death, his hand-written prayers were discovered among his papers, as excerpted below:

> Merciful Father, who desirest not the death of the sinner, but will have all men to be saved and to come to the knowledge of the truth, give me grace so to draw nigh unto thee as that thou wilt condescend to draw nigh unto me; and enable me to offer unto Thee, through thy beloved Son, supplication and thanksgiving acceptably ...Above all, I thank Thee for Thy mercy to our fallen race, as declared in Thy Holy Gospel, by Thy beloved Son, 'who gave Himself a ransom for all.' I thank Thee for the hope of the remission of sins, of regeneration, and of life and happiness everlasting, through the merits and intercession of our Saviour... Let Thy Holy Spirit purify and unite me to my Saviour forever, and enable me to cling unto Him as my very life, as indeed He is. Perfect and confirm my faith, my trust, and hope of salvation in Him and in Him only.[8]

JOHN JAY - NEW YORK

After the original painting of John Jay by Gilbert Stuart, in the National Gallery of Art, Washington, D.C.

139

Officially Recorded Presidential Inaugural Scriptures:

Theodore Roosevelt's second inauguration took place on March 4, 1905. Below Chief Justice Fuller's signature, the President had dedicated this inaugural Bible to his son as follows:

> To Theodore Roosevelt, Jr. from his father March 4, 1905.

The Clerk of the Supreme Court jotted down for posterity, James 1:22-23 as Roosevelt's choice of inaugural Scripture:

> But be ye doers of the word, and not merely hearers only, deceiving your own selves. For if any be a hearer of the word, and not a doer, he is like unto a man beholding his natural face in a glass: for once he has looked at himself and gone away, he has immediately forgotten what kind of person he was.

Franklin D. Roosevelt's Bible, dated 1686, is the oldest of all inaugural Bibles, and the only one written in a modern foreign language. This Biblia Hollandica (Dutch) version of Scripture was used by the President during all four inaugurations. It was opened each time to I Corinthians 13:

> If I speak with the tongues of men and of angels but do not have love, I have become a noisy gong or a clanging cymbal. And if I have the gift of prophecy, and know all mysteries and all knowledge; and if I have all faith, so as to remove mountains, but do not have love, I am nothing. And if I give all my possessions to feed the poor, and if I deliver my body to be burned, but do not have love, it profits me nothing. Love is patient, love is kind, and is not jealous; love does not brag and is not arrogant, does not act unbecomingly; it does not seek its own, is not provoked, does not take into account a wrong suffered, does not rejoice in unrighteousness, but rejoices with the truth; bears all things, believes all things, hopes all things, endures all things. Love never fails; but if there are gifts of prophecy, they will be done away; if there are tongues, they will cease; if there is knowledge, it will be done away. For we know in part, and we prophesy in part; but when the perfect comes, the partial will be done away. When I was a child, I used to speak as a child, think as a child, reason as a child; when I became a man, I did away with childish things. For now we see in a mirror dimly, but then face to face; now I know in part, but then I shall know fully just as I also have been fully known. But now abide faith, hope, love, these three; but the greatest of these is love. (I Corinthians 13) New American Standard Version

United States Presidents: Martin van Buren (8th); Millard Fillmore (13th); Grover Cleveland (22nd, 24th); Theodore Roosevelt (26th); Franklin Delano Roosevelt (32nd).

CHARLES BRANTLEY AYCOCK, 1859-1912, NORTH CAROLINA

After the Original Sculpture in the Hall of Fame, U.S. Capitol, Washington, D.C.

141

NORTH CAROLINA

(after the Latin word
"Carolus" meaning Charles
- Charles II of England)

The Preamble to the Constitution of the State of North Carolina states that, *We the people of the State of North Carolina, grateful to Almighty God, the Sovereign Ruler of the Nations, for the preservation of the American Union and the existence of our civil, political and religious liberties, and acknowledging our dependence upon Him for the continuance of those blessings to us and our posterity, do ordain and establish this Constitution.*

North Carolina joined the Union on November 21, 1789 as the 12th State.

State Capital: Raleigh.

State Motto:
"Esse Quam Videri," translated from Latin to mean, "To be Rather Than to Seem."[1] The words "Esse Quam Videri," along with the date "May 20, 1775," is placed with North Carolina's Coat of Arms upon the Great Seal of the State of North Carolina.

State Seal:
The Great Seal of North Carolina is two and one-quarter inches in diameter. The two women figures in the foreground of the seal are Liberty and Plenty. Liberty, standing upright, is holding a scroll with the word "Constitution" inscribed upon it. This depicts the foundation upon which our government is based. Plenty, the sitting figure, holds three sheaves of grain in her right hand and her left hand rests on the small end of her "horn of plenty" - with the contents spilling out. This depicts the abundance of North Carolina's agricultural products. In the background are mountains on the left with the ocean to the right. A three-masted ship is moored behind Plenty's left shoulder. The mountains, the ocean and the grassy plain upon which Liberty and Plenty are placed, represent the three geographical regions of the State. The ship stands for the means by which most of North Carolina's early settlers came to the State, as well as for the importance of shipbuilding and "naval stores" in the development of North Carolina. Along the lower perimeter of the seal are the words "Esse Quam Videri," the State Motto, translated from Latin to mean, "To be Rather Than to Seem." The upper date of May 20, 1775, and the lower date of April 12, 1776, represent the dates of the Mecklenburg Declaration and the Halifax Resolves, respectively.[2]

State Flag:

An Act to Establish a State Flag
The General Assembly of North Carolina do enact:
SEC. 1. That the flag of North Carolina shall consist of a blue union, containing in the centre thereof a white star with the letter N in gilt on the left and the letter C in gilt on the right of said star, the circle containing the same to be one-third the width of the union.

SEC. 2. That the fly of the flag shall consist of two equally proportioned bars; the upper bar to be red, the lower bar to be white; that the length of the bars horizontally shall be equal to the perpendicular length of the union, and the total length of the flag shall be one-third more than its width.

SEC. 3. That above the star in the centre of the union there shall be a gilt scroll in semi-circular form, containing in black letters the inscription, "May 20th, 1775," and that below the star there shall be a similar scroll containing in black letters the inscription: "April 12th, 1776."

SEC. 4. That this act shall take effect from and after its ratification. In the General Assembly read three times and ratified this 9th day of March, A.D. 1885.[3]

The shades of red and blue found on the North Carolina State Flag and the United States Flag are the official state colors.[4]

State Song:

THE OLD NORTH STATE
by William Gaston

Carolina! Carolina! Heaven's blessings attend her.
While we live we will cherish, protect and defend her.
Tho' the scorner may sneer at and witlings defame her.
Still our hearts swell with gladness whenever we name her.
Hurrah! Hurrah! The Old North State forever. Hurrah!
The good Old North State.

Tho' she envies not others, their merited glory.
Say whose name stands the foremost in liberty's story.
Tho' too true to herself e'er to crouch to oppression.
Who can yield to just rule a more loyal submission.
Hurrah! Hurrah! The Old North State forever. Hurrah!
The good Old North State.

Then let all those who love us, love the land that we live in.
As happy a region as on this side of Heaven,
Where plenty and peace, love and joy smile before us.
Raise aloud, raise together the heart thrilling chorus.
Hurrah! Hurrah! The Old North State forever.
Hurrah! Hurrah! The good Old North State.[5]

First "Christian Heritage Week:" March 17-23, 1996, proclaimed by the Governor.

Of Historic Interest:

Charles Brantley Aycock (1859-1912) was chosen by the citizens of North Carolina as their greatest hero in the U.S. Capitol's Hall of Fame. As a young lad, he and six older brothers walked two miles to school each day. It is recorded that Aycock remembered his patient, loving mother having made a mark in lieu of signing her name - North Carolina being devoid of State schools. From thence on, his life's work became education, believing that every child had the right to being educated as he or she had the right to be free.[6]

Aycock's family was Baptist, humbly practising foot-washing, and firmly believing that God would convert the heathen, if He so chose.[7]

Charles was sent to an academy nearby in order to prepare for college; subsequently entering the Sophomore Class of the *University of North Carolina,* from which he graduated with honors in oratory and essay writing. When he entered college, Edwin A. Alderman, later to become President of the University of North Carolina, and the *University of Virginia,* respectively, was a Senior. Alderman was struck by Aycock's openness and strong spirituality, befriending him for life. While in college, Charles became a member of the local Baptist Church, practising his Christian faith on campus. As a member of the College Debating Club, he was once falsely accused of an untruth. His fellow-members took steps to ensure the withdrawal of his opponent's statement. His accuser reports: "Aycock crossed the hall, dropped into the seat next to me, and putting his arm around my shoulder, said, 'It's all right, Jim . . . I know you didn't mean it, and it shan't affect our friendship.' "[8]

He was elected College Marshall in his Junior year, as the highest social honor bestowed by his fellow-colleagues; later becoming editor of the *University Magazine,* and also editing *The Chapel Hill Ledger.* Aycock's studies encompassed law, becoming a lawyer at 21. To support himself, he became a teacher, excelling to the extent that he was appointed Superintendent of Schools in Wayne County. His law practice also thrived.

At 31, he was elected Governor of North Carolina. During his four-year term, it is reported that a new schoolhouse was constructed each day of his administration, totalling almost 3,000. His educational reforms were extensive - Normal schools were founded, teaching methods enhanced, teacher salaries doubled and school terms were lengthened. He successfully combatted illiteracy for both white and black children.[9]

Said Governor Aycock, "the people of North Carolina have given me some degree of honor and influence . . . and this position of mine is not for sale . . . money cannot buy it."

Addressing an assembly of thousands of teachers of the *American Teachers' Association* in Birmingham, Alabama, his last words dealt with "the equal right of every child born on earth to have the opportunity to burgeon out all there is within him," after which he died of sudden heart failure, aged 53. Charles Brantley Aycock, Christian, Educator, Lawyer and Statesman is known as "the Educational Governor of North Carolina."[10]

The Origins of the Phrase: "Tar Heel State"
During its early history, North Carolina was best known for products derived from pine trees, particularly tar pitch and turpentine, which were crucial naval supplies in the days of wooden sailing ships. A popular State tradition holds that during the First Battle of Manassas in 1861, a charge by federal troops against part of the Confederate Army's lines broke through a Virginia regiment, causing its soldiers to flee to the rear in panic. The North Carolina regiments holding the line next to the shattered Virginia regiment, however, held their ground, stemming the Union Army's breakthrough.

After the battle, the North Carolinians, who had successfully fought it out alone, were greeted by the chagrined derelict regiment with the question: "Any more tar down in the Old North State, boys?" Quick as a flash came the answer: "No, not a bit, old Jeff's bought it all up." "Is that so? What is he going to do with it?" the Virginians asked. "He's going to put it on you-uns' heels to make you stick better in the next fight."

It is reported that General Robert E. Lee, upon hearing of the incident, said, "God bless the Tar Heel boys," and that the name stuck to all North Carolina troops serving in the Army of Northern Virginia from thence on.[11]

144

ROBERT E. LEE, 1807-1870, VIRGINIA

After the Bronze Statue in the Hall of Fame, U.S. Capitol, Washington, D.C.

Officially Recorded Presidential Inaugural Scripture:
Immediately following President Lincoln's death, **Andrew Johnson** was sworn into office at the Kirkwood Hotel on April 14, 1865. His inaugural Bible is the King James Version, published by C.J. Clay, at the University Press, London.

Inscribed on the front inside board of the Bible are the words:

> Andrew Johnson's Inaugural Bible. When oath was taken his hand rested on Chapter 20 and 21 of Proverbs. The King's heart is in the hand of the Lord, as the rivers of water; he turneth it withersoever he will. Every way of a man is right in his own eyes: But the Lord pondereth the hearts. To do justice and judgment is more acceptable to the Lord than sacrifice.
>
> Proverbs 21:1-3.

United States Presidents: James Knox Polk, born in North Carolina (11th); Andrew Johnson, born in North Carolina (17th).

JOHN BURKE
1859-1937

After the Bronze Statue of John Burke in the Hall of Fame, U.S. Capitol, Washington, D.C.

147

NORTH DAKOTA
(from the Indian, "Allies")

The Preamble to the Constitution of the State of North Dakota states that, *We, the people of North Dakota, grateful to Almighty God for the blessings of civil and religious liberty, do ordain and establish this Constitution.*

North Dakota joined the Union on November 2, 1889 as the 39th State.

State Capital: Bismarck.

State Motto:

"Liberty and Union, Now and Forever, One and Inseparable." This was similar to the motto used by the Dakota Territory and was adopted when North Dakota became a State. The motto of the Dakota Territory was "Liberty and Union, One and Inseparable, Now and Forever." This motto was suggested by Dr. Joseph Ward of Yankton who was quoting a reply from Daniel Webster. However, the motto that was used by the Territory had two of the phrases turned around. When North Dakota became a State, the error was corrected.

State Seal:

The Great Seal of the state of North Dakota is described in Article XI, Section 2, of the North Dakota Constitution, as follows:

> A tree in the open field, the trunk of which is surrounded by three bundles of wheat; on the right a plow, anvil and sledge; on the left, a bow crossed with three arrows, and an Indian on horseback pursuing a buffalo toward the setting sun; the foliage of a tree arched by a half circle of forty-two stars surrounded by the motto: "Liberty and Union, Now and Forever, One and Inseparable"; the words, "Great Seal" at the top; the words "State of North Dakota" at the bottom; "October 1st" on the left and "1889" on the right. The seal to be two and one-half inches in diameter.[1]

State Flag:

The Flag of North Dakota "shall consist of a field of blue silk or material which will withstand the elements four feet four inches on the pike and five feet six inches on the fly, with a border of knotted yellow fringe two and one-half inches wide. On each side of said flag in the center thereof, shall be embroidered or stamped an eagle with outspread wings and with opened beak. The eagle shall be three feet four inches from tip to tip of wing, and one foot ten inches from top of head to bottom of olive branch hereinafter described. . .The left foot of the eagle shall grasp a sheaf of arrow, the right foot shall grasp an olive branch showing three red berries. On the breast of the eagle shall be displayed a shield, the lower part showing seven red and six white stripes placed alternately. Through the open beak of the eagle shall pass a scroll bearing the words 'E Pluribus Unum.' Beneath the eagle there shall be a scroll on which shall be borne the words 'North Dakota.' Over the scroll carried through the eagle's beak shall be shown thirteen five-pointed stars, the whole device being surmounted by a sunburst."[2]

State Coat of Arms:
The description and significance of the State Coat of Arms is as follows:

Device: On an Indian arrowhead point to base or a bend vert charged with three mullets of the first, in base a fleur-de-lis of the second.

Crest: On a wreath or an azure, a sheaf of three arrows argent armed and flighted gules behind a stringed bow fessways or with grip of the second (gules).

Motto: Strength from the soil.

Significance: The colors of yellow-gold and green are indicative of the great agricultural State of North Dakota and has particular reference to ripening grain and the abundant grazing areas. The Indian arrowhead forms the shield of the Coat of Arms and symbolizes the "Sioux State."

The three stars denote the three branches of government, the legislative, executive and judicial. Each star in the bend is given the heraldic value of thirteen which signifies the thirteen original States, and the cumulative numerical value of the three stars indicates that North Dakota was the thirty-ninth state admitted to the Union. The stars also allude to the history of the Territory under three foreign flags. Three stars are borne upon the Coat of Arms of Merriwether Lewis of the Lewis and Clark expedition and also on the Coat of Arms of Lord Selkirk, head of the first permanent settlement in this state. The fleur-de-lis alludes to La Verendrye, a French explorer who was the first known explorer to visit the territory of this state. The blue and gold wreath in the crest reflects the history of the territory as part of the Louisiana purchase. The crest which shall constitute the military crest of the State of North Dakota is a motif taken from the State Seal, and the Sioux Indian tribes signify mighty warriors.[3]

State Hymn:
"North Dakota Hymn" was written through a request by Minnie J. Nielson, North Dakota Superintendent of Public Instruction. In 1926 she approached James W. Foley, a former noted North Dakota poet who was living in California, and asked him to compose a song about North Dakota. He agreed and wrote the poem "North Dakota Hymn" which could be sung to the tune of "Austrian Hymn." Upon seeing the words to the poem, Dr. C.S. Putnam, music conductor for the *North Dakota Agriculture College Band* set out to compose the music. The combined work of Foley and Putnam was first presented publicly at the Bismarck City Auditorium in 1927.[4]

NORTH DAKOTA HYMN
North Dakota, North Dakota, With thy prairies wide and free,
All thy sons and daughters love thee, Fairest state from sea to sea.

Hear thy children singing, Songs of happiness and praise,
Far and long the echoes ringing, Through the vastness of thy ways.

Onward, onward, onward going, Light of courage in thine eyes,
Sweet the winds above thee blowing, Green thy fields and fair thy skies

God of freedom, all victorious, Give us souls serene and strong,
Strength to make the future glorious, Keep the echo of our song;

North Dakota, North Dakota, In our hearts forever long.
North Dakota, North Dakota, In our hearts forever long.

First "Christian Heritage Week:" November 5-11, 2000 proclaimed by the Governor.

Of Historic Interest:
John Burke (1859-1937) won recognition in pioneering days for his crusading effort which resulted in the overthrow of corrupt political control. He became legislator, Governor, Supreme Court Justice and Treasurer of the United States.

On June 27, 1963, at the acceptance of the statue of **John Burke** (Honest John Burke) as North Dakota's greatest hero in the Hall of Fame, Senator Carl Hayden delivered the following speech:

> ... This is a proud and inspiring day. It belongs not only to John Burke and North Dakota, but to our entire nation, for here at this ceremony, we witness the admission of a new member to that exclusive group of patriots — makers of our noble history — who have been selected by their States and their country for enshrinement in Statuary Hall.
>
> The eloquent and glowing praises which John Burke earned by his dedicated public service must come from others more articulate than I. There are perhaps few here, however, who more vividly recall the development of his career or who more sincerely appreciate this honor which he so richly merits.
>
> I was twelve years of age when North Dakota was admitted to statehood in 1889. John Burke was then thirty years of age and a homespun country lawyer. In 1912, when I came to Washington as the first Representative of the new State of Arizona, John Burke was serving his sixth year as Governor of North Dakota. The breadth of his vision, the force of his personality, and the high quality of his leadership had already characterized him as a man of national prominence and respect. It came as no surprise, therefore, when President Woodrow Wilson appointed him as the Treasurer of the United States, the office in which he served so ably from 1913 to 1921.
>
> As I accept this statue, I congratulate the good people of North Dakota. In their name and on behalf of Americans everywhere, I thank God for blessing this country of ours with patriots like John Burke. They are our finest heritage.

GARFIELD

1831 – 1881

After the Marble Statue of James Abram Garfield in the Hall of Fame,
U.S. Capitol, Washington, D.C.

151

OHIO
(great)

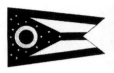

The Constitution of the State of Ohio states that, We, the people of the State of Ohio, grateful to Almighty God for our freedom, to secure its blessings, and promote our common welfare, do establish this Constitution... All men have a natural and indefeasible right to worship Almighty God according to the dictates of their own conscience...Religion, morality, and knowledge, however, being essential to good government, it shall be the duty of the general assembly to pass suitable laws to protect every religious denomination in the peaceable enjoyment of its own mode of public worship, and to encourage schools and the means of instruction.

Ohio joined the Union on March 1, 1803 as the 17th State.

State Capital: Columbus.

State Motto:
"With God all Things are Possible." (Matthew 19:26), Act of the 103rd General Assembly. In 1958, Jimmie Mastronardo, a 12-year-old, sixth-grade student at *The Hartwell School* in Cincinnati, was concerned about Ohio having no State Motto, among all other States in the Union. Jimmy's teacher had pointed this out to his History Class. It was thus that Jimmy decided that something had to be done about the matter. With the help of his parents, Mr. and Mrs. John Mastronardo, Jimmy selected an ideal State Motto from Matthew's Gospel, Chapter 19, verse 26: "With God all Things are Possible." [1] These are Jesus' words to His disciples, who were astonished at His statement that "It is easier for a camel to go through the eye of a needle, than for a rich man to enter into the Kingdom of God." In Matthew's Gospel account, Jesus added, "With men this is impossible, but with God all things are possible."

State Coat of Arms:
The Coat of Arms of the State shall consist of the following device: a circular shield; on the right foreground of the shield a full sheaf of wheat bound and standing erect; in the left foreground, a cluster of seventeen arrows bound in the center and resembling in form the sheaf of wheat; in the background, a representation of Mount Logan, Ross County, as viewed from Adena State Memorial; over the mount, a rising sun, three-quarters exposed and radiating seventeen rays, the exterior extremities of which form a semi-circle; and uniting the background and foreground, a representation of the Scioto River and cultivated fields.
The 107th General Assembly. [2]

State Flag:
The flag of the State of Ohio shall be pennant shaped. It shall have three red and two white horizontal stripes; the union of the flag shall be seventeen five-point stars, white, in a blue triangular field, the base of which shall be the staff end or vertical edge of the flag, and the apex of which shall be the center of the middle red stripe. The stars shall be grouped around a red disc superimposed upon a white circular "O" . . . The proportional dimensions of the flag and of its various parts shall be according to the official design thereof on file in the office of the Secretary of State.
The 75th General Assembly. [3]

First "Christian Heritage Week:" April 14-20, 1996, proclaimed by the Governor.

Of Historic Interest:
  James Abram Garfield (1831-1881) is Ohio's greatest hero in the Hall of Fame. He served as twentieth U.S. President, dying tragically through the bullet of his assassin — a demented, disappointed office-seeker. Garfield was born in a log cabin in western Ohio, his father being a descendant of the Massachusetts settlers under John Winthrop. His mother traced her ancestry to Roger Williams, founder of Rhode Island. At age two, his father died; James learning to read at age three, attending school at four, undertaking manual labor at ten and doing farm work for wages at age sixteen. Attending school for a few months each winter, he became an avid reader, knowing his Bible well. He was a member of the Disciples of Christ Church.[4]

  At age eighteen he attended a local academy, the following year entering the *Eclectic Institute* in Hiram, Ohio, where, working as janitor, doing odd jobs and teaching at a public school, he was able to pay for his education and save $350.00. Garfield entered the Junior Class at *Williams College* in Massachusetts, graduating three years later as valedictorian; having served as teacher in order to pay his tuition. Garfield led prayer meetings on campus and was also President of his debating society and editor of the *Williams Quarterly*.[5]

  Returning to the *Eclectic Institute*, Garfield taught Latin and Greek, while studying law. At 26 he was elected to President of the *Eclectic Institute*, which became *Hiram College*. He mastered the art of oratory. He was a frequent preacher of the Gospel in churches, it being reported that throughout a twenty-seven-day time span, he preached as many sermons; seven students accepting Jesus Christ as their personal Savior.[6]

  His wife, Lucretia Rudolph Garfield, bore him five children who survived. One of his sons became President of *Williams College*, while another became Secretary of the Interior. Garfield, an anti-slavery advocate, was elected in 1859 to the Ohio State Senate. During the Civil War he gained the reputation of "preacher-soldier." He also gained the distinction of attaining the highest rank among Army Volunteers, that of Major-General.[7]

  At the suggestion of Abraham Lincoln, he took his place as delegate in the U.S. House of Representatives, favoring the Library of Congress, from which, it is said, he consulted more books than any other congressman except Charles Sumner. Garfield led the cause for a new Library of Congress historic building, which was inaugurated in 1897, after his death.

  At a speech in New York after Lincoln's assassination, he quieted the fears of the people by proclaiming: "Fellow citizens, God reigns, and the government in Washington still lives."

  In June, 1880, Garfield was nominated for the Presidency. While serving as twentieth U.S. President, he boldly exposed financial frauds and authorized a thorough investigation of scandals in the Postal Star Routes. He encouraged the "Good Neighbor" policy with South America, as well as the Panama Canal.[8]

  The untimely death of Ohio's greatest hero was mourned nationally and internationally.

Other Notable Ohians:
  William Holmes McGuffey (1800-1873) was active in higher education as professor, and president of Cincinnati College in 1836 and Ohio College from 1839-1843. His text-

book series, written for the first six grades of elementary school, helped shape American Christian education and morals for nearly a century. His eclectic readers sold an estimated 120 million copies. The National Education Association (NEA) honored McGuffey with the following resolution at his death:

> In the death of William H. McGuffey,...this Association feels that they have lost one of the great lights of the profession whose life was a lesson full of instruction; an example and model to American teachers. His labors in the cause of education, extending over a period of half a century, in several offices as teacher of common schools, college professor and college president, and as author of text books; his almost unequalled industry; his power in the lecture room; his influence upon his pupils and community; his care for the public interests of education; his lofty devotion to duty; his conscientious Christian character—all these have made him one of the noblest ornaments of our profession in this age, and entitle him to the grateful remembrance of this Association and of the teachers of America.
>
> Elmira, New York, August 7, 1873.[9]

Astronaut John Glenn was the first American to orbit the earth in 1962.

Oficially Recorded Presidential Inaugural Scriptures:
Ulysses S. Grant was sworn into office for the second time on March 4, 1873. On the second blank leaf of his Inaugural Bible is inscribed:

> To Miss Nellie Grant from D.W. Middleton Clerk Sup. Ct. U.S. used for the administration of the oath, on the Second Inauguration of General U.S. Grant, as President of the United States March 4, 1873

The Bible was opened at the beautiful Messianic prophecy of Isaiah, which reads:

> And there shall come forth a rod out of the stem of Jesse, and a Branch shall grow out of his roots; And the Spirit of the Lord shall rest upon Him, the Spirit of wisdom and understanding, the Spirit of counsel and might, the Spirit of knowledge and the fear of the Lord. Isaiah 11:1-2

The General is purported to have been pleased with this coincidence, as he was the son of Jesse.

On the 5th of March, 1877, **Rutherford B. Hayes** was sworn into office as the nineteenth President of the United States. The Bible upon which he took the oath of office was a King James Version, printed in London by George E. Eyre and William Spottiswoode, printers to the Queen's Most Excellent Majesty. A single electoral vote won this difficult election for Hayes. Due to the closeness of the election, Psalm 118:11-13 might have been chosen as the Inaugural Scripture:

> They compassed me about; yea, they compassed me about but in the name of the Lord I will destroy them. They compassed me about like bees; they are quenched as the fire of thorns; for in the name of the Lord I will destroy them. Thou hast thrust sore at me that I might fall, but the Lord helped me.
>
> Psalm 118:11-13

Inscribed upon the second front blank leaf are these words:

> To Mrs. Hayes with the Compliments of D.W. Middleton Clerk Sup.
> Court U.S. Used for the administration of the oath on the inaugura-
> tion of Rutherford B. Hayes as President of the United States. 5th
> March 1877.

Below, in pencil is the notation:

> See 118 Psalm 11 verse etc.
> "   Psalm 101

James A. Garfield swore allegiance to the Constitution of the United States on March 4, 1881. His Inaugural Bible is the King James Version, S.S. Teacher's Edition, printed at the University Press, Oxford.

A Certification on the second front blank leaf reads:

> Bible used at the inauguration of James A. Garfield 20th President of
> the United States 4th March A.D. 1881. James H. McKenney Clerk
> Supreme Court U.S. (L.S.) To Mrs. J.A. Garfield with compliments
> James H. McKenney

The left margin holds the following handwritten comment:

> See Proverb XXI

To the left of Proverbs 21, the following notation appears in the same hand:

> "Verse 1, chapter 21 kissed by President Garfield when taking oath
> of office."

The verse referred to reads:

> The king's heart is in the hand of the Lord, as rivers of water; He
> turneth it withersoever he will. Proverbs 21:1

Benjamin Harrison was inaugurated into office as President of the United States on March 4, 1889. His inaugural Bible is the S.S. Teacher's Edition of the King James Version published by the Oxford University Press. An official inscription on the first blank leaf of his Bible reads:

> I certify that this Bible was used in the administration of the oath of
> office on the fourth day of March, A.D. 1889, to Benjamin Harrison,
> the twenty-third President of the United States. Melville W. Fuller
> James H. McKenney Clerk of the Supreme Court of the United States.
> To Mrs. Benjamin Harrison with the compliments of the Clerk.

The following lines are from Psalm 121, verses 1-6:

> I will lift up mine eyes unto the hills, from whence cometh my help.

155

My help cometh from the Lord, which made heaven and earth. He will not suffer thy foot to be moved; he that keepeth thee will not slumber. Behold, he that keepeth Israel shall neither slumber nor sleep. The Lord is thy keeper; the Lord is thy shade upon thy right hand. The sun shall not smite thee by day, nor the moon by night.

Psalm 121:1-6

William McKinley was sworn into office on March 4, 1897. Justice Fuller's certification, without the seal, is inscribed upon the first blank leaf of McKinley's first inaugural Bible, as follows:

I certify that this Bible was used by me in admastering the oath of office to William McKinley as President of the United States on the fourth day of March, A.D. 1897. Melville W. Fuller Chief Justice of the United States

The President's choice of Scripture passage is then pencilled in, to read:

II Chronicles 1:10

An article appearing in the *Washington Post* of March 5, 1897, elaborates upon this auspicious event:

Sworn on a Bishop's Bible presented to Mr. McKinley on behalf of African Methodist Episcopal Church. Supreme Court usually provides the Book on which President takes oath of office.

II Chronicles 1:10 reads as follows: "Give me now wisdom and knowledge that I may go out and come in before this people, for whom can judge this thy people that is so great?"

This is the verse in the Bible that Mr. McKinley kissed yesterday, when Chief Justice Fuller had administered to him the oath of office. It is the 10th verse of the first chapter of II Chronicles. Clerk McKenny held the sacred book which fell open at this chapter, and when the newly made President bent forward his lips were directed to this verse, probably the most appropriate in the book.

"It is a much larger Bible than you had four years ago," remarked Mr. Cleveland who had stood by to Mr. McKenny. "Yes," replied Mr. McKenny, who had carried the large volume about for an hour or so. "I think it has been growing all that time." The Bible is an unusually handsome and costly copy of the Testaments, made especially for the occasion in Ohio, and presented to the new President by Bishop Arnett, of Wilberforce College, a colored institution in the Buckeye State, on behalf of the African Methodist Episcopal Church. Its covers are of blue morocco with satin linings, white satin panels and gilt edges. A gold plate in the center will be engraved with the following inscription: William McKinley, President of the United States of America. Inaugurated March 4, 1897.

On March 4, 1901, **McKinley** swore allegiance to the U.S. Constitution with his left hand upon his second inaugural Bible. Beneath the usual certification by Chief Justice Melville

W. Fuller, a pencilled inscription reads:

> Proverbs 16:20 and 21.

This beautiful and appropriate inaugural Scripture, chosen by the President, reads as follows;

> He that handleth a matter wisely shall find good; and whoso trusteth in the Lord, happy is he. The wise in heart shall be called prudent; and the sweetness of the lips increaseth learning.

William Howard Taft was the only U.S. President to later become Chief Justice of the Supreme Court of the United States. Inscribed on the third sheet of his own Bible are these lines:

> I, William Howard Taft, do solemnly swear that I will faithfully execute the office of President of the United States, and will, to the best of my ability, preserve, protect and defend the Constitution of the United States. Wm H. Taft

> I certify that this Bible was used by me in administering the oath of office to William Howard Taft as President of the United States on the 4th day of March, Nineteen hundred and nine. Melville W. Fuller, Chief Justice of the United States (L.S.)

I Kings 3:9-11, marked and dated March 4, 1909, was the passage selected by Taft for his oath of Office:

> Give therefore thy servant an understanding heart to judge thy people, that I may discern between good and bad; for who is able to judge this thy so great a people? And the speech pleased the Lord, that Solomon had asked this thing. And God said unto him, because thou hast asked this thing, and hast not asked for thyself long life; neither hast asked riches for thyself, nor hast asked the life of thine enemies; but has asked for thyself understanding to discern judgment;...
>
> I Kings 3:9-11

President Warren G. Harding was sworn into office on Washington's Inaugural Bible, opened at Micah 6:8:

> He hath showed thee, O man, what is good; and what doth the Lord require of thee, but to do justly, and to love mercy, and to walk humbly with thy God? Micah 6:8

United States Presidents: Ulysses Simpson Grant (18th); Rutherford B. Hayes (19th); James Abram Garfield (20th); Benjamin Harrison (23rd); William McKinley (25th); William Howard Taft (27th); Warren Gamaliel Harding (29th).

OKLAHOMA
(from the Indian, "red people")

OKLAHOMA

The Preamble to the Constitution of the State of Oklahoma states that, *Invoking the guidance of Almighty God, in order to secure and perpetuate the blessing of liberty...we, the people of the State of Oklahoma, do ordain and establish this Constitution.*

Oklahoma joined the Union on November 16, 1907 as the 46th State.

State Capital: Oklahoma City.

State Motto:
"Labor Omnia Vincit" translated from Latin to mean, "Labor Conquers all Things."[1]

State Seal:
Centered by a five-sided star, each ray contains the seal of each of the five Indian Tribes. In the center of the star, an Indian and a pioneer shake hands under the figure holding balanced scales, representing Justice.

In the center shall be a five pointed star, with one ray directed upward. The center of the star shall contain the central device of the seal of the Territory of Oklahoma, including the words, "Labor Omnia Vincit." The upper left-hand ray shall contain the symbol of the ancient seal of the Cherokee Nation, namely: A seven pointed star partially surrounded by a wreath of oak leaves. The ray directed upward shall contain the symbol of the ancient seal of the Chickasaw Nation, namely: An Indian warrior standing upright with bow and shield. The lower left-hand ray shall contain the symbol of the ancient seal of the Creek Nation, namely: A sheaf of wheat and a plow. The upper right-hand ray shall contain the symbol of the ancient seal of the Choctaw Nation, namely: A tomahawk, bow, and three crossed arrows. The lower right hand ray shall contain the symbol of the ancient seal of the Seminole Nation, namely: A village with houses and a factory beside a lake upon which an Indian is paddling a canoe. Surrounding the central star and grouped between its rays shall be forty-five small stars, divided into five clusters of nine stars each, representing the forty-five states of the Union, to which the forty-sixth is now added. In a circular band surrounding the whole device shall be inscribed, GREAT SEAL OF THE STATE OF OKLAHOMA 1907.[2]

State Flag:
The basic design is an Osage warrior's buckskin shield, decorated with pendant eagle feathers. Over the shield, the crossed positions are an Indian peace pipe (the Indian symbol for peace) and an olive branch (the pioneers' symbol for peace). The flag is a rich sky blue. The word "Oklahoma" is white. The Osage war shield is tan, outlined in red, the peace pipe is white with red tips, and the olive branch is green. [3]

State Song: "OKLAHOMA."

OKLAHOMA
by Rodgers and Hammerstein

Brand new state! Brand new state, gonna treat you great!
Gonna give you barley, carrots and pertaters,
Pasture fer the cattle, Spinach and Temayters!
Flowers on the prairie where the June bugs zoom,
Plen'y of air and plen'y of room,
Plen'y of room to swing a rope!
Plen'y of heart and plen'y of hope...
Oklahoma, ev'ry night my honey lamb and I
Sit alone and talk and watch a hawk makin' lazy circles in the sky.
We know we belong to the land
And the land we belong to is grand!
And when we say—Yeeow! A-yip-i-o-ee-ay!
We're only sayin' You're doin' fine, Oklahoma! Oklahoma—O.K.

First "Christian Heritage Week:" April 2-8, 1995, proclaimed by the Governor.

Of Historic Interest:
Oklahoma has a **State Musical Instrument** — the fiddle; and **State Colors** — green and white.

Will Rogers (1879-1935) was chosen by the citizens of Oklahoma as their hero in the Hall of Fame. Humorist, philosopher and patriot, his friends were among the lowly, as well as the powerful and affluent, alike.[4]

Rogers was entertained by three different Presidents in the White House, as also by King George and Queen Mary of England. He declined an honorary degree from Columbia University, stating that the colleges "gave honorary degrees for all kinds of ignorance" but not for his brand of ignorance.[5]

Will was generous to the poor and needy, giving freely to cow-hands and beggars. His head was never turned by fame. In Buffalo, he was detained by a beggar to whom he gave pennies prior to entering a Barber Shop. While tending to the beggar's needs, the building collapsed, killing all within. Rogers stated that his life had been saved by a beggar.[6]

The following are some of his sayings:

No man can ever rise above his surroundings, and if you put a man in that was elected on nothing but campaign speeches, you are going to have nothing but wind to represent you. — Dec. 26, 1926

Farmers starve three years out of four, but the good year is always election year. — Sept. 9, 1926

We are always reading statistics and figures. Half of America do nothing but prepare propaganda for the other half to read.
— Feb. 24, 1929

I love a dog. He does nothing for political reasons.— Dec. 3, 1933

The short memories of the American voter is what keeps our politicians in office. —April 7, 1930

An economist is a man who can tell you what can happen under any given conditions, and his guess is liable to be just as good as anybody else's. — May 26, 1935

Everything is changing in America. People are taking their comedians seriously and the politicians as a joke, when it used to be vice versa.

— Will Rogers

After the Bronze Statue of Reverend Jason Lee in the Hall of Fame,
U.S. Capitol, Washington, D.C. He holds a Bible in his left hand.

OREGON
(beautiful water)

The Constitution of the State of Oregon states that, *All men shall be secure in the natural right, to worship Almighty God according to the dictates of their own consciences...and no law shall in any case whatever control the free exercise and enjoyment of religious opinions or interfere with the rights of conscience.*

Oregon joined the Union on February 14, 1859 as the 33rd State.

State Capital: Salem.

State Motto:
"The Union."[1]

State Seal:
The State Seal consists of a shield supported by 33 stars and divided by a ribbon with the inscription "The Union." Above the shield are the mountains and forests of Oregon, an elk with branching antlers, a covered wagon and ox team, the Pacific Ocean with setting sun, a departing man-of-war signifying the departure of British influence in the region and an arriving American Merchant ship signifying the rise of American power. Below the shield is a quartering with a sheaf of wheat, plow and pickax, which represent Oregon's mining and agricultural resources. The crest is the American Eagle. Around the perimeter of the seal is the wording: "State of Oregon, 1859."[2]

State Flag:
The Oregon State Flag, adopted in 1925, is navy blue with gold lettering and symbols. Blue and gold are the State colors. On the flag's face the wording, "STATE OF OREGON" is written above a shield which is surrounded by 33 stars. Below the shield, which is part of the State Seal, is written "1859," the year of Oregon's admission to the Union as the 33rd State.[3]

State Song:

OREGON, MY OREGON
Land of the Empire Builders, Land of the Golden West
Conquered and held by Free men, Fairest and the best
Onward and upward ever, Forward and on and on;
Hail to the land of heroes, My Oregon.

Land of the Rose and sunshine, Land of the summer's breeze
Laden with health and vigor, Fresh from Western seas.
Blest by the blood of martyrs, Land of the setting sun;
Hail to the Land of Promise, My Oregon.[4]

First "Christian Heritage Week:"   March 30 - April 5, 1997.

Of Historic Interest:
Oregon's greatest hero, chosen by its citizens to represent them in the U.S. Capitol's

Hall of Fame, is **Reverend Jason Lee (1803-1845),** first missionary to Oregon Territory, who brought the Gospel of Jesus Christ to the Indians. Orphaned at age 3 and self-supporting at 13, Jason Lee's character and accomplishments were eulogized by Thomas A. McBride, Justice of Oregon State Supreme Court, at the unveiling of his portrait:

> The precious jewel of a Commonwealth; the one thing above all others which it would treasure, and the memory of those grand and self-sacrificing men and women who laid the foundations of its greatness and prosperity. One of these treasured memories, is the life and work of Jason Lee, the founder of American civilization in Oregon...Lee combined the fervor of a missionary, the foresight of a seer, and the patriotism of a loyal citizen.[5]

Governor of Oregon, Ben Olcott, accepted the portait for the people of his state, with these stirring words:

> Unhesitatingly I say that Jason Lee was Oregon's most heroic figure. By every right of acheivement, by every right of peaceful conquest, this portrait of Jason Lee should adorn the halls of the Capitol building in our state, as long as those Capitol buildings stand.[6]

PETER VON MUHLENBERG, PENNSYLVANIA

After the Marble Statue of General Peter von Muhlenberg in
the Hall of Fame, U.S. Capitol, Washington, D.C.

164

PENNSYLVANIA

("Penn's Woodland," named
by Charles II, after
Admiral Penn, father of
William Penn, founder of Commonwealth)

The Preamble to the Constitution of the Commonwealth of Pennsylvania states that, *We, the people of the Commonwealth of Pennsylvania, grateful to Almighty God for the blessings of civil and religious liberty, and humbly invoking His guidance, do ordain and establish this Constitution.*

Pennsylvania joined the Union on December 12, 1787 as the 2nd State.

Capital of Commonwealth: Harrisburg.

Motto of Commonwealth:
"Virtue, Liberty, and Independence."[1]

Seal of Commonwealth:
The State Seal has two faces: the obverse, which is the more familiar face and the one most often referred to as the "State Seal" and the reverse, or counter-seal, which is used less frequently. When Pennsylvania was still a province of England, its seals were those of William Penn and his descendants. The transition from this provincial seal to a state seal began when the State Constitutional Convention of 1776 directed that "all commissions shall be . . . sealed with the State Seal," and appointed a committee to prepare such a seal for future use. By 1778 there was in use a seal similar to the present one.[2] The seal received legal recognition from the General Assembly in 1791, when it was designated the official State Seal.[3]

The obverse of the seal contains a shield, upon which are emblazoned a sailing ship, a plough, and three sheaves of wheat. To the left of the shield is a stalk of Indian corn, to the right, an olive branch. The shield's crest is an eagle, and the entire design is encircled by the inscription "Seal of the State of Pennsylvania." These three symbols - the plough, the ship and the sheaves of wheat - have, despite minor changes through the years, remained the traditional emblems of Pennsylvania's State Seal. They were first found in the individual seals of several colonial Pennsylvania counties which mounted their own identifying crests above the existing Penn Coat of Arms. Chester County's crest was a plough; Philadelphia County's crest was a ship under full sail; Sussex County, Delaware (then part of provincial Pennsylvania) used a sheaf of wheat as its crest. The shield of the City of Philadelphia contained both a sheaf of wheat and a ship under sail. It was a combination of these sources that provided the three emblems now forming the obverse of the State Seal. *The reverse* of the first seal shows a woman who represents Liberty. Her left hand holds a wand topped by a liberty cap, a French symbol of liberty. In her right hand is a drawn sword. She is tramping upon Tyranny, represented by a lion. The entire design is encircled by the words, "Both Can't Survive."

Coat of Arms of Commonwealth:
Pennsylvania's Coat of Arms, while not used in the same official capacity as the State Seal (although it contains the emblems of the seal), is perhaps a more familiar symbol of the

Commonwealth of Pennsylvania. It appears on countless documents, letterheads, and publications, and forms the design on Pennsylvania's State Flag. Provincial Pennsylvania's Coat of Arms was that of the Penn family. A State Coat of Arms first appeared on state paper money issued in 1777. This first Coat of Arms was nearly identical to the State Seal, without the inscription. In 1778, Caleb Lownes of Philadelphia prepared a Coat of Arms. Heraldic in design, it consisted of a shield, which displayed the emblems of the State Seal - the ship, plough, and sheaves of wheat, an eagle for the crest; two black horses as supporters; and the motto, "Virtue, Liberty and Independence." An olive branch and a cornstalk were crossed below the shield. Behind each horse was a stalk of corn, but these were omitted after 1805. Numerous modifications were made to this Coat of Arms between 1778 and 1873, chiefly in the position and color of the supporting horses. In 1874, the legislature noted these variations and lack of uniformity and appointed a commission to establish an official Coat of Arms for the Commonwealth. In 1875, the commission reported that it had

adopted almost unchanged, the Coat of Arms originally designed by Caleb Lownes 96 years earlier. This is the Coat of Arms in use today.

Flag of Commonwealth:
Pennsylvania's State Flag is composed of a blue field on which is embroidered the State Coat of Arms. The first State Flag bearing the State Coat of Arms was authorized by the General Assembly in 1799. During the Civil War many Pennsylvania regiments carried flags modeled after the U.S. Flag, but substituted Pennsylvania's Coat of Arms for the field of stars. An Act of the General Assembly of June 13, 1907, standardized the flag and required that the blue field match the blue of Old Glory.

State Song:

PENNSYLVANIA

Verse 1
Pennsylvania, Pennsylvania,
Mighty is your name,
Steeped in glory and tradition,
Object of acclaim.
Where brave men fought the foe of freedom,
Tyranny decried,
'Til the bell of Independence
Filled the countryside.

Chorus
Pennsylvania, Pennsylvania,
May your future be,
Filled with honor everlasting
As your history.

Verse 2
Pennsylvania, Pennsylvania,
Blessed by God's own hand,
Birthplace of a mighty nation,
Keystone of the land.
Where first our country's flag unfolded,

166

Freedom to proclaim,
May the voices of tomorrow
Glorify your name.

Chorus
Pennsylvania, Pennsylvania,
May your future be
Filled with honor everlasting
As your history.[4]

First "Christian Heritage Week:"   October 11-17, 1992.

Of Historic Interest:
The phrase **"Keystone State"** comes from the word "keystone" in architecture, and refers to the central, wedge-shaped stone in an arch which holds all other stones in place. The application of the term "Keystone State" to Pennsylvania cannot be traced to any single source. It was commonly accepted soon after 1800. At a Jefferson Republican victory rally in October 1802, Pennsylvania was toasted as "the keystone in the federal union," and in the newspaper *Aurora,* the following year, the state was referred to as "the keystone in the democratic arch." The modern persistence of this designation is justified in view of the key position of Pennsylvania as "birthplace of liberty."

"Commonwealth:" Pennsylvania shares with Virginia, Kentucky and Massachusetts, the designation "Commonwealth." The word is of English derivation and refers to the common "weal" or well-being of the public. The State Seal of Pennsylvania does not use the term, but it is a traditional, official designation used in referring to the state, and legal processes are in the name of the Commonwealth. In 1776, the first State Constitution referred to Pennsylvania as both "Commonwealth" and "State," a pattern of usage that was perpetuated in the Constitutions of 1790, 1838, 1874 and 1968. Today, "State" and "Commonwealth" are correctly used interchangeably. The distinction between them has been held to have no legal significance.

William Penn (1644-1713), founder of Pennsylvania, won the love and respect of the Indians. He visited them in their lands and ate with them. Like Roger Williams, he believed that the Indians should be paid for their lands. Accordingly, he made them rich gifts and entered into solemn treaties with their chiefs, to include his famous 1682 Treaty.[5] The Indians said of Penn: "We will live peacably with William Penn and his children as long as the moon and the sun shall endure." If the Indians admired a European, they said, "He is like William Penn."[6]

With the establishment of free government and freedom of Protestant Christians to worship in their own mode, hundreds of German families escaped persecution to "Penn's Woods," their descendants today being known as the "Pennsylvania Dutch."[7]

It can be said of William Penn that no other one man, at his own expense, had planted so great a Colony in the wilds of America, as he had. Few nobler men ever lived than William Penn.[8]

William Penn's greatest work, **"No Cross, No Crown"** was written from prison, where he had been confined due to his preaching the Gospel without a license. It gives insight into his own conversion account, and the basis for his desire to establish a Christian colony in the New World, free from persecution:

...Christ's cross is Christ's way to Christ's crown. This is the subject of the following discourse, first written during my confinement in the Tower of London in the year 1668, now reprinted with great enlargement of matter and testimonies, that thou mayest be won to Christ, or if won already, brought nearer to him. It is a path which God in his everlasting kindness guided my feet into, in the flower of my youth, when about two and twenty years of age. He took me by the hand and led me out of the pleasures, vanities and hopes of the world. I have tasted of Christ's judgments, and of his mercies, and of the world's frowns and reproaches. I rejoice in my experience, and dedicate it to thy service in Christ.

Though the knowledge and obedience of the doctrine of the cross of Christ be of infinite moment to the souls of men, being the only door to true Christianity and the path which the ancients ever trod to blessedness, yet it is little understood, much neglected, and bitterly contradicted, by the vanity, superstition, and intemperance of professed Christians.

The unmortified Christian and the heathen are of the same religion, and the deity they truly worship is the god of this world. What shall we eat? What shall we drink? What shall we wear? And how shall we pass away our time? Which way may we gather and perpetuate our names and families in the earth? It is a mournful reflection, but a truth which will not be denied, that these worldly lusts fill up a great part of the study, care and conversation of Christendom. The false notion that they may be children of God while in a state of disobedience to his holy commandments, and disciples of Jesus though they revolt from his cross, and members of his true church, which is without spot or wrinkle, notwithstanding their lives are full of spots and wrinkles, is of all other deceptions upon themselves the most pernicious to their eternal condition for they are at peace in sin and under a security in their transgression.[9]

Pennsylvania's Heroes:
Benjamin Franklin's Speech given to the Constitutional Convention in Philadelphia in 1787, while deliberating the framing of the U.S. Constitution, reads as follows:

Mr. President:

The small progress we have made, after four or five weeks' close attendance, and continual reasonings with each other, our different sentiments producing as many noes as ayes is, methinks, a melancholy proof of the imperfection of human understanding. We indeed seem to feel our own want of political wisdom, since we have been running around in search of it. We have gone back to ancient history for models of government, and examined the different forms of those republics which, having been originally formed with the seeds of their own dissolution, now no longer exist, and we have viewed modern states all round Europe, but find none of their constitutions suitable to our circumstances.

In this situation of this assembly, groping, as it were in the dark, to find political truth, and scarce able to distinguish it when presented to us, how has it happened, sir, that we have not hitherto once thought of humbly applying to the Father of Lights, to illuminate our understandings? In the beginning of the contest with Britain, when we were sensible of danger, we had daily prayers in this room for Divine protection. Our prayers, sir, were heard, and they were graciously answered. All of us who were engaged in the struggle must have observed frequent instances of a superintending Providence in our favor. To that kind Providence we owe this happy opportunity of consulting in peace on the means of establishing our future national felicity. And have we now forgotten that powerful Friend? or do we imagine we no longer need His assistance? I have lived, sir, a long time, and the longer I live the more convincing proofs I see of this truth, that God governs the affairs of men. And if a sparrow cannot fall to the ground without His notice, is it probable that an empire can rise without His aid? We have been assured, sir, in the sacred writings that "except the Lord build the house, they labor in vain that build it." (Psalm 127:1) I firmly believe this, and I also believe that without His concurring aid we shall succeed in this political building no better than the builders of Babel; we shall be divided by our little, partial, local interests, our projects will be confounded, and we ourselves shall become a reproach and a by-word down to future ages. And, what is worse, mankind may hereafter, from this unfortunate instance, despair of establishing government by human wisdom, and leave it to chance, war, and conquest.

I therefore beg leave to move —

That henceforth prayers, imploring the assistance of Heaven and its

BENJAMIN AND DEBORAH FRANKLIN'S TOMB, CHRIST CHURCH, PHILADELPHIA

169

blessings on our deliberations, be held in this assembly every morning before we proceed to business; and that one or more of the clergy of this city be requested to officiate in that service.[10]

— Benjamin Franklin

EMMANUEL EPISCOPAL CHURCH, WOOD STOCK, ON THE SITE OF MUHLENBERG'S CHURCH

Peter von Muhlenberg (1746-1807) was chosen by the citizens of Pennsylvania as their greatest hero in the U.S. Capitol's Hall of Fame. He was known as "The Fighting Parson."

On Thursday, April 1, 1976, the *Religious News Service* circulated this press release in respect to Peter von Muhlenberg:

> Washington, D.C. —— A memorial will be erected here to honor Peter Muhlenberg, remembered in American history as "the fighting parson of the American Revolution"...A clergyman who dramatically pulled open his clerical vestments at the close of a sermon 200 years ago to reveal the uniform of a colonel in the Continental Army, Muhlenberg went on to serve a total of eight years' military service for the then fledgling country...Ultimately promoted to the rank of Major General, John Peter Gabriel Muhlenberg was the eldest of eleven children of Henry Melchior Muhlenberg, who has been referred to as the "patriarch" of Lutherans in this country. The younger Muhlenberg was ordained by the Lutheran ministerium of Pennsylvania in 1768, serving parishes in New Germantown, Pennsylvania and Bedminister, New Jersey. Then moving to Woodstock, Virginia, he was asked by the Anglican Church to serve German-speaking settlers there, agreeing to be ordained as an Anglican minister in 1772. It was at the close of a four-year ministry at the Anglican Church in Woodstock in 1776 that he threw off his black clerical robe and revealed his Continental Army uniform, quoting the Bible from the Book of Ecclesiastes, Chapter 3, verse 8: "There is a time for peace and a time for war."[11]

United States President: James Buchanan (15th).

170

After the Original Marble Sculpture of Roger Williams in the Hall of Fame, U.S. Capitol, Washington, D.C.

RHODE ISLAND

("red" island,
named for its red clay)

The Preamble to the Constitution of the State of Rhode Island states that, *We, the people of the State of Rhode Island and Providence Plantations, grateful to Almighty God for the civil and religious liberty which He hath so long permitted us to enjoy, and looking to Him for a blessing upon our endeavors to secure and to transmit the same unimpaired to succeeding generations, do ordain and establish this constitution of government.*

Rhode Island joined the Union on May 29, 1790 as the 13th State.

State Capital: Providence.

State Motto:
 "Hope."

State Seal:
 "There shall continue to be one seal for the public use of the state; the form of an anchor shall be engraven thereon; the motto thereof shall be the word "Hope;" and in a circle around the outside shall be engraven the words, 'Seal of the State of Rhode Island and Providence Plantations, 1636.' "[1]

Coat of Arms:
 The Coat of Arms is a golden anchor on a blue field, and the motto thereof is the word "Hope."[2]

State Flag:
 The Flag of the State of Rhode Island and Providence Plantations as it presently exists was formally adopted by the General Assembly at the January Session of 1897. Rhode Island was the third of the original thirteen colonies to formally adopt a State Flag. New Jersey and New York having done so in 1896. Although of such recent origin, it incorporates all the features which from time to time have been prescribed by the General Assembly. The colors, white and blue, are the same as those used in the flags carried by the regiments of the State of Rhode Island during the Revolution, the War of 1812 and the Mexican War. The stars which represent the thirteen original states were also used on flags of the Continental Regiments from Rhode Island during the Revolution. The anchor has been connected with Rhode Island since its foundation. In 1647, the Assembly, acting under Roger Williams' Patent of 1643 setting up the Providence Plantations, adopted the anchor as the seal of the province. In 1644, when another charter was granted by King Charles II to the Colony of Rhode Island and Providence Plantations, the anchor was again chosen for the seal but the word "Hope" was added over the head of the anchor.[3]

State Song:
 "The song entitled 'Rhode Island,' words and music by T. Clarke Brown, shall be and is hereby established as, and declared to be the state song."[4]

First "Christian Heritage Week:" September 19-25, 1999, proclaimed by the Governor.

Of Historic Interest:

Roger Williams, founder of Rhode Island, was chosen by the citizens of Rhode Island to represent them in the U.S. Capitol's Hall of Fame.

Today, an 11-foot-tall bronze statue entitled "The Independent Man," representing Roger Williams, stands atop the State House dome. It is a symbol of the State's enduring commitment to freedom.

Williams' greatest work: *The Bloudy Tenent of Persecution, for Cause of Conscience,* was published in 1644 by Gregory Dexter. It was written in answer to Cotton's work upholding the right and enforcing the duty of the civil magistrate to regulate the doctrines of the church. This able Christian apologist prefaces his cause as follows:

> Whether Persecution for cause of Conscience be not against the Doctrine of Jesus Christ the King of Kings. The Scriptures and reasons are these.
>
> Because Christ commandeth that the tares and wheat (which some understand are those that walke in the truth, and those that walke in lies) should be let alone in the world, and not plucked up until the harvest, which is the end of the world, Matt. 13.30.38.&c.
>
> The same commandeth Matt.15.14. that they that are blinde (as some interpret, led on in false religion, and are offended with him for teaching true religion) should be let alone, referring their punishment unto their falling into the ditch.
>
> Againe, Luke 9.55.56. hee reproved his disciples who would have had fire come downe from heaven and devour those Samaritans who would not receive Him, in these words: Ye know not what manner of Spirit ye are of, for the Son of Man is not come to destroy men's lives but to save them...All civill states with their officers of justice in their respective constitutions and administrations are proved essentially civill and therefore not Judges, Governours or Defendours of the spirituall or Christian state of worship...[5]

The above work encapsulates Williams' stance for freedom of religion, being the first great American statesman to preach and advocate, *Separation of Church (from Interference by) the State.*

The First Baptist Church in America, founded by Roger Williams in Providence, Rhode Island. (c. 1638)

173

JOHN C. CALHOUN, 1782-1850, SOUTH CAROLINA

After the Original Marble Statue in the Hall of Fame, U.S. Capitol, Washington, D.C.

SOUTH CAROLINA
(Named after
Charles II of England)

The Constitution of the State of South Carolina states that, *All political power is vested in and derived from the people only, therefore, they have the right at times to modify their form of government,* and that *The General Assembly shall make no law respecting an establishment of religion or prohibiting the free exercise thereof...*

South Carolina joined the Union on May 23, 1788 as the 8th State.

State Capital: Columbia.

State Motto:
"While I Breathe I Hope."

State Seal:
On March 26, 1776, the Provincial Congress of South Carolina set up an independent government, electing John Rutledge as President. On April 2, 1776, the President and Privy Council were authorized by Resolution of the General Assembly "to design and cause to be made a Great Seal of South Carolina."[1]

After the Declaration of Independence, a design for the arms of an official great seal, prepared by William Henry Drayton, a member of the Privy Council, was accepted, together with a design for the reverse, said to have been designed by Arthur Middleton. Both designs were turned over to an engraver in Charles Town and engraved as a great seal, which was used by President Rutledge for the first time on May 22, 1777.

ST. MICHAEL'S EPISCOPAL CHURCH

John Rutledge is buried in the Church Gravesite. George Washington Worshipped the Lord at this Church during the Revolutionary War (Pew No. 43).

175

The Seal was made in the form of a circle, four inches in diameter, and four-tenths of an inch thick.

Both the arms and reverse symbolize the battle fought on June 28, 1776, between the unnamed, and unfinished fort at Sullivan's Island (now Fort Moultrie), and the British Fleet.

The Great Seal's design shows a Palmetto tree growing on the seashore erect (symbolic of the fort on Sullivan's Island, built on Palmetto logs); at its base, a torn up oak tree, its branches lopped off, prostrate, typifying the British Fleet, constructed of oak timbers and defeated by the fort; both proper. Just below the branches of the Palmetto, two shields; pendant; one of them on the viewer's left side is inscribed MARCH 26, (the date of ratification of the Constitution of South Carolina) — the other on the viewer's right side JULY 4, (the date of the Declaration of Independence): Twelve spears proper, are bound crosswise to the stem of the Palmetto, their points raised, (representing the 12 states first acceding to the Union); the band uniting them together bearing the inscription QUIS SEPARABIT (Who Shall Separate?). Under the prostrate oak, is inscribed MELIOREM LAPSA LOCAVIT (having fallen it has set up a better); below which appears in large figures, 1776 (the year the Constitution of South Carolina was passed, the year of the Battle at Sullivan's Island and of the Declaration of Independence, and the year in which the Seal was ordered and made). At the summit of the Seal are the words SOUTH CAROLINA; and at the bottom of the same ANIMIS OPIBUSQUE PARATI (Prepared in Mind and Resources.)

A woman walking on the seashore, over swords and daggers (typifying Hope overcoming dangers, which the sun, just rising, was about to disclose); she holds in her dexter hand a laurel branch, (symbolic of the honors gained at Sullivan's Island), and in her sinister hand, the folds of her robe; she looks toward the sun, just rising above the sea, (indicating that the battle was fought on a fine day, and also bespeaking blessing); all proper. On the upper part is the sky azure. At the summit of the seal, are the words DUM SPIRO SPERO (While I Breathe I Hope) and within the field below the figure, is inscribed the word SPES (Hope).

State Flag:
Asked by the Revolutionary Council of Safety in the Fall of 1775 to design a flag for the use of South Carolina troops, **Colonel William Moultrie** chose a blue which matched the color of their uniforms and a crescent which reproduced the silver emblem worn on the front of their caps. The palmetto tree was added later to represent Moultrie's heroic defence of the palmetto-log fort on Sullivan's Island against the attack of the British fleet on June 28, 1776.[2]

State Song:

CAROLINA
Call on thy children of the hill
Wake swamp and river, coast and rill,
Rouse all thy strength and all thy skill,
Carolina! Carolina!

Hold up the glories of thy dead;
Say how thy elder children bled,
And point to Eutaw's battle-bed.
Carolina! Carolina!

Thy skirts indeed the foe may part,
Thy robe be pierced with sword and dart,
They shall not touch thy noble heart,
Carolina! Carolina!

Throw thy bold banner to the breeze!
Front with thy ranks the threatening seas
Like thine own proud armorial trees
Carolina! Carolina!

Girt with such wills to do and bear,
Assured in right, and mailed in prayer,
Thou wilt not bow thee to despair,
Carolina! Carolina![3]

Salute to the Flag of South Carolina:
"I salute the Flag of South Carolina and pledge to the Palmetto State love, loyalty and faith."[4]

First "Christian Heritage Week:" May 8-14, 1994, proclaimed by the Governor.

Of Historic Interest:
John C. Calhoun (1782-1850), South Carolina's greatest statesman and hero, was chosen by the people of South Carolina to represent them in statuary form in our U.S. Capitol's Hall of Fame. John C. Calhoun's education took place at the famous Waddell log cabin school, of which his brother-in-law, Reverend Moses Waddell, was the headmaster, receiving a Christian foundation in his formative years.[5] Discerning that John was a thoughtful and able youth, his mother and brothers determined that he should be educated for the law.[6] At age eighteen, John was sent to the *Wellington Academy,* formerly the Waddell school. He studied so well, that in two years he was prepared to enter the Junior Class of Yale, graduating from this university at age 22. He took a lively part in debates at college, questioning and evaluating the powers extended to each State in the union, under the U.S. Constitution. Reverend Timothy Dwight, the greatest president Yale has ever produced, left us this testimony: "Mr. Calhoun was one of the very few in a class of more than seventy who had the firmness openly to avow and maintain the opinion of the Republican party... that the people were the only legitimate source of political power."[7]

Seeing how ably Calhoun debated his views, Reverend Dwight believed that the youth would achieve great heights.[8] Having been a student at Yale during the presidency of Reverend Dwight, no doubt Calhoun's values, virtues and morals were directly influenced by this great Christian educator.

Calhoun spent two more years at the *Litchfield Law School* at Litchfield, Connecticut, thereafter beginning his law practice in Abbeville, South Carolina. Those who knew John Calhoun related that he was tall in stature, bright, energetic, and possessed gracious manners.[9]

In 1811, he became a member of the 12th Congress of the House of Representatives as delegate from South Carolina, serving his country for forty years. Sixteen of these years were dedicated to national issues. He also distinguished himself as Secretary of War under President Monroe and eight more years as Vice-President of the United States under Presidents John Quincy Adams and Andrew Jackson – remarkable terms of service to the nation.[10]

According to those who knew him well, Calhoun's conversation was "fascinating." He had clarity of speech and excellent diction. He was always courteous and amiable. The

177

great Daniel Webster, one of his contemporaries, said of him: "If he had aspirations they were high, honorable and noble." Clay said that he "possessed an elevated genius of the highest order." Jefferson Davis stated that he was "the wisest man I ever knew." He loved his State, South Carolina, however, more that he loved the Union, debating and defending her interests to the end.[11]

At Calhoun's death on March 29, 1850, the grandest and most imposing pageant that ever took place in Charleston, South Carolina, was witnessed by many thousands of spectators. The City Hall was shrouded for mourning, his mortal remains being placed therein so that thousands of citizens could pay their last respects to this illustrious statesman. On the 26th of April, he was buried in the graveyard of *St. Phillips Church,* Charleston, where he rests in a sarcophagus to this day. Americans throughout the nation mourned his death. His great contemporaries, Clay and Webster, wept over his remains, testifying to his great and exalted worth.[12] A eulogy given at his death praises Calhoun, as follows:

"Honesty, morality, genius, love of country and devoted service for forty years, will entitle him to the universal wail of sorrow, with which his death was but recently announced."

General Thomas Sumter:
A 1908 Library of Congress book entitled, *Report of the Commission Appointed by the General Assembly of South Carolina to Mark the Grave of General Thomas Sumter,* records the following Address regarding this Revolutionary War hero:

Address by Hon. A.J. Montague
Upon this interesting occasion it is difficult to shut out of mind a realizing sense of that dominant force which so early gave power and identity of an American civilization, and in behalf of which the life we today commemorate spent its austere patriotism and military genius.

The fifteenth century loosened the quickening power of the two mighty events, akin in historic time and purpose, the invention of printing and the discovery of America; the two being new ways of thinking and new ways of living unto countless thousands, and bringing a new and structural concept of liberty unto the civilizations of the world...

Liberty finds its concrete genius and strength in local self-government, in constitutional sanctions and limitations, in the guaranty of equality of individual opportunity, and in the appreciation and practice of personal and social responsibility. George the Third realized the secret sources of this buoyant and reforming force, and quickly began to lay upon it his oppressive and heavy hand, only to be met by the tactful, vigorous, and finally revolutionary dissent of his American colonies.

Injustice nearly always sows the seed of justice, and tyranny nearly always kindles the flame of liberty. The law of relativity holds in the political world, and the pendulum of society will swing back and forth. So the Colonists were early conscious of their wrongs and daring in expressions of enlarged conceptions of their rights. Nathaniel Bacon, a good hundred years before 1776, was crying into the ears

178

of the royal governor of Virginia some of the identical notes which were to peal forth in the Great Declaration — that governments were made for man, and not man for governments; and that all just governments must rest upon the consent of the governed. From this time on the Colonists waxed and strengthened in the care and keeping of these great politics, and grew restive and defiant under the arbitrary exactions of the royal government.

South Carolina early and aggressively stood for the substitution of the consent of the governed for the will of an hereditary sovereign. Her voice was potential in calling the first Continental Congress in opposition to the Stamp Act. Her Assembly quickly approved of the resolve of this Congress in behalf of the 'cause of freedom and union,' and boldly transmitted them to England. Her Legislature voted a statue to Pitt, that lofty and inspiring apostle of English liberty. She published the names of her citizens who would not sign the non-importation agreement. She remitted 10,500 pounds to the Society of London for supporting the Bill of Rights in the protection of the liberty of Great Britain and America. And her Rutledge, her Gadsden and her Laurens came back with fire upon their lips to tell that they had heard at Westminster the voices of Burke and Chatham, of Richmond and Rockingham, pleading the cause of the colonies, and declaring that cause right and just...

South Carolina was, therefore, no uncongenial soil to Thomas Sumter, who came from Virginia to the high hills of the Santee about the year 1765; and it may be truthfully affirmed that your great State has received into its life no nobler spirit than that of this man, who was born in the County of Hanover, the birthplace of Patrick Henry, and of Henry Clay, and near the homes of Thomas Jefferson, John Taylor and Edmund Pendleton. He early drew his sword for his native colony in the French and Indian wars and witnessed with Washington the deserved defeat of the reckless Braddock, thus schooling himself for the arduous and brilliant service afterwards rendered his adopted State.

The beginning of the ending of the Revolution is embraced within the four years from 1777 to 1781, from Saratoga to Yorktown, a period during which active war was transferred almost entirely from the North to the South. The early portion of this period was most discouraging. Augusta and Savannah had fallen; General Prevost was harrying the country with a warfare of barbarism as only a buccaneer of his type could wage; the disastrous and ignominious defeat of Gates at Camden saw the destruction of our second army within three months; the Tories were ruthless in their atrocities, and the Patriots retorted with unjustifiable reprisals. The Congress was a meddlesome debating society, relying upon words more than swords, hampering Washington, and capriciously bestowing its rewards; the treason of Arnold was striking dismay into the country...

Yet at this time the struggle was assuming international connections and complications beneficial to America. Franklin had consummated a treaty between France and the Colonies. Frederick the

Great had not only opened the port of Dantzic to our cruisers, but had prohibited the Hessian soldiers passing through his dominion, thus summarily cutting off this powerful source of supply to the British army. These conditions, together with the marvelous resiliency of the Colonies, alarmed England, and to the amazement and disgust of Parliament, Lord North turned a political somersault, bringing in a programme which, if earlier presented and adopted, would have prevented or ended the war. Commissioners of North's ministry came to America only to find this mission so belated as to be unavailing, and completed their work by issuing truculent and threatening manifestoes, which were no negligible cause of the subsequent atrocities of the British soldiery in South Carolina, which so harried the State that Mr. Fiske says, 'The fit ground for wonder is that in spite of such adverse circumstances, the State of South Carolina should have shown as much elastic strength as she did under the severest military stress which any American State was called upon to withstand during the Revolutionary War...

We soon again hear of Sumter's brilliant exploit in cutting Cornwallis' line of communication and capturing his supply train, which, however, was neutralized by the surprise and defeat of Sumter by Tarleton at Fishing Creek a few days thereafter. Sumter made his escape and went immediately to York to recruit, and was ready to participate in the memorable battle of King's Mountain. Within a short time his star was again in the ascendant, and the people were quickly thrilled by his capture of Major Weymiss on Broad Road. Tarleton at once undertook to retrieve this defeat only to find himself outgeneraled and his whole command destroyed by Sumter at Black Stock Hill. After the commencement of this fight Sumter changed his plan of battle, thus exhibiting his military genious in turning unexpected exigencies to his advantage. Yet the victory was saddened by the dear price of a severe wound which he received in the breast, and which disabled him for some months.

Immediately upon the recovery of his health he resumed his work. The British considered him their worst enemy. They burned his home and turned his wife and son out of doors. But these misfortunes only strengthened his inflexible will and fired his inspiring activity. The battle of Cowpens, displaying the brilliant strategy and execution of Daniel Morgan, now came to give high hope to the country, and the battle of Guilford Court House followed to turn the tide of the American Revolution. Cornwallis' plan of campaign was now broken. With his Southern army he was to effect a junction with Clinton in Virginia, thus crushing between the two British armies the small American force. But Cowpens and Guilford Court House rudely shattered a scheme which was adopted by Grant and Sherman a century later. The battle of Guilford was claimed by the British, but Charles Fox, with dramatic eloquence, declared that 'Another such victory would destroy the British army.' Thus were Cornwallis' troops hurriedly and unwillingly removed from the Carolinas, and his surrender in October following brought to the full conscience of the American people the patience, the sagacity and the strategy of Washington in accomplishing one of the world's greatest achievements, with which Sumter's name, and fame, and glory will be indissolubly associated.

The termination of hostilities, however, did not end Sumter's public life. His courage, his probity, his candor, his freedom from vicissitudes of opinion or purpose, his opulent faith in the practical efficiency of self-government, and his military fame, gave him an immediate and sure place in the confidence of the people.

In his mission to England in 1762 for the Cherokee Indians he had exhibited, at an early age, an aptitude for public affairs, and his entrance into the Continental Congress after the Revolution must have been made with a confidence that he was not unfitted for legislative service...

But this monument is yet more to us. It is a symbol of the dear old unrestrained days — days happily, after bloody interruption, now come back to stay forever more. Here the children of a perfect Union may gather to drink, not of the blood of war but of the cup of peace, and to hear, not the tocsin of strife but the music of fraternity. Here we can come to revive in the days of our strength that religious patriotism which we relied upon without fail in the days of our weakness...

United States President: Andrew Jackson, born in South Carolina (7th).

JOSEPH WARD, 1838–1889

After the Marble Statue of Dr. Joseph Ward in the Hall of Fame, U.S. Capitol, Washington, D.C.

SOUTH DAKOTA
(alliance with friends)

The Preamble to the Constitution of the State of South Dakota states that, *We, the people of South Dakota, grateful to Almighty God for our civil and religious liberties...and preserve to ourselves and to our posterity the blessings of liberty...*

South Dakota joined the Union on November 2, 1889 as the 40th State.

State Capital: Pierre.

State Seal:
   The state seal serves as a symbol of life in South Dakota. It depicts the state's bounty: farming, ranching, industries, lumbering, manufacturing and mining. It bears the motto: "Under God the People Rule."[1]

   The design of the Great Seal of South Dakota and its motto, "Under God the People Rule," were the creation of Dr. Joseph Ward, the great South Dakotan who founded Yankton College. Article XXI, Miscellaneous, Section 1, reads: "Seal and Coat of Arms. The design of the Great Seal of South Dakota shall be as follows: A circle within which shall appear in the left foreground, a smelting furnace and other features of mining work. In the left background, a range of hills. In the right background, a herd of cattle and a field of corn. Between the two parts thus described shall appear a river bearing a steamboat. Properly divided between the upper and lower edges of the circle shall appear the words, 'Under God the People Rule,' which shall be the motto of the State of South Dakota. Exterior to this circle and within a circumscribed circle shall appear in the upper part the words, 'Great Seal' and the date in numerals of the year in which the state shall be admitted to the Union."

State Flag:
   The South Dakota flag features the great seal of the state surrounded by a golden blazing sun in a field of sky blue. Golden letters reading "South Dakota, The Sunshine State," are arranged in a circle around the sun.[2]

   The flag has been carried proudly into battle by South Dakotan infantry men, flying on tanks, overhead in all manner of aircraft, and in all types of naval craft from the river patrol to the largest aircraft carriers.

   The flag of South Dakota flies over state buildings, schools and institutions, over the SAC base at Ellsworth, South Dakota and all National Guard installations. Flags are presented by the Governor to new industries, building dedications, to state dignitaries and other outstanding South Dakotans.

State Pledge of Allegiance:
   "I pledge loyalty and support to the flag and state of South Dakota, land of sunshine, land of infinite variety."[3]

State Song:
   "Hail, South Dakota."[4]

First "Christian Heritage Week:" November 5-11, 1995, proclaimed by the Governor.

Of Historic Interest:
The program for the *Unveiling and Presentation Ceremony* of the statue of **Dr. Joseph Ward (1838-1889),** South Dakota's greatest hero in the Hall of Fame, gave him these titles: Churchman, Educator, Statesman.

Ward's father, Dr. Jabez Ward, was the country doctor and beloved physician of Perry Centre, a town in Western New York State. Dr. Ward ministered to both the body and soul of those who sought his help. His account books revealed extremely hard work for sparse compensation. He not only prescribed medicines, but also prepared them for his patients, receiving meagre returns. Ward's sister wrote this account of Perry Centre, ". . . the strict keeping of Saturday night as the beginning of Holy Time, the nightly ringing of the curfew, the tolling of the bell on the death of anyone in the parish — all these were more conscientiously observed than in many Massachusetts towns." Most of all, the community loved and worshipped the Lord in church; prayer, praise and Bible Study being a way of life.[5]

When Joseph was five years old, his father died of pneumonia, having left his sick bed to assist the birth of a child. His widowed mother, although an invalid, displayed Christian character and integrity, molding her son's future, as she patiently resigned her soul into the hands of her blessed Redeemer. Her incurable disease caused increasing pain and helplessness.

It was thus that Ward's magnificent character was developed, attending daily to his mother's needs with tenderness, gentleness, and faithfulness, until the age of fifteen. The constant watchfulness at her bedside and the thought of impending death wrought in him a clear perception of immortality through Christ's atonement. He also acquired a taste for reading good books while attending his mother's needs. Joseph had already devoured *Josephus' History of Israel*, Milton's *Paradise Lost* and other great works at eight years of age. It is said that Ward possessed a remarkable memory, later becoming a Latin scholar. *Blackstone's Commentaries* also interested him.[6]

Ward's preparation for the ministry began at *Phillips Academy* in Andover, Massachusetts, where he became the foremost Latin scholar. He spent eleven years in academy, college and seminary. After graduation from *Phillips Academy* in 1861, he matriculated at Providence, Rhode Island's *Brown University.* Teaching at the Sunday School of the church which his sister's husband, Reverend Stewart Sheldon, pastored, Ward fell in love with Sarah Wood, daughter of the Sunday School Superintendent, the Honorable Joseph Wood.

In 1865, Ward entered *Andover Theological Seminary,* which was then infused with missionary zeal. He became a great champion of missions, being described by Dr. C.F.P. Bancroft:

> As a Theological student he showed the same traits which made him
> subsequently the effective home missionary, the faithful pastor, the
> enterprising and sagacious college president. There was the same
> candor of judgment, the same frankness and openness of expres-

sion, quickness of sympathy, abounding good humor, fertility of resources, the same turn for practical business, the same integrity and
solidarity of character and robust but gracious piety.

He was married to Sarah Frances Wood in Rhode Island in 1868, shortly after graduating
from Andover. The couple soon accepted a call to missionary service in Yankton, the capital of Dakota Territory, which was at that time a village comprising a few hundred residents
in the far west of civilization. The first Congregational Church having just been formed at
Yankton, Ward preached his first sermon in the bare lower room of the old Capitol building,
from a pulpit made of a draped dry-goods box, his text coming from I Corinthians 3:11,
"For other foundation can no man lay than that is laid, which is Jesus Christ." His diary
records indicate that it was a bitterly cold, snowy day, thirty-three persons being in attendance.[7]

Yankton was visited thrice weekly by a stage coach from Sioux City. During the sum-
mertime, river traffic was the only means by which supplies and freight were transported
thither. Soon a missionary church was organized by him in Bon Homme. He also preached
at Elm Grove, Nebraska; and Green Island, Dakota.

Through his leadership a Congregational Association in Dakota was formed encompassing the above churches, as well as churches which had sprung up at Canton, Sioux Falls,
Dell Rapids, Vermillian, Springfield on the Missouri and the Indian Mission at Santee,
Nebraska. It was thus that Joseph Ward gained the reputation of "father of Congregational-
ism in Dakota," being the pioneer-minister and organizer of the earliest churches, together
with the work of Dakota missions throughout the period of immigration. Interested in
Indian Missions, he became the champion of the Indians' welfare.[8]

In 1872, he organized the *Yankton Academy,* forerunner of *Yankton College.* It was the
foremost academic institution of Dakota Territory and continued in its academic excellence.

The motto Dr. Ward chose for the College was, "Christ for the World" and the widely
known and sung hymn from which the phrase originated became the College Hymn. The
College bell then had a verse from this hymn inscribed upon it:

> At morn, at noon at twilight dim,
> My voice shall sound, the earth around,
> Christ for the world, the world for Him.

On Thanksgiving Day, 1879, the leaders and inspirers of South Dakota's statehood movement convened at Yankton. They met in the home of Reverend Stewart Sheldon, brother-
in-law of Joseph Ward. These leaders comprised Joseph Ward, the Honorable William A.
Howard, Governor of the Territory of Dakota, General Hugh J. Campbell, United States
Attorney for Dakota, General W.H.H. Beadle, Territorial Superintendent of Public Instruction, Mr. E.P. Wilcox, Mr. H. Smith and a few others. This meeting was the beginning of
plans resulting in the admission of South Dakota to the Union.

At this Convention, Dr. Ward was chairman of the Committee on Arrangement and Phraseology of the Constitution, as well as member of the Committee on Seal and Coat of Arms.
South Dakota owes a great debt of gratitude to Joseph Ward for its Motto, inscribed upon

the State Seal, "Under God the People Rule." This Motto signifies the spirit of the people of South Dakota in the movement for Statehood, which was Christian in nature, stating the fact that under God's authority (His Word) the people maintained their rights.[9]

The Constitution formed by the 1885 Sioux Falls Convention, in time became the Constitution for the State of South Dakota. However, the struggle for statehood continued for four additional years prior to South Dakota's admission into the Union.

On Thanksgiving Day, 1889, returning from a visit to Sioux Falls for preaching engagements, Joseph Ward preached once more at the Union Service of the Yankton churches. However, on December 11, 1889, Ward's sudden death from blood poisoning was no doubt hastened by his steadfast, loyal and unrelenting hard labor in the mission of Dakota. During the last hours of his life he delivered a special message of love and encouragement to each family member as well as each faculty member of *Yankton College.* His last message to the Trustees of the College was: "Do not stop anything for me. The work must go on no matter what becomes of the workers."[10]

Among the many tributes paid to this great man was that of Judge Hugh J. Campbell, his longtime friend and fellow worker in the struggle for statehood. It was a message which proved to be prophetic:

> Joseph Ward is the greatest man intellectually as well as morally whom the Dakotas have produced. He is the most noble, loyal, faithful and royal soul whom I have met, whose more than kingly crown was the simple crown of service to you, to me, to all of us...If South Dakota ever rears in her mansion of statehood any statues in memory of her sons who have done the State signal service in critical times of danger, and helped most to shape the destinies for good; foremost and highest among them all will stand the noble, genial, powerful form of Joseph Ward.

On September 27, 1963, a welcome and statement of greeting was given by the Honorable John F. Kennedy, President of the United States at the unveiling of this statue in the Rotunda of the United States Capitol. This was followed by a reading of the poem, "Ward of Dakota."

Ward of Dakota

The winds sang welcome on the waiting prairie
When Joseph Ward came journeying to Dakota;
Not he the hunter, armed and predatory.
Not he the seeker of a gilded future.
Not he the emissary of greedy empires;
Compassion was his guide, and love his mission.

Out of the east he came, a knight un-knighted,
Clad in invisible armor, God-directed:
And where his journey ceased, his hands created,
With sweat and toil, a citadel of learning.
A nursery of thought, a spring of knowledge;

186

Whose broad far-reaching gains are yet uncounted.

To him as builder, leader, youth-inspirer,
To him as seer and prophet of high vision,
To him as never-wearying burden-bearer,
To him as seeker of new paths, and opener
Of blinded eyes, with courage never flagging
Waging a war to banish wrong and evil
Wherever found, by letting light and truth in:
Homage is due, and love, and long remembrance.

— Mabel Frederick, Sioux Falls

The following *History of the United States of America* is inscribed upon a handsome bronze plaque on the Terrace overlooking Gutsom Borglum's four U.S. Presidents — George Washington, Thomas Jefferson, Abraham Lincoln, and Theodore Roosevelt — in the black hills of South Dakota.

HISTORY OF THE UNITED STATES OF AMERICA - MOUNT RUSHMORE HISTORIC PLAQUE

Almighty God, from this pulpit of stone the American people render thanksgiving and praise for the new era of civilization brought forth upon this continent. Centuries of tyrannical oppression sent to these shores God-fearing men to seek in freedom the guidance of the benevolent hand in the progress toward wisdom, goodness toward men, and piety toward God.

1776 - Consequently, on July 4, 1776, our forefathers promulgated a principle never before successfully asserted, that life, liberty, equality and pursuit of happiness were the birthrights of all mankind. In this Declaration of Independence, formulated by Jefferson, beat a heart for all humanity. It declared this country free from British rule and announced the inalienable sovereignty of the people. Freedom's soldiers victoriously consecrated this land with their life's blood to be free forevermore.

1787 - Then, in 1787, for the first time a government was formed that derived its just powers from the consent of the governed. General Washington and representatives from the thirteen states formed this sacred constitution, which embodies our faith in God and in mankind by giving equal participation in government to all citizens, distributing the powers of governing threefold, securing freedom of speech and of the press, establishing the right to worship the Infinite according to conscience, and assuring this nation's general welfare against an embattled world. This chart of national guidance has for 145 years weathered the ravages of time. Its supreme trial came under pressure of Civil War, 1861-65. The deadly doctrines of secession and slavery were then purged away in blood. The seal of the union's finality set by President Lincoln, was accomplished like all our triumphs of law and humanity, through the wisdom and the power of an honest, Christian heart.

Farsighted American statesmanship acquired by treaties, vast wilderness territories where progressive, adventurous Americans spread civilization and Christianity.

1850 - Texas willingly ceded the disputed Rio Grande region, thus

187

ending the dramatic acquisition of the west.

1867 - Alaska was purchased from Russia.

1904 - The Panama Canal Zone was purchased as authorized by President Theodore Roosevelt, whereupon our people built a navigable highway to conveniently enable the world's people to share the fruits of the earth and of human industry. Now, these areas are welded into a nation possessing unity, liberty, power, integrity and faith in God with responsible development of character and the steady performance of humanitarian duty.

Holding no fear of the economic and political, chaotic clouds hovering over the earth, the consecrated Americans dedicate this nation before God, to exalt righteousness and to maintain mankind's constituted liberties so long as the earth shall endure.

–William Andrew Burkett
Author

This 560-word "History of the United States of America, 1776-1904," was chosen in 1935 by a nationwide competition conducted by the Mount Rushmore National Memorial Inscription Committee, the President of the United States, Chairman. This plaque was presented by the National Historical Foundation, July 4, 1971.

MT. RUSHMORE, BLACK HILLS, SOUTH DAKOTA

ANDREW JACKSON

After the Original Bronze Sculpture of Andrew Jackson in the Hall of Fame, U.S. Capitol, Washington, D.C.

TENNESSEE
(the name of a Cherokee village)

The Constitution of the State of Tennessee states, *That all power is inherent in the people, and all free governments are founded on their authority, and instituted for their peace, safety, and happiness...That all men have a natural and indefeasible right to worship Almighty God according to the dictates of their own conscience; that no man can of right be compelled to attend, erect, or support any place of worship, or to maintain any minister against his consent...;*

Tennessee joined the Union on June 1, 1796 as the 16th State.

State Capital: Nashville.

State Seal:
   The Roman numerals XVI signify that Tennessee was the 16th State to enter the Union. The plow, the sheaf of wheat and a cotton stalk symbolize the importance of agriculture, while the riverboat attests to the importance of its rivers in commerce.[1]

State Flag:
   The flag features three stars representing the grand divisions of the state: East, Middle, and West. The stars are bound together in indissoluble unity by an unending white band.[2]

State Song:
   "My Homeland, Tennessee."[3]

First "Christian Heritage Week:" August 29 - September 3, 1993, proclaimed by the Governor.

Of Historic Interest:
   General Andrew Jackson (1767-1845), 7th U.S. President, finds his place in the Hall of Fame as Tennessee's greatest hero. The following eulogy, given to the U.S. Senate on June 8, 1845, gives credence to his true Christian identity:

> The last moment of his life on earth is at hand. It is the Sabbath of the Lord: When he first felt the hand of death upon him, 'may my enemies,' he cried, 'find peace; may the liberties of my country endure forever.'
>
> When his exhausted system, under the excess of pain, sunk, for a moment from debility, 'Do not weep,' said he to his adopted daughter; 'my sufferings are less than those of Christ upon the cross;' for he, too, as a disciple of the cross, could have devoted himself, in sorrow, for mankind...His two little grandchildren were absent at Sunday School. He asked for them; and as they came, he prayed for them, and kissed them and blessed them...And that dying man, thus surrendered, in a gush of fervid eloquence, spoke with inspiration of God, of the Redeemer, of salvation, through the atonement, of immortality, of heaven. For he ever thought that pure and undefiled

religion was the foundation of private happiness, and the bulwark of republican institutions.

Having spoken of immortality in perfect consciousness of his own approaching end, he bade them all farewell. 'Dear children,' such were his final words, 'dear children, servants and friends, I trust to meet you all in heaven, both white and black—all, both white and black.' And having borne his testimony to immortality, he bowed his mighty head, and without a groan, the spirit of the greatest man of his age, escaped to the bosom of His God. In life, his career had been like the blaze of the sun in the fierceness of its noonday glory; his death was lonely as the mildest sunset of the summer's evening, when the sun goes down in tranquil beauty without a cloud...[4]

From the diary of **James Knox Polk** during his presidency, 1845-1849, we glean this great American statesman's regular attendance at Sunday worship service, his partaking of the Lord's Supper and his commendation of the preaching of God's Word. Here are some excerpts:

Sunday, 7th September, 1845: Attended the First Presbyterian Church with Mrs. Polk at 4 o'clock p.m. when the sacrament of the Lord's Supper was administered," and again...Sunday, 31st May, 1846: Attended the dedication of a new Presbyterian Church near the Patent Office today, under the pastoral care of the Reverend Mr. Tuston. Mrs. Polk, her niece, Miss Rucker and my nephew, Marshall T. Polk, accompanied me. The sermon (an excellent one) was delivered by the Reverend Mr. Balch of Virginia, who is the brother of the Honorable Alfred Balch of Tennessee.

Andrew Johnson

From the Minutes of Proceedings of a called meeting of Ministers of all Christian denominations in the *First Baptist Church* on 13th Street, at the death of Abraham Lincoln; April 17, 1865, we learn these historic facts on the life and character of Andrew Johnson:

...After a pause and in perfect silence of the interested group of nearly 60 ministers of all denominations, the President, evidently oppressed by his emotions, began somewhat slowly, in a low voice, which grew earnest as he proceeded, and reached every heart, nearly as follows:

'Gentlemen: I feel overwhelmed by this occasion, and utterly incompetent to the task before me, of making a suitable reply to you; and may it be that silence and the deep feelings of my own heart are the best answer I can give you. I thank you for this visit and this expression of your sentiments. I feel deeply solemn in view of this whole scene, and in listening to the eloquent words which have been spoken and read to me. I feel overwhelmed by thoughts of the position in which I am so suddenly placed, and the duties which have devolved upon me. But amid all this natural feeling, the assurance which you have been pleased to give me, that I shall have the countenance, the assistance, and the prayers of such a body as this, is most gratifying to my heart. It is possible, it is natural, that you should desire to know something of the future administration of affairs, and I can only say to you, as I have said to others, that my course in the past must be a guaranty of what I hope to do in the future. I call upon you to take notice, that I have entered upon my office with no manifesto - no proclamation, with no propositions of changes or new policy of my own. In entering on the performance of duties so important and responsible as those before me, I can only say to you, that the course of events must decide, as they arise, what shall be the measures best adapted to promote the good of the country. My whole life has been based on the profound belief, in which I have never wavered, that there is a great principle of right, which lies at the basis of all things. I have always trusted to that principle as the certain support of all who abide by it - the great principle of right, and justice and truth. I shall trust to it, and guide the administration of public affairs in conformity to it. I should feel anxious for the future, but I have an abiding confidence in the strength of that principle, and in Him who founded it...I say again that I put my trust in the great principle which underlies all our institutions, and believe that we shall come out of this struggle to a better and higher life. The government has not accomplished its mission - but under the benignant smiles of the Almighty it will yet fulfill it. The country will triumph in the end, and these great principles will be firmly established...I trust that, in confidence, in the great principles of which I have spoken, and with your countenance and prayers, I shall be enabled to succeed in restoring peace and concord to this now distracted and unhappy country.'

The individuals present responded to certain portions of his remarks with a fervent Amen, and at their conclusion again approached, and with each word of encouragement and blessing, took leave of the President...

Site of the Brainerd Mission to the Cherokee Indians, Chattanooga:

Plaques and memorials to distinguished missionaries and educators, who labored tirelessly among the Cherokee Indians at the *Brainerd Mission* read as follows:

The Reverend Stephen Foreman

"He labored with the Cherokees and walked with God"
Born October 22, 1807, in the Cherokee Nation near the present site of Rome, Georgia, of Scotch-Cherokee parentage. Died December 8, 1881, at Park Hill Indian Territory and is buried at the Stephen Foreman Cemetery there. A gentleman of the Old Southern type, a scholar of much culture and learning, a writer of prominence. Educated College of Richmond, Virginia and Princeton Theological Seminary. Licensed to preach September 23, 1835 by Union Presbytery, Tennessee. Served "old nation" as associate editor of the *Cherokee Phoenix*. Translated into Cherokee the New Testament, and part of the Old, also many tracts and hymns. Worked with the missionaries at Brainerd and preached for 46 years among his people. Had charge of Train of Wagons at the removal of Cherokees 1838. Organized Cherokee National Public School System and was first Superintendent of Education west of the Mississippi River. Elected to Supreme Court of the Cherokee Nation October 11, 1884. Executive Councillor 1847-1855 and held many other places of trust and honor. Established *First Presbyterian Church* at Tah Lequah. In memory of this great Cherokee who did so much for his people along the lines of

Religion, education and good fellowship, this tablet is lovingly dedicated by his children, grandchildren and great grandchildren. September 21, 1938.

Here upon a small clearing in the wilderness in 1817, *Brainerd Mission* was founded among the Cherokee Indians by the American Board of Foreign Missions. First called *Chickamaugah*. Changed to *Brainerd* in 1818. Maintained with aid of the United States Government until the removal of the Indians in 1838. Here 40 buildings were erected and hundreds of Indians were christianized and educated. This Mission was visited in 1819 by President Monroe.

Its work was successfully carried on by Eastern Missionaries among whom were Reverend Ard Hoyt, first Superintendent, and Samuel Austin Worcester, who inspired the use of Sequoyah's syllabary in printing. Scientific agriculture, trades and domestic arts were taught to several hundred children, and through their influence, Christian ideals were spread throughout the Cherokee nation.

Brainerd Missionaries (1817-1838)
Friends and Students of Brainerd Mission:

Prominent among the friends and students at *Brainerd Mission* were: Charles A. Hicks, Assistant Principal Chief of the Cherokee Nation, the most powerful man of his time among the tribe. Charles Reece, second member of the Brainerd Church and interpreter for the missionaries; David Brown (A-Wih). Brilliant student, interpreter, orator and translator. Elias Boudinot (Kill-Kee-Nah), student, prominent in Cherokee National Affairs, editor of *Cherokee Phoenix*. Stephen Foreman, Minister, employed by the American Board. John Huss, distinguished warrior who studied here and became a minister. Lydia Lavery, student, wrote the first Cherokee hymn, married Milo Hoyt. David Carter (Ta-Wah), student, Judge of the Cherokee Supreme Court, Editor of the *Cherokee Advocate*. Thomas Basil (Tools-oo-Wan), student and interpreter. Elijah Hicks, interpreter and editor of the *Cherokee Phoenix*.

The Mission played an important part in the educational development and Christianizing of the Cherokee. Brainerd Cemetery contains graves of whites and Indians who died at the Mission.

–Tennessee Historical Commission

United States Presidents: Andrew Jackson (7th); James K. Polk (11th); Andrew Johnson (17th).

193

After the Marble Statue of Samuel Houston in the Hall of Fame, U.S. Captiol, Washington, D.C.

TEXAS
(friend)

The Preamble to the Constitution of the State of Texas states that, *Humbly invoking the blessings of Almighty God, the people of the State of Texas, do ordain and establish this Constitution.*

Texas joined the Union on December 29, 1845 as the 28th State.

State Capital: Austin.

State Motto:
"Remember the Alamo."

State Seal:
"There shall be a Seal of the State which shall be kept by the Secretary of State, and used by him officially under the direction of the Governor. The Seal of the State shall be a star of five points, encircled by olive and live oak branches, and the words, 'The State of Texas.' "[1]

Reverse of the State Seal:
The Daughters of the Republic of Texas proposed a design for the reverse side of the state seal that was adopted by the Fifty-Seventh Legislature, Second Called Session. Governor Price Daniel approved this concurrent resolution on August 26, 1961. Sarah R. Farnsworth designed the art for the seal's reverse. This design was unusual because the legislature adopted the art itself as the reverse of the state seal, as opposed to the usual practice of adopting a description, or blazon, which is later rendered by an artist.

The Seventy-Second Legislature modified the description of the reverse of the State Seal as follows:

> RESOLVED, That the design for the reverse side of the Great Seal of Texas shall consist of a shield, the lower half of which is divided into two parts; on the shield's lower left is a depiction of the cannon of the Battle of Gonzales; on the shield's lower right is a depiction of Vince's Bridge; on the upper half of the shield is a portrayal of the Alamo; the shield is circled by live oak and olive branches, and the unfurled flags of the Kingdom of France, the Kingdom of Spain, the United Mexican States, the Republic of Texas, the Confederate States of America, and the United States of America; above the shield is emblazoned the motto, "REMEMBER THE ALAMO," and beneath

195

the shield are the words, "TEXAS ONE AND INDIVISIBLE;" over the entire shield, centered between the flags, is a white, five-pointed star...[2]

State Flag:
The Republic of Texas adopted the Lone Star Flag in 1839. In 1844, the State of Texas adopted the flag. The colors of the Texas State flag depict the following: **red** for courage, **white** for purity and **blue** for allegiance.

State Song:
"Texas, Our Texas."

First "Christian Heritage Week:" September 12-18, 1993, proclaimed by the Governor.

Of Historic Interest:
Both **Samuel Houston** and **Stephen Austin** were chosen by the citizens of Texas to represent them as their greatest heroes in the U.S. Capitol's Hall of Fame.

From a speech delivered on February 28, 1859 to the United States Senate by **General Sam Houston (1793-1863)**, of Texas, refuting calumnies produced and circulated against his character as Commander-in-Chief of the Army of Texas, we note this great American Christian hero's use of God's Word to validate his actions. Quoting from the original:

> ...The Commander-in-Chief, on that occasion, was not aware that he had the approval of Holy Writ for the course he adopted, though he subsequently became apprised of the fact; for we find that, after Elisha had smitten the Syrians and conducted them into the midst of Samaria and had ordered their eyes to be opened, the King of Israel, Jehoram, said to the prophet: 'My father, shall I smite them? Shall I smite them?' And he answered: 'Thou shalt not smite them; wouldst thou smite those who thou hast taken captive with thy sword and with thy bow? Set bread and water before them, that they may eat and drink, and go to their master.' Sir, that sanctioned the course of the Commander-in-Chief on that occasion; and though he was not as familiar with the subject as he ought to have been, yet, when apprised of it afterwards, he was rejoiced to know that he had the authority of Holy Writ for his conduct...

And again, in the same discourse, we see Sam Houston's humble dependence upon Almighty God as he prays that our United States Senators be endowed with light, knowledge, wisdom and patriotism, as they work to secure His blessings upon our nation:

> I know the high and important duties that devolve upon Senators, and I have confidence that their attention and their great abilities will be called to the discharge of those duties; that they will, on great national subjects, harmonize so as to give vigor to, and cement our institutions, and that they will keep pace in their efforts to advance the country with the progress that seems to invite it onward. My prayers will remain with them, that light, knowledge, wisdom and patriotism may guide them, and that their efforts will be perpetually employed for blessings to our country; that under their influence and their exertions the nation will be blessed, the people happy, and the perpetuity of the Union secured to the latest posterity. (Applause in the galleries).

Sam Houston's life and deeds live on in the hearts of many Americans. They are worthy to be resuscitated and emulated by our nation's youth. This is just another indication of God's hand upon America during the development era of the nation.

On August 1, 1854 in a speech given by the **Honorable Sam Houston** of Texas to the United States Senate, this American son stated:

> ...One arm and one leg I have given to be crushed in the defense of my country...

Houston's strength and bravery did not detract from his need for a personal Savior. He accepted Jesus Christ as his personal Lord and Redeemer in early November, 1854, during a Revival conducted in his home town by Independence Church. It is reported that Houston responded to the minister's appeal, and, weeping and repenting of his sins, professed his faith in Christ. On Sunday, November 19, the father of Texas was baptized by Pastor Rufus Burleson of Independence Church in Little Rocky Creek, two miles south of the town.

Stephen Fuller Austin (1793-1836), is the second great Texan hero in our U.S. Capitol's Hall of Fame. As one of the Commissioners of Texas, he delivered an address at Louisville, Kentucky on March 7, 1836. From its contents we learn that he, too, knew Almighty God had stamped his law of self-government (precluding tyranny) upon man's heart:

> ...It is with the most unfeigned and heartfelt gratitude that I appear before this enlightened audience, to thank the citizens of Louisville, as I do in the name of the people of Texas, for the kind and generous sympathy they have manifested in favor of the cause of that struggling country; and to make a plain statement of facts explanatory of the contest in which Texas is engaged with the Mexican government...Our cause is just, and is the cause of light and liberty; the same holy cause for which our forefathers fought and bled: the same that has an advocate in the bosom of every freeman, no matter in what country, or by what people it may be contended for...Our forefathers in 1776 flew to arms for much less. They resisted a principle, "the theory of oppression," but in our case it was the reality; it was a denial of justice and of our guaranteed rights - it was oppression itself...In further support of this subject, I will present an extract from a report made by me to the provisional government of Texas on the 30th November last, communicating the said decree of 3rd October...That every people have the right to change their government...If they submit to a forcible and unconstitutional destruction of the social compact, which they have sworn to support, they violate their oaths. If they submit to be tamely destroyed, they disregard their duty to themselves, and violate the first law which God stamped upon the heart of man, civilized or savage, which is the law or the right of self-preservation...Ours is most truly and emphatically the cause of liberty, which is the cause of philanthropy, of religion, of mankind; for in its train follow freedom of conscience, pure morality, enterprise, the arts and sciences, all that is dear to the noble-minded and the free, all that renders life precious,...With these claims to the approbation and moral support of the free of all nations, the people of Texas have taken up arms in self defense, and they submit their cause to the judgment of an impartial world, and

to the protection of a just and omnipotent God.

The above also shows Austin's love and adherence to pure morality, freedom of conscience and nobility of mind; his speech ending with a humble plea to the overruling justice of Almighty God, who, through His protective care, would undertake to secure Texas' liberty.

The Seal of the city of Austin contains the cross of Jesus Christ; being the Coat of Arms of its illustrious father, Stephen Austin.

Lt. General William W. Momyer, USAF, delivered the following *Pilgrimage Address at the Alamo* to the House of Representatives on April 18, 1966:

PILGRIMAGE ADDRESS AT THE ALAMO

We are assembled here to give tribute to the men who defended the Alamo. Some 130 years ago, a group of almost 200 men gave their lives in one of the most stirring battles of our history. The men of Colonel Travis' command fought off a superior force of more than 2,500 troops for 13 days. The gallant defense of the Alamo stands as a living memorial to all men of courage. Knowing that no help could reach them in time, *these men laid down their lives so Sam Houston might have time to gather additional forces for other battles to be fought.* We know that the valuable time the defense of the Alamo gave Sam Houston, permitted him to defeat Santa Anna at San Jacinto and, thereby, established the Republic of Texas. American history is punctuated with the outstanding courage of its fighting men. When men fight in defense of their freedom, courage and dedication to their fellow men are characteristic. The strength of our country is in our people and the willingness to fight for those ideals that have made us the greatest country on earth. Whenever our ideals have been threatened we have responded with heroic self-sacrifice in defense of those precious things...Our fighting men have faced difficult battles in the past and shall face even more difficult ones in the future. Sam Houston didn't become discouraged because of the severity of the struggle. His cause and determination to succeed swept all obstacles aside. Our fighting men are led by the same dedicated leadership today...I think we need have no fear of the strength and will of our fighting men. We can all be proud of the example set by that heroic group of volunteers at the *Alamo*. Their display of self-sacrifice for a more noble cause should be a source of inner strength for all of us as we face the future, and an individual determination that we will courageously defend our freedom no matter how small or great the challenge. Yes, we remember the *Alamo*, because without the strength of character displayed by men like Travis, Crockett, Bowie, and Bonham there would be no freedom to defend...[3]

United States Presidents: Dwight D. Eisenhower (34th), born in Texas; Lyndon Baines Johnson (36th); George Bush (41st).

Michael O. Leavitt
Governor

Declaration

Whereas, the Preamble to the Constitution of the state of Utah states that "Grateful to Almighty God for life and liberty, we, the people of Utah, in order to secure and perpetuate the principles of free government, do ordain and establish this Constitution"; and

Whereas, Benjamin Franklin, at the Constitutional Convention in 1787 stated: "It is impossible to build an empire without our Father's aid. I believe the sacred writing which say that 'Except the Lord build the house, they labor in vain that build it'" (Psalm 127:1); and

Whereas, George Washington enunciated: "animated alone by the pure spirit of Christianity, and conducting ourselves as the faithful subjects of our free government, we may enjoy every temporal and spiritual felicity"; and

Whereas, Thomas Jefferson, author of the Declaration of Independence, wrote: "Can the liberties of a nation be secure when we have removed the conviction that these liberties are the gift of God?"; and

Whereas, James Madison, father of the U.S. Constitution, advocated "the diffusion of the light of Christianity in our nation" in his Memorial and Remonstrance; and

Whereas, Patrick Henry quoted Proverbs 14:34 for your nation: "Righteousness alone can exalt a nation, but sin is a disgrace to any people"; and

Whereas, George Mason, in his Virginia Declaration of Rights, forerunner to our U.S. Bill of Rights, affirmed: "That it is the mutual duty of all to practice Christian forbearance, love and charity towards each other"; and

Whereas, these, and many other truly great men and women of America, giants in the structuring of American history, were Christian statesmen of calibor and integrity who did not hesitate to express their faith;

Now, Therefore, I, Michael O. Leavitt, Governor of the state of Utah, do hereby declare September 19 through 25, 1999, as

Christian Heritage Week

in Utah.

Governor: *Michael O. Leavitt*

Utah's First Annual "Christian Heritage Week, September 19-25, 1999" Proclaimed by the Governor.

UTAH
(from the Indian word "upper")

The Preamble to the Constitution of the State of Utah states that, *Grateful to Almighty God for life and liberty, we, the people of Utah, in order to secure and perpetuate the principles of free government, do ordain and establish this Constitution.*

Utah joined the Union on January 4, 1896 as the 45th State.

State Capital: Salt Lake City.

State Motto:
"Industry." Officially adopted on March 4, 1959.

State Emblem:
The Beehive. Industry is associated with the symbol of the beehive. The early pioneers had few material resources at their disposal and therefore had to rely on their own hard work and resources, representative of "industry." The beehive was chosen as the emblem for the provisional State of Deseret in 1848 and was maintained along with the word "industry" on the Seal and Flag when Utah became a state in 1896.

State Seal:
"The great seal of the State of Utah shall be two and one-half inches in diameter, and of the following device: the center a shield and perched thereon an American eagle with outstretched wings; the top of the shield pierced by six arrows crosswise; under the arrows the motto 'Industry'; beneath the motto a beehive, on either side growing sego lilies; below the beehive the figures '1847'; and on either side of the shield an American flag; encircling all, near the outer edge of the seal, beginning at the lower left-hand portion, the words 'The Great Seal of the State of Utah', with the figures '1896' at the base." [1]

State Flag:
The original Utah State Flag consisted of a solid white state seal on a light blue background which was adopted by the State Legislature in 1896 and revised in 1913. [2] The Utah State Flag, as we know it today, was originally designed for the battleship "Utah" in 1912. It was later made the official flag of the state in 1913. The American Eagle with outstretched wings, has six arrows in its talons and indicates protection. The beehive symbolizes industry. The Sego Lily represents peace. The draped American Flag is representative of Utah's support for the Union. "1896" is the year Utah joined the Union as the 45th State (January 4, 1896).

State Song:
"Utah We Love Thee" by Evan Stephens. This song was written to commemorate Utah's statehood as the 45th State.

First "Christian Heritage Week:" September 19-25, 1999, proclaimed by the Governor.

Of Historic Interest:

In 1540, Garcia Lopez de Cardenas entered the region from the south. He reached the Colorado River, but soon returned to Coronado, the leader of the exploring expedition, with unfavorable reports about the country. The Utah region was really opened by representatives of British and American fur companies from the Oregon country and the upper Missouri. In 1825, Great Salt Lake was discovered by James Bridger, and he was followed (if not preceded) by Etienne Provot, preacher of the Gospel, **"Bible Totin' " Jedediah Smith** and Peter Skene Ogden. About the same time William Ashley of the Rocky Mountain Fur Company followed the Green River nearly to present-day Greenriver. The expeditions of Captain B.L.E. Benneville in 1832-43 were the first to leave permanent records. In 1841 the first emigrant train to California crossed the Salt Desert after leaving the Oregon Trail.[3]

Lake Utah, a fresh water lake in Utah County, is situated 30 miles south east of the Great Salt Lake, into which it discharges by the Jordan River. It has a length of 25 miles from north to south, an extreme width of 13 miles, and an area of 150 square miles. Provo is situated on its eastern shore.[4]

ETHAN ALLEN 1737~1789 VERMONT

After the Original Marble Sculpture of Ethan Allen in the
Hall of Fame, U.S. Capitol, Washington, D.C.

202

VERMONT
(from the French "Verd Mont,"
meaning "Green Mountain")

> **The Constitution of the State of Vermont states,** *That all men have a natural and unalienable right to worship Almighty God according to the dictates of their own consciences and under-standings, as in their opinion shall be regulated by the Word of God;...Nevertheless, every sect or denomination of Christians ought to observe the Sabbath or Lord's day, and keep up some sort of religious worship, which to them shall seem most agree-able to the revealed will of God.*

Vermont joined the Union on March 4, 1791 as the 14th State.

State Capital: Montpelier.

State Motto:
"Freedom and Unity," derived from the fact that the individual States should be free, but united.[1]

State Seal:
The most dominant feature of the seal is the central pine. The pine trees of that time were tall trees, sometimes looming a hundred feet higher than the other trees around them. The pine was used on pine tree shillings, samplers, platters and other familiar objects.

The peculiar cutting of the Vermont seal tree shows fourteen distinct branches, none a leader. It is interesting to examine possible reasons for this. The national flag adopted in 1777 had focused attention on the number "thirteen," representing the original thirteen states. Since Vermont felt so strongly on the subject of admission to the Union that she marked her coins "Quarta Decima Stella," or fourteenth star, it is easy to imagine that Ira Allen picked the New England Pine as a proper symbol for the United States, and deliberately made it a pine of fourteen branches to indicate that Vermont should be a member of the Union; that the Union should have no one dominant state, and that it was a living and growing organiza-tion, capable of adding branch after branch as it went higher and grew stronger.[2]

State Coat of Arms:
The first Vermont Coat of Arms was an engraving for use on military commissions, made in 1821 when the original state seal was revised by rearranging some of the features in pictorial form. It placed the picture in a shield surmounted by the stag's head crest, with the motto beneath, and the whole was put under the outspread wings of the American eagle with full panoply of war. The crest was a new feature, possibly invented by Secretary of the Governor and Council, Robert Temple, or by the Boston engraver who designed the com-mission. Although no law provided for a Coat of Arms, it was in official use in this form, with slight modifications, until 1862.

When the Civil War began, a Coat of Arms and crest for military purposes was needed. The crest had been used for some years on military buttons, but search for an authentic descrip-tion of the Coat of Arms revealed that there was no law making this provision. Professor George W. Benedict of Burlington wrote a description in quasi-heraldic terms, and this was confirmed by law in 1862.[3]

The law does not specify any particular mountains or view. The shield may be of any shape, with any sort of border or none. There must be a landscape of natural color in the foreground or base, with high mountains of blue above and extending into a yellow sky. There must be a pine tree of natural color extending from near the base to the top; sheaves of grain, three in number and yellow, placed diagonally on the right side; and a red cow standing on the left side of the field. The motto, badge, crest, and scroll must conform to the description.

State Flag:
The history of the Vermont state flag must include a reference to the United States flag, adopted on June 14, 1777, and described as follows: "The flag of the United States shall be thirteen stripes, alternate red and white, that the union be thirteen stars, white in a blue field."

The first Stars and Stripes Flag known to have been used in the Revolutionary War was carried by the Green Mountain Boys of Vermont at the Battle of Bennington, August 16, 1777, and is now the most cherished possession of the Bennington Historical Museum, Bennington, Vermont.

The first distinct Vermont flag was a state militia flag created on October 31, 1803.   Tennessee and Ohio had now been admitted into the Union and, apparently anticipating that the U.S. Flag would continue to add stripes and stars for each addition, Vermont authorized a flag of seventeen stripes and seventeen stars, "with the word 'VERMONT' in capitals above the said stripes and stars." However, in April, 1818, Congress authorized our present United States flag of thirteen stripes, with a star for each state.

The second Vermont flag, then, was authorized on October 20, 1837, and contained "Thirteen stripes, alternate red and white, and a union of one large star, white in a blue field, with the Coat of Arms of the State of Vermont therein." This remained the state flag until 1919, when the design of the official state flag was approved.[4]

State Song:
"Hail, Vermont!"

First "Christian Heritage Week:" October 24-30, 1999, proclaimed by the Governor.

Of Historic Interest:
Ethan Allen (1737-1789) is Vermont's greatest hero in the U.S. Capitol's Hall of Fame. At the beginning of the Revolutionary War, Allen, with eighty-three men at dawn, without firing a shot or losing a man, captured Fort Ticonderoga at the head of Lake Champlain. On entering the fort, he was fired at directly by the guard. However, the cap fused, and he was spared. The following winter, the captured cannon, powder and shot were forwarded by sled to Boston. Washington used this equipment to remove the British from that city.[5]

Years later, Ethan Allen recounts that when the commander of Fort Ticonderoga asked him by what authority the fort was called to surrender, he responded, "In the name of the Great Jehovah and the Continental Congress."[6]

Allen stated the following:

> I am as resolutely determined to defend the Independence of Vermont as Congress are that of the United States, and rather than fail, will retire with hardy Green Mountain Boys into the desolate caverns of the mountains and wage war with human nature at large. 1781.[7]

Vermont's second great hero, chosen to represent them in the Hall of Fame, is **Jacob Collamer (1792-1865).** Following are excerpts from the *Unveiling Ceremonies* program which took place at the U.S. Capitol:

> He gave a half century of varied and distinguished service to State and Nation
>
> ORATOR, JURIST, STATESMAN
>
> Born at Troy, New York, 1792
> Family moved to Burlington, VT, 1795
> Country school; earned University expense
> Graduate, University of Vermont, 1810
> Served in militia on Canadian Frontier, 1812
> To Woodstock, VT: admitted to the bar, 1813
> Member, VT Assembly, 1821-1822; 1827-1828
> Justice of the VT Supreme Court, 1833-1842
> Delegate to VT Constitutional Conv., 1836
> Member, U.S. House of R., 1843-1849
> Postmaster General, by Pres. Taylor, 1949-1950
> Justice of the VT Supreme Court, 1850-1854
> Member, U.S. Senate till death, 1855-1865
> Died, Woodstock, VT (brief illness), 1865
> Marble statue accepted by Congress, 1881
> Statue located in Hall of Columns

His friend and colleague stated of him:

> The distinguished statesman, Jacob Collamer, whose statue is now presented under the Act of Congress of 1865 by the State of Vermont, I knew well and intimately for several years. We entered Congress together in 1843 and remained in the House together until 1849 when he was appointed to the office of Postmaster General. During the three Congresses of our joint service, we occupied adjacent seats. I well recollect Judge Collamer's first speech in the House. This speech, not over thirty minutes in length, was so pointed, clear, logical and conclusive, that it put him at once in the front rank of debaters, lawyers and jurists in the House. Jacob Collamer was a man of great probity, of most exemplary conduct and of sincere piety.[8]

In 1928, **Calvin Coolidge**, Thirtieth President of the United States, asserted the following regarding Vermont:

If the Spirit of Liberty should vanish in other parts of the Union and support of our institutions should languish, it could all be replenished from the generous store held by the people of this brave little State of Vermont.[9]

Officially Recorded Presidential Inaugural Scriptures:
   Chester Arthur was sworn into office privately in New York City after the death of President Garfield on September 20, 1881, and a second time in Washington, D.C. on September 22 of the same year. His Inaugural Bible was a King James Version, published by George E. Eyre and William Spottiswoode of London. A statement by the Clerk of the Supreme Court appears near the front:

> Upon this Bible the Chief Justice administered the oath of office to Chester A. Arthur 21st President of the United States. (L.S.) James H. McKenney Clerk of the Supreme Court of the United States.

Psalm 31:1-2, the Scripture chosen by the President for his inauguration, is marked in pencil:

> In thee, O Lord, do I put my trust; let me never be ashamed; deliver me in thy righteousness. Bow down thine ear to me; deliver me speedily; be thou my strong rock, for a house of defense to save me. Psalm 31:1-2

   Calvin Coolidge's second inauguration took place on March 4, 1925. The Bible he used was a gift from his mother when he was but a boy. The President's wife, Grace Coolidge, jotted down these lines in pencil on a blank sheet near the front of the Bible:

> This is the Bible upon which the President's hand rested as he took the oath of office March 4, 1925 at Washington, D.C. G.C.

The Clerk of the Supreme Court listed the Gospel according to John, Chapter I as the President's choice of Scripture passage for his swearing in:

> In the beginning was the Word, and the Word was with God, and the Word was God. The same was in the beginning with God. All things were made by him; and without him was not any thing made that was made. In him was life; and the life was the light of men. And the light shineth in darkness; and the darkness comprehended it not. There was a man sent from God, whose name was John. The same came for a witness, to bear witness of the Light, that all men through him might believe. He was not that Light, but was sent to bear witness of that Light. That was the true Light, which lighteth every man that cometh into the world. He was in the world, and the world was made by him, and the world knew him not. He came unto his own, and his own received him not. But as many as received him, to them gave he power to become the sons of God, even to them that believe on his name: Which were born, not of blood, nor of the will of the flesh, nor of the will of man, but of God. And the Word was made flesh, and dwelt among us, and we beheld his glory, the glory as of the only begotten of the father, full of grace and truth. John 1:1-14

A front page column in the *New York Times*, dated March 4, 1925, gives interesting insight into the Presidential choice:

> Coolidge will kiss Bible he first read: His grandfather's book will be opened at the first Chapter of St. John. His aged father arrives. Colonel is calm and silent but does remark that President was quiet, even as a boy.

> President Coolidge will kiss the Bible at the first Chapter of St. John when he takes the oath of office tomorrow. The Bible is one that belonged to his grandfather, from which is it said, the President learned to read between four and five years of age. According to a friend, the Coolidges were accustomed to read the Bible daily, and as a child, Mr. Coolidge took to reading it as his first book. It appears that he frequently read it to his grandfather, who died when he was about five years of age. The section which he first read was the first chapter of St. John. It had been announced that Colonel Coolidge, the President's father, would bring the family Bible containing the births and deaths of the Coolidges, for use in the ceremonies tomorrow. This proved to be incorrect, and the Bible which is in the possession of the President is his grandfather's which his grandfather later gave to the President. It is a book about the size of the Bible-class, Oxford edition. It is not the bulky family Bible of tradition. Colonel Coolidge, who administered the oath to his son under the kerosene lamp in his Vermont home in August, 1923, arrived late this evening to be present at the ceremonies tomorrow. He declined to make any comment on things political and did not seem to be any more aroused over the event than he was when his son established the summer White House at Plymouth. He displays no more emotion than the President, and is the same, silent stamp of sturdy citizen. (*New York Times*, March 4, 1925)

United States Presidents: Chester A. Arthur (21st); Calvin Coolidge (30th).

GEORGE WASHINGTON.

The General Assembly of the Commonwealth
of Virginia have caused this Statue to be erected.
as a monument of affection and gratitude to
GEORGE WASHINGTON:
who, uniting to the endowments of the Hero
the virtues of the Patriot, and exerting both
in establishing the Liberties of his Country
has rendered his name dear to his Fellow Citizens.
and given the world an immortal example
of true Glory. Done, in the year of
CHRIST.
One thousand seven hundred and eighty eight
and in the year of. the Commonwealth the twelfth

Taken from the Original Statue of George Washington by Jean Antoine
Houdon in the Hall of Fame, U.S. Capitol, Washington, D.C.

THE COMMONWEALTH OF VIRGINIA
(After Elizabeth I, Virgin Queen of England)

The Constitution of the Commonwealth of Virginia states, *That religion, or the duty which we owe to our Creator, and the manner of discharging it, can be directed only by reason and conviction; not by force or violence; and, therefore, all men are equally entitled to the free exercise of religion, according to the dictates of conscience; and that it is the mutual duty of all to practice Christian forbearance, love and charity towards each other.*

Virginia joined the Union on June 25, 1788 as the 10th State.

State Capital: Richmond.

State Motto:
"Sic Semper Tyrannis," translated from Latin to mean, "Ever thus to Tyrants."

State Seal:
"The Great Seal of the Commonwealth of Virginia shall consist of two metallic discs, two inches and one-fourth in diameter, with an ornamental border one-fourth of an inch wide, with such words and figures engraved thereon as will, when used, produce impressions to be described as follows: On the obverse, Virtue, the genius of the Commonwealth, dressed as an Amazon, resting on a spear in her right hand, point downward, touching the earth; and holding in her left hand, a sheathed sword or parazonium, pointing upward; her head erect and face up-turned; her left foot on the form of Tyranny, represented by the prostrate body of a man, with his head to her left, his fallen crown nearby, a broken chain in his left hand, and a scourge in his right. Above the group and within the border conforming therewith, shall be the word Virginia, and, in the space below, on a curved line, shall be the motto, 'Sic Semper Tyrannis.' On the reverse, shall be placed a group consisting of Libertas, holding a wand and pileus in her right hand; on her right, Aeternitas, with a globe and phoenix in her right hand, on the left of Libertas, Ceres, with a cornucopia in her left hand, and an ear of wheat in her right; over this device, in curved line, the word 'Perseverando.' "[1]

From the pen of the Honorable Thomas Moncure, Jr. came the following historic lines: "It is the figure of Virtue, standing over the dead body of Tyranny, that dominates the Great Seal of the Commonwealth."

The Seal, designed by George Wythe, a signer of the Declaration of Independence and first Professor of Law at the College of William and Mary; as well as mentor to Thomas Jefferson, was first adopted in 1776 and modified in 1930.

The Lesser Seal:
The Lesser Seal of the Commonwealth shall be one and nine-sixteenths inches in diameter, and have engraved thereon the device and inscriptions contained in the obverse of the Great Seal.[2]

Of greatest importance, Virginia's founders envisioned that the people would possess certain traits, namely, "a firm adherence to Justice, Moderation, Temperance, Frugality and Virtue." No concept was more central than that of public or civil virtue. The civically virtuous citizen was self-reliant and self-determinative, while recognizing a duty to the general welfare or common good of the community.[3]

State Flag:

The flag of Virginia contains the state seal in a field of blue. It was first used in the 1800's, but not officially adopted until 1930.

> The flag of the Commonwealth shall hereafter be made of bunting or merino. It shall be a deep blue field with a circular white centre of the same material. Upon this circle shall be painted or embroidered, to show on both sides alike, the Coat of Arms of the State, as described in Section 7.1.26 for the obverse of the great seal of the Commonwealth, and there shall be a white silk fringe on the outer edge, further from the flag-staff. This shall be known and respected as the flag of Virginia.[4]

State Song:
"Carry Me Back to Old Virginia."[5]

First "Christian Heritage Week:" March 13-19, 1994, Proclaimed by the Governor.

Of Historic Interest:

The first permanent Protestant Christian settlement in America was established at Jamestown in 1607. Their **First Virginia Charter,** dated April 10, 1606, is excerpted as follows: ". . . We, greatly commending, and graciously accepting of so noble a work, which may, by the Providence of Almighty God, hereafter tend to the glory of His Divine Majesty, in propagating of Christian Religion to such people, as yet live in darkness and miserable ignorance of the true knowledge and worship of God . . ." The first representative legislative assembly in America took place in the 1607 Jamestown Church on July 30, 1619.

George Washington (1732-1799), first U.S. President and General of the Continental Army during the American Revolution, was born on February 22, 1732. This illustrious "Father of his Country" has left for posterity hand-written prayers, composed for the morning and the evening. His *Sunday Evening Prayer,* is hereunder reprinted. It gives insight into this hero's true Christianity:

> O MOST GLORIOUS GOD, in Jesus Christ my merciful & loving father, I acknowledge and confess my guilt, in the weak and imperfect performance of the duties of this day. I have called on thee for pardon and forgiveness of sins, but so coldly & carelessly, that my prayers are become my sin and stand in need of pardon. I have heard thy holy word, but with such deadness of spirit that I have been an unprofitable and forgetful hearer, so that, O Lord, tho' I have done thy work, yet it hath been so negligently that I may rather expect a curse than a blessing from thee. But, O God, who art rich in mercy and plenteous in redemption, mark not, I beseech thee, what I have done amiss; remember I am but dust, and remit my transgressions negligences & ignorances, and cover them all with the absolute obedience of thy dear Son, that those sacrifices which I have offered may be accepted by thee, in and for the sacrifice Jesus Christ offered upon the cross for me; for his sake, ease me of the burden of my sins, and give me grace that by the call of the Gospel I may rise from the

slumber of sin unto newness of life. Let me live according to those holy rules which thou hast this day prescribed in thy holy word; make me to know what is acceptable in thy sight and therein to delight. Open the eyes of my understanding, and help me thoroughly to examine myself concerning my knowledge, faith and repentance. Increase my faith, and direct me to the true object, Jesus Christ the way, the truth and the life. Bless, O Lord, all the people of this land, from the highest to the lowest, particularly those whom thou hast appointed to rule over us in church & state. Continue thy goodness to me this night. These weak petitions I humbly implore thee to hear, accept and answer for the sake of thy Dear Son, Jesus Christ our Lord. Amen[6]

Officially Recorded Presidential Inaugural Scriptures:

George Washington was sworn into office on April 30, 1789. The Bible upon which the first President of the United States swore allegiance to the U.S. Constitution was published in London in 1767 by Mark Baskett. This King James Version of Holy Scripture is handsomely illustrated with biblical scenes. After taking the oath of office, Washington kissed the Bible, which had been opened at random to Genesis, Chapters 49-50, due to haste. The page of the Bible which Washington kissed is indicated by the leaf being turned down.

Verses 22-25c, excerpted from Genesis 49, read as follows:

Joseph is a fruitful bough, even a fruitful bough by a well; whose branches run over the wall; The archers have sorely grieved him and shot at him, and hated him; But his bow abode in strength, and the arms of his hands were made strong by the hands of the mighty God of Jacob; (from thence is the shepherd, the stone of Israel;) Even by the God of thy father, who shall help thee; and by the Almighty, who shall bless thee with blessings of heaven above...

Interior of Pohick Church. George Washington's Pew (No. 28) is closest to the Communion Rail. The Lord's Prayer, the Ten Commandments and the Apostles' Creed are calligraphied upon the Wall behind the Altar.

George Washington's Inaugural Worship Service was held at *St. Paul's Chapel* of *Trinity Episcopal Church* in New York, where Washington and members of his government worshipped the Lord. Many served as wardens and vestrymen. Washington's pew can still be seen at *St. Paul's Chapel.*

George Washington's and George Mason's Pew Bench Cushions. Pohick Church (c.1774).

Woodrow Wilson's Inaugural Bible was first used in his swearing in as Governor of the State of New Jersey, and is dated 11 January 1911. At his first inauguration, in 1913, the passage of Scripture chosen by Wilson was Psalm 119:43-46:

> And take not the word of truth utterly out of my mouth; for I have hoped in thy judgments. So shall I keep thy law continually for ever and ever. And I will walk at liberty: for I seek thy precepts. I will speak of thy testimonies also before Kings, and will not be ashamed.

A Senate document of March 5, 1917 records President Wilson's second oath-taking in graphic detail:

Mrs. Wilson rode at Wilson's side in the parade, both to and from the Capitol, and also sat beside him at the time he stood reviewing the parade. Both Mrs. Wilson and Mrs. Marshall, the wife of the Vice President, rode through the parade with the President and Vice President. The fact that the grand Marshall, Major General Hugh L. Scott, Chief of Staff of the Army, stood beside the President all during the review of the parade was also an innovation. Promptly at 11 o'clock the President and his personal party came from the White House. He stepped into an open landau drawn by two mettlesome bay horses, which champed and pawed the ground fretfully. Beside him sat Mrs. Wilson, and in the same carriage were Senator Lee S. Overman of North Carolina, and Representative William W. Rucker of Missouri, Chairmen, respectively, of the Senate and House Inaugural Committees. With Vice President and Mrs. Marshall rode Senator Hoke Smith of Georgia, and Francis E. Warren of Wyoming, members of the Senate Committee. In the Senate Chamber the President was seated in front of the Vice President's desk, and the committee on arrangements occupied seats on his right and left.

It was found, when the President ended his solemn obligation, that he had kissed the Bible upon this passage. "The Lord is our refuge, a very present help in time of trouble." (Psalm 46:1)

As the Chief Justice came to the conclusion of the oath, which the President repeated after him, very slowly, a few words at a time, the Chief Justice paused for a pronounced period, lowered his voice, and said solemnly: "So help you God." The President slowly and solemnly repeated:

"So — help — me — God..."

United States Presidents: George Washington (1st); Thomas Jefferson (3rd); James Madison (4th); James Monroe (5th); William Henry Harrison (9th); John Tyler (10th); Zachary Taylor (12th); and Woodrow Wilson (28th).

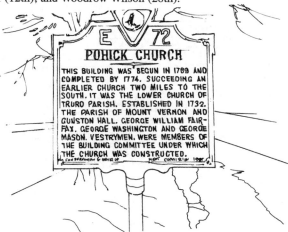

Historical Marker outside Pohick Church (c.1774).

213

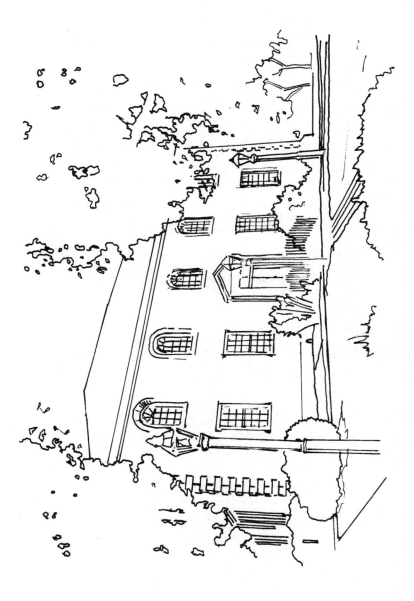

Pohick Church (c.1774) of Truro Parish. George Washington, George Mason and William Fairfax were on the Building Committee of this Church.

MARCUS WHITMAN

After the Original Bronze Sculpture of Marcus Whitman in the Hall of Fame, U.S. Capitol, Washington, D.C. He holds a Bible in his right hand, medical equipment in the left.

WASHINGTON
(After George Washington)

The Preamble to the Constitution of the State of Washington states that, *We the people of the State of Washington, grateful to the Supreme Ruler of the Universe for our liberties, do ordain this Constitution.*

Washington joined the Union on November 11, 1889 as the 42nd State.

State Capital: Olympia.

State Motto:
"Alki," translated from Indian to mean "bye and bye."

State Seal:
The State Seal was first designed in 1889 by an Olympia jeweler called Charles Talcott. The latter used an ink bottle and a silver dollar to draw the rings of the seal, and then pasted a postage stamp, with the portrait of George Washington by celebrated artist, Gilbert Stuart, in the center. His brother, Grant Talcott lettered the words, "The Seal of the State of Washington 1889" and another brother cut the printing die.

State Flag:
When the Legislature approved a law in 1923 setting forth the design of the official state flag, it stipulated that the flag "shall be of dark green silk or bunting, bearing in its center a reproduction of the seal of the state of Washington . . ." The original law allowed the option of using green fringe on the flag; two years later, the Legislature changed the fringe color to gold. In the seal used on the state flag, the portrait of George Washington has a blue background and is encircled by a gold ring with black lettering.[1]

State Song:
In 1909, "Washington Beloved" was adopted by the Legislature. Professor Edmond Meany, historian, wrote the words and Reginald de Koven wrote the music. This song was never formally introduced as a bill, however, and so it is not part of the State's code of law. In 1959, a State Senator from South Bend introduced a bill to make "Washington My Home," by Helen Davis, the state song.

State Ship:
"President Washington." In 1983, the "President Washington" was proclaimed the official state ship, and is the first container ship to be adopted by a state. The 860-foot vessel is one of the largest container ships ever built in the United States and has a 43,000 horsepower diesel engine. The 23-foot propeller weighs 98,000 pounds. The ship's route on the Pacific Ocean expands the natural geographical advantage of trade shipping between Washington State and Pacific Ocean countries.

First "Christian Heritage Week:" October 19-25, 1997, proclaimed by the Governor.

Of Historic Interest:

In 1923, President Warren Gamaliel Harding gave a speech eulogizing **Marcus Whitman (1802-1847),** Washington State's greatest hero in the Hall of Fame, as follows:

Living history records many indissoluble links, to one of which it seems fitting that I should direct your attention today. Of the many rooms in the White House, which possess the peculiar charm of association with epochal happenings, the one most fascinating to me is that which formerly comprised the Cabinet Room and the President's study...Before my mind's eye as I stood in that heroic chamber a few days ago appeared the vivid picture. I beheld seated at his desk, immaculately attired, the embodiment of dignity and courtliness, John Tyler, 10th President of the United States. Facing him, from a chair constructed for a massive frame, his powerful spirit gleaming through his cavernous eyes, was the lion-visaged Daniel Webster, Secretary of State. The door opened and there appeared before the amazed statesmen a strange and astonishing figure. It was that of a man of medium height and sturdy build, deep chested, broad shouldered, yet lithe in movement and soft in step. He was clad in a coarse fur coat, buckskin breeches, fur leggings, and boot moccasins, looking much the worse for wear. But it was the countenance of the visitor, as he stood for an instant in the doorway, that riveted the perception of the two Chiefs of State. It was that of a religious enthusiast, tenaciously earnest yet revealing no suggestion of fanaticism, bronzed from exposure to pitiless elements and seamed with deep lines of physical suffering, a rare combination of determination and gentleness—obviously a man of God, but no less a man among men.

Such was Marcus Whitman, the pioneer missionary hero of the vast, unsettled, unexplored Oregon country, who had come out of the West to plead that the State should acquire for civilization the Empire that the churches were gaining for Christianity...

It was more than a desperate and perilous trip that Marcus Whitman undertook. It was a race against time. Public opinion was rapidly crystallizing into a judgement that the Oregon country was not worth claiming, much less worth fighting for; that even though it could be acquired against the insistence of Great Britain, it would prove to be a liability rather than an asset...

And he did not hesitate to speak plainly as one who knew, even like the prophet Daniel. "Mr. Secretary," he declared, "you would better give all New England for the cod and mackerel fisheries of Newfoundland than to barter away Oregon."

Then turning to the President in conclusion, he added quietly but beseechingly:

"All I ask is that you will not barter away Oregon or allow English interference until I can lead a band of stalwart American settlers across the plains. For this I shall try to do!"

The manly appeal was irresistible. He sought only the privilege of proving his faith. The just and considerate Tyler could not refuse.

"Dr. Whitman," he rejoined sympathetically, "your long ride and frozen limbs testify to your courage and your patriotism. Your credentials establish your character. Your request is granted!"

...Never in the history of the world has there been a finer example of civilization following Christianity. The missionaries led under the banner of the cross, and the settlers moved close behind under the star-spangled symbol of the Nation. Among the records of the evangelizing effort as the forerunner of human advancement, there is none so impressive as this of the early Oregon mission and its marvelous consequences. To the men and women of that early day whose first thought was to carry the gospel to the Indians—to the Lees, the Spauldings, the Grays, the Walkers, the Leslies, to Fathers DeSmet and Blanchet and DeMars, and to all the others of that glorious company who found that in serving God they were also serving their country and their fellowmen—to them we pay today our tribute; to them we owe a debt of gratitude, which we can never pay, save partially through recognition such as you have recorded it today...I rejoice particularly in the opportunity afforded me of voicing my appreciation both as President of the United States and as one who honestly tries to be a Christian soldier, of the signal service of the martyred Whitman. And finally, as just a human being, I wish I could find words to tell you how glad I am to see you all, and reflecting as you do, from untroubled eyes, and happiness of spirit breathed by your own best song:

There are no new worlds to conquer,
Gone is the last frontier,
And the steady grind of the wagon-train,
Of the sturdy pioneer.
But their memories live like a thing divine,
Treasured in Heaven above,
For the Trail that led to the storied West,
Was the wonderful trail of Love.

Warren Gamaliel Harding
President of the United States
(1865-1923)[2]

218

FRANCIS H. PIERPONT
1814 - 1899

After the Original Marble Sculpture of Governor Francis Pierpont in the Hall of Fame, U.S. Capitol, Washington, D.C.

219

WEST VIRGINIA

The Preamble to the Constitution of the State of West Virginia states that, *We the people of West Virginia, through Divine Providence, enjoy the blessings of liberty and reaffirm our faith in and constant reliance upon God.*

West Virginia joined the Union on June 20, 1863 as the 35th State.

State Capital: Charleston.

State Motto:
"Montani Semper Liberi," translated from Latin to mean, "Mountaineers are Always Free."

State Seal:
On West Virginia's Coat of Arms, the rock and ivy represent stability and continuity. The rock bears the inscription "June 20, 1863," the date West Virginia became a state. To the right of the rock stands a farmer. His right hand rests on a plow and his left arm supports an axe. These symbolize West Virginia agriculture, farming and timbering. To the left of the rock stands a miner with a pick-axe on his shoulder. The anvil, minerals and sledge-hammer at his feet, represent the development of West Virginia's natural resources. On the ground in front of the rock are two crossed rifles with a Liberty Cap at the point of intersection. These indicate that the state won her freedom and will fight to defend it. The Coat of Arms is bordered below by a wreath of rhododendrons, and above by a ribbon, upon which is lettered "Montani Semper Liberi," translated from Latin to mean, "Mountaineers Are Always Free."[1]

State Flag:
There are two state symbols on the State flag. The coat of arms (the State seal), and the rhododendron (the State flower). Across the top, lettered on a ribbon, are the words "State of West Virginia." The white background is bordered on all four sides by a strip of blue and all sides to be trimmed in gold fringe for parade.

State Song:

THE WEST VIRGINIA HILLS

I
Oh, the West Virginia hills
How majestic and how grand
With their summits bathed in glory,
Like our Prince Immanuel's land!
Is it any wonder then, That my heart
 with rapture thrills,
As I stand once more with loved ones
On those West Virginia hills.

II
Oh, the West Virginia hills
Where my girlhood's hours were pass'd
Where I often wander'd lonely,

And the future tried to cast;
Many are our visions bright
Which the future ne'er fulfills;
But how sunny were my day-dreams
On those West Virginia hills.

III
Oh, the West Virginia hills!
How unchang'd they seem to stand
With their summits pointed skyward,
To the Great Almighty's Land!
Many changes I can see,
Which my heart with sadness fills,
But no changes can be noticed
In those West Virginia hills.

IV
Oh, the West Virginia hills,
I must bid you now adieu
In my home beyond the mountains
I shall ever dream of you;
In the evening time of life,
If my Father only wills,
I shall still behold the vision
Of those West Virginia hills.

Chorus
O the hills, beautiful hills,
How I love those West Virginia hills
Beautiful hills
If o'er sea or land I roam,
Still I'll think of happy home,
And the friends among the West Virginia hills.

First "Christian Heritage Week:" March 8-14, 1992, signed and proclaimed by Governor Gaston Caperton at the request of the author, via a formal letter, which included credentials as an historian.

Of Historic Interest:
   Governor Francis Harrison Pierpont (1814-1899) was chosen by the citizens of West Virginia as their greatest hero in the Hall of Fame. Pierpont, an anti-slavery advocate and a leading member of the Methodist Protestant Church, wrote the following lines to President Lincoln:

Wheeling, VA., Dec. 31, 1862

President Lincoln: I am in hopes you will sign the bill to make West Virginia a new State. The loyal people of the State have their hearts set on it. The soldiers in the army have their hearts set on it. If the bill fails, God only knows the result. I fear general demoralization. I am clear, the consequence is in your hands.

F.H. Pierpont, Gov.[2]

The program of the *Pierpont Statue Unveiling, Washington, April 30th, 1910,* contained the following poem dedicated to the life and work of Francis H. Pierpont:

You are standing midst the mighty in the Great White Hall of Fame;
On the Nation's list of heroes they have written high your name,
And the powers and princes pass you and they give you meed of praise
But 'twas Freedom you were wooing, and not Fame, in those dark days.

Filled with manhood's high ideals, by a slave-block you stood near,
Watched the virgin crouching on it, saw her trembling, felt her fear,
And your spirit rose within you, as one led the maid away,
And you gave yourself to Freedom — life and soul and strength — that day.

When the loud alarm of battle flung a challenge to the North,
Home and childish hands clung to you, but your country called you forth;
On the strong God lays the burden when He makes a people free,
And on hearts that are most tender doth He write His stern decree.

In the shout and din of battle she was born, the brave free State;
Humble men stood sponsor for her, but their every deed was great —
West Virginia, child of Freedom! Many a brave man's life was given
Ere the chains with which foul slavery sought to hold you could be riven.

But it must be, up in Heaven, that the holy angels know
Of the struggles and the triumphs of those toiling here below;
And men's hearts were moved to action, so they placed you, Statesman, there,
That the world might know and feel it, what is wrought by work and prayer.

A.P.S.[3]

John Brown's name and deeds are intricately connected with the historic events at Harper's Ferry, West Virginia, preceding the outbreak of the Civil War.

From his account of his childhood, we read that during the war with England, a circumstance occurred that in the end made him a most determined Abolitionist, and led him to declare eternal war against slavery. He was staying for a short time with a very gentlemanly landlord, a U.S. Marshall, who held a slave boy near his own age, who was active, intelligent and of good feeling, and to whom John was under considerable obligation for numerous acts of kindness. The master made a great pet of John; brought him to table with his distinguished guests and friends; called their attention to every little smart thing he said or did; and to the fact of his being more than a hundred miles from home with a company of cattle alone; while the slave boy (who was fully, if not more than his equal) was poorly clothed, badly fed; lodged in cold weather and beaten before his eyes with iron shovels, or any other thing that came first to hand. This brought John to reflect on the wretched, hopeless condition of fatherless and motherless slave children; for such children have neither fathers nor mothers to protect and provide for them. He, at times, would raise the question, "Is God their Father?"[4]

Following are some of John Brown's last words from prison, recorded for posterity, prior to his execution for anti-slavery activities:

John Brown's Last Letter to His Family:

Charlestown Prison, Jefferson County, Virginia
November 30, 1859

My dearly beloved wife, sons and daughters, everyone:
As I now begin probably what is the last letter I shall ever write to
any of you, I conclude to write to all at the same time...I beseech you
all to live in habitual contentment with moderate circumstances and
gains of wordly store, and earnestly to teach this to your children and
children's children after you, by example as well as precept. Be determined to know by experience, as soon as may be, whether Bible
instruction is of Divine origin or not. Be sure to owe no man anything, but to love one another. John Rogers wrote to his children,
"Abhor that arrant whore of Rome." John Brown writes to his children to abhor, with undying hatred also, that sum of all villanies —
slavery.

Remember, "he that is slow to anger is better than the mighty," and
"he that ruleth his spirit than he that taketh a city." Remember also
that they being wise shall shine, and they that turn many to righteousness, as the stars forever and ever."
And now, dearly beloved family, to God and the work of his grace I
commend you all.

Your affectionate husband and father,
John Brown[5]

The last paper written by **John Brown,** and handed to one of the guards on the morning
of his execution, reads thus:

Charlestown, Virginia
December 2, 1859

I, John Brown, am now quite certain that the crimes of this *guilty
land* will never be purged away but with *blood.* I had, as I now think
vainly, flattered myself that without very much bloodshed it might
be done.

John Brown[6]

ROBERT M. LA FOLLETTE, SR., 1855-1925

After the Marble Sculpture of Robert M. La Follette in the Hall of Fame, U.S. Capitol, Washington, D.C.

WISCONSIN
(Indian for "gathering of the waters")

The Preamble to the Constitution of the State of Wisconsin states that, *We, the people of Wisconsin, grateful to Almighty God for our freedom, in order to secure its blessings, form a more perfect government, insure domestic tranquility and promote the general welfare, do establish this Constitution.*

Wisconsin joined the Union on May 29, 1848 as the 30th State.

State Capital: Madison.

State Motto:
"Forward."[1]

State Seal:
The State Seal features a sailor with a coiled rope and a yeoman, with a pick, who both symbolize labor on water and land. The two figures support a shield containing the symbols for agriculture, mining, manufacturing and navigation, representing a plow, pick and shovel, arm and hammer and anchor, respectively. In the center of the shield is a small Coat of Arms of the United States, reflecting Wisconsin's loyalty to the Union. At the base, a horn of plenty portrays abundance and blessing, while a triangle of 13 lead ingots shows forth mineral prosperity, and the 13 original States. Above the shield is a badger, the state animal. A banner above the badger proclaims Wisconsin's State Motto, "Forward." 13 stars undergird the Seal, which bears the words on its outer border: GREAT SEAL OF THE STATE OF WISCONSIN.[2]

State Coat of Arms:
The State Coat of Arms is an integral part of the State Seal as also the State Flag.

State Flag:
The State Flag is an integral part of the State Seal. In 1979, the word WISCONSIN and the date of her statehood, 1848, were inserted in white letters and numbers, above and below the official Coat of Arms, respectively, by the Legislature.[3]

State Song:
"On, Wisconsin!" Its music was composed by William T. Purdy in 1909. The State Song was officially adopted in 1959.[4]

First "Christian Heritage Week:" September 20-26, 1992, proclaimed by the Governor.

Of Historic Interest:
Robert M. La Follette (1855-1925) was chosen by the citizens of Wisconsin as their greatest hero in the Hall of Fame. The Wisconsin Legislature passed this Memorial Resolution:

Chapter 410, Laws of 1925
An Act

Section 1. Robert M. La Follette is hereby designated as one of the deceased residents of Wisconsin of historic renown worthy of the national commendation of having their statues placed in the old hall of the House of Representatives now generally known as the Hall of Fame, or as Statuary Hall, in the national capitol.

Section 2. The Governor is hereby authorized and directed to have placed in the said hall a statue of Robert M. La Follette.

La Follette was Governor of Wisconsin, U.S. Senator and a candidate for the presidency. Senator La Follette made this statement:

Evil and corruption thrive in the dark. Many, if not most of the arts of legal dishonesty which have made scandalous the proceedings of Congress and State legislature, could never have reached the first stage had they not been caused and properly consummated in secret conferences, secret caucuses, secret sessions of committees and then carried through the legislative body with little or no discussion.

At his death, the following words appeared in *La Follette's Magazine*:

Wisconsin mourns the death of its most illustrious son, its Senior Senator, Robert Marion La Follette. La Follette and Wisconsin are inseparable in the minds of the American people. This State has had other great leaders, men of ability and vision. No other of its sons, however, influenced so profoundly the history of the State and the Nation.

ESTHER HOBART MORRIS 1813-14
1902

*After the Original Bronze Sculpture of Esther Hobart Morris in the
Hall of Fame, U.S. Capitol, Washington, D.C.*

227

WYOMING
(from the Indian, "end of the plains")

The Preamble to the Constitution of the State of Wyoming states that, *We the people of the State of Wyoming, grateful to God for our civil, political and religious liberties, and desiring to secure them to ourselves and perpetuate them to our posterity, do ordain and establish this Constitution.*

Wyoming joined the Union on July 10, 1890 as the 44th State.

State Capital: Cheyenne.

State Insignia:
The Bucking Horse and Rider.

State Seal:
The two dates on the Great Seal, 1869 and 1890, commemorate the organization of the Territorial government and Wyoming's admission into the Union. The woman in the center holds a banner proclaiming "Equal Rights," Wyoming having been the first government to grant equal civil and political rights to women. The male figures typify the livestock and mining industries of the State. Upon a five-pointed star the number "44" appears, being the number of admission into the Union. On top of the pillars rest lamps from which burn the Light of Knowledge. Scrolls encircling the two pillars bear the words "Oil," "Mines," "Livestock," and "Grain," four of Wyoming's major industries.[1]

State Flag:
Red Border: The red border is symbolic of the blood of the pioneers shed in giving their lives to establish Christianity, preceding civilization.

Blue Area: The blue area, which is found in the bluest blue of the Wyoming skies and the distant mountains, has throughout the ages been symbolic of fidelity, justice and strength.

White Area: White is a symbol of purity and righteousness over Wyoming.

Heart of the Flag: The Great Seal of the State of Wyoming is the heart of the flag.

Bison: The bison represents the animal of the plains.

The Wyoming State Flag was designed in 1916 by Mrs. Verna Keyes of Casper, Wyoming.[2]

First "Christian Heritage Week:" November 1-7, 1998, proclaimed by the Governor.

Of Historic Interest:
Quoted from the program for the Unveiling Ceremonies of the statue of **Esther Hobart Morris (1814-1902),** Wyoming's greatest heroine in the Hall of Fame, is this tribute:

Much of the history of the American people in the expansive nineteenth century is recorded in the life of Esther Hobart Morris. Born of New England stock in New York in 1814, she lived successively in New York, Illinois and Wyoming, mirroring the migration of New Englanders across the northern United States. In moving, New Englanders carried with them to the far places of the continent a penchant for reform. This New England preoccupation with individual dignity touched Esther Hobart Morris early. Before she was twenty, she defied those threatening to burn a Baptist church because it was the site of meetings dedicated to the abolition of slavery. Later, as a successful business woman in her own right, she went to Illinois to settle the estate of her husband, Artemus Slack, a civil engineer. She found that, under the law, even a woman of demonstrated capability was treated, with respect to her property, almost as a minor. The difficulties she encountered in settling her husband's estate seemingly dedicated her to the freeing of women from such legal disabilities.

One of the greatest of these, of course, was the denial of the right to vote. In moving with her second husband, John Morris, an Illinois merchant, to the far reaches of the great plains in 1869, Esther Morris was to have opportunity in a newly created territory to assist in striking this particular shackle. Mrs. Morris and her family arrived at South Pass in time to take part in the election of the first legislators for the Wyoming Territory. During the campaign, she organized a tea party for the 40 or so electors and the two candidates for the first territorial legislature. To both, she put the question of women vote. As the successful candidate was to write in later years: "Of course, we both pledged ourselves to introduce a women vote bill, and received the applause of all present." Whatever the force of the promise secured, Colonel William Bright, the successful candidate, introduced the bill. It passed, and Governor John Campbell signed it on December 10, 1869, thus Wyoming's women were given the vote, the first women so recognized by any government in the world. In addition, Mrs. Morris was influential also in securing the passage of bills which permitted women in Wyoming to hold property in their own right, as well as legislation to correct other legal disabilities.

By her own performance in public office, she is entitled to more renown than that of the symbol of the passage of women vote. In 1870, she was appointed Justice of the Peace of the South Pass District, the first woman to hold judicial office in the modern world. She presided over the justice court for eight and a half months in a manner which commended her to her contemporaries and to those who have studied her record since.

Esther Morris lived out her long and active life in Wyoming. She died in Cheyenne in 1902. In the words of her son: "Her quest for truth in this world...ended. Her mission in life has been fulfilled. The work she did for the elevation of womankind will be told in the years to come, when the purpose will be better understood."

Another commentary on **Esther Hobart Morris'** life and work, entitled *Woman of the Century*, gives further insight into her ability as a judge:

> ...In 1869 she joined her husband and three sons in South Pass, Wyoming, and there she administered justice in a little court that became famous throughout the world. During her term of office, which covered a period of one year, Judge Morris tried about fifty cases, and no decision of hers was ever reversed by a higher court on appeal...

Wyoming's "Firsts:"

Wyoming had the first National Park, Yellowstone National Park, in 1872. It was the first national park in the world.

Wyoming was the first State to have a County Public Library System: The Laramie County Public Library System was organized in August, 1886.

By Act of Congress signed by President Benjamin Harrison in 1891, Shoshone National Forest became the first National Forest. Wyoming now has 9 national forests.

The first National Monument in northeastern Wyoming was designated by President Theodore Roosevelt in 1906.

Wyoming is a fisherman's paradise with 15,846 miles of fishing streams and 297,633 acres of fishing lakes. Nearly one million big game animals, including elk, deer, moose, antelope, bighorn sheep and mountain goats, winter in Wyoming. Black bear, grizzly bear and mountain lions are also found.

CHRISTIAN HERITAGE WEEK
- A History -

The first "Christian Heritage Week" took place in Albuquerque, New Mexico, November 10-16, 1991. *Citizens for Excellence in Education* and *Christian Heritage Ministries* worked hand-in-hand to make this week a true revival of the Christian principles, values and virtues upon which this nation under God was founded.

The event was extremely significant for our nation, as it is the first official proclamation signed by a State Governor, recognizing the Christian principles upon which our country was founded, and thus glorifying the God of our fathers and resuscitating the historic, biblical legacy which is ours.

More than one thousand Christian (and non-Christian) students, teachers, homeschoolers, parents and educators attended the seminar and slide presentations which I conducted. One non-Christian private school had two hundred and fifty students, teachers and parents in attendance. We were able to minister to numerous young people who had important and pressing questions pertaining to the true history of America, as opposed to its modern revised versions permeating our nation's school system. The breakthroughs for Christ were gratifying and encouraging. As our Lord Jesus says in John's gospel, Chapter 8 verses 31 and 32: "If you abide in my Word . . . the Truth shall make you free." And again: "Where the Spirit of the Lord is, there is liberty" (II Cor. 3:17).

Upon returning to Washington, God gave me the task to research each of the 50 State Constitutions at the International Law Library of the Library of Congress. The Preamble to all 50 State Constitutions glorifies God as the Father and sustainer of our liberties as Americans. All State Proclamations were then formulated, citing each State's Christian heritage, followed by the founding fathers' use of Scripture and their reliance upon Almighty God in prayer. These were then put into the hands of Christian Heritage Ministries' State Coordinators at God's appointed time for each Governor's signature, in order to celebrate their first "Christian Heritage Week."

Schools, both public and Christian, homeschoolers, ministries, churches, and the public-at-large are thus impacted with historic fact from the original documents of our founders.

Christian Heritage Ministries begins our youth-oriented, grassroots, community-involved "Christian Heritage Week" celebrations in early September of each academic school year, through May of the successive year, *excluding* summer holidays, Thanksgiving and Christmas weeks, when the schools of America are closed or preoccupied with holidays of major national significance. We have celebrated "Christian Heritage Week" on a state-wide level in 50 individual states to date. A number of these states have celebrated their fifth, sixth and seventh "Christian Heritage Week," to include Virginia, Pennsylvania, Kentucky, Indiana, South Dakota, New York, Mississippi, Illinois, Arkansas and Idaho, while Delaware celebrated her "Eighth Annual Christian Heritage Week," December 5-11, 1999.

We have given our slide presentations to many public schools, who have welcomed the exciting experience of learning about America's authentic history from original records. All 50 States in the Union have now celebrated a statewide "Christian Heritage Week" during the academic year.

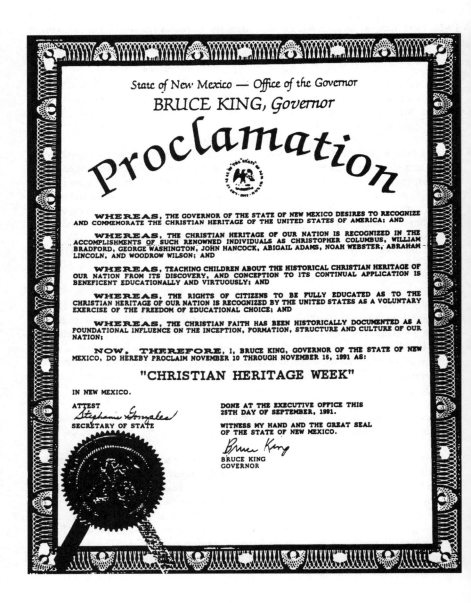

State of New Mexico — Office of the Governor

BRUCE KING, *Governor*

Proclamation

WHEREAS, THE GOVERNOR OF THE STATE OF NEW MEXICO DESIRES TO RECOGNIZE AND COMMEMORATE THE CHRISTIAN HERITAGE OF THE UNITED STATES OF AMERICA; AND

WHEREAS, THE CHRISTIAN HERITAGE OF OUR NATION IS RECOGNIZED IN THE ACCOMPLISHMENTS OF SUCH RENOWNED INDIVIDUALS AS CHRISTOPHER COLUMBUS, WILLIAM BRADFORD, GEORGE WASHINGTON, JOHN HANCOCK, ABIGAIL ADAMS, NOAH WEBSTER, ABRAHAM LINCOLN, AND WOODROW WILSON; AND

WHEREAS, TEACHING CHILDREN ABOUT THE HISTORICAL CHRISTIAN HERITAGE OF OUR NATION FROM ITS DISCOVERY, AND CONCEPTION TO ITS CONTINUAL APPLICATION IS BENEFICENT EDUCATIONALLY AND VIRTUOUSLY; AND

WHEREAS, THE RIGHTS OF CITIZENS TO BE FULLY EDUCATED AS TO THE CHRISTIAN HERITAGE OF OUR NATION IS RECOGNIZED BY THE UNITED STATES AS A VOLUNTARY EXERCISE OF THE FREEDOM OF EDUCATIONAL CHOICE; AND

WHEREAS, THE CHRISTIAN FAITH HAS BEEN HISTORICALLY DOCUMENTED AS A FOUNDATIONAL INFLUENCE ON THE INCEPTION, FORMATION, STRUCTURE AND CULTURE OF OUR NATION;

NOW, THEREFORE, I, BRUCE KING, GOVERNOR OF THE STATE OF NEW MEXICO, DO HEREBY PROCLAIM NOVEMBER 10 THROUGH NOVEMBER 16, 1991 AS:

"CHRISTIAN HERITAGE WEEK"

IN NEW MEXICO.

ATTEST
Stephanie Gonzales
SECRETARY OF STATE

DONE AT THE EXECUTIVE OFFICE THIS 25TH DAY OF SEPTEMBER, 1991.

WITNESS MY HAND AND THE GREAT SEAL OF THE STATE OF NEW MEXICO.

Bruce King
BRUCE KING
GOVERNOR

New Mexico was the first State in the Union to celebrate "Christian Heritage Week" with a Governer's signed proclamation, November 10-16, 1991.

PROCLAMATION

BY THE GOVERNOR

WHEREAS, the Preamble to the state Constitution says "We, the people of the state of Alabama, in order to establish justice, insure domestic tranquility, and secure the blessings of liberty to ourselves and to our posterity, invoking the favor and guidance of Almighty God, do ordain and establish the following Constitution and form of government for the state of Alabama;" and

WHEREAS, Benjamin Franklin, at the Constitutional Convention in 1787 said, "It is impossible to build an empire without our Father's aid. I believe the sacred writings which say that 'Except the Lord build the house, they labor in vain that build it'" (Psalm 127:1); and

WHEREAS, George Washington enunciated "animated alone by the pure spirit of Christianity, and conducting ourselves as the faithful subjects of our free government, we may enjoy every temporal and spiritual felicity;" and

WHEREAS, Thomas Jefferson, author of the Declaration of Independence, wrote: "Can the liberties of a nation be secure when we have removed the conviction that these liberties are the gift of God?" and

WHEREAS, James Madison, father of the U.S. Constitution, advocated "the diffusion of the light of Christianity in our nation" in his memorial and remonstrance; and

WHEREAS, Patrick Henry quoted Proverbs 14:34 for our nation: "Righteousness alone can exalt a nation, but sin is a disgrace to any people;" and

WHEREAS, George Mason, in his Virginia Declaration of Rights, forerunner to our U.S. Bill of Rights, affirmed: "That it is the mutual duty of all to practice Christian forbearance, love and charity toward each other;" and

WHEREAS, these and many other great men and women of America, giants in the structuring of American history, were Christian statesmen of caliber and integrity who did not hesitate to express their faith:

NOW, THEREFORE, I, Guy Hunt, Governor of the State of Alabama, do hereby proclaim March 14 through March 20, 1993, as

CHRISTIAN HERITAGE WEEK

in Alabama.

GIVEN UNDER MY HAND, and the Great Seal of the Governor's Office at the State House in the City of Montgomery on this the 23rd day of December, 1992.

GUY HUNT

STATE OF ARKANSAS
EXECUTIVE DEPARTMENT

PROCLAMATION

TO ALL TO WHOM THESE PRESENTS SHALL COME -- GREETINGS:

WHEREAS, The Preamble to the Constitution of the State of Arkansas states that "We the people of the State of Arkansas, *grateful to Almighty God for the privilege of choosing our own form of government, for our civil and religious liberty, and desiring to perpetuate its blessings and secure the same to ourselves and posterity,* do ordain and establish this Constitution."; and

WHEREAS, Benjamin Franklin, at the Constitutional Convention in 1787 stated: "It is impossible to build an empire without our Father's aid. I believe the sacred writings which say that 'Except the Lord build the house, they labor in vain that build it'" (Psalm 127:1); and

WHEREAS, George Washington enunciated: "animated alone by the pure spirit of Christianity, and conducting ourselves as the faithful subjects of our free government, we may enjoy every temporal and spiritual felicity"; and

WHEREAS, Thomas Jefferson, author of the Declaration of Independence, wrote: "Can the liberties of a nation be secure when we have removed the conviction that these liberties are the gift of God?"; and

WHEREAS, James Madison, father of the U.S. Constitution, advocated "the diffusion of the light of Christianity in our nation" in his Memorial and Remonstrance; and

WHEREAS, Patrick Henry quoted Proverbs 14:34 for our nation: "Righteousness alone can exalt a nation, but sin is a disgrace to any people"; and

WHEREAS, George Mason, in his Virginia Declaration of Rights, forerunner to our U.S. Bill of Rights, affirmed: "That it is the mutual duty of all to practice Christian forbearance, love and charity towards each other"; and

WHEREAS, These, and many other truly great men and women of America, giants in the structuring of American history, were Christian statesmen of calibre and integrity who did not hesitate to express their faith;

NOW, THEREFORE, I, Mike Huckabee, Acting Governor of the State of Arkansas, do proclaim **February 27th** through **March 5th, 1994**, as:

CHRISTIAN HERITAGE WEEK

in the State of Arkansas.

IN WITNESS WHEREOF, I have hereunto set my hand and caused the Great Seal of the State of Arkansas to be affixed at the Capitol in Little Rock on this 1st day of February in the year of our Lord nineteen hundred and ninety-four.

_____
ACTING GOVERNOR

_____
SECRETARY OF STATE

234

STATE OF COLORADO

Bill Owens
Governor

HONORARY PROCLAMATION

CHRISTIAN HERITAGE WEEK
October 10-16, 1999

WHEREAS, the preamble to the Constitution of the State of Colorado states that "We, the people of Colorado, with profound reverence for the Supreme Ruler of the Universe, in order to form a more independent and perfect government; establish justice; insure tranquility; provide for the common defense; promote the general welfare and secure the blessings of liberty to ourselves and our posterity, for ordain and establish this Constitution for the State of Colorado; and

WHEREAS, George Washington enunciated: "animated alone by the pure spirit of Christianity, and conducting ourselves as the faithful subjects of our free government, we may enjoy every temporal and spiritual felicity"; and

WHEREAS, Thomas Jefferson, author of the Declaration of Independence, wrote: "Can the liberties of a nation be secure when we have removed the conviction that these liberties are the gift of God?";

Now Therefore, I, Bill Owens, Governor of the State of Colorado, do hereby proclaim October 10-16, 1999, as

CHRISTIAN HERITAGE WEEK

in the State of Colorado.

GIVEN under my hand and the Executive Seal of the State of Colorado, this twenty seventh day of April 1999

Bill Owens
Governor

235

STATE OF DELAWARE

STATEMENT
IN OBSERVANCE OF
CHRISTIAN HERITAGE WEEK

Whereas, our Nation was founded on the belief that religious freedom was an inherent right of all citizens; and

Whereas, the Constitution of the State of Delaware states that "Through Divine Goodness, all men have by nature the rights of worshipping and serving their Creator according to the dictates of their consciences..."; and

Whereas, Benjamin Franklin, at the Constitutional Convention in 1787 stated: "It is impossible to build an empire without our Father's aid. I believe the sacred writings which say that 'Except the Lord build the house, they labor in vain that build it'" (Psalm) 127:1); and

Whereas, George Washington enunciated: "animated alone by the pure spirit of Christianity, and conducting ourselves as the faithful subjects of our free government, we may enjoy every temporal and spiritual felicity"; and

Whereas, Thomas Jefferson, author of the Declaration of Independence, wrote: "Can the liberties of a nation be secure when we have removed the conviction that these liberties are the gift of God?"; and

Whereas, James Madison, father of the U.S. Constitution, advocated "the diffusion of the light of Christianity in our nation" in his Memorial and Remonstrance; and

Whereas, Patrick Henry quoted Provers 14:34 for our nation: "Righteousness alone can exalt a nation, but sin is a disgrace to any people"; and

Whereas, George Mason, in his Virginia Declaration of Rights, forerunner to our U.S. Bill of Rights, affirmed: "That it is the mutual duty of all to practice Christian forbearance, love and charity towards each other"; and

Whereas, these, and many other truly great men and women of America, giants in the structuring of American history, were Christian statesman of calibre and integrity who relied on their religious beliefs for guidance, strength and comfort.

Now, Therefore, We, Thomas R. Carper, Governor, and Ruth Ann Minner, Lieutenant Governor, of the State of Delaware, do hereby declare November 14-20, 1993, as:

CHRISTIAN HERITAGE WEEK

in the State of Delaware, and urge all citizens to recognize the importance of this event.

Thomas R. Carper, Governor

Ruth Ann Minner, Lieutenant Governor

Proclamation

WHEREAS, the Preamble to the Constitution of the State of Hawaii states, "We, the people of Hawaii, Grateful for Divine Guidance...;" and

WHEREAS, the State Motto, *"Ua mau ke ea o ka `aina i ka pono"* -- The Life of the Land is Perpetuated in Righteousness -- was first uttered by Queen Ke`opuolani as she was baptized into the Christian faith before her death in 1825; and

WHEREAS, King Kamehameha III reiterated his mother's dying words, *"Ua mau ke ea o ka `aina i ka pono,"* as he gave thanks to God at Kawaiaha`o Church for the return of his kingdom in 1843; and

WHEREAS, the first Hawaiian Christian, Henry Opukahai`a's zeal for Christ and love for the Hawaiian people inspired the first American Board mission to Hawaii in 1820; and

WHEREAS, amid much solemnity and rejoicing the remains of Henry Opukahai`a were returned to Hawaii in 1993, 175 years after his death in Connecticut, and were reinterred at Napo`opo`o, Kona, Hawaii; and

WHEREAS, the influence of Christianity helped to bring about medical aid, public health policies, public education, law and order, political stability and the principles of democracy to the Hawaiian Kingdom; and

WHEREAS, the founding fathers of the United States and many of the leaders who shaped the modern history of Hawaii readily acknowledged their Christian religious heritage as a guiding force in their daily lives and in the conduct of their professional and personal pursuits; and

WHEREAS, the Hawaii Association of Evangelicals has set aside a period in February, 1994, for activities and events to educate the public about the Christian roots of our country and our state; and

WHEREAS, this period -- designated as Christian Heritage Week -- has been chosen because it is between the birthdays of Presidents Lincoln and Washington, deeply religious leaders who drew great strength and inspiration from their Christian beliefs, and within this period also falls the anniversary of the death of Henry Opukahai`a, recognized as one of the pivotal persons in Hawaii's history;

NOW, THEREFORE, I, JOHN WAIHEE, Governor of the State of Hawaii, do hereby proclaim the period February 12 through February 22, 1994, to be

CHRISTIAN HERITAGE WEEK IN HAWAII

DONE at the State Capitol, in the Executive Chambers, Honolulu, State of Hawaii, this Thirtieth day of December, 1993.

STATE OF INDIANA

EXECUTIVE DEPARTMENT
INDIANAPOLIS

PROCLAMATION

Executive Order

TO ALL TO WHOM THESE PRESENTS MAY COME, GREETING:

WHEREAS, the Preamble to the Constitution of the State of Indiana states that "We, the people of the State of Indiana, grateful to Almighty God for the free exercise of the right to choose our own form of government, do ordain this Constitution;" and

WHEREAS, Benjamin Franklin, at the Constitutional Convention in 1787 stated: "It is impossible to build an empire without our Father's aid. I believe the sacred writings that say that 'Except the Lord build the house, they labor in vain that build it' (Psalm 127:1)"; and

WHEREAS, George Washington said: "animated alone by the pure spirit of Christianity, and conducting ourselves as the faithful subjects of our free government, we may enjoy every temporal and spiritual felicity"; and

WHEREAS, Thomas Jefferson, author of the Declaration of Independence, wrote: "Can the liberties of a nation be secure when we have removed the conviction that these liberties are the gift of God?"; and

WHEREAS, these, and many other truly great men and women of the United States, giants in the structuring of American history, were Christian statesmen of caliber and integrity who did not hesitate to express their faith;

NOW, THEREFORE, I, FRANK O'BANNON, Governor of the State of Indiana, do hereby proclaim the week of May 25 - 31, 1997 as

CHRISTIAN HERITAGE WEEK

in the State of Indiana.

IN TESTIMONY WHEREOF, I have hereunto set my hand and caused to be affixed the Great Seal of the State of Indiana at the Capitol in Indianapolis on this 10th day of February, 1997.

Frank O'Bannon

BY THE GOVERNOR: Frank O'Bannon
Governor of Indiana

ATTEST: Sue Anne Gilroy
Secretary of State

SF 18322R

State of Iowa

Executive Department

IN THE NAME AND BY THE AUTHORITY OF THE STATE OF IOWA
PROCLAMATION

WHEREAS, THE CONSTITUTION OF THE STATE OF IOWA STATES THAT "WE THE PEOPLE OF THE STATE OF IOWA, GRATEFUL TO THE SUPREME BEING FOR THE BLESSINGS HITHERTO ENJOYED, AND FEELING OUR DEPENDENCE ON HIM FOR A CONTINUATION OF THOSE BLESSINGS, DO ORDAIN AND ESTABLISH A FREE AND INDEPENDENT GOVERNMENT..." AND

WHEREAS, BENJAMIN FRANKLIN, AT THE CONSTITUTIONAL CONVENTION IN 1787 STATED: "IT IS IMPOSSIBLE TO BUILD AN EMPIRE WITHOUT OUR FATHER'S AID. I BELIEVE THE SACRED WRITINGS WHICH SAY THAT 'EXCEPT THE LORD BUILD THE HOUSE THE WORKERS LABOR IN VAIN THAT BUILD IT" (PSALM 127:1); AND

WHEREAS, GEORGE WASHINGTON ENUNCIATED, "ANIMATED ALONE BY THE PURE SPIRIT OF CHRISTIANITY, AND CONDUCTING OURSELVES AS THE FAITHFUL SUBJECTS OF OUR FREE GOVERNMENT, WE MAY ENJOY EVERY TEMPORAL AND SPIRITUAL FELICITY;" AND

WHEREAS, THOMAS JEFFERSON, AUTHOR OF THE DECLARATION OF INDEPENDENCE, WROTE: "CAN THE LIBERTIES OF A NATION BE SECURE WHEN WE HAVE REMOVED THE CONVICTION THAT THESE LIBERTIES ARE THE GIFT OF GOD?" AND

WHEREAS, JAMES MADISON, FATHER OF THE U.S. CONSTITUTION, ADVOCATED "THE DIFFUSION OF THE LIGHT OF CHRISTIANITY IN OUR NATION" IN HIS MEMORIAL REMONSTRANCE; AND

WHEREAS, PATRICK HENRY QUOTED PROVERBS 14:34 FOR OUR NATION: "RIGHTEOUSNESS ALONE CAN EXALT A NATION, BUT SIN IS A DISGRACE TO ANY PEOPLE;" AND

WHEREAS, GEORGE MASON, IN HIS VIRGINIA DECLARATION OF RIGHTS, FORERUNNER TO OUR U.S. BILL OF RIGHTS, AFFIRMED: "THAT IT IS THE MUTUAL DUTY OF ALL TO PRACTICE CHRISTIAN FOREBEARANCE, LOVE AND CHARITY TOWARD EACH OTHER:" AND

WHEREAS, THESE, AND MANY OTHER TRULY GREAT MEN AND WOMEN OF AMERICA, GIANTS IN THE STRUCTURING OF AMERICAN HISTORY, WERE CHRISTIAN STATESMEN OF CALIBER AND INTEGRITY WHO DID NOT HESITATE TO EXPRESS THEIR FAITH:

NOW, THEREFORE, I, TERRY E. BRANSTAD, GOVERNOR OF THE STATE OF IOWA, DO HEREBY PROCLAIM SEPTEMBER 20 - 26, 1998, AS

CHRISTIAN HERITAGE WEEK

IN TESTIMONY WHEREOF, I HAVE HEREUNTO SUBSCRIBED MY NAME AND CAUSED THE GREAT SEAL OF THE STATE OF IOWA TO BE AFFIXED. DONE AT DES MOINES THIS 10TH DAY OF MARCH IN THE YEAR OF OUR LORD ONE THOUSAND NINE HUNDRED NINETY-EIGHT.

GOVERNOR

ATTEST:

SECRETARY OF STATE

239

STATE OF KANSAS

PROCLAMATION
BY THE
GOVERNOR

TO THE PEOPLE OF KANSAS, GREETINGS:

WHEREAS, The Preamble to the Constitution of the State of Kansas states that, "We, the people of Kansas, *grateful to Almighty God* for our civil and religious privileges . . ."; and

WHEREAS, Benjamin Franklin, at the Constitutional Convention in 1787 stated: "It is impossible to build an empire without our Father's aid. I believe the sacred writings which say that 'Except the Lord build the house, they labor in vain that build it.'" (Psalm 127:1); and

WHEREAS, George Washington enunciated: "animated alone by the pure spirit of Christianity, and conducting ourselves as the faithful subjects of our free government, we may enjoy every temporal and spiritual felicity"; and

WHEREAS, Thomas Jefferson, author of the Declaration of Independence, wrote: "Can the liberties of a nation be secure when we have removed the conviction that these liberties are the gift of God?"; and

WHEREAS, James Madison, father of the U.S. Constitution, advocated "the diffusion of the light of Christianity in our nation" in his Memorial and Remonstrance; and

WHEREAS, Patrick Henry quoted Proverbs 14:34 for our nation: "Righteousness alone can exalt a nation, but sin is a disgrace to any people"; and

WHEREAS, George Mason in his Virginia Declaration of Rights, forerunner to our U.S. Bill of Rights, affirmed: "That it is the mutual duty of all to practice Christian forbearance, love and charity towards each other"; and

WHEREAS, these, and many other truly great men and women of America, giants in the structuring of American history, were Christian statesmen of calibre and integrity who did not hesitate to express their faith:

NOW, THEREFORE, I, BILL GRAVES, GOVERNOR OF THE STATE OF KANSAS, do hereby proclaim the week of April 23-29,1995 as

Christian Heritage Week

in Kansas, and urge that all citizens join in the observance.

DONE At the Capitol in Topeka under the Great Seal of the State this 2nd day of February, A.D. 1995

BY THE GOVERNOR: _____

Ron Thornburgh
Secretary of State

_____
Assistant Secretary of State

Proclamation

by

Paul E. Patton
Governor

of the

Commonwealth of Kentucky

To All To Whom These Presents Shall Come:

WHEREAS, The Preamble to the Constitution of the State of Kentucky states that "We the people of the Commonwealth of Kentucky, grateful to Almighty God for the civil, political and religious liberties we enjoy, and invoking the continuance of these blessings, do ordain and establish this Constitution"; and

WHEREAS, Benjamin Franklin, at the Constitutional Convention in 1787, stated, "It is impossible to build an empire without our Father's aid. I believe the sacred writings which say that Except the Lord build the house, they labor in vain that build it"; and

WHEREAS, George Washington enunciated, "Animated alone by the pure spirit of Christianity, and conducting ourselves as the faithful subjects of our free government, we may enjoy every temporal and spiritual felicity."; and

WHEREAS, Thomas Jefferson, author of the Declaration of Independence, wrote, "Can the liberties of a nation be secure when we have removed the conviction that these liberties are the gift of God?"; and

WHEREAS, Patrick Henry quoted Proverbs 14:34 for our nation, "Righteousness alone can exalt a nation, but sin is a disgrace to any people"; and

WHEREAS, These, and many other truly great men and women of America, giants in the structuring of American history, were Christian statesmen of calibre and integrity who did not hesitate to express their faith.

NOW, THEREFORE, I, PAUL E. PATTON, Governor of the Commonwealth of Kentucky, do hereby proclaim May 18 - 24, 1997, as

CHRISTIAN HERITAGE WEEK

in Kentucky.

DONE AT THE CAPITOL, in the City of Frankfort, this the 12th day of December, in the year of Our Lord One Thousand Nine Hundred Ninety-Six and in the 205TH year of the Commonwealth

PAUL E. PATTON
GOVERNOR

John Y. Brown III, Secretary of State

State of Louisiana

M. J. "Mike" Foster, Jr.
Governor

Proclamation

WHEREAS, the Preamble of the Constitution of the State of Louisiana states that "We, the people of Louisiana, grateful to Almighty God for the civil, political, economic and religious liberties we enjoy...and secure the blessings of freedom and justice to ourselves and our posterity, do ordain and establish this Constitution."; and

WHEREAS, Benjamin Franklin stated: "It is impossible to build an empire without our Father's aid. I believe the sacred writings which say that 'Except the Lord build the house, they labor in vain that build it'"; and

WHEREAS, George Washington enunciated: "animated alone by the pure spirit of Christianity, and conducting ourselves as the faithful subjects of our free government, we may enjoy every temporal and spiritual felicity"; and

WHEREAS, Thomas Jefferson wrote: "Can the liberties of a nation be secure when we have removed the conviction that these liberties are the gift of God?"; and

WHEREAS, James Madison, father of the U.S. Constitution, advocated "the diffusion of the light of Christianity in our nation" in his Memorial and Remonstrance; and

WHEREAS, Patrick Henry quoted Proverbs 14:34 for our nation: "Righteousness alone can exalt a nation, but sin is a disgrace to any people"; and

WHEREAS, George Mason, in his Virginia Declaration of Rights, affirmed: "That it is the mutual duty of all to practice Christian forbearance, love and charity towards each other"; and

WHEREAS, many Americans in the structuring of our history, were Christian statesmen of calibre and integrity who did not hesitate to express their faith.

NOW, THEREFORE, I, M.J. "MIKE" FOSTER, JR., Governor of the State of Louisiana, do hereby proclaim May 26 through June 1, 1996, as

CHRISTIAN HERITAGE WEEK

in the State of Louisiana.

In Witness Whereof, I have hereunto set my hand officially and caused to be affixed the Great Seal of the State of Louisiana, at the Capitol, in the City of Baton Rouge, on this the 22ND day of JANUARY A.D., 1996

Governor of Louisiana

Attest By
The Governor

Secretary of State

242

Proclamation

WHEREAS: The Preamble to the Constitution of the State of Minnesota states that "We the people of the State of Minnesota, grateful to God for our civil and religious liberty, and desiring to perpetuate its blessings and secure the same to ourselves and our posterity, do ordain and establish this Constitution"; and

WHEREAS: Benjamin Franklin, at the Constitutional Convention in 1787 stated: "It is impossible to build an empire without our Father's aid. I believe the sacred writings which say that 'Except the Lord build the house, they labor in vain that build it'" (Psalm 127:1); and

WHEREAS: George Washington enunciated, "animated alone by the pure spirit of Christianity, and conducting ourselves as the faithful subjects of our free government, we may enjoy every temporal and spiritual felicity; and

WHEREAS: Thomas Jefferson, author of the Declaration of Independence, wrote, "Can the liberties of a nation be secure when we have removed the conviction that these liberties are the gift of God?; and

WHEREAS: James Madison, father of the U.S. Constitution, advocated "the diffusion of the light of Christianity in our nation" in his Memorial and Remonstrance; and

WHEREAS: Patrick Henry quoted Proverbs 14:34 for our nation: "Righteousness alone can exalt a nation, but sin is a disgrace to any people"; and

WHEREAS: George Mason, in his Virginia Declaration of Rights, forerunner to our U.S. Bill of Rights, affirmed, "That it is the mutual duty of all to practice Christian forbearance, love and charity towards each other"; and

WHEREAS: These and many other truly great men and women of America, giants in the structuring of American history, were Christians who did not hesitate to express their faith;

NOW, THEREFORE I, ARNE H. CARLSON, Governor of the State of Minnesota, do hereby proclaim September 21-27, 1997 to be

Christian   Heritage   Week

in Minnesota.

IN WITNESS WHEREOF, I have hereunto set my hand and caused the Great Seal of the State of Minnesota to be affixed at the State Capitol this twenty-first day of September in the year of our Lord one thousand nine hundred and ninety-seven, and of the State the one hundred thirty-ninth.

_____
GOVERNOR

_____
SECRETARY OF STATE

STATE OF MISSISSIPPI

Office of the Governor

A PROCLAMATION
BY GOVERNOR
KIRK FORDICE

Whereas, the Constitution of the State of Mississippi states that "We the people of Mississippi in convention assembled, grateful to Almighty God, and invoking His blessing on our work, do ordain and establish this Constitution . . . no preference shall be given to by law to any religious sect or mode of worship; but the free enjoyment of all religious sentiments and the different modes of worship shall be held sacred. The rights hereby secured shall not be construed to justify acts of licentiousness injurious to morals or dangerous to the peace and safety of the State, or to exclude the Holy Bible from use in any public school of this State"; and

Whereas, at the Constitutional Convention in 1787, Benjamin Franklin stated, "It is impossible to build an empire without our Father's aid. I believe the sacred writings which say that 'Except the Lord build the house, they labor in vain that build it'" *(Psalm 127:1); and*

Whereas, George Washington enunciated: "animated along by the pure spirit of Christianity, and conducting ourselves as the faithful subjects of our free government, we may enjoy every temporal and spiritual felicity"; and

Whereas, Thomas Jefferson, author of the Declaration of Independence, wrote: "Can the liberties of a nation be secure when we have removed the conviction that these liberties are the gift of God?"; and

Whereas, James Madison, father of the U.S. Constitution, advocated "the diffusion of the light of Christianity in our nation" in his Memorial and Remonstrance; and

Whereas, Patrick Henry quoted Proverbs 14:34 for our nation: "Righteousness alone can exalt a nation, but sin is a disgrace to any people"; and

Whereas, George Mason, in his Virginia Declaration of Rights, forerunner to our U.S. Bill of Rights, affirmed: "That it is the mutual duty of all to practice Christian forbearance, love, and charity toward each other"; and

Whereas, these and many other truly great men and women of America, giants in the structuring of American history, were Christian statesmen of caliber and integrity, who did not hesitate to express their faith:

Now, therefore, I, Kirk Fordice, Governor of the State of Mississippi, hereby proclaim in the State of Mississippi, September 29 through October 5, 1996, as

CHRISTIAN HERITAGE WEEK

IN WITNESS WHEREOF, I have hereunto set my hand and caused the Great Seal of the State of Mississippi to be affixed.

DONE in the City of Jackson, January 10, 1996, in the two hundred and twentieth year of the United States of America.

KIRK FORDICE

GOVERNOR

244

Office of the Governor
State of Missouri

Proclamation

WHEREAS, the preamble of the Missouri Constitution states, "We the people of Missouri, with profound reverence for the Supreme Ruler of the Universe, and grateful for His goodness, do establish this Constitution for the better government of the State"; and

WHEREAS, Benjamin Franklin, at the Constitutional Convention in 1787, said, "It is impossible to build an empire without our Father's aid"; and

WHEREAS, George Washington was quoted as saying, "Animated alone by the pure spirit of Christianity, and conducting ourselves as the faithful subjects of our free government, we may enjoy every temporal and spiritual felicity"; and

WHEREAS, Thomas Jefferson wrote, "Can the liberties of a nation be secure when we have removed the conviction that these liberties are the gift of God?"; and

WHEREAS, these men, and many other great leaders of American history, were Christian patriots of caliber and integrity who did not hesitate to express their faith:

NOW, THEREFORE, I, MEL CARNAHAN, GOVERNOR OF THE STATE OF MISSOURI, do hereby proclaim May 2 – 8, 1999, to be

CHRISTIAN HERITAGE WEEK

in Missouri.

IN TESTIMONY WHEREOF, I have hereunto set my hand and caused to be affixed the Great Seal of the State of Missouri, in the City of Jefferson, this 12th day of January, 1999.

_____
Governor

Attest: _____
Secretary of State

Proclamation

WHEREAS,	The Preamble to the Constitution of the State of Nebraska states that "We, the people, grateful to Almighty God for our freedom, do ordain and establish the following declaration of rights and frame of government;" and
WHEREAS,	Benjamin Franklin, at the Constitutional Convention in 1787, stated: "It is impossible to build an empire without our Father's aid. I believe the sacred writings which say that 'Except the Lord build the house, they labor in vain that build it'" (Psalm 127:1); and
WHEREAS,	George Washington enunciated: "animated alone by the pure spirit of Christianity, and conducting ourselves as the faithful subjects of our free government, we may enjoy every temporal and spiritual felicity;" and
WHEREAS,	Thomas Jefferson, author of the Declaration of Independence, wrote: "Can the liberties of a nation be secure when we have removed the conviction that these liberties are the gift of God?;" and
WHEREAS,	James Madison, father of the U.S. Constitution, advocated "the diffusion of the light of Christianity in our nation" in his Memorial and Remonstrance; and
WHEREAS,	George Mason, in his Virginia Declaration of Rights, forerunner to our U.S. Bill of Rights, affirmed: "That it is the mutual duty of all to practice Christian forbearance, love and charity towards each other;" and
WHEREAS,	These and many other truly great men and women of America, giants in the structuring of American history, were Christian statesmen of caliber and integrity who did not hesitate to express their faith.
NOW, THEREFORE,	I, Mike Johanns, Governor of the State of Nebraska, DO HEREBY PROCLAIM the week of August 29th through September 4th, 1999, as
	CHRISTIAN HERITAGE WEEK
	in Nebraska, and I do hereby urge all citizens to take due note of the observance.
	IN WITNESS WHEREOF, I have hereunto set my hand, and cause the Great Seal of the State of Nebraska to be affixed this Seventh day of May, in the year of our Lord One Thousand Nine Hundred and Ninety-Nine.

Attest:

_____
Secretary of State

_____
Governor

STATE OF NEVADA

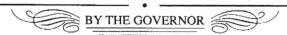

A Proclamation

BY THE GOVERNOR

Whereas, the Preamble to the Constitution of the State of Nevada states that "We the people of the State of Nevada, grateful to Almighty God for our freedom, in order to secure its blessings, insure domestic tranquility, and form a more perfect Government, do establish this Constitution"; and

Whereas, Benjamin Franklin, at the Constitutional Convention in 1787 stated: "It is impossible to build an empire without our Father's aid. I believe the sacred writings which say that "Except the Lord build the house, they labor in vain that build it"; (Psalm 127:1); and

Whereas, George Washington enunciated: "animated alone by the pure spirit of Christianity, and conducting ourselves as the faithful subjects of our free government, we may enjoy every temporal and spiritual felicity"; and

Whereas, Thomas Jefferson, author of the Declaration of Independence, wrote: "Can the liberties of a nation be secured when we have removed the conviction that these liberties are the gift of God"; and

Whereas, James Madison, father of the U.S. Constitution, advocated "the diffusion of the light of Christianity in our nation" in his Memorial Remonstrance; and

Whereas, Patrick Henry quoted Proverbs 14:34 for our nation: "Righteousness alone can exalt a nation, but sin is a disgrace to any people"; and

Whereas, George Mason, in his Virginia Declaration of Rights, forerunner to our U.S. Bill of Rights, affirmed: "That it is the mutual duty of all to practice Christian forbearance, love and charity towards each other"; and

Whereas, these, and many other truly great men and women of America, giants in the structuring of American history, were Christian statesmen of caliber and integrity who did not hesitate to express their faith;

NOW, THEREFORE, I, BOB MILLER, GOVERNOR OF THE STATE OF NEVADA, do hereby proclaim August 30 – September 6, 1997 as

"CHRISTIAN HERITAGE WEEK"
In The State Of Nevada

In Witness Whereof, I have hereunto set my hand and caused the Great Seal of the State of Nevada to be affixed at the State Capitol in Carson City, this ....21st day of ....July........ in the year of Our Lord one thousand nine hundred and ninety ....seven

....
Governor

Attest:...
Secretary of State

247

State of New York

Executive Chamber

The Constitution of the State of New York states that "We, the people of the State of New York, grateful to Almighty God for our Freedom, in order to secure its blessings, do establish this Constitution."

Benjamin Franklin at the Constitutional Convention in 1787 stated: "It is impossible to build an empire without our Father's aid. I believe the sacred writings which say that 'Except the Lord build the house, they labor in vain that build it." (Psalm 127:1)

George Washington enunciated: "animated alone by the pure spirit of Christianity and conducting ourselves as the faithful subjects of our free government, we may enjoy every temporal and spiritual felicity."

Thomas Jefferson, author of the Declaration of Independence, wrote: "Can the liberties of a nation be secure when we have removed the conviction that these liberties are the gift of God."

James Madison, father of the U.S. Constitution, advocated "the diffusion of the light of Christianity in our nation" in his Memorial and Remonstrance.

Patrick Henry quoted Proverbs 14:34 for our nation: "Righteousness alone can exalt a nation, but sin is a disgrace to any people."

George Mason, in his Virginia Declaration of Rights, forerunner to our U.S. Bill of Rights, affirmed: "That it is the mutual duty of all to practice Christian forbearance, love and charity towards each other."

These and many other truly great men and women of America, giants in the structuring of American history, were Christian statesmen of calibre and integrity who did not hesitate to express their faith.

NOW, THEREFORE, I, George E. Pataki, Governor of the State of New York, do hereby recognize April 13-19, 1997 as

CHRISTIAN HERITAGE WEEK

in the Empire State.

George E. Pataki

GOVERNOR

STATE OF OKLAHOMA

EXECUTIVE DEPARTMENT

Proclamation

Whereas, the Preamble to the Constitution of the State of Oklahoma states that *"Invoking the guidance of Almighty God, in order to secure and perpetuate the blessing of liberty,...we, the people of the State of Oklahoma, do ordain and establish this Constitution, "* and

Whereas, Benjamin Franklin, at the Constitutional Convention in 1787 stated: "It is impossible to build an empire without our Father's aid. I believe the sacred writings which say that "Except the Lord build the house, they labor in vain that build it" (Psalm 127:1); and

Whereas, George Washington enunciated: "animated alone by the pure spirit of Christianity, and conducting ourselves as the faithful subjects of our free government, we may enjoy every temporal and spiritual felicity: " and

Whereas, Thomas Jefferson, author of the Declaration of Independence, wrote: " Can the liberties of a nation be secure when we have removed the conviction that these liberties are the gift of God?" and

Whereas, James Madison, father of the U.S. Constitution, advocated "the diffusion of the light of Christianity in our nation" in his Memorial and Remonstrance; and

Whereas, Patrick Henry quoted proverbs 14:34 for our nation: "Righteousness alone can exalt a nation, but sin is a disgrace to any people;" and

Whereas, George Mason, in his Virginia Declaration of Rights, forerunner to our U.S. Bill of Rights, affirmed: "That it is the mutual duty of all to practice Christian forbearance, love and charity towards each other," and

Whereas, these, and many other truly great men and women of America, giants in the structuring of American history, were Christian statesmen of calibre and integrity who did not hesitate to express their faith,

Now, Therefore, I Frank Keating, Governor of the Great State of Oklahoma, do proclaim and announce April 2 through April 8, 1995 in Oklahoma as:

Christian Heritage Week

in the state of Oklahoma.

In Witness Whereof, I have hereunto set my hand and caused the Great Seal of the State of Oklahoma to be affixed.

Done at the Capitol, in the City of Oklahoma City, this 31st day of January, in the Year of Our Lord one thousand nine hundred and ninety five, and of the State of Oklahoma the eighty seventh year

ATTE̲ST̲

ASSISTANT SECRETARY OF STATE

GOVERNOR

249

Commonwealth of Pennsylvania

Governor's Office

PROCLAMATION

CHRISTIAN HERITAGE WEEK
March 9 - 15, 1997

WHEREAS, The Preamble to the Constitution of the State of Pennsylvania states that "We, the people of the Commonwealth of Pennsylvania, grateful to Almighty God for the blessings of civil and religious liberty, and humbly invoking His guidance, do ordain and establish this Constitution; and

WHEREAS, Benjamin Franklin, at the Constitutional Convention in 1787 stated: "It is impossible to build an empire without our Father's aid. I believe the sacred writings which say that 'Except the Lord build the house, they labor in vain that build it'"(Psalm 127:1); and

WHEREAS, George Washington enunciated: "animated alone by the pure spirit of Christianity, and conducting ourselves as the faithful subjects of our free government, we may enjoy every temporal and spiritual felicity;" and

WHEREAS, Thomas Jefferson, author of the Declaration of Independence, wrote: "Can the liberties of a nation be secure when we have removed the conviction of these liberties are the gift of God?" and

WHEREAS, James Madison, father of the U.S. Constitution, advocated "the diffusion of the light of Christianity in our nation" in his Memorial and Remonstrance; and

WHEREAS, Patrick Henry quoted Proverbs 14:34 for our nation: "Righteousness alone can exalt a nation, but sin is a disgrace to any people;" and

WHEREAS, George Mason, in his Virginia Declaration of Rights, forerunner of our U.S. Bill of Rights, affirmed: "That it is the mutual duty of all to practice Christian forbearance, love and charity towards each other;" and

WHEREAS, these and many other truly great men and women of America, giants in the structuring of American history were Christian statesmen of calibre and integrity who did not hesitate to express their faith.

THEREFORE, I, Tom Ridge, Governor of the Commonwealth of Pennsylvania, do hereby proclaim March 9 - 15, 1997, as CHRISTIAN HERITAGE WEEK in Pennsylvania.

GIVEN under my hand and the Seal of the Governor, at the City of Harrisburg, on this twentieth day of February in the year of our Lord one thousand nine hundred and ninety-seven and of the Commonwealth the two hundred and twenty-first.

Tom Ridge

TOM RIDGE
Governor

250

State of Rhode Island and Providence Plantations

GUBERNATORIAL PROCLAMATION

Whereas, The Constitution of the State of Rhode Island states that, "We the people of the State of Rhode Island and Providence Plantations, grateful to almighty God for the civil and religious liberty which He hath so long permitted us to enjoy, and looking to Him for a blessing upon our endeavors to secure and to transmit the same unimpaired to succeeding generations, do ordain and establish this constitution of government;" and,

Whereas, Benjamin Franklin, at the Constitutional Convention in 1787 stated: "It is impossible to build an empire without our Father's aid. I believe the sacred writings which say that 'Except the Lord build the house, they labor in vain that build it" (Psalm 127:1); and,

Whereas, George Washington enunciated: "Animated alone by the pure spirit of Christianity, and conducting ourselves as the faithful subjects of our free government, we may enjoy every temporal and spiritual felicity"; and,

Whereas, Thomas Jefferson, author of the Declaration of Independence, wrote: "Can the liberties of a nation be secure when we have removed the conviction that these liberties are the gift of God?"; and,

Whereas, James Madison, father of the U.S. Constitution, advocated "the diffusion the light of Christianity in our nation'"in his Memorial and Remonstrance; and,

Whereas, Patrick Henry quoted Proverbs 14:34 for our nation: "Righteousness alone can exalt a nation, but sin is a disgrace to any people"; and,

Whereas, George Mason, in his Virginia Declaration of Rights, forerunner to our U.S. Bill of Rights, affirmed: "That it is the mutual day of all to practice Christian forbearance, love and charity towards each other"; and,

Whereas, These, and many other truly great men and women of America, giants in the structuring of American history, were Christian statesmen of calibre and integrity who did not hesitate to express their faith;

NOW, THEREFORE, I, LINCOLN ALMOND, GOVERNOR OF THE STATE OF RHODE ISLAND AND PROVIDENCE PLANTATIONS, DO HEREBY PROCLAIM,

September 19 - 25, 1999
as
Christian Heritage Week

in the State of Rhode Island and encourage all of its citizens to join me in recognizing the importance of this week for all Christians.

In recognition whereof I have hereby set my hand and caused the Seal of the State of Rhode Island and Providence Plantations to be hereunto affixed this 19th day of September, 1999.

Lincoln Almond
Governor

James R. Langevin
Secretary of State

251

PROCLAMATION BY
GOVERNOR CARROLL A. CAMPBELL, JR.
ON
CHRISTIAN HERITAGE WEEK

WHEREAS, the Constitution of the State of South Carolina states that "All political power is vested in and derived from the people only, therefore, they have the right at times to modify their form of government" and that "The general assembly shall make no law respecting an establishment of religion or prohibiting the free exercise thereof..."; and

WHEREAS, Benjamin Franklin, at the Constitutional Convention in 1787 stated: "It is impossible to build an empire without our Father's aid. I believe the sacred writings which say that 'Except the Lord build the house, they labor in vain that build it" (Psalm 127:1); and

WHEREAS, George Washington enunciated: "animated alone by the pure spirit of Christianity, and conducting ourselves as the faithful subjects of our free government, we enjoy every temporal and spiritual felicity"; and

WHEREAS, Thomas Jefferson, author of the Declaration of Independence, wrote: "Can the liberties of a nation be secure when we have removed the conviction that these liberties are the gift of God?"; and

WHEREAS, James Madison, father of the U.S. Constitution, advocated "the diffusion of the light of Christianity in our nation" in his Memorial and Remonstrance; and

WHEREAS, Patrick Henry quoted Proverbs 14:34 for our nation: "Righteousness alone can exalt a nation, but sin is a disgrace to any people"; and

WHEREAS, George Mason, in his Virginia Declaration of Rights, forerunner to our U.S. Bill of Rights, affirmed: "That it is the mutual duty of all to practice Christian forbearance, love and charity towards each other"; and

WHEREAS, these, and many other truly great men and women of America, giants in the structuring of American history, were Christian statesmen of calibre and integrity who did not hesitate to express their faith.

NOW, THEREFORE, I, Carroll A. Campbell, Jr., Governor of the state of South Carolina, do hereby proclaim May 8-14, 1994 as

CHRISTIAN HERITAGE WEEK

in South Carolina.

Carroll A. Campbell, Jr.
Governor

State of South Carolina
Office of the Governor

252

Executive Proclamation
State of South Dakota
Office of the Governor

WHEREAS, The Preamble to the Constitution of the State of South Dakota states that "We, the people of South Dakota, grateful to Almighty God for our civil and religious liberties...and preserve to ourselves and to our posterity the blessings of liberty...;" and,

WHEREAS, Benjamin Franklin, at the Constitutional Convention in 1787 stated: "It is impossible to build an empire without our Father's aid. I believe the sacred writings which say that 'Except the Lord build the house, they labor in vain that built it'" (Psalm 127:1); and,

WHEREAS, George Washington enunciated: "Animated alone by the pure spirit of Christianity, and conducting ourselves as the faithful subjects of our free government, we may enjoy every temporal and spiritual felicity;" and,

WHEREAS, Thomas Jefferson, author of the Declaration of Independence, wrote: "Can the liberties of a nation be secure when we have removed the conviction that these liberties are the gift of God?;" and,

WHEREAS, James Madison, father of the U.S. Constitution, advocated "the diffusion of the light of Christianity in our nation" in his Memorial and Remonstrance; and,

WHEREAS, Patrick Henry quoted Proverbs 14:34 for our nation: "Righteousness alone can exalt a nation, but sin is a disgrace to any;" and,

WHEREAS, George Mason, in his Virginia Declaration of Rights, forerunner to our U.S. Bill of Rights, affirmed: "That it is the mutual duty of all to practice Christian forbearance, love and charity toward each other;" and,

WHEREAS, These, and many other truly great men and women of America, giants in the structuring of American history, were Christian statesmen of caliber and integrity who did not hesitate to express their faith:

NOW, THEREFORE, I, WILLIAM J. JANKLOW, Governor of the State of South Dakota, do hereby proclaim November 5 through November 11, 1995, as

CHRISTIAN HERITAGE WEEK

in South Dakota.

IN WITNESS WHEREOF, I have hereunto set my hand and caused to be affixed the Great Seal of the State of South Dakota, in Pierre, the Capital City, this Fourteenth Day of June, in the Year of Our Lord, Nineteen Hundred and Ninety-Five.

WILLIAM J. JANKLOW, GOVERNOR

ATTEST:

JOYCE HAZELTINE, SECRETARY OF STATE

253

STATE OF TENNESSEE

PROCLAMATION

BY THE GOVERNOR

WHEREAS, the Constitution of the State of Tennessee states that "All power is inherent in the people, and all free governments are founded on their authority, and instituted for their peace, safety, and happines...That all men have a natural and indefeasible right to worship Almighty God according to the dictates of their own conscience; that no man can of right be compelled to attend, erect, or support any place of worship, or to maintain any minister against his consent..."; and

WHEREAS, Benjamin Franklin, at the Constitutional Convention in 1787 stated: "It is impossible to build an empire without our Father's aid. I believe the sacred writings which say that 'Except the Lord build the house, they labor in vain that build it' (Psalm 127:1); and

WHEREAS, George Washington enunciated: "animated alone by the pure spirit of Christianity, and conducting ourselves as the faithful subjects of our free government, we may enjoy every temporal and spiritual felicity;" and

WHEREAS, Thomas Jefferson, author of the Declaration of Independence, wrote: "Can the liberties of a nation be secure when we have removed the conviction that these liberties are the gift of God?" and

WHEREAS, James Madison, father of the U.S. Constitution, advocated "the diffusion of the light of Christianity in our nation" in his Memorial and Remonstrance; and

WHEREAS, Patrick Henry quoted Proverbs 14:34 for our nation: "Righteousness alone can exalt a nation, but sin is a disgrace to any people;" and

WHEREAS, George Mason, in his Virginia Declaration of Rights, forerunner to our U.S. Bill of Rights, affirmed: "that it is the mutual duty of all to practice Christian forbearance, love and charity towards each other"; and

WHEREAS, these, and many other truly great men and women of America, giants in the structuring of American history, were Christian statesmen of calibre and integrity who did not hesitate to express their faith;

NOW THEREFORE, I, Ned McWherter, as Governor of the State of Tennessee do hereby proclaim August 29 through September 4, 1993, as

CHRISTIAN HERITAGE WEEK

in Tennessee and urge all citizens to join me in this worthy observance.

IN WITNESS WHEREOF, I HAVE HEREUNTO SET MY HAND AND CAUSED THE GREAT SEAL OF THE STATE OF TENNESSEE TO BE AFFIXED AT NASHVILLE ON THIS 21ST DAY OF JUNE, 1993.

_____
GOVERNOR

_____
SECRETARY OF STATE

254

CERTIFICATE of RECOGNITION

By virtue of the authority vested by the Constitution in the Governor of the
Commonwealth of Virginia, there is hereby officially recognized:

THE 7TH ANNUAL CHRISTIAN HERITAGE WEEK

WHEREAS, the Constitution of Virginia states, "That religion or the duty which we owe to our Creator, and the manner of discharging it, can be directed only by reason and conviction; not by force or violence; and therefore all men are equally entitled to the free exercise of religion, according to the dictates of conscience"; and

WHEREAS, George Washington, our nation's first President, proclaimed that we are, "animated alone by the pure spirit of Christianity, and conducting ourselves as the faithful subjects of our free government, we may enjoy every temporal and spiritual felicity"; and

WHEREAS, Thomas Jefferson, author of the *Declaration of Independence* posed the question, "Can the liberties of a nation be secure when we have removed the conviction that these liberties are the gift of God?"; and

WHEREAS, James Madison, who is known as the father of the *Constitution of the United States of America*, advocated "the diffusion of the light of Christianity in our nation" in his *Memorial and Remonstrance*; and

WHEREAS, Patrick Henry quoted Proverbs 14:34 for our nation, saying, "Righteousness alone can exalt a nation, but sin is a disgrace to any people"; and

WHEREAS, George Mason affirmed in the Virginia *Declaration of Rights*, forerunner to our United States *Bill of Rights*, "That it is the mutual duty of all to practice Christian forbearance, love and charity towards each other"; and

WHEREAS, these Virginians, and many other truly great men and women of America, were statesmen of caliber and integrity, giants in the structuring of American government and history and men unafraid to express their Christian faith in Almighty God;

NOW, THEREFORE, I, James S. Gilmore, III, do hereby recognize March 5-11, 2000 as **THE 7TH ANNUAL CHRISTIAN HERITAGE WEEK** in the **COMMONWEALTH OF VIRGINIA**, and I call this observance to the attention of all our citizens.

_____
Governor

_____
Secretary of the Commonwealth

255

The State of Wisconsin

OFFICE OF THE GOVERNOR

A PROCLAMATION

WHEREAS, the Preamble to the Constitution of the State of Wisconsin states that "We, the people of Wisonsin, grateful to Almighty God for our freedom, domestic tranquility and promote the general welfare, do establish this Constitution"; and

WHEREAS, Benjamin Franklin, at the Constitutional Convention in 1787 stated: "It is impossible to build an empire without our Father's aid. I believe the sacred writings which say that 'Except the Lord build the house, they labor in vain that build it'" (Psalm 127:1); and

WHEREAS, George Washington enunciated: "animated alone by the pure spirit of Christianity, and conducting ourselves as the faithful subjects of our free government, we may enjoy every temporal and spiritual felicity"; and

WHEREAS, Thomas Jefferson, author of the Declaration of Independence, wrote: "Can the liberties of a nation be secure when we have removed the conviction that these liberties are the gift of God?"; and

WHEREAS, James Madison, father of the U.S. Constitution, advocated "the diffusion of the light of Christianity in our nation" in his Memorial and Remonstrance; and

WHEREAS, Patrick Henry quoted Proverbs 14:34 for our nation: "Righteousness alone can exalt a nation, but sin is a disgrace to any people"; and

WHEREAS, George Mason, in his Virginia Declaration of Rights, forerunner to our U.S. Bill of Rights, affirmed: "That it is the mutual duty of all to practice Christian forbearance, love and charity towards each other"; and

WHEREAS, these, and many other truly great men and women of America, giants in the structuring of American history, were Christian statesmen of calibre and integrity who did not hesitate to express their faith;

NOW, THEREFORE, I, TOMMY G. THOMPSON, Governor of the State of Wisconsin, do hereby proclaim October 3 through October 9, 1993

CHRISTIAN HERITAGE WEEK

in the State of Wisconsin, and I commend this observance to all citizens.

IN TESTIMONY WHEREOF, I have hereunto set my hand and caused the Great Seal of the State of Wisconsin to be affixed. Done at the Capitol in the City of Madison this twentieth day of September in the year one thousand nine hundred ninety-three.

TOMMY G. THOMPSON

By the Governor:

DOUGLAS LA FOLLETTE
Secretary of State

256

Governor's Proclamation

THE PREAMBLE TO THE CONSTITUTION OF THE STATE OF WYOMING *states: "We, the people of the State of Wyoming, grateful to God for our civil, political, and religious liberties, and desiring to secure them to ourselves and perpetuate them to our posterity, do ordain and establish this Constitution."*

THE DECLARATION OF INDEPENDENCE OF THE UNITED STATES OF AMERICA *states: "We hold these truths to be self-evident. That all men are created equal, that they are endowed by their Creator with certain unalienable rights, that among these are life, liberty and the pursuit of happiness."*

ON JUNE 21, 1776, JOHN ADAMS *wrote, "Statesmen, my dear Sir, may plan and speculate for liberty, but it is religion and morality alone, which can establish the principles upon which freedom can securely stand."*

GEORGE WASHINGTON *enunciated, "Animated alone by the pure spirit of Christianity, and conducting ourselves as the faithful subjects of our free government, we may enjoy temporal and spiritual felicity."*

THOMAS JEFFERSON, *author of the Declaration of Independence, wrote, "Can the liberties of a nation be secure when we have removed the conviction that these liberties are the gift of God?"*

JAMES MADISON, *father of the U.S. Constitution, advocated "the diffusion of the light of Christianity" in our nation" in his Memorial and Remonstrance.*

PATRICK HENRY *quoted Proverbs 14:34 for our nation: "Righteousness alone can exalt a nation, but sin is a disgrace to any people."*

GEORGE MASON *in his Virginia Declaration of Rights, forerunner to our Bill of Rights, affirmed "That it is the mutual duty of all to practice Christian forbearance, love and charity toward each other."*

THESE, AND MANY OTHER *truly great men and women of America, giants in the structuring of American history, were Christian statesmen of caliber and integrity who did not hesitate to express their faith.*

FOR THESE SIGNIFICANT REASONS, I, JIM GERINGER, *Governor of the State of Wyoming, do hereby proclaim October 31 through November 6, 1999 to be*

"CHRISTIAN HERITAGE WEEK"

in Wyoming.

IN WITNESS WHEREOF, *I have hereunto set my hand and caused the Great Seal of the State of Wyoming to be affixed this 23rd day of September, 1999.*

_____
Governor

ATTEST:

_____
Secretary of State

257

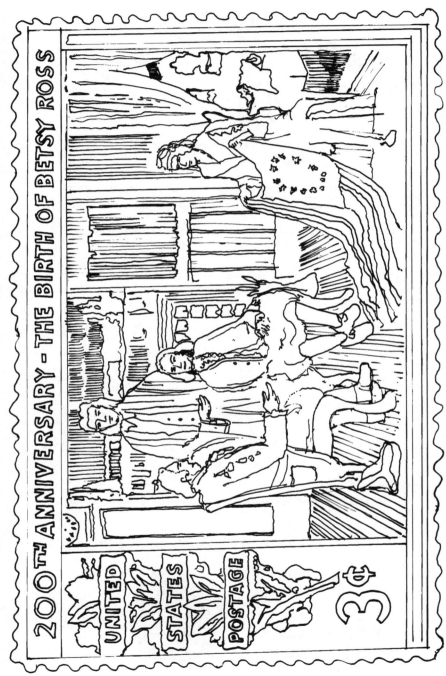

The 200th Anniversary of the Birth of Betsy Ross Commemorative Postage Stamp. Bureau of Engraving and Printing, Washington, D.C.

OUR FLAG

How did the United States Flag Originate? — Betsy Ross and the Stars and Stripes:
At 239 Arch Street in historic Philadelphia, stands the restored colonial home of **Betsy Ross.** Here she received a committee from Continental Congress comprised of **George Washington, Colonel George Ross and Robert Morris,** who commissioned her to make the first American flag in 1776. It was Washington's desire to have a six-pointed star. However, when Betsy Ross, with a deft snip of her scissors, cut a perfect, five-pointed star for him, the committee, unanimously impressed, opted for five points in each star of our star-spangled banner.

The large Ross family consisted of seven children. Betsy's family Bible is on permanent display in the Ross home, showing forth in whom she and her family placed their trust. Betsy Ross and her family were members of Christ Church — "the nation's church" — in Philadelphia. A plaque in that church designates her family pew, not far from George and Martha Washington's pew, together with a depiction of the original 13-star flag, and the inscription:

Here Worshipped Mrs. Elizabeth Ross
Who, Under the Direction of a
Committee of Continental Congress
Composed of:
George Washington
Robert Morris
and
George Ross
Was the Maker of the
First American Flag
1777

Francis Scott Key and the Star Spangled Banner:
On September 14, 1814, Christian Patriot, **Francis Scott Key,** wrote his heaven-inspired poem at an inn in Baltimore harbor, portraying America's flag — her foremost symbol, representing our origins, dependence upon Almighty God and the value system as a nation. Ever since he came ashore from a ship after watching the American flag fly triumphantly through the bombardment of Fort McHenry, his immortal poem has been cherished by Americans with the deepest patriotic devotion. It is interesting that many people are only familiar with the first stanza of this poem. However, the remaining stanzas clearly speak of the relationship of God to our nation and our dependence upon Him. It is here printed in its entirety:

The Star-Spangled Banner

O say! Can you see, by the dawn's early light,
What so proudly we hailed at the twilight's last gleaming?
Whose broad stripes and bright stars through the perilous fight,
O'er the ramparts we watched were so gallantly streaming?
And the rocket's red glare, the bomb bursting in air,
Gave proof through the night that our flag was still there.
O say, does that Star-Spangled Banner yet wave
O'er the land of the free and the home of the brave?

The Francis Scott Key Commemorative Postage Stamp.

260

On the shore, dimly seen through the mists of the deep,
Where the foe's haughty host in dread silence reposes,
What is that which the breeze, o'er the towering steep,
As it fitfully blows half conceals, half discloses?
Now it catches the gleam of the morning's first beam,
In full glory reflected now shines in the stream,
'Tis the Star-Spangled Banner–O Long may it wave
O'er the land of the free and the home of the brave!

And where is that band who so vauntingly swore,
That the havoc of war and the battle's confusion
A home and a Country should leave us no more?
Their blood has washed out their foul footsteps' pollution.
No refuge could save the hireling and slave
From the terror of flight or the gloom of the grave,
And the Star-Spangled Banner in triumph doth wave
O'er the land of the free and the home of the brave.

O thus be it ever when free men shall stand
Between their loved homes and war's desolation!
Blest with victory and peace may the heaven rescued land
Praise the Power that hath made and preserved us a nation!
Then conquer we must when our cause it is just
And this be our motto: "In God is our trust."
And the Star-Spangled Banner in triumph shall wave
O'er the land of the free and the home of the brave.

These magnificent words, depicting love of God and country, were adapted to the inspiring music of John Stafford Smith (c.1780).[1]

On March 3, 1931, an Act to make the Star-Spangled Banner the national anthem of the United States of America, was resolved by the Senate and House of Representatives in Congress assembled (36 U.S.C. Sec. 170).[2]

Millions of Americans throughout the ensuing years have paid homage to our flag — the Star-Spangled Banner, by singing the National Anthem, giving full expression to their love of Almighty God and their homeland.

Poems of Francis Scott Key[3]
Author of "The Star Spangled Banner"

On Reading Lines by Fawcett
On Revisiting Scenes of Early Life

So sings the world's fond slave! so flies the dream
Of life's gay morn; so sinks the meteor ray
Of fancy into darkness; and no beam
Of purer light shines on the wanderer's way.

So sings not he who soars on other wings
Than fancy lends him; whom a cheering faith
Warms and sustains, and whose freed spirit springs
To joys that bloom beyond the reach of death.

And thou would'st live again! again dream o'er
The wild and feverish visions of thy youth
Again to wake in sorrow, and deplore
Thy wanderings from the peaceful paths of truth!

Yet yield not to despair! be born again,
And thou shalt live a life of joy and peace,
Shall die a death of triumph, and thy strain
Be changed to notes of rapture ne'er to cease.

"All Things Are Yours."

I Corinthians 3:21

Behold the grant the King of kings
Hath to his subjects given:
"All things are yours," it saith; all things
That are in earth and heaven.

The saints are yours, to guide you home,
And bless you with their prayers;
The world is yours, to overcome
Its pleasures and its cares;

And life is yours, to give it all
To works of faith and love;
And death is yours, a welcome call
To higher joys above;

All present things are yours: whate'er
God's providence decreed.
Is from his treasures culled with care,
And sent to suit thy need;

And things to come are yours: and all
Shall ever ordered be,
To keep thee safe, whate'er befall,
And work for good to thee;

And Christ is yours — his sacrifice,
To speak your sins forgiven:
His righteousness the only price
That thou canst pay for heaven.

Thus God is yours — thus reconciled,
His love your bliss secures,
The Father looks upon the child
And saith, "All things are yours."

Efficacy of Prayer

"When I called upon thee thou heardest me, and enduedst
my soul with much strength." — Psalm ciii, 3

When troubles, wave on wave, assailed,
And fear my soul appalled,
I knew the Lord would rescue me,
And for deliverance called.

Still onward, onward came the flood;
Again I sought the Lord,

And prayed that he the waves would still
By his resistless word.

But still they rushing came; again
Arose my earnest prayer,
And then I prayed for faith and strength
Whate'er he willed, to bear.

Then his felt presence was my strength,
His outstretched arm was nigh;
My head he raised, my heart he cheered,
"Fear not," he said, "'tis I."

Strong in that strength, I rose above
The tempest's fierce alarms;
It drove me to a port of peace,
Within a Saviour's arms.

Life

If life's pleasures cheer thee,
Give them not thy heart,
Lest the gifts ensnare thee
From thy God to part:
His praises speak, his favor seek,
Fix there thy hopes' foundation;
Love him, and he shall ever be
The rock of thy salvation.

If sorrow e'er befall thee,
Painful though it be,
Let not fear appal thee:
To thy Saviour flee;
He, ever near, thy prayer will hear,
And calm thy perturbation;
The waves of woe shall ne'er o'erflow
The rock of thy salvation.

Death shall never harm thee,
Shrink not from his blow,
For thy God shall arm thee,
And victory bestow:
For death shall bring to thee no sting,
The grave no desolation;
'Tis gain to die, with Jesus nigh,
The rock of thy salvation.

Man

"The days of man are but as grass; for he flourisheth
as a flower of the field.
"For as soon as the wind goeth over it, it is gone, and
the place thereof shall know it no more.
"But the merciful goodness of the Lord endureth
forever and ever upon them that fear him, and his
righteousness upon children's children;
"Even upon such as keep his covenant and think upon
his commandments to do them.
"The Lord hath prepared his seat in heaven, and his
kingdom ruleth over all." — Psalm 103:15-19

Such are thy days — so shall they pass away —
As flowers that bloom at morn, at eve decay;
But then, there comes a life that knows no end —
Rich in unfading joys that far transcend
Thy highest thoughts or warmest wishes — given
To those whose days on earth have fitted them for heaven.

Home

O! Where can the soul find relief from its foes,
A shelter of safety, a home of repose?
Can earth's brightest summit, or deepest hid vale,
Give a refuge no sorrow nor sin can assail?
      No, no, there's no home!
There's no home on earth; the soul has no home.

Shall it leave the low earth, and soar to the sky,
And seek an abode in the mansions on high?
In the bright realms of bliss shall a dwelling be given,
And the soul find a home in the glory of heaven?
      Yes, yes, there's a home!
There's a home in high heaven: the soul has a home!

O! holy and sweet its rest shall be there,
Free forever from sin, from sorrow and care;
And the loud hallelujahs of angels shall rise
To welcome the soul to its home in the skies.
      Home, home, home of the soul!
The bosom of God is the home of the soul.

Hymn

Lord, with glowing heart I'd praise thee
For the bliss thy love bestows,
For the pardoning grace that saves me,
And the peace that from it flows.
Help, O God! my weak endeavor,
This dull soul to rapture raise;
Thou must light the flame, or never
Can my love be warmed to praise.

Praise, my soul, the God that sought thee,
Wretched wanderer, far astray;
Found thee lost, and kindly brought thee
From the paths of death away.

Praise, with love's devoutest feeling,
Him who saw thy guilt-born fear,
And, the light of hope revealing,
Bade the blood-stained cross appear.

Lord! this bosom's ardent feeling
Vainly would my lips express;
Low before thy foot-stool kneeling,
Deign thy suppliant's prayer to bless.
Let thy grace, my soul's chief treasure,
Love's pure flame within me raise;
And, since words can never measure,
Let my life show forth thy praise.

O say can you see, ~~through~~ by the dawn's early light,
What so proudly we hail'd at the twilight's last gleaming,
Whose broad stripes & bright stars through the perilous fight
O'er the ramparts we watch'd, were so gallantly streaming?
    And the rocket's red glare, the bomb bursting in air,
    Gave proof through the night that our flag was still there,
    O say does that star spangled banner yet wave
    O'er the land of the free & the home of the brave?

On the shore dimly seen through the ~~mists~~ of the deep,
    Where the foe's haughty host in dread silence reposes,
What is that which the breeze, o'er the towering steep,
    As it fitfully blows, half conceals, half discloses?
        Now it catches the gleam of the morning's first beam,
        In full glory reflected now shines in the stream,
    'Tis the star-spangled banner — O long may it wave
    O'er the land of the free & the home of the brave!

And where is that band who so vauntingly swore,
    That the havoc of war & the battle's confusion
A home & a Country should leave us no more?
    ~~Their~~ ~~blood~~
    — Their blood has wash'd out their foul footstep's pollution.
    No refuge could save the hireling & slave
    From the terror of flight or the gloom of the grave,
    And the star-spangled banner in triumph doth wave
    O'er the land of the free & the home of the brave.

O thus be it ever when freemen shall stand
    Between their lov'd home & the war's desolation!
Blest with vict'ry & peace may the heav'n rescued land
    Praise the power that hath made & preserv'd us a nation!
        Then conquer we must when our cause it is just,
        And this be our motto — "In God is our trust,"
    And the star-spangled banner in triumph shall wave
    O'er the land of the free & the home of the brave. —

The above piece is the Original Star Spangled Banner,
written on the back of an old letter, by my great uncle

The Original Star-Spangled Banner (Written on the Back of an Old
Letter) by Francis Scott Key

265

The Original Poem "On Reading Lines by Fawcett" (being "Born Again") by Francis Scott Key

Origins of the Pledge of Allegiance to the Flag

The Pledge of Allegiance to the Flag
I pledge allegiance to the flag of the United States of
America and to the Republic for which it stands, one nation
under God, indivisible, with liberty and justice for all.

On October 21, 1892, Francis Bellamy, a Minister of the Gospel who had been ordained in the *First Baptist Church of Little Falls,* New York, wrote a pledge of allegiance to America's flag — the Star-Spangled Banner.

I pledge allegiance *to my* flag and to the Republic for which it
stands, one nation, indivisible with liberty and justice for all.[4]

The pledge he wrote was first used at the dedication of the World's Fair grounds in Chicago on October 21, 1892, the 400th anniversary of the discovery of America, and has been recited from that day to this, with some changes, by school children throughout our land. Reverend Bellamy's original wording was altered slightly by the First and Second National Flag Conferences in 1923 and 1924 and his work was officially designated, as the Pledge of Allegiance to the Flag by Public Law 287, 79th Congress, approved December 28, 1945. On June 14, 1954, Flag Day, President Dwight D. Eisenhower signed into law House Joint Resolution 243, which added to the Pledge of Allegiance the compelling and meaningful words: under God.[5] This came about after Eisenhower and his wife had attended the Sunday, February 7, 1954, Lincoln Day Observance Service at the *New York Avenue Presbyterian Church* — the sermon topic, **"Under God,"** being preached by Pastor George Docherty, D.D. So moving are these lines, that they are here excerpted for the reader to assess:

> ...And where did all this come from? It has been with us so long, we have to recall it was brought here by the people who laid stress on the fundamentals. They called themselves Puritans because they wished to live the pure and noble life purged of all idolatry and enslavement of the mind, even by the church. They did not realize that in fleeing from tyranny and setting up a new life in a new world they were to be the fathers of a mighty nation.

> These fundamental concepts of life had been given to the world from Sinai, where the moral law was graven upon tables of stone, symbolizing the universal application to all men; and they came from the New Testament, where they heard in the words of Jesus of Nazareth the living Word of God for the world.

> This is the American way of life. Lincoln saw this clearly. History for him was the Divine Comedy, though he would not use that phrase. The providence of God was being fulfilled.

> Wherefore, he claims that it is under God that this nation shall know a new birth of freedom. And by implication, it is under God that "government of the people, by the people and for the people shall not perish from the earth." For Lincoln, since God was in His Heaven all must ultimately be right for his country...

> Russia claims to have liberty. You will never understand the

Communist mind until you realize this aberration of their judgment. Marx in his dialectic, makes it clear that the communist state is only an imperfect stage toward true socialism. When that day comes, the state will wither away and thus socialism will reign forever. Utopia will have dawned. Until that day there must be personal limitations. As the capitalist state limits freedom in the day of war, so must the workers of the world accept this form of restricted freedom. Besides, claims Marx, trouble arises when you give men their unrestricted freedom. Human freedom always proliferates into license and gives rise to greed and war. They might claim that their servitude is perfect freedom.

Again the Communists claim there is justice in Russia. They have their law courts. They have their elections with universal suffrage. When pressed to the point, they will admit there is really only one candidate because the people are so unanimous about that way of life.

They call their way of life "democratic." One of the problems statesmen find in dealing with Russia is one of semantics, of definition. Russia says she is democratic and we are Fascist; we claim to be democratic and call Russia communist.

What, therefore, is missing in the Pledge of Allegiance that Americans have been saying off and on since 1892, and officially since 1942? The one fundamental concept that completely and ultimately separates Communist Russia from the democratic institutions of this country. This was seen clearly by Lincoln. Under God this people shall know a new birth of freedom, and **"under God"** are the definitive words.

Now, Lincoln was not being original in that phrase. He was simply reminding the people of the basis upon which the Nation won its freedom in its Declaration of Independence. He went back to Jefferson as he did in a famous speech delivered at Independence Hall in Philadelphia on February 22, 1861, two years before the Gettysburg Address. "All the political sentiments I entertain have been drawn from the sentiments which originated and were given to the world from this hall. I have never had a feeling politically that did not spring from sentiments embodied in the Declaration of Independence."

Listen again to the fundamentals of this Declaration:

"We hold these truths to be self-evident, that all men are created equal, that they are endowed by their Creator with certain unalienable rights; that among these are life, liberty, and the pursuit of happiness..."

In Jefferson's phrase, if we deny the existence of the God who gave us life, how can we live by the liberty He gave us at the same time? This is a God-fearing nation. On our coins, bearing the imprint of Lincoln and Jefferson are the words "In God we trust." Congress is opened with prayer. It is upon the Holy Bible the President takes his oath of office. Naturalized citizens, when they take their oath of allegiance, conclude, solemnly, with the words "so help me God."

This is the issue we face today: A freedom that respects the rights of the minorities, but is defined by a fundamental belief in God. A way of life that sees man, not as the ultimate outcome of a mysterious concantenation of evolutionary process, but a sentient being created by God and seeking to know His will, and "Whose soul is restless till he rest in God...

The meaningful and compelling words: ***One nation under God,*** denoting dependence and reliance upon Almighty God, our Benefactor and Sustainer, were adapted from Abraham Lincoln's famed Gettysburg Address, where he describes America as "this nation under God."

The song, "Pledge of Allegiance to the Flag," composed by Irving Caesar, ASCAP, was sung for the first time on the floor of the House of Representatives on Flag Day, June 14, 1955, by the official Air Force choral group, the "Singing Sergeants," under the direction of Captain Robert L. Landers, AFRES, in special Flag Day ceremonies.[6]

Webster's New Twentieth Century Dictionary states that "to dip the flag" means "to salute by lowering the flag and immediately returning it to place. It is done in token of courtesy, welcome, or respect." The commentary goes on to explain that "to strike or lower the flag" means to "lower the flag as a sign of surrender; hence, to capitulate, to give up."

The Star-Spangled Banner has a proud Christian heritage. It was designed by a Christian patriot, George Washington, and first made by a Christian patriot, Betsy Ross, both of whom were members of Christ Church in Philadelphia. Our flag has been honored and stamped with America's national motto: ***In God is our Trust,*** both verbally and musically. It is thus the foremost symbol of a nation whose primary allegiance is to Almighty God, and whose people bow the knee to God alone; for, as the Pledge of Allegiance states: we are the One nation under God.

Flag Holidays

The flag should be displayed on all days, especially . . .

New Year's Day, January 1
Inauguration Day, January 20
Lincoln's Birthday, February 12
Washington's Birthday, third Monday in February
Easter Sunday, (variable)
Mother's Day, second Sunday in May
Armed Forces Day, third Saturday in May
Memorial Day (half-staff until noon), the last Monday in May
Flag Day, June 14
Independence Day, July 4
Labor Day, first Monday in September
Constitution Day, September 17
Columbus Day, second Monday in October
Navy Day, October 27
Veterans Day, November 11
Thanksgiving Day, fourth Thursday in November
Christmas Day, December 25

. . . such other days as may be proclaimed by the President of the United States: the birthdays of States (date of admission); and on State holidays.

The rules and customs presented herein are in accordance with the July 7, 1976 amendment to the Flag Code (Public Law 94, 344, 94th Congress, S.J. Res. 49).

ROOTED IN THE PAST
BUILDING IN THE PRESENT
REACHING TO THE FUTURE
FIRST BAPTIST CHURCH – 1829
LITTLE FALLS, NEW YORK

Reverend Francis Bellamy, Minister of the Gospel and Author of the Pledge of Allegiance to our Flag, pastored this Church.

"IN GOD WE TRUST"
— On America's Coins and Currency —

The following correspondence addressed to Hon. S.P. Chase, Secretary of the Treasury, and dated November 13, 1861, reveals how even America's coins came to be symbolic of our Christian heritage:

> Dear Sir:
>
> You are about to submit your annual report to Congress respecting the affairs of the national finances.
>
> One fact touching our currency has hitherto been seriously overlooked. I mean the recognition of the Almighty God in some form on our coins.
>
> You are probably a Christian. What if our Republic were now shattered beyond reconstruction? Would not the antiquaries of succeeding centuries rightly reason from our past that we were a heathen nation? ...What I propose...next inside the 13 stars a ring inscribed with the words "perpetual union," within this ring...the American flag, bearing in its field stars equal to the number of the States united; in the folds of the bars the words "God, liberty, law"...This would make a beautiful coin, to which no possible citizen could object. This would relieve us from the ignominy of heathenism. This would place us openly under the Divine protection we have personally claimed. From my heart I have felt our national shame in disowning God as not the least of our present national disasters.
>
> To you first I address a subject that must be agitated.
>
> (sgd) M.R. Watkinson
Minister of the Gospel
Ridleyville, PA[1]

A few days after reading its contents, the Secretary of the Treasury addressed his response to the Director of the Mint in Philadelphia, as follows:

> Dear Sir:
>
> No nation can be strong except in the strength of God or safe except in His defense. The trust of our people in God should be declared on our national coins.
>
> You will cause a device to be prepared without unnecessary delay with a motto expressing in the fewest and tersest words possible this national recognition.
>
> Yours truly,
(Sgd). S.P. Chase[2]

A further letter from the Secretary of the Treasury to James Pollock, Director of the Mint, dated December 9, 1863, finalizes the conviction that our nation's strength lies in Almighty God and His defense. He writes:

I approve your mottos, only suggesting that on that with the Washington obverse the motto should begin with the word 'Our,' so as to read:

"Our God and our Country." And on that with the shield, it should be changed so as to read: "In God we Trust."[3]

Thus it was that by Act of Congress, dated March 3, 1865, **"In God We Trust"** was inscribed upon the United States coins. The truth of its poignant message is a daily reminder to Americans where our allegiance lies: upon Almighty God and His providence (blessings) upon our land.

FOOTNOTES

Alabama
[1] Act. No. 244 of the State Legislature, 1953.
[2] Act of the State Legislature, 1876.
[3] Act No. 140 of the State Legislature, March 14, 1939.
[4] Adopted by the State Legislature, 1853. The Bible is kept in the Alabama Department of Archives and History. When not in use, it is on exhibit in the department's third floor Nineteenth Century Gallery.
[5] Act of the State Legislature, adopted 1895.
[6] Act No. 128, House Joint Resolution 74, March 3, 1931. Author: Julia S. Tutwiler. Music: Edna Gockell-Gussen.
[7] Official Documentation. Office of the Architect of the Capitol, Washington, D.C.
[8] Ibid.
[9] Ibid.

Alaska
[1] Act of the Alaska Legislature, May 2, 1927. Later approved by the Constitution of the State of Alaska.
[2] Act of the Alaska Legislature, 1955. Author: Marie Drake, written in 1935. Music: Elinor Dusenbury.

Arizona
[1] Adopted by the State Legislature, 1917.
[2] Adopted by the Fourth State Legislature, February 28, 1919.
[3] Official Documentaion. Office of the Architect of the Capitol, Washington, D.C.
[4] Ibid.
[5] Ibid.

Arkansas
[1] Adopted in 1864. Act of the State Legislature, 1907.
[2] Adopted February 26, 1913. Act of the State Legislature.
[3] Adopted in 1987. Act of the General Assembly. Author: Wayland Holyfield.
[4] Official Documentation. Office of the Architect of the Capitol, Washington, D.C.
[5] Ibid.
[6] Ibid.

California
[1] Adopted by Act of the State Legislature, 1911.
[2] First sung publicly in 1913. Lyrics and music by Silverwood and Frankenstein.

Colorado
[1] Adopted by the First Territorial Assembly, November 6, 1861.
[2] Adopted June 5, 1911. Act of the State Legislature.

Connecticut

[1] Act of the General Assembly, May, 1784. Chapter 54 of the Public Acts, 1931.

[2] Act of the General Assembly, 1897.

[3] Act of the General Assembly, October, 1985.

[4] Official Documentation. Office of the Architect of the Capitol, Washington, D.C.

[5] Ibid.

[6] Ibid.

[7] Ibid.

[8] Ibid.

[9] Hooker, Thomas. *A Survey of the Summe of Church Discipline.* Boston: Old South Leaflets No. 55, 1896, p. 15.

[10] Ibid.

[11] Ibid.

[12] Ibid.

[13] Hooker, Thomas. (Late pastor of the Church at Hartford upon Connecticut, in N.E.). *A Survey of the Summe of Church Discipline, wherein the Way of Churches of New England is warranted out of the Word and all exceptions of weight, which are made against it, answered.* London: A.M. for John Bellamy, 1648, Preface.

Delaware

[1] Acts of the Delaware State Legislature, 1847 and 1907 respectively.

[2] Ibid.

[3] Murdock, Myrtle Cheney. *"Statuary Hall" - Delaware - Caesar Rodney.* Office of the Architect of the Capitol, Washington, D.C.

[4] Lord, Frank B. *Little Sung Heroes of Independence.* The Washington Post, June 28, 1931, p. 3.

[5] Ibid.   [6] Ibid., p. 11   [7] Ibid., p. 3   [8] Ibid.

Florida

[1] Article XVI, Section 20 of the State Constitution, 1868. Article XVI, Section 12 of the State Constitution, 1885.

[2] State Constitution of 1900.

[3] Act of the State Legislature, 1935. Stephen Collins Foster's composition.

[4] Twenty-fourth Annual Reunion of the Association of the Graduates of the United States Military Academy, at West Point, New York, June 9, 1893. Saginaw, Michigan: Seeman & Peters, Printers and Binders, 1893.

[5] Noll, Arthur Howard. *General Kirby-Smith.* The University Press, at the University of the South, Sewanee, Tennessee, 1907, p. 175.

[6] *A Narrative of the Expedition of Hernando de Soto into Florida by a Gentleman of Elvas*, published at Evora in 1557. Translated from the Portugese by Richard Hackluyt, London, 1609, p. 117.

Georgia

[1] Act of the State Legislature, 1799.

[2] Mace, William J. *Mace's Primary History - Stories of Heroism.* Rand McNally & Co., 1909. pp. 112-114.

[3] Ibid.

[4] Ibid.

Hawaii

[1] Joint Resolution 4, 30th Territorial Legislature, May 1, 1959.

[2] Act 272 of the Territorial Legislature, May 1, 1959. The Coat of Arms of the Kingdom was adopted in May, 1845.

[3] Act 301 of the Legislature, 1967.

[4] Bingham, Hiram, A.M. (Member of the American Oriental Board). *Residence of Twenty-one Years in the Sandwich Islands*; or The Civil, Religious and Political History of Those Islands: Comprising a particular view of the Christianity and Civilization among the Hawaian people. New York: Herman Converse, 1848, pp. 58-59.

[5] Ibid., pp. 69-70.

Idaho

[1] Act of the First State Legislature, 1891.

[2] Act of the State Legislature, 1907.

[3] Act of the State Legislature, 1931. Author: McKinley Helm. Music: Alice Bessee.

Illinois

[1] Act of the State Legislature, February 19, 1819.

[2] Flag Act of the General Assembly of 1915. Act of the General Assembly, September 17, 1969.

[3] Wanamaker, John. *The Wanamaker Primer of Abraham Lincoln*. New York: John Wanamaker, 1909, pp. 98-100.

[4] Edgington, Frank E. *A History of the New York Avenue Presbyterian Church, One Hundred Fifty-Seven Years, 1803-1961*. Published by the New York Avenue Presbyterian Church, Washington, D.C., 1961, p. 244.

[5] Congressional Record - U.S. Senate, April 23, 1926, p. 2095.

Indiana

[1] State Constitutions of 1816 and 1851 (Article 15, Section 5). Act of the General Assembly, 1963.

[2] Act of the General Assembly.

[3] Adopted by the General Assembly, 1913. Indiana Code 1-2-6.

[4] Act of the General Assembly, 1963. Poet: Arthur Franklin Mapes.

[5] Official Documentation. Office of the Architect of the Capitol, Washington, D.C.

Iowa

[1] Act of the State Legislature, 1847.

[2] Ibid.

[3] Act of the State Legislature, 1921.

[4] Official Documentation. Office of the Architect of the Capitol, Washington, D.C.

[5] Ibid.

[6] Ibid.

[7] Ibid.

Kansas

[1] Joint Resolution of the State Legislature, May 25, 1861.

[2] Act of the State Legislature, 1927.

[3] Act of the State Legislature, 1947. Words: Dr. Brewster Higley. Music: Dan Kelly.

Kentucky

[1] Approved by the Kentucky General Assembly and Governor Isaac Shelby (1792-1796), December 20, 1792.

[2] Act of the General Assembly, March 26, 1918.

[3] Official Documentation. Office of the Architect of the Capitol, Washington, D.C.

[4] Ibid.

[5] Ibid.

[6] Ibid.

[7] Ibid.

[8] Ibid.

Louisiana

[1] Adopted by the Louisiana State Legislature in 1912.

[2] Scott, Walter Dill, B.A., Ph.D., LL.D. (ed.), President Emeritus, Northwestern University. *The American People's Encyclopedia. Battle of New Orleans. War of 1812.* Chicago: The Spencer Press, Inc., 1948, pp. 14-574-575.

[3] Ibid.

[4] Ibid.

[5] Ibid.

Maine

[1] Laws of 1820.

[2] Ibid.

[3] Act of the State Legislature, 1909.

[4] Words and Music by Roger Vinton Snow.

[5] Official Documentation. Office of the Architect of the Capitol, Washington, D.C.

[6] Ibid.

[7] Ibid.

Maryland

[1] Joint Resolution No. 5. Acts of the State Legislature, 1876.

[2] Adopted by an Act of the State Legislature, Chapter 48, Acts of 1904.

[3] Act of the State Legislature. Chapter 451, Code State Government Article, Sec. 13-307, 1939. Poet: James Ryder Randall, written in 1861; set to the traditional tune of "Lauriger Horatius."

Massachusetts

[1] Adopted in 1775 by the Provincial Congress.

[2] Adopted by Governor John Hancock and the Council on December 13, 1780. Made official by the General Court on June 4, 1885.

[3] Act of the Legislature, 1971. Act of the Legislature, July, 1981. (Official song of the Commonwealth since September, 1966).

[4] Franklin, Benjamin. *Franklin's Boyhood in Boston, from His Autobiography* — "Twyford, at the Bishop of St. Asaph's, 1771." Old South Leaflets. Volume VII. Boston: Published by the Directors of the Old South Work. Old South Meeting House, n.d.

[5] *Handbook of Christ Church* - Second Street Above Market, Philadelphia. 1695-1920. Philadelphia: Christ Church, 1920, p. 29.

Michigan
[1] Adopted by the State Legislature, June 2, 1835.
[2] Ibid.
[3] Official Documentation. Office of the Architect of the Capitol, Washington, D.C.
[4] Ibid.
[5] Ibid.
[6] Ibid.

Minnesota
[1] Act of the State Legislature, 1945.
[2] Official Documentation. Office of the Architect of the Capitol, Washington, D.C.
[3] Ibid.
[4] Ibid.

Mississippi
[1] Laws of Mississippi, First Session, First General Assembly, 1817-1818.
[2] Legislative Action, February 7, 1894.
[3] Ibid.
[4] Section 37-13-7, Mississippi Code of 1972.
[5] Chapter 654, General Laws of Mississippi of 1962. Author: Houston Davis.
[6] Lattimore, Ralston B. (ed.) *The Story of Robert E. Lee, as Told in his Own Words and Those of his Contemporaries. Washington, D.C.: Colortone Press, 1964, p. 13.*

Missouri
[1] Act of the State Legislature.
[2] Act of the Forty-seventh General Assembly, 1913.
[3] Act of the State Legislature.

Montana
[1] Section 1-1-501 Montana Code Annotated, 1893.
[2] Lyrics by Charles C. Cohen. Melody by Joseph E. Howard.

Nebraska
[1] Act of the State Legislature, June 15, 1867.
[2] Ibid.
[3] Act of the State Legislature, March 28, 1925.
[4] Act of the State Legislature, June 12, 1967. Words and Music by Jim Fras of Lincoln, a Russian refugee who came to Nebraska in 1952.
[5] Act of the State Legislature, 1935.
[6] Official Documentation. Office of the Architect of the Capitol, Washington, D.C.
[7] Ibid.
[8] Ibid.
[9] Ibid.

Nevada
[1] Act of the State Legislature, 1866.
[2] Act of the State Legislature, February 24, 1866.
[3] Act of the State Legislature, March 21, 1929.

[4] Act of the State Legislature, February 6, 1933. Composer: Mrs. Bertha Raffetto of Reno.

New Hampshire
[1] Section 3:8 of the Revised Statutes Annotated of the State Legislature.
[2] Section 3:9 of the Revised Statutes Annotated of the State Legislature.
[3] Section 3:1 of the Revised Statutes Annotated of the State Legislature.
[4] Section 3:2 of the Revised Statutes Annotated of the State Legislature.
[5] Section 3:7 of the Revised Statutes Annotated of the State Legislature.
[6] Library of Congress documentation.
[7] Ibid.
[8] Nichols, Roy Franklin, Professor of History, University of Pennsylvania. *Franklin Pierce, Young Hickory of the Granite Hills.* Philadelphia: University of Pennsylvania Press, 1931, p. 528.

New Jersey
[1] Minutes of the New Jersey General Assembly, March 11, 1896.
[2] Official Documentation. Office of the Architect of the Capitol, Washington, D.C.
[3] Ibid.
[4] Ibid.
[5] Ibid.
[6] Ibid.
[7] Montague, Marie Louise. *Witherspoon, Signer of the Declaration of Independence.* Washington, D.C.: H.C. and J.B. McQueen, Inc., 1932, p. 2.

New Mexico
[1] Act of the Territorial Legislature, 1887.
[2] Act of the First State Legislature, 1912.
[3] Act of the State Legislature, March, 1925.
[4] Act of the State Legislature, 1917.

New York
[1] Act of the State Legislature, No. 70.
[2] New York State Museum documentation, Albany, New York.
[3] Official Documentation. Office of the Architect of the Capitol, Washington, D.C.
[4] Ibid.
[5] Ames, Seth (ed.). *Works of Fisher Ames with a Selection from his Speeches and Correspondence.* Edited by his son, Seth Ames. Vol. I. Boston: Little, Brown & Company, 1854, p. 34.
[6] Official Documentation, Office of the Architect of the Capitol, Washington, D.C.
[7] Ibid.
[8] *The Christian Statesmen of America.* Boston: Massachusetts Sabbath School Society, 1861, pp. 117-118.

North Carolina
[1] Chapter 145 of the General Assembly.
[2] Act of the General Assembly, 1883.
[3] Act of the General Assembly, March 9, 1885.
[4] Act of the General Assembly.

[5] Act of the General Assembly, 1927.
[6] Official Documentation. Office of the Architect of the Capitol, Washington, D.C.
[7] Ibid.
[8] Ibid.
[9] Ibid.
[10] Ibid.
[11] Clark, Walter. *Histories of North Carolina Regiments.* Vol. III.

North Dakota
[1] Article XI, Section 2 of the North Dakota Constitution.
[2] Sections 54-02-02 of the NDCC.
[3] Sections 54-41-01 and 54-41-02 of the NDCC.
[4] Adopted on March 15, 1947. Section 54-02-04 of the NDCC.

Ohio
[1] Act of the 103rd General Assembly.
[2] Act of the 107th General Assembly.
[3] Act of the 75th General Assembly.
[4] Official Documentation. Office of the Architect of the Capitol, Washington, D.C.
[5] Ibid.
[6] Ibid.
[7] Ibid.
[8] Ibid.
[9] Westerhoff, John H. *McGuffey and his Readers - Piety, Morality and Education in 19th Century America.* Nashville: Abingdon Press, n.d., p. 13.

Oklahoma
[1] Constitution, Article 6, No. 35.
[2] Ibid.
[3] Oklahoma Statutes.
[4] Official Documentation. Office of the Architect of the Capitol, Washington, D.C.
[5] Ibid.
[6] Ibid.

Oregon
[1] Act of the State Legislature, 1937.
[2] Act of the State Legislature.
[3] Act of the State Legislature, 1925.
[4] Act of the State Legislature, 1927. Authors: J.A. Buchanan and Henry B. Murtagh.
[5] Barker, Burt Brown. *Oregon, Prize of Discovery, Exploration, Settlement.* Salem: State Printing Section, 1952, p. 38
[6] Ibid.

Pennsylvania
[1] State Constitutional Convention, 1776.
[2] Original design of 1778 by Caleb Lownes.
[3] Act of the General Assembly, 1791.
[4] Act of the General Assembly, November 29, 1990. (Written and composed by Eddie Khoury and Ronnie Banner).

5 Mace, William H. *Mace's Primary History - Stories of Heroism.* New York: Rand McNally, Inc., 1909, p. 110.

6 Ibid., p. 111.

7 Ibid.

8 Ibid.

9 Cope, Thomas Pryne (ed.) *Passages in the Life and Writings of William Penn.* Philadelphia: Friends Bookstore, 1882.

10 Rogers, George L. (ed.) Benjamin Franklin. *The Art of Virtue.* Acorn Publishing Company, 1990, pp. 69-70.

11 Religious News Service. April 1, 1976. *Memorial in Capital Planned to Honor "Fighting Parson."*

Rhode Island

1 General Laws, Section 42.4.2.

2 General Laws, 42.4.1.

3 General Laws, 42.4.3.

4 General Laws, 42.4.4.

5 Williams, Roger. *The Bloudy Tenent of Persecution for Cause of Conscience, discussed, in a Conference betweene Truth and Peace,* Who, in all tender affection, present to the High Court of Parliament. Printed by Gregory Dexter, 1644, Preface.

South Carolina

1 Act of the Privy Council, April 2, 1776.

2 Act of the Revolutionary Council of Safety, 1775. Act of the General Assembly. 1861.

3 Words by Henry Timrod. Music by Anne Custis Burgess.

4 Act of the General Assembly, January 28, 1966.

5 Official Documentation. Office of the Architect of the Capitol, Washington, D.C.

6 Ibid.   7 Ibid.   8 Ibid.

9 Ibid.   10 Ibid.   11 Ibid.

12 Ibid.

South Dakota

1 Act of the State Legislature, 1885.

2 Act of the State Legislature, 1909.

3 Act of the State Legislature, July 1, 1987.

4 Adopted by the State Legislature, March 5, 1943. Words and Music: Deecort Hammitt.

5 Official Documentation. Office of the Architect of the Capitol, Washington, D.C.

6 Ibid.   7 Ibid.   8 Ibid.

9 Ibid.   10 Ibid.

Tennessee

1 Act of the State Legislature, 1905.

2 Act of the State Legislature.

3 Ibid.

4 Eulogy on Andrew Jackson given in the U.S. Senate, June 8, 1845.

Texas

1 Texas Constitution, Article IV, Section 19.

2 Act of the State Legislature, August 26, 1961. Resolution, June 14, 1991.

[3] *Congressional Record* - House of Representatives - *Pilgrimage Address at the Alamo, April 18, 1966.* Address by Lt. Gen. William W. Momyer, USAF, p. A2367.

Utah

[1] Adopted on April 3, 1896, at the First Regular Session of the Legislature.

[2] House Joint Resolution I in 1913 signed by Governor William Spry.

[3] Scott, Walter Dill, B.A., Ph.D., LL.D. (ed.) President Emeritus, Northwestern University. *The American People's Encyclopedia.* Chicago: The Spencer Press, Inc., 1948, p. 19-464.

[4] Ibid.

Vermont

[1] Adopted with State Seal in 1779.

[2] Provided for by the first Constitution, 1777; First design established 1779.

[3] Statutes No. 11 of the Acts of 1862.

[4] No. 8 of the Acts of 1919.

[5] Official Documentation. Office of the Architect of the Capitol, Washington, D.C.

[6] Ibid.

[7] Plaque within the State Capitol, Monpelier, Vermont.

[8] Official Documentation. Office of the Architect of the Capitol, Washington, D.C.

[9] Plaque within the State Capitol, Montpelier, Vermont.

Virginia

[1] Adopted in 1776 as the original composition of George Wythe, signer of the Declaration of Independence.

[2] Ibid.

[3] The Honorable Thomas M. Moncure, Jr.

[4] Act of the Legislature, 1930.

[5] Act of the Legislature.

[6] Burk, W. Herbert, D.D. *Washington's Prayers.* (Facsimile of the original.) Published for the benefit of Washington Memorial Chapel, Norristown, PA., 1907.

Washington

[1] Adopted by the State Legislature, 1923.

[2] Harding, Warren Gamaliel. *A Government Document.* Washington, D.C.: Government Printing Office, 1923.

West Virginia

[1] Constitution of West Virginia, Article 2, Section 7.

[2] Official Documentation. Office of the Architect of the Capitol, Washington, D.C.

[3] Ibid.

[4] Old South Leaflets. *The Words of John Brown.* Volume IV. 76-100. Boston: Published by the Directors of the Old South Work. Old South Meeting House, n.d.

[5] Ibid.

[6] Ibid.

Wisconsin

[1] Section 1.07 of the Statutes, 1851.

[2] Chapter 280, Laws of 1881. Sections 1.07 and 14.45 of the Statutes.

[3] Joint Resolution 4, 1863. Chapter 111, Laws of 1913.

[4] Chapter 170, Laws of 1959. Section 1.10 of the Statutes.

Wyoming

[1] Adopted by the Second Legislature in 1893.

[2] Designed in 1916 by Mrs. Verna Keyes of Casper, Wyoming. Mrs. Keyes won the Flag Design Contest sponsored by the DAR. Adopted January 31, 1917 by the 14th Legislature and approved by Governor Robert D. Carey.

Our Flag

[1] Hearings before Subcommittee No. 4 of the Committee of the Judiciary, 85th Congress, 2nd Session. May 21, 22 and 28, 1958, p. 6.

[2] Ibid., p. 1.

[3] Key, Francis Scott. *Poems of the late Francis S. Key, Esq.*, Author of "The Star-Spangled Banner." With an Introductory letter by Chief Justice Taney. New York: Robert Carter & Brothers, 1857.

[4] Inscribed upon a bronze plaque on the outer wall of the *First Baptist Church* of Little Falls, New York.

[5] Hearings before Subcommittee No. 4 of the Committee of the Judiciary, 85th Congress, 2nd Session. May 21, 22 and 28, 1958, p. 138.

[6] Ibid.

"In God We Trust"
- On America's Coins and Currency -

[1] Watkinson, M.R., Minister of the Gospel to Hon. S. P. Chase, Secretary of the Treasury. November 13, 1861.

[2] Hon. S. P. Chase, Secretary of the Treasury to Director of the Mint. Philadelphia, November 20, 1861.

[3] Secretary of the Treasury to Director of the Mint. Philadelphia, December 9, 1863.

The Continental Congress

[1] Official Documentation. Office of the Architect of the Capitol, Washington, D.C.

Appendix I

[1] Adams, John Quincy. *The Jubilee of the Constitution – A Discourse*, delivered at the request of the New York Historical Society, in the city of New York, on Tuesday, the 30th of April, 1839, being the 50th anniversary of the inaugural of George Washington as President of the United States, on Thursday the 30th of April, 1789. New York: Published by Samuel Colman, MDCCCXXXIX, pp. 8-39.

THE NATIONAL HYMN

GOD OF OUR FATHERS
Author: Daniel C. Roberts   Music: George W. Warren

God of our fathers, whose Almighty Hand
Leads forth in beauty all the starry band
Of shining worlds in splendor thro' the skies,
Our grateful songs before Thy throne arise.

Thy love divine hath led us in the past.
In this free land by Thee our lot is cast.
Be Thou our Ruler, Guardian, Guide, and Stay,
Thy Word our law, Thy paths our chosen way.

From war's alarms, from deadly pestilence,
Be Thy strong arm our ever sure defense.
Thy true religion in our hearts increase;
Thy bounteous goodness nourish us in peace.

Refresh Thy people on their toilsome way.
Lead us from night to never ending day.
Fill all our lives with love and grace divine;
And glory, laud, and praise be ever Thine.

AMERICA
PATRIOTIC HYMN

On May 4, 1932, by Act of Congress (S.J. Res. 113), our 72nd Congress, 1st Session, passed a Joint Resolution to Commemorate the one hundredth anniversary of the first public singing of "**America**," showing, once again, our true identity as a Christian nation. It reads as follows:

WHEREAS, the 4th of July, 1932, marks the one hundredth anniversary of the first public singing in Park Street Church, Boston, Massachusetts, by a chorus of children, of the great and thrilling patriotic hymn "**America;**" and

WHEREAS this significant event already is promised splendid recognition at Detroit, Michigan, where the contributions of patriotic school children have provided a beautiful monument to the hymn and to its author, which will be appropriately dedicated upon Independence Day; and

WHEREAS it is the sense of the Congress that there should be general observance of this anniversary because of the incalculable inspiration which has touched the life of the Nation through the countless millions of voices, in peace and in war, which have sung "My Country, 'Tis of Thee" across the century: Therefore be it Resolved by the Senate and House of Representatives of the United States of America in Congress assembled, That this one hundredth anniversary of the first public singing of "**America**" be commended to all citizens for appropriate recognition in connection with the celebration of Independence Day on the 4th day of July, 1932.

AMERICA

Author: Katherine Lee Bates   Music: Samuel A. Ward

O beautiful for spacious skies,
For amber waves of grain,
For purple mountain majesties
Above the fruited plain!
America! America! God shed His grace on thee,
And crown thy good with brotherhood
From sea to shining sea!

O beautiful for pilgrim feet,
Whose stern, impassioned stress
A thoroughfare for freedom beat
Across the wilderness!
America! America! God mend thine every flaw,
Confirm thy soul in self-control,
Thy liberty in law!

O beautiful for heroes proved
In liberating strife,
Who more than self their country loved,
And mercy more than life!
America! America! May God thy gold refine
Till all success be nobleness
And every gain divine!

O beautiful for patriot dream
That sees beyond the years
Thine alabaster cities gleam,
Undimmed by human tears!
America! America! God shed His grace on thee
And crown thy good with brotherhood
From sea to shining sea! Amen.

BATTLE HYMN OF THE REPUBLIC

Author: Julia Ward Howe   Music: William Steffe

Mine eyes have seen the glory
of the coming of the Lord;
He is trampling out the vintage
where the grapes of wrath are stored;
He hath loosed the fateful lightning
of His terrible swift sword;
His truth is marching on.

Glory! glory! Hallelujah!
Glory! glory! Hallelujah!
Glory! glory! Hallelujah!
His truth is marching on.

I have seen Him in the watchfires
of a hundred circling camps;
They have builded Him an altar
in the evening dews and damps;
I can read His righteous sentence
by the dim and flaring lamps.
His day is marching on.

I have read a fiery gospel
writ in burnished rows of steel:
"As ye deal with My condemners,
so with you My grace shall deal;
Let the Hero, born of woman,
crush the serpent with His heel,
Since God is marching on."

He has sounded forth the trumpet
that shall never call retreat;
He is sifting out the hearts of men
before His judgment seat;
O be swift, my soul, to answer Him!
be jubilant, my feet!
Our God is marching on.

In the beauty of the lilies
Christ was born across the sea,
With a glory in His bosom
that transfigures you and me:
As He died to make men holy,
let us die to make men free,
While God is marching on.

MY COUNTRY 'TIS OF THEE

Author: Samuel F. Smith   Music: Henry Carey

My country, 'tis of Thee,
Sweet land of liberty,
Of thee I sing:
Land where my fathers died,
Land of the pilgrims' pride,
From every mountain side
Let freedom ring!

My native country, thee,
Land of the noble, free,
Thy name I love;
I love thy rocks and rills,
Thy woods and templed hills;
My heart with rapture thrills,
Like that above.

Let music swell the breeze,
And ring from all the trees
Sweet freedom's song;
Let mortal tongues awake;
Let all that breathe partake;
Let rocks their silence break,
The sound prolong.

Our fathers' God, to Thee,
Author of liberty,
To Thee we sing:
Long may our land be bright
With freedom's holy light;
Protect us by Thy might,
Great God, our King. Amen.

THE CONTINENTAL CONGRESS[1]

Place and Time of Meeting

Philadelphia, Pa	From September 5, 1774, to October 26, 1774
Philadelphia, Pa	From May 10, 1775, to December 12, 1776
Baltimore, Md	From December 20, 1776, to March 4, 1777
Philadelphia, Pa	From March 5, 1777, to September 18, 1777
Lancaster, Pa	September 27, 1777 (one day only)
York, Pa	From September 30, 1777, to June 27, 1778
Philadelphia, Pa	From July 2, 1778, to June 21, 1783
Princeton, N.J.	From June 30, 1783, to November 4, 1783
Annapolis, Md	From November 26, 1783, to June 3, 1784
Trenton, N.J.	From November 1, 1784, to December 24, 1784
New York City	From January 11, 1785, to November 4, 1785
New York City	From November 7, 1785, to November 3, 1786
New York City	From November 6, 1786, to October 30, 1787
New York City	From November 5, 1787, to October 21, 1788
New York City	From November 3, 1788, to March 2, 1789

Presidents of the Congress

Peyton Randolph,[1] of Virginia	Elected September 5, 1774
Henry Middleton, of South Carolina	Elected October 22, 1774
Peyton Randolph,[2] of Virginia	Elected May 10, 1775
John Hancock, of Massachusetts	Elected May 24, 1775
Henry Laurens, of South Carolina	Elected November 1, 1777
John Jay, of New York	Elected December 10, 1778
Samuel Huntington, of Connecticut	Elected September 28, 1779
Thomas McKean, of Delaware	Elected July 10, 1781
John Hanson, of Maryland	Elected November 5, 1781

(9th President; 1st to serve after the ratification of the Articles of Confederation.)

Elias Boudinot, of New Jersey	Elected November 4, 1782
Thomas Mifflin, of Pennsylvania	Elected November 3, 1783
Richard Henry Lee, of Virginia	Elected November 30, 1784
John Hancock,[3] of Massachusetts	Elected November 23, 1785
Nathaniel Gorham, of Massachusetts	Elected June 6, 1786
Arthur St. Clair, of Pennsylvania	Elected February 2, 1787
Cyrus Griffin, of Virginia	Elected January 22, 1788

Secretary of the Congress

Charles Thomson, of Pennsylvania	Elected September 5, 1774

---

[1] Resigned October 22, 1774.
[2] Departed Congress May 28, 1775, to resume duties as Speaker of the Virginia House of Burgesses.
[3] Resigned May 29, 1786, having never served owing to illness.

The Northwest Ordinance

An ORDINANCE for the GOVERNMENT of the TERRITORY of the UNITED STATES, North-West of the RIVER OHIO.

BE IT ORDAINED by the United States in Congress assembled, That the said territory, for the purposes of temporary government, be one district; subject, however, to be divided into two districts, as future circumstances may, in the opinion of Congress, make it expedient.

Be it ordained by the authority aforesaid, That the estates both of resident and non-resident proprietors in the said territory, dying intestate, shall descend to, and be distributed among their children, and the descendants of a deceased child in equal parts; the descendants of a deceased child or grand-child, to take the share of their deceased parent in equal parts among them: And where there shall be no children or descendants, then in equal parts to the next of kin, in equal degree; and among collaterals, the children of a deceased brother or sister of the intestate, shall have in equal parts among them their deceased parents share; and there shall in no case be a distinction between kindred of the whole and half blood; saving in all cases to the widow of the intestate, her third part of the real estate for life, and one third part of the personal estate; and this law relative to descents and dower, shall remain in full force until altered by the legislature of the district. ——— And until the governor and judges shall adopt laws as herein after mentioned, estates in the said territory may be devised or bequeathed by wills in writing, signed and sealed by him or her, in whom the estate may be, (being of full age) and attested by three witnesses; —— and real estates may be conveyed by lease and release, or bargain and sale, signed, sealed, and delivered by the person being of full age, in whom the estate may be, and attested by two witnesses, provided such wills be duly proved, and such conveyances be acknowledged, or the execution thereof duly proved, and be recorded within one year after proper magistrates, courts, and registers shall be appointed for that purpose; and personal property may be transferred by delivery, saving, however, to the French and Canadian inhabitants, and other settlers of the Kaskaskies, Saint Vincent's, and the neighbouring villages, who have heretofore professed themselves citizens of Virginia, their laws and customs now in force among them, relative to the descent and conveyance of property.

Be it ordained by the authority aforesaid, That there shall be appointed from time to time, by Congress, a governor, whose commission shall continue in force for the term of three years, unless sooner revoked by Congress; he shall reside in the district, and have a freehold estate therein, in one thousand acres of land, while in the exercise of his office.

There shall be appointed from time to time, by Congress, a secretary, whose commission shall continue in force for four years, unless sooner revoked, he shall reside in the district, and have a freehold estate therein, in five hundred acres of land, while in the exercise of his office; it shall be his duty to keep and preserve the acts and laws passed by the legislature, and the public records of the district, and the proceedings of the governor in his executive department; and transmit authentic copies of such acts and proceedings, every six months, to the secretary of Congress: There shall also be appointed a court to consist of three judges, any two of whom to form a court, who shall have a common law jurisdiction, and reside in the district, and have each therein a freehold estate in five hundred acres of land, while in the exercise of their offices; and their commissions shall continue in force during good behaviour.

The governor and judges, or a majority of them, shall adopt and publish in the district, such laws of the original states, criminal and civil, as may be necessary, and best suited to the circumstances of the district, and report them to Congress, from time to time, which laws shall be in force in the district until the organization of the general assembly therein, unless disapproved of by Congress; but afterwards the legislature shall have authority to alter them as they shall think fit.

The governor for the time being, shall be commander in chief of the militia, appoint and commission all officers in the same, below the rank of general officers; all general officers shall be appointed and commissioned by Congress.

Previous to the organization of the general assembly, the governor shall appoint such magistrates and other civil officers, in each county or township, as he shall find necessary for the preservation of the peace and good order in the same: After the general assembly shall be organized, the powers and duties of magistrates and other civil officers shall be regulated and defined by the said assembly; but all magistrates and other civil officers, not herein otherwise directed, shall, during the continuance of this temporary government, be appointed by the governor.

For the prevention of crimes and injuries, the laws to be adopted or made shall have force in all parts of the district, and for the execution of process, criminal and civil, the governor shall make proper divisions thereof—and he shall proceed from time to time, as circumstances may require, to lay out the parts of the district in which the Indian titles shall have been extinguished, into counties and townships, subject, however, to such alterations as may thereafter be made by the legislature.

So soon as there shall be five thousand free male inhabitants, of full age, in the district, upon giving proof thereof to the governor, they shall receive authority, with time and place, to elect representatives from their counties or townships, to represent them in the general assembly; provided that for every five hundred free male inhabitants there shall be one representative, and so on progressively with the number of free male inhabitants, shall the right of representation increase, until the number of representatives shall amount to twenty-five, after which the number and proportion of representatives shall be regulated by the legislature; provided that no person be eligible or qualified to act as a representative, unless he shall have been a citizen of one of the United States three years and be a resident in the district, or unless he shall have resided in the district three years, and in either case shall likewise hold in his own right, in fee simple, two hundred acres of land within the same:——Provided also, that a freehold in fifty acres of land in the district, having been a citizen of one of the states, and being resident in the district; or the like freehold and two years residence in the district shall be necessary to qualify a man as an elector of a representative.

The representatives thus elected, shall serve for the term of two years, and in case of the death of a representative, or removal from office, the governor shall issue a writ to the county or township for which he was a member, to elect another in his stead, to serve for the residue of the term.

The general assembly, or legislature, shall consist of the governor, legislative council, and a house of representatives. The legislative council shall consist of five members, to continue in office five years, unless sooner removed by Congress, any three of whom to be a quorum, and the members of the council shall be nominated and appointed in the following manner, to wit: As soon as representatives shall be elected, the governor shall appoint a time and place for them to meet together, and, when met, they shall nominate ten persons, residents in the district, and each possessed of a freehold in five hundred acres of land, and return their names to Congress; five of whom Congress shall appoint and commission to serve as aforesaid; and whenever a vacancy shall happen in the council, by death or removal from office, the house of representatives shall nominate two persons, qualified as aforesaid, for each vacancy, and return their names to Congress, one of whom Congress shall appoint and commission for the residue of the term; and every five years, four months at least before the expiration of the time of service of the members of council, the said house shall nominate ten persons, qualified as aforesaid, and return their names to Congress, five of whom Congress shall appoint and commission to serve as members of the council five years, unless sooner removed. And the governor, legislative council, and house of representatives, shall have authority to make laws in all cases for the good government of the district, not repugnant to the principles and articles in this ordinance established and declared. And all bills having passed by a majority in the house, and by a majority in the council, shall be referred to the governor for his assent; but no bill or legislative act whatever, shall be of any force without his assent. The governor shall have power to convene, prorogue and dissolve the general assembly, when in his opinion it shall be expedient.

The governor, judges, legislative council, secretary, and such other officers as Congress shall appoint in the district, shall take an oath or affirmation of fidelity, and of office, the governor before the president of Congress, and all other officers before the governor. As soon as a legislature shall be formed in the district, the council and house, assembled in one room, shall have authority by joint ballot to elect a delegate to Congress, who shall have a seat in Congress, with a right of debating, but not of voting, during this temporary government.

And for extending the fundamental principles of civil and religious liberty, which form the basis whereon these republics, their laws and constitutions are erected; to fix and establish those principles as the basis of all laws, constitutions and governments, which forever hereafter shall be formed in the said territory;—to provide also for the establishment of states, and permanent government therein, and for their admission to a share in the federal councils on an equal footing with the original states, at as early periods as may be consistent with the general interest:

It is hereby ordained and declared by the authority aforesaid, That the following articles shall be considered as articles of compact between the original states and the people and states in the said territory, and forever remain unalterable, unless by common consent, to wit:

Article the First. No person, demeaning himself in a peaceable and orderly manner, shall ever be molested on account of his mode of worship or religious sentiments in the said territory.

Article the Second. The inhabitants of the said territory shall always be entitled to the benefits of the writ of habeas corpus, and of the trial by jury; of a proportionate representation of the people in the legislature, and of judicial proceedings according to the course of the common law; all persons shall be bailable unless for capital offences, where the proof shall be evident, or the presumption great; all fines shall be moderate, and no cruel or unusual punishments shall be inflicted; no man shall be deprived of his liberty or property but by the judgment of his peers, or the law of the land; and should the public exigencies make it necessary for the common preservation to take any person's property, or to demand his particular services, full compensation shall be made for the same;—and in the just preservation of rights and property it is understood and declared, that no law ought ever to be made, or have force in the said territory, that shall in any manner whatever interfere with, or affect private contracts or engagements, bona fide and without fraud previously formed.

Article the Third. Religion, morality and knowledge, being necessary to good government and the happiness of mankind, schools and the means of education shall forever be encouraged. The utmost good faith shall always be observed towards the Indians; their lands and property shall never be taken from them without their consent; and in their property, rights and liberty, they never shall be invaded or disturbed, unless in just and lawful wars authorized by Congress; but laws founded in justice and humanity shall from time to time be made, for preventing wrongs being done to them, and for preserving peace and friendship with them.

Article the Fourth. The said territory, and the states which may be formed therein, shall forever remain a part of this confederacy of the United States of America, subject to the articles of confederation, and to such alterations therein as shall be constitutionally made; and to all the acts and ordinances of the United states in Congress assembled, conformable thereto. The inhabitants and settlers in the said territory, shall be subject to pay a part of the federal debts contracted or to be contracted, and a proportional part of the expences of government, to be apportioned on them by Congress, according to the same common rule and measure by which apportionments thereof shall be made on the other states; and the taxes for paying their proportion, shall be laid and levied by the authority and direction of the legislatures of the district or districts or new states, as in the original states, within the time agreed upon by the United States in Congress assembled. The legislatures of those districts, or new states, shall never interfere with the primary disposal of the soil by the United States in Congress assembled, nor with any regulations Congress may find necessary for securing the title in such soil to the bona fide purchasers. No tax shall be imposed on lands the property of the United States; and in no case shall non-resident proprietors be taxed higher than residents. The navigable waters leading into the Mississippi and St. Lawrence, and the carrying places between the same shall be common highways, and forever free, as well to the inhabitants of the said territory, as to the citizens of the United States, and those of any other states that may be admitted into the confederacy, without any tax, impost or duty therefor.

Article the Fifth. There shall be formed in the said territory, not less than three nor more than five states; and the boundaries of the states, as soon as Virginia shall alter her act of cession and consent to the same, shall become fixed and established as follows, to wit: The western state in the said territory, shall be bounded by the Mississippi, the Ohio and Wabash rivers; a direct line drawn from the Wabash and Post Vincent's due north to the territorial line between the United States and Canada, and by the said territorial line to the lake of the Woods and Mississippi. The middle state shall be bounded by the said direct line, the Wabash from Post Vincent's to the Ohio; by the Ohio, by a direct line drawn due north from the mouth of the Great Miami to the said territorial line, and by the said territorial line. The eastern state shall be bounded by the last mentioned direct line, the Ohio, Pennsylvania, and the said territorial line: Provided however, and it is further understood and declared, that the boundaries of these three states, shall be subject so far to be altered, that if Congress shall hereafter find it expedient, they shall have authority to form one or two states in that part of the said territory which lies north of an east and west line drawn through the southerly bend or extreme of lake Michigan: and whenever any of the said states shall have sixty thousand free inhabitants therein, such state shall be admitted by its delegates into the Congress of the United states, on an equal footing with the original states in all respects whatever; and shall be at liberty to form a permanent constitution and state government: Provided the constitution and government so to be formed, shall be republican, and in conformity to the principles contained in these articles; and so far as it can be consistent with the general interest of the confederacy, such admission shall be allowed at an earlier period, and when there may be a less number of free inhabitants in the state than sixty thousand.

Article the Sixth. There shall be neither slavery nor involuntary servitude in the said territory, otherwise than in punishment of crimes whereof the party shall have been duly convicted: Provided always, that any person escaping into the same, from whom labor or service is lawfully claimed in any one of the original states, such fugitive may be lawfully reclaimed and conveyed to the person claiming his or her labor or service as aforesaid.

Be it ordained by the authority aforesaid, That the resolutions of the 23d of April, 1784, relative to the subject of this ordinance, be, and the same are hereby repealed and declared null and void.

DONE by the UNITED STATES in CONGRESS assembled, the 13th day of July, in the year of our Lord 1787, and of their sovereignty and independence the 12th.

Cha. Thomson secy

The
Constitution
of
The United States
of America

The Constitution of the United States of America

*

IN the earlier years of the Revolution, after the Declaration of Independence, the Continental Congress exercised executive, legislative, and even, to a small extent, judiciary power, without definition of those powers in any formal document. Then the Congress framed the Articles of Confederation, under which the country was governed from March 1, 1781 on. The great defects of this loose league soon became apparent. The central government which it provided had no effectual power to raise money or regulate commerce. It did not operate on individuals, but only on states. It could not compel observance of its treaties, nor effectively execute its decrees. The articles could not be amended but by unanimous consent of all thirteen states. Therefore, after a preliminary convention at Annapolis in 1786, a Federal Convention of representatives from all the states was summoned to meet at Philadelphia on May 14, 1787, and to provide a more effectual union. The Convention chose George Washington as its president. Among the most influential members were James Madison, Alexander Hamilton, James Wilson, William Samuel Johnson, William Paterson, and Charles Pinckney. A tentative plan was laid before the Convention by Governor Edmund Randolph, chairman of the Virginia delegation. This, with three other plans proposed by individuals, was discussed by the Convention for several weeks. The great struggle was over the question whether in the legislative body, the Congress, representation should be by states, as in the Continental Congress, or proportional to population. By a compromise mainly due to the Connecticut members it was settled that there should be equal representation of the states in the Senate, representation proportional to population in the House of Representatives. Then, July 26, the results thus far reached were given over to a Committee of Detail, which, on August 6, reported a draft which, after further discussion and modifications, was on September 8 referred to a committee of five (Johnson, Hamilton, Madison, Rufus King, and Gouverneur Morris) "to revise the style and arrange the articles which had been agreed to by the House." On September 17, 1787, the Constitution in its final form was adopted by the Convention and submitted to the Continental Congress, to be laid before the people of the states. Its last article provided that it should go into effect when it had been ratified by conventions in nine states. After much discussion and struggle this was achieved in the ensuing June and on March 4, 1789, government under the new Constitution began. It is now (with the exception of that of Massachussetts) the oldest political constitution in present operation. Modified in various particulars by some twenty amendments, this Constitution, framed by sagacious leaders for a population of less than four millions, is still in all essentials the fundamental document of a union embracing, one hundred and fifty years later, a population of 130,000,000.

J. FRANKLIN JAMESON
Chief, Division of Manuscripts
LIBRARY OF CONGRESS

WASHINGTON, MAY 1, 1935

AFTER signing, the Constitution of the United States was transferred by President Washington of the Constitutional Convention to President Arthur St. Clair of the Continental Congress. It remained in its custody until the Federal Government was established, March 4, 1789, and placed in charge of the new Department of State.

The seat of the Government was transferred, in 1800, from Philadelphia, Pa., to the District of Columbia; and the Constitution has remained continuously in Washington since that year to the present time, except for the few weeks when it was carried into Virginia, with other governmental records, to escape capture by the British in 1814.

Both the Constitution and the Declaration of Independence were transferred from the Department of State to the Library of Congress by Executive Order, of September 29, 1921, upon the recommendation of the Secretary of State. They were placed on permanent exhibition in the Library of Congress, February 28, 1924, in a Shrine for which Congress appropriated $12,000 (by Act approved March 20, 1922), "For providing a safe, permanent repository of appropriate design, within the Library of Congress Building, for the originals of the Declaration of Independence and the Constitution of the United States."

The Shrine, designed by Mr. Francis H. Bacon, is in the Main Hall, second floor, on the west side.

The photograph of the Constitution, from which this facsimile was made, was taken by Levin C. Handy, Washington, D. C.

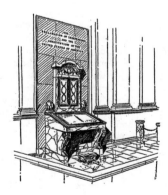

We the People

of the United States, in order to form a more perfect Union, establish Justice, insure domestic Tranquility, provide for the common defence, promote the general Welfare, and secure the Blessings of Liberty to ourselves and our Posterity, do ordain and establish this Constitution for the United States of America.

Article. I.

Section. 1. All legislative Powers herein granted shall be vested in a Congress of the United States, which shall consist of a Senate and House of Representatives.

Section. 2. The House of Representatives shall be composed of Members chosen every second Year by the People of the several States, and the Electors in each State shall have the Qualifications requisite for Electors of the most numerous Branch of the State Legislature.

No Person shall be a Representative who shall not have attained to the Age of twenty five Years, and been seven Years a Citizen of the United States, and who shall not, when elected, be an Inhabitant of that State in which he shall be chosen.

Representatives and direct Taxes shall be apportioned among the several States which may be included within this Union, according to their respective Numbers, which shall be determined by adding to the whole Number of free Persons, including those bound to Service for a Term of Years, and excluding Indians not taxed, three fifths of all other Persons. The actual Enumeration shall be made within three Years after the first Meeting of the Congress of the United States, and within every subsequent Term of ten Years, in such Manner as they shall by Law direct. The Number of Representatives shall not exceed one for every thirty Thousand, but each State shall have at Least one Representative; and until such enumeration shall be made, the State of New Hampshire shall be entitled to chuse three, Massachusetts eight, Rhode Island and Providence Plantations one, Connecticut five, New York six, New Jersey four, Pennsylvania eight, Delaware one, Maryland six, Virginia ten, North Carolina five, South Carolina five, and Georgia three.

When vacancies happen in the Representation from any State, the Executive Authority thereof shall issue Writs of Election to fill such Vacancies.

The House of Representatives shall chuse their Speaker and other Officers; and shall have the sole Power of Impeachment.

Section. 3. The Senate of the United States shall be composed of two Senators from each State, chosen by the Legislature thereof, for six Years; and each Senator shall have one Vote.

Immediately after they shall be assembled in Consequence of the first Election, they shall be divided as equally as may be into three Classes. The Seats of the Senators of the first Class shall be vacated at the Expiration of the second Year, of the second Class at the Expiration of the fourth Year, and of the third Class at the Expiration of the sixth Year, so that one third may be chosen every second Year; and if Vacancies happen by Resignation, or otherwise, during the Recess of the Legislature of any State, the Executive thereof may make temporary Appointments until the next Meeting of the Legislature, which shall then fill such Vacancies.

No Person shall be a Senator who shall not have attained to the Age of thirty Years, and been nine Years a Citizen of the United States, and who shall not, when elected, be an Inhabitant of that State for which he shall be chosen.

The Vice President of the United States shall be President of the Senate, but shall have no Vote, unless they be equally divided.

The Senate shall chuse their other Officers, and also a President pro tempore, in the Absence of the Vice President, or when he shall exercise the Office of President of the United States.

The Senate shall have the sole Power to try all Impeachments. When sitting for that Purpose, they shall be on Oath or Affirmation. When the President of the United States is tried, the Chief Justice shall preside: And no Person shall be convicted without the Concurrence of two thirds of the Members present.

Judgment in Cases of Impeachment shall not extend further than to removal from Office, and disqualification to hold and enjoy any Office of honor, Trust or Profit under the United States: but the Party convicted shall nevertheless be liable and subject to Indictment, Trial, Judgment and Punishment, according to Law.

Section. 4. The Times, Places and Manner of holding Elections for Senators and Representatives, shall be prescribed in each State by the Legislature thereof; but the Congress may at any time by Law make or alter such Regulations, except as to the Places of chusing Senators.

The Congress shall assemble at least once in every Year, and such Meeting shall be on the first Monday in December, unless they shall by Law appoint a different Day.

Section. 5. Each House shall be the Judge of the Elections, Returns and Qualifications of its own Members, and a Majority of each shall constitute a Quorum to do Business; but a smaller Number may adjourn from day to day, and may be authorized to compel the Attendance of absent Members, in such Manner, and under such Penalties as each House may provide.

Each House may determine the Rules of its Proceedings, punish its Members for disorderly Behaviour, and, with the Concurrence of two thirds, expel a Member.

Each House shall keep a Journal of its Proceedings, and from time to time publish the same, excepting such Parts as may in their Judgment require Secrecy; and the Yeas and Nays of the Members of either House on any question shall, at the Desire of one fifth of those Present, be entered on the Journal.

Neither House, during the Session of Congress, shall, without the Consent of the other, adjourn for more than three days, nor to any other Place than that in which the two Houses shall be sitting.

Section. 6. The Senators and Representatives shall receive a Compensation for their Services, to be ascertained by Law, and paid out of the Treasury of the United States. They shall in all Cases, except Treason, Felony and Breach of the Peace, be privileged from Arrest during their Attendance at the Session of their respective Houses, and in going to and returning from the same; and for any Speech or Debate in either House, they shall not be questioned in any other Place.

No Senator or Representative shall, during the Time for which he was elected, be appointed to any civil Office under the Authority of the United States, which shall have been created, or the Emoluments whereof shall have been encreased during such time; and no Person holding any Office under the United States, shall be a Member of either House during his Continuance in office.

Section. 7. All Bills for raising Revenue shall originate in the House of Representatives; but the Senate may propose or concur with Amendments as on other Bills.

Every Bill which shall have passed the House of Representatives and the Senate, shall, before it become a Law, be presented to the President of the

United States; If he approve he shall sign it, but if not he shall return it, with his Objections to that House in which it shall have originated, who shall enter the Objections at large on their Journal, and proceed to reconsider it. If after such Reconsideration two thirds of that House shall agree to pass the Bill, it shall be sent, together with the Objections, to the other House, by which it shall likewise be reconsidered, and if approved by two thirds of that House, it shall become a Law. But in all such Cases the Votes of both Houses shall be determined by yeas and Nays, and the Names of the Persons voting for and against the Bill shall be entered on the Journal of each House respectively. If any Bill shall not be returned by the President within ten Days (Sundays excepted) after it shall have been presented to him, the Same shall be a Law, in like Manner as if he had signed it, unless the Congress by their Adjournment prevent its Return, in which Case it shall not be a Law.

Every Order, Resolution, or Vote to which the Concurrence of the Senate and House of Representatives may be necessary (except on a question of Adjournment) shall be presented to the President of the United States; and before the Same shall take Effect, shall be approved by him, or being disapproved by him, shall be repassed by two thirds of the Senate and House of Representatives, according to the Rules and Limitations prescribed in the Case of a Bill.

Section. 8. The Congress shall have Power To lay and collect Taxes, Duties, Imposts and Excises, to pay the Debts and provide for the common Defence and general Welfare of the United States; but all Duties, Imposts and Excises shall be uniform throughout the United States;

To borrow Money on the credit of the United States;

To regulate Commerce with foreign Nations, and among the several States, and with the Indian Tribes;

To establish an uniform Rule of Naturalization, and uniform Laws on the subject of Bankruptcies throughout the United States;

To coin Money, regulate the Value thereof, and of foreign Coin, and fix the Standard of Weights and Measures;

To provide for the Punishment of counterfeiting the Securities and current Coin of the United States;

To establish Post Offices and post Roads;

To promote the Progress of Science and useful Arts, by securing for limited Times to Authors and Inventors the exclusive Right to their respective Writings and Discoveries;

To constitute Tribunals inferior to the supreme Court;

To define and punish Piracies and Felonies committed on the high Seas, and Offences against the Law of Nations;

To declare War, grant Letters of Marque and Reprisal, and make Rules concerning Captures on Land and Water;

To raise and support Armies, but no Appropriation of Money to that Use shall be for a longer Term than two Years;

To provide and maintain a Navy;

To make Rules for the Government and Regulation of the land and naval Forces;

To provide for calling forth the Militia to execute the Laws of the Union, suppress Insurrections and repel Invasions;

To provide for organizing, arming, and disciplining, the Militia, and for governing such Part of them as may be employed in the Service of the United States, reserving to the States respectively, the Appointment of the Officers, and the Authority of training the Militia according to the discipline prescribed by Congress;

To exercise exclusive Legislation in all Cases whatsoever, over such District (not exceeding ten Miles square) as may, by Cession of particular States, and the Acceptance of Congress, become the Seat of the Government of the United States, and to exercise like Authority over all Places purchased by the Consent of the Legislature of the State in which the Same shall be, for the Erection of Forts, Magazines, Arsenals, dock-Yards, and other needful Buildings;— And

To make all Laws which shall be necessary and proper for carrying into Execution the foregoing Powers, and all other Powers vested by this Constitution in the Government of the United States, or in any Department or Officer thereof.

Section. 9. The Migration or Importation of such Persons as any of the States now existing shall think proper to admit, shall not be prohibited by the Congress prior to the Year one thousand eight hundred and eight, but a Tax or duty may be imposed on such Importation, not exceeding ten dollars for each Person.

The Privilege of the Writ of Habeas Corpus shall not be suspended, unless when in Cases of Rebellion or Invasion the public Safety may require it.

No Bill of Attainder or ex post facto Law shall be passed.

No Capitation, or other direct, Tax shall be laid, unless in Proportion to the Census or Enumeration herein before directed to be taken.

No Tax or Duty shall be laid on Articles exported from any State.

No Preference shall be given by any Regulation of Commerce or Revenue to the Ports of one State over those of another: nor shall Vessels bound to, or from, one State, be obliged to enter, clear, or pay Duties in another.

No Money shall be drawn from the Treasury, but in Consequence of Appropriations made by Law; and a regular Statement and Account of the Receipts and Expenditures of all public Money shall be published from time to time.

No Title of Nobility shall be granted by the United States: And no Person holding any Office of Profit or Trust under them, shall, without the Consent of the Congress, accept of any present, Emolument, Office, or Title, of any kind whatever, from any King, Prince, or foreign State.

Section. 10. No State shall enter into any Treaty, Alliance, or Confederation; grant Letters of Marque and Reprisal; coin Money; emit Bills of Credit; make any Thing but gold and silver Coin a Tender in Payment of Debts; pass any Bill of Attainder, ex post facto Law, or Law impairing the Obligation of Contracts, or grant any Title of Nobility.

No State shall, without the Consent of the Congress, lay any Imposts or Duties on Imports or Exports, except what may be absolutely necessary for executing its inspection Laws: and the net Produce of all Duties and Imposts, laid by any State on Imports or Exports, shall be for the Use of the Treasury of the United States; and all such Laws shall be subject to the Revision and Controul of the Congress.

No State shall, without the Consent of Congress, lay any Duty of Tonnage, keep Troops, or Ships of War in time of Peace, enter into any Agreement or Compact with another State, or with a foreign Power, or engage in War, unless actually invaded, or in such imminent Danger as will not admit of delay.

Article. II.

Section. 1. The executive Power shall be vested in a President of the United States of America. He shall hold his Office during the Term of four Years, and, together with the Vice President, chosen for the same Term, be elected, as follows:

Each State shall appoint, in such Manner as the Legislature thereof may direct, a Number of Electors, equal to the whole Number of Senators and Representatives to which the State may be entitled in the Congress: but no Senator or Representative, or Person holding an Office of Trust or Profit under the United States, shall be appointed an Elector.

The Electors shall meet in their respective States, and vote by Ballot for two Persons, of whom one at least shall not be an Inhabitant of same State with themselves. And they shall make a List of all the Persons voted for, and of the Number of Votes for each; which List they shall sign and certify, and transmit sealed to the Seat of the Government of the United States, directed to the President of the Senate. The President of the Senate shall, in the Presence of the Senate and House of Representatives, open all the Certificates, and the Votes shall then be counted. The Person having the greatest Number of Votes shall be the President, if such Number be a Majority of the whole Number of Electors appointed; and if there be more than one who have such Majority, and have an equal Number of Votes, then the House of Representatives shall immediately chuse by Ballot one of them for President; and if no Person have a Majority, then from the five highest on the List the said House shall in like Manner chuse the President. But in chusing the President, the Votes shall be taken by States, the Representation from each State having one Vote; A quorum for this Purpose shall consist of a Member or Members from two thirds of the States, and a Majority of all the States shall be necessary to a Choice. In every Case, after the Choice of the President, the Person having the greatest Number of Votes of the Electors shall be the Vice President. But if there should remain two or more who have equal Votes, the Senate shall chuse from them by Ballot the Vice President.

The Congress may determine the Time of chusing the Electors, and the Day on which they shall give their Votes; which Day shall be the same throughout the United States.

No Person except a natural born Citizen, or a Citizen of the United States, at the time of the Adoption of this Constitution, shall be eligible to the Office of President; neither shall any Person be eligible to that Office who shall not have attained to the Age of thirty five Years, and been fourteen Years a Resident within the United States.

In Case of the Removal of the President from Office, or of his Death, Resignation, or Inability to discharge the Powers and Duties of the said Office, the Same shall devolve on the Vice President, and the Congress may by Law provide for the Case of Removal, Death, Resignation or Inability, both of the President and Vice President, declaring what Officer shall then act as President, and such Officer shall act accordingly, until the Disability be removed, or a President shall be elected.

The President shall, at stated Times, receive for his Services, a Compensation, which shall neither be increased nor diminished during the Period for which he shall have been elected, and he shall not receive within that Period any other Emolument from the United States, or any of them.

Before he enter on the Execution of his Office, he shall take the following Oath or Affirmation:— "I do solemnly swear (or affirm) that I will faithfully execute the Office of President of the United States, and will to the best of my Ability, preserve, protect and defend the Constitution of the United States."

Section. 2. The President shall be Commander in Chief of the Army and Navy of the United States, and of the Militia of the several States, when called into the actual Service of the United States; he may require the Opinion, in writing, of the principal Officer in each of the executive Departments, upon any Subject relating to the Duties of their respective Offices, and he shall have Power to grant Reprieves and Pardons for Offences against the United States, except in Cases of Impeachment.

He shall have Power, by and with the Advice and Consent of the Senate, to make Treaties, provided two thirds of the Senators present concur; and he shall nominate, and by and with the Advice and Consent of the Senate, shall appoint Ambassadors, other public Ministers and Consuls, Judges of the supreme Court, and all other Officers of the United States, whose Appointments are not herein otherwise provided for, and which shall be established by Law: but the Congress may by Law vest the Appointment of such inferior Officers, as they think proper, in the President alone, in the Courts of Law, or in the Heads of Departments.

The President shall have Power to fill up all Vacancies that may happen during the Recess of the Senate, by granting Commissions which shall expire at the End of their next Session.

Section. 3. He shall from time to time give to the Congress Information of the State of the Union, and recommend to their Consideration such Measures as he shall judge necessary and expedient; he may, on extraordinary Occasions, convene both Houses, or either of them, and in Case of Disagreement between them, with Respect to the Time of Adjournment, he may adjourn them to such Time as he shall think proper; he shall receive Ambassadors and other public Ministers; he shall take Care that the Laws be faithfully executed, and shall Commission all the Officers of the United States.

Section. 4. The President, Vice President and all civil Officers of the United States, shall be removed from Office on Impeachment for, and Conviction of, Treason, Bribery, or other high Crimes and Misdemeanors.

Article III.

Section. 1. The judicial Power of the United States, shall be vested in one supreme Court, and in such inferior Courts as the Congress may from time to time ordain and establish. The Judges, both of the supreme and inferior Courts, shall hold their Offices during good Behaviour, and shall, at stated Times, receive for their Services, a Compensation, which shall not be diminished during their Continuance in Office.

Section. 2. The judicial Power shall extend to all Cases, in Law and Equity, arising under this Constitution, the Laws of the United States, and Treaties made, or which shall be made, under their Authority;— to all Cases affecting Ambassadors, other public Ministers and Consuls;— to all Cases of admiralty and maritime Jurisdiction;— to Controversies to which the United States shall be a Party;— to Controversies between two or more States;— between a State and Citizens of another State;— between Citizens of different States,— between Citizens of the same State claiming Lands under Grants of different States, and between a State, or the Citizens thereof, and foreign States, Citizens or Subjects.

In all Cases affecting Ambassadors, other public Ministers and Consuls, and those in which a State shall be Party, the supreme Court shall have original Jurisdiction. In all the other Cases before mentioned, the supreme Court shall have appellate Jurisdiction, both as to Law and Fact, with such Exceptions, and under such Regulations as the Congress shall make.

The Trial of all Crimes, except in Cases of Impeachment, shall be by Jury; and such Trial shall be held in the State where the said Crimes shall have been committed; but when not committed within any State, the Trial shall be at such Place or Places as the Congress may by Law have directed.

Section. 3. Treason against the United States, shall consist only in levying War against them, or in adhering to their Enemies, giving them Aid and Comfort. No Person shall be convicted of Treason unless on the Testimony of two Witnesses to the same overt Act, or on Confession in open Court.

The Congress shall have Power to declare the Punishment of Treason, but no Attainder of Treason shall work Corruption of Blood, or Forfeiture except during the Life of the Person attainted.

Article IV.

Section. 1. Full Faith and Credit shall be given in each State to the public Acts, Records, and judicial Proceedings of every other State. And the

Congress may by general Laws prescribe the Manner in which such Acts, Records and Proceedings shall be proved, and the Effect thereof.

Section. 2. The Citizens of each State shall be entitled to all Privileges and Immunities of Citizens in the several States.

A Person charged in any State with Treason, Felony, or other Crime, who shall flee from Justice, and be found in another State, shall on Demand of the executive Authority of the State from which he fled, be delivered up, to be removed to the State having Jurisdiction of the Crime.

No Person held to Service or Labour in one State, under the Laws thereof, escaping into another, shall, in Consequence of any Law or Regulation therein, be discharged from such Service or Labour, but shall be delivered up on Claim of the Party to whom such Service or Labour may be due.

Section. 3. New States may be admitted by the Congress into this Union; but no new State shall be formed or erected within the Jurisdiction of any other State; nor any State be formed by the Junction of two or more States, or Parts of States, without the Consent of the Legislatures of the States concerned as well as of the Congress.

The Congress shall have Power to dispose of and make all needful Rules and Regulations respecting the Territory or other Property belonging to the United States; and nothing in this Constitution shall be so construed as to Prejudice any Claims of the United States, or of any particular State.

Section. 4. The United States shall guarantee to every State in this Union a Republican Form of Government, and shall protect each of them against Invasion; and on Application of the Legislature, or of the Executive (when the Legislature cannot be convened) against domestic Violence.

Article. V.

The Congress, whenever two thirds of both Houses shall deem it necessary, shall propose Amendments to this Constitution, or, on the Application of the Legislatures of two thirds of the several States, shall call a Convention for proposing Amendments, which, in either Case, shall be valid to all Intents and Purposes, as Part of this Constitution, when ratified by the Legislatures of three fourths of the several States, or by Conventions in three fourths thereof, as the one or the other Mode of Ratification may be proposed by the Congress; Provided that no Amendment which may be made prior to the Year One thousand eight hundred and eight shall in any Manner affect the first and fourth Clauses in the Ninth Section of the first Article; and that no State, without its Consent, shall be deprived of its equal Suffrage in the Senate.

Article. VI.

All Debts contracted and Engagements entered into, before the Adoption of this Constitution, shall be as valid against the United States under this Constitution, as under the Confederation.

This Constitution, and the Laws of the United States which shall be made in Pursuance thereof; and all Treaties made, or which shall be made, under the Authority of the United States, shall be the supreme Law of the Land; and the Judges in every State shall be bound thereby, any Thing in the Constitution or Laws of any State to the Contrary notwithstanding.

The Senators and Representatives before mentioned, and the Members of the several State Legislatures, and all executive and judicial Officers, both of the United States and of the several States, shall be bound by Oath or Affirmation, to support this Constitution; but no religious Test shall ever be required as a Qualification to any Office or public Trust under the United States.

Article. VII.

The Ratification of the Conventions of nine States, shall be sufficient for the Establishment of this Constitution between the States so ratifying the Same.

The Word "the", being interlined between the seventh and eighth Lines of the first Page, The Word "Thirty" being partly written on an Erazure in the fifteenth Line of the first Page. The Word "is" tried "being interlined between the thirty second and thirty third Lines of the first Page and the Word "the" being interlined between the forty third and forty fourth Lines of the second Page.

done in Convention by the Unanimous Consent of the States present the Seventeenth Day of September in the Year of our Lord one thousand seven hundred and Eighty seven and of the Independence of the United States of America the Twelfth In witness whereof We have hereunto subscribed our Names.

attest William Jackson Secretary

Delaware
Geo: Read
Gunning Bedford jun
John Dickinson
Richard Bassett
Jaco: Broom

Maryland
James McHenry
Dan of St Thos Jenifer
Danl Carroll

Virginia
John Blair—
James Madison Jr.

North Carolina
Wm Blount
Richd Dobbs Spaight.
Hu Williamson

South Carolina
J. Rutledge
Charles Cotesworth Pinckney
Charles Pinckney
Pierce Butler.

Georgia
William Few
Abr Baldwin

G. Washington—Presidt and deputy from Virginia

New Hampshire
John Langdon
Nicholas Gilman

Massachusetts
Nathaniel Gorham
Rufus King

Connecticut
Wm Saml Johnson
Roger Sherman

New York
Alexander Hamilton

New Jersey
Wil: Livingston
David Brearley
Wm Paterson
Jona: Dayton

Pennsylvania
B Franklin
Thomas Mifflin
Robt Morris
Geo. Clymer
Thos FitzSimons
Jared Ingersoll
James Wilson
Gouv Morris

In Convention Monday September 17th. 1787.

Present

The States of

New Hampshire, Massachusetts, Connecticut, Mr. Hamilton from New York, New Jersey, Pennsylvania, Delaware, Maryland, Virginia, North Carolina, South Carolina and Georgia.

Resolved.

That the preceding Constitution be laid before the United States in Congress assembled, and that it is the Opinion of this Convention, that it should afterwards be submitted to a Convention of Delegates, chosen in each State by the People thereof, under the Recommendation of its Legislature, for their Assent and Ratification; and that each Convention assenting to, and ratifying the same, should give Notice thereof to the United States in Congress assembled.

Resolved, That it is the Opinion of this Convention, that as soon as the Conventions of nine States shall have ratified this Constitution, the United States in Congress assembled should fix a Day on which Electors should be appointed by the States which shall have ratified the same, and a Day on which the Electors should assemble to vote for the President, and the Time and Place for commencing Proceedings under this Constitution. That after such Publication the Electors should be appointed, and the Senators and Representatives elected: That the Electors should meet on the Day fixed for the Election of the President, and should transmit their Votes certified, signed, sealed and directed, as the Constitution requires, to the Secretary of the United States in Congress assembled; that the Senators and Representatives should convene at the Time and Place assigned; that the Senators should appoint a President of the Senate, for the sole Purpose of receiving, opening and counting the Votes for President; and, that after he shall be chosen, the Congress, together with the President, should, without Delay, proceed to execute this Constitution.

W. Jackson Secretary.

By the unanimous Order of the Convention

G⁰. Washington Presidt.

297

The Constitution of the United States of America
Amendments

ONE

Congress shall make no law respecting an establishment of religion, or prohibiting the free exercise thereof; or abridging the freedom of speech, or of the press; or the right of the people peaceably to assemble, and to petition the Government for a redress of grievances.

TWO

A well regulated Militia, being necessary to the security of a free State, the right of the people to keep and bear Arms, shall not be infringed.

THREE

No Soldier shall, in time of peace be quartered in any house, without the consent of the Owner, nor in time of war, but in a manner to be prescribed by law.

FOUR

The right of the people to be secure in their persons, houses, papers, and effects, against unreasonable searches and seizures, shall not be violated, and no Warrants shall issue, but upon probable cause, supported by Oath or affirmation, and particularly describing the place to be searched, and the persons or things to be seized.

FIVE

No person shall be held to answer for a capital, or otherwise infamous crime, unless on a presentment or indictment of a Grand Jury, except in cases arising in the land or naval forces, or in the Militia, when in actual service in time of War or public danger; nor shall any person be subject for the same offence to be twice put in jeopardy of life or limb; nor shall be compelled in any criminal case to be a witness against himself, nor be deprived of life, liberty, or property, without due process of law; nor shall private property be taken for public use, without just compensation.

SIX

In all criminal prosecutions, the Accused shall enjoy the right to a speedy and public trial, by an impartial jury of the State and district wherein the crime shall have been committed, which district shall have been previously ascertained by law, and to be informed of the nature and cause of the accusation; to be confronted with the witnesses against him; to have compulsory process for obtaining witnesses in his favor, and to have the Assistance of Counsel for his defence.

SEVEN

In Suits at common law, where the value in controversy shall exceed twenty dollars, the right of trial by jury shall be preserved, and no fact tried by a jury, shall be otherwise re-examined in any court of the United States, than according to the rules of the common law.

EIGHT

Excessive bail shall not be required, nor excessive fines imposed, nor cruel and unusual punishments inflicted.

NINE

The enumeration in the Constitution, of certain rights, shall not be construed to deny or disparage others retained by the people.

TEN

The powers not delegated to the United States by the Constitution, nor prohibited by it to the States, are reserved to the States respectively, or to the people.

ELEVEN

The Judicial power of the United States shall not be construed to extend to any suit in law or equity commenced or prosecuted against one of the United States by Citizens of another State, or by Citizens or Subjects of any Foreign State.

Submitted March 5, 1794. Ratified January 8, 1798

TWELVE

The Electors shall meet in their respective states, and vote by ballot for President and Vice-President, one of whom, at least, shall not be an inhabitant of the same state with themselves; they shall name in their ballots the person voted for as President, and in distinct ballots the person voted for as Vice-President, and they shall make distinct lists of all persons voted for as President, and of all persons voted for as Vice-President, and of the number of votes for each, which lists they shall sign and certify, and transmit sealed to the seat of Government of the United States directed to the president of the Senate;—The president of the Senate shall, in the presence of the Senate and House of Representatives,

★The First Ten Amendments to the Constitution of the United States were submitted to the legislatures of the several states by the First Congress by a resolution passed on the 25th of September, 1789, and were ratified by the States between that date and December 15, 1791.

Congressional Record

United States of America

PROCEEDINGS AND DEBATES OF THE 82^d CONGRESS, FIRST SESSION

he Greatest Subversive Plot in History—Report to the American People on UNESCO

EXTENSION OF REMARKS
OF

HON. JOHN T. WOOD
OF IDAHO

IN THE HOUSE OF REPRESENTATIVES
Thursday, October 18, 1951

Mr. WOOD of Idaho. Mr. Speaker, m herewith appending an article pubsed by the American Flag Committee, Granite Street, Philadelphia, Pa., ring the title "A Report to the erican People on UNESCO."

Now anyone who venerates and loves Glory as the symbol of the deathmarch of the United States through years to fulfill its destiny as a free d independent Republic can read this umented evidence of the greatest most malignant plot in history inst the future of this country, and children's children, is more than I am e to comprehend.

ust how careless and unthinking can be that we permit this band of spies traitors to exist another day in this d we all love? Are there no limits to callousness and neglect of palpable evident treason stalking rampant ough our land, warping the minds imaginations of even our little chiln, to the lying propaganda and palle untruths we allow to be fed to m through this monstrous poison?

t is my sincere hope that every parent very child in America may be able to d the inroads that this infamous plot already made in the educational tem of America, and, reading, may impelled to do something about it, h locally and nationally; and parlarly at the voting booth.

REPORT TO THE AMERICAN PEO-PLE ON UNESCO BY THE AMERICAN FLAG COMMITTEE

NESCO, the United Nations Educational, ntific, and Cultural Organization, is a versive association. It is consciously hering a campaign calculated to pervert teaching profession in this country, and estroy the worth and integrity of Amerifirst bulwark of freedom—our tax-supd public schools.

rong words? Yes, but not strong enough ert you and the American people to a

proper understanding of the UNESCO menace, which, unless met squarely and eradicated by the concerted action of parents, teachers and the general public, may shortly transform our schools into laboratories for the systematic destruction of all sense of national allegiance and loyalty in the minds and hearts of America's school children.

SCHEME TO PERVERT PUBLIC EDUCATION

UNESCO's scheme to pervert public education appears in a series of nine volumes, titled "Toward World Understanding," which presume to instruct kindergarten and elementary grade teachers in the fine art of preparing our youngsters for the day when their first loyalty will be to a world government, of which the United States will form but an administrative part. The booklets bear the following individual numbers and titles:

I. Some Suggestions on Teaching About the U. N. and Its Specialized Agencies.
II. The Education and Training of Teachers.
III. A Selected Bibliography.
IV. The U. N. and World Citizenship.
V. In the Classroom With Children Under 13 Years of Age.
VI. The Influence of Home and Community on Children Under 13 Years of Age
VII. Some Suggestions on the Teaching of Geography.
VIII. A Teachers' Guide to the Declaration of Human Rights.
IX. Some Suggestions on the Teaching of World History.

COLUMBIA HOTBED OF BRITISH FABIANISM

These booklets are cheaply priced for maximum distribution and are printed by Columbia University Press, New York. This seems appropriate, considering the role Columbia's Teachers College has long played in developing new methods for radicalizing and internationalizing public education in this country. The institution has become well-known as a hotbed of British Fabianism, that peculiar type of creeping socialism which sired the present Labor Government which has reduced England to a fourth-rate power and a star boarder in the European section of America's world charity ward.

TEACH DISLOYALTY TO CHILDREN

UNESCO's booklets read like the propaganda put out by United World Federalists, Inc., which has been denied tax exemption because of its specifically political nature.

They begin by advancing the totally un-American doctrina that the prime function of public education in the United States must be that of capturing the minds of our children, at the earliest possible age, for the cause of political world government. The teacher is urged to devote every classroom minute to this end, and every subject taught must serve, or be revised in such a manner that it is made to serve, this same central objective.

The program is quite specific. The teacher is to begin by eliminating any and all words, phrases, descriptions, pictures, maps, classroom material or teaching methods of a sort causing his pupils to feel or express a particular love for, or loyalty to, the United States of America. Children exhibiting such prejudice as a result of prior home influences—UNESCO calls it the outgrowth of the narrow family spirit—are to be dealt an abundant measure of counter propaganda at the earliest possible age. Booklet V, on page 9, advises the teacher that: "The kindergarten or infant school has a significant part to play in the child's education. Not only can it correct many of the errors of home training, but it can also prepare the child for membership, at about the age of seven, in a group of his own age and habits—the first of many such social identifications that he must achieve on his way to membership in the world society."

POISONING THE MINDS OF TEACHERS

Following this same line of attack upon patriotism and its parental encouragement, the same booklet, on pages 58-60, goes on to further poison the minds of our teachers by adding:

"As we have pointed out, it is frequently the family that infects the child with extreme nationalism. The school should therefore use the means described earlier to combat family attitudes that favor jingoism. Education for world-mindedness is not a problem that the school can solve within its own walls or with its own means. It is a political problem even more than an educational one, and the present position of teachers does not, in general, permit them to intervene in the field of politics with the requisite authority. We thought with cautious optimism that educators could also try to influence public opinion. Certain members of our group thought that educators might now besiege the authorities with material demands in the manner of a trade union. In our opinion it is essential that, on the one hand, a children's charter should secure for all children such education as is summarized in this report, which alone can create the atmosphere in which development of world-mindedness is conceivable, and that, on the other hand, a teacher's charter should secure for all members of the teaching profession the liberty to provide such an education by the means they decide upon, as well as the right of access to commissions and councils responsible for the organization of public education."

Aside from encouraging the public school teachers to make war upon the ideals of patriotic national devotion which UNESCO sees as infecting our children in the home, precisely what kind of instruction would the authors of these UNESCO booklets introduce by influencing public opinion, besieging the authorities with material demands in the manner of a trade-union, and by pressing for a Children's Charter and a Teachers' Charter, which refer to instruments prepared in treaty form. making UNESCO principles the supreme law of the United States? Let's see.

TEACHERS URGED TO SUPPRESS AMERICAN HISTORY

First of all, teachers are urged to suppress American history and American geography, which might enhance pro-American sentiments which UNESCO wishes to sterilize. Here is how booklet V, on page 11, treats the problem as it affects children aged 3 to 13 years:

"In our view, history and geography should be taught at this stage as universal history and geography. Of the two, only geography lends itself well to study during the years prescribed by the present survey. The study of history, on the other hand, raises problems of value which are better postponed until the pupil is freed from the nationalist prejudices which at present surround the teaching of history."

Translated into less abstruse phraseology, the teacher is instructed to purge American geography from the elementary school classroom, by divorcing it from its national element, and to completely ignore the teaching of history until the pupil enters high school, since this subject cannot be similarly internationalized, and so is too risky to advance until the youngsters' patriotic spirit has been thoroughly emasculated. Parents who take a bit of time to investigate may find (as we found in eastern Pennsylvania) that a number of elementary schools have already dropped American history as a standard, required subject.

LOGICAL TEACHING METHODS TO BE DISCARDED

Logical and orderly teaching methods are also to be discarded if found to obstruct UNESCO'S program for de-Americanizing the minds and hearts of little children. Discussing the usual method of teaching geography, booklet V, page 11, continues:

"One method much in use now is to teach geography in a series of widening circles, beginning with local geography (i. e., the classroom, the school building and its surroundings, the village, the country) and proceeding to a study of the nation and the continent. Only when that routine has been accomplished is the child introduced to the rest of the world.

"This progress from the particular and the immediate to the general and the remote may be logical, but does it serve our purpose?"

The booklet goes on to conclude that it certainly does not, since it is found that this manner of presentation will lead pupils to the mistaken conclusion that what is nearest to them is the most important and vice versa. UNESCO-indoctrinated teachers must therefore reverse the procedure, upset the rule of logical sequence, and begin by teaching the 3-year old child about the distribution of land and water, of air and sea currents, hydrography, climate, occupations, etc. But, even before this, and certainly before the

youngsters are given any kind of formal study of their own country, every opportunity should be taken to enlarge the child's imagination and encourage him in an interest in all that is remote and strange. This is accomplished by occupying the impressionable mind of the very young child with the games, occupations, tools, domestic animals, etc., of foreign lands. The purpose of this is not simply to teach our kindergarten and elementary pupils about alien peoples, but to cause them to identify themselves in their imagination with people different from themselves.

TRUTH IS TO BE SUPPRESSED

Truth, like orthodox and reasonable teaching methods, is to be suppressed wherever and whenever it stands in the way of glorifying those things which are foreign above those which are particularly American. On page 14, booklet V, there appears the following advice:

"Certain delicate problems, however, will arise in these studies and explorations. Not everything in foreign ways of living can be presented to children in an attractive light. At this stage, though, the systematic examination of countries and manners can be postponed, and the teacher need seek only to insure that his children appreciate, through abundant and judicious examples, that foreign countries, too, possess things of interest and beauty, and that many of them resemble the beauty and interest of his own country. A child taught thus about the different countries of the world will gradually lose those habits of prejudice and contempt which are an impediment to world-mindedness."

And there you have the UNESCO instructions on geography and history: Suppress American studies in these fields; accentuate, by abundant and judicious examples, all that is especially worth while and attractive in foreign modes of living; but, as soon as the point of unfavorable reporting seems to be approaching, simply postpone further study, leaving the children with the false and truly prejudiced notion that the nations of the other continents are paragons of virtue, beauty and over-all perfection.

LIKE A PASSAGE FROM MARX COMMUNIST MANIFESTO

What else does UNESCO's teachers' guides recommend that our little ones be taught? For one thing (booklet V, p. 16), "the methods for putting the resources of the globe at the disposal of all people," which reads like a passage from Marx Communist Manifesto. Following the same line, page 51 of the same work proposes an international anthem for American classrooms (and tomorrow (for) all the inhabitants of the world). It is interesting to note that the booklet we are reviewing was prepared in 1949, and that a United Nations anthem was previewed by the U. N. in 1950, being presented to the public on October 1 of that year in California's giant Hollywood Bowl. The anthem describes how things will be when its flag (the spiderweb banner of the U. N.—editor) waves o'er every land.

We have quoted extensively from booklet V, because it contains the most flagrant of UNESCO's anti-American propaganda, and develops it the most extensively. Now, in the space left us, let's quote from other volumes in the series:

OBJECTIVE: A ONE-WORLD GOVERNMENT

Booklet IV, on pages 13–14, sympathetically deals with the various methods for converting the United Nations into an actual world state. The original concept of the U. N. as an assembly of delegates representing free and sovereign governments is being challenged, teachers are informed, in an ef-

fort to break up the concentration of political power in the hands of national governments, especially the great-power governments, which include the United States and America. There are two alternative proposals. The first, to popularly elect U. N. representatives; the second, to appoint representatives who will be organized specialists in limited fields. The latter proposal follows the Fascist ideology which developed the corporate state of Italy, under Benito Mussolini. UNESCO is not perturbed on this score, however, since "it would be a beginning of functional world government based on transnational rather than international cooperation."

CORRUPTING THE MORALS OF YOUR CHILDREN

Booklet VI contains a series of research suggestions which indicate an intention to stimulate ultimate classroom expedition into the field of detailed sex education. Here are a few samples of the type of questions which UNESCO, which is heavily subsidized by the tax dollars of many Americans who feel that sex training rests within the domain of the home or of the tenets of their own particular religious faith, propounds our public-school teachers: "Are there services * * * for limiting the family?" "What are supposed to be the typical feelings of pregnant women?" "Do parents undress before the child?" "What is he (the child) told about where babies come from? A sense of propriety prohibits us from quoting the even less modest projects which appear with the above.

YOUR JOB AS A LOYAL AMERICAN

Space does not permit us to further examine the other booklets in the series, but this brief analysis should serve to alert any citizen to the menacing nature of UNESCO activities. Once alerted, then, it is his job—your job as a loyal American—to take the next step. Contact your friends and neighbors, show them this Newsletter, ask them to join with you in forming a local committee to obtain further data and fight this danger. Order those nine booklets of UNESCO; also the heavier paper-bound book titled Handbook for the Improvement of Textbooks and Teaching Materials," which suggested another UNESCO project (to eliminate Americanism from schoolroom reading material) which we may deal with in the very near future. Read this material for yourselves; then, as a committee, go into action.

Firstly, prepare your own report and submit it to your local school board. Introduce the matter before your parent-teacher association. Interview the teachers in your community and ask their assistance in obtaining action. Join with the American Flag Committee in demanding that your United States Senators introduce and support legislation withdrawing our Government from UNESCO membership and terminating its activities in this country. Many other ways will occur to you, in which you can help safeguard our American system of public education from infiltration and undermining by UNESCO's America I propagandists.

UNESCO MUST ASSUME RESPONSIBILITY

One further word remains to be added. Several of the booklets discussed bear a preface which states that the views expressed are those of their authors, and that they are not those of the official views of UNESCO. If this weak-kneed attempt to avoid responsibility is brought to your attention by a UNESCO apologist, tell him that one who administers poison to a Nation's youth is guilty of a crime, whether the prescription is official or other.

To the People of the United States.

O. Friends and Fellow-Citizens,

The period for a new election of a citizen, to administer the executive government of the United States, being not far distant; and the time actually arrived, when your thoughts must be employed in designating the person, who is to be cloathed with that important trust, it appears to me proper, especially as it may conduce to a more distinct expression of the public voice, that I should now apprise you of the resolution I have formed, to decline being considered among the number of those, out of whom a choice is to be made. —

I beg you, at the same time, to do me the justice to be assured, that this resolution has not been taken, without a strict regard to all the considerations appertaining to the relation, which binds a dutiful citizen to his Country; and that, in withdrawing the tender of service which silence in my situation might imply, I am influenced by no diminution of zeal for your future interest; no deficiency of grateful respect for your past kindness; but am supported by a full conviction that the step is compatible with both. —

The acceptance of, and continuance hitherto in the office to which your suffrages have twice called me, have been a uniform sacrifice of inclination to the opinion of duty, and to a deference for what appeared to be your desire. I constantly hoped, that it would have been much earlier in my power, consistently with motives, which I was not at liberty to disregard, to return
to

to that retirement, from which I had been reluctantly drawn. The strength of my inclination to do this, previous to the last election, had even led to the preparation of an Address to declare it to you; but mature reflection on the, then perplexed and critical posture of our affairs with foreign nations, and the unanimous advice of persons entitled to my confidence, impelled me to abandon the idea.

I rejoice, that the state of your concerns, external as well as internal, no longer renders the pursuit of inclination incompatible with the sentiment of duty, or propriety; and am persuaded whatever partiality may be retained for my services, that in the present circumstances of our Country, you will not disapprove my determination to retire.

The impressions with which I first undertook the arduous trust, were explained on the proper occasion. In the discharge of this trust, I will only say, that I have with good intentions, contributed towards the organization and administration of the government, the best exertions of which a very fallible judgment was capable. Not unconscious in the outset, of the inferiority of my qualifications, experience in my own eyes, perhaps still more in the eyes of others, has strengthened the motives to diffidence of myself; and every day the encreasing weight of years admonishes me more and more, that the shade of retirement is as necessary to me as it will be welcome. Satisfied that if any circumstances have given peculiar value to my services, they

302

they were temporary, I have the consolation to beleive, that while choice and prudence invite me to quit the political scene, patriotism does not forbid it. —

In looking forward to the moment, which is intended to terminate the career of my public life, my feelings do not permit me to suspend the deep acknowledgment of that debt of gratitude which I owe to my beloved Country, for the many honours it has conferred upon me; still more for the stedfast confidence with which it has supported me; and for the opportunities I have thence enjoyed of manifesting my inviolable attachment, by services faithful and persevering, though in usefulness unequal to my zeal. If benefits have resulted to our Country from these services, let it always be remembered to your praise, and as an instructive example in our annals, that under circumstances in which the passions, agitated in every direction, were liable to mislead, amidst appearances sometimes dubious, — vicissitudes of fortune often discouraging, — in situations in which, not unfrequently want of success has countenanced the spirit of criticism — the constancy of your support was the essential prop of the efforts, and a guarantee of the plans by which they were effected. — Profoundly penetrated with this idea, I shall carry it with me to my grave; as a strong incitement to unceasing vows that Heaven may continue to you the choicest tokens of its beneficence — that your union and brotherly affection may be perpetual — that the free Constitution, which is the work of your hands, may be sacredly maintained — that its administration in every department may be

stamped

stamped with wisdom and virtue — that, in fine, the happiness of the people, of these states, under the auspices of Liberty, may be made complete; by so careful a preservation and so prudent a use of this blessing as will acquire to them the glory of recommending it to the applause, the affection and adoption of every nation which is yet a stranger to it. —

Here, perhaps, I ought to stop. But a solicitude for your welfare, which cannot end but with my life, and the apprehension of danger, natural to that solicitude, urge me on an occasion like the present, to offer to your solemn contempla= tion, and to recommend to your frequent review, some sentiments, which are the result of much reflection, of no inconsiderable observation, and which appear to me all-important to the perma= nency of your felicity as a people. — These will be offered to you with the more freedom, as you can only see in them the disinterested warnings of a parting friend, who can possibly have no personal motive to bias his Council. Nor can I forget, as an encouragement to it, your indulgent reception of my sentiments on a former and not dissimilar occasion. —

Interwoven as is the love of Liberty with every ligament of your hearts, no recom= mendation of mine is necessary to fortify or confirm the attachment.

The unity of Government which constitutes you one people, is also now dear
to

to you. It is justly so; for it is a main pillar in the edifice of your real independence, the support of your tranquility at home, your peace abroad; of your safety; of your prosperity; of that very Liberty which you so highly prize. But as it is easy to foresee, that from different causes and from different quarters, much pains will be taken, many artifices employed, to weaken in your minds the conviction of this truth; as this is the point in your political fortress against which the batteries of internal and external enemies will be most constantly and actively (though often covertly and insidiously) directed, it is of infinite moment, that you should properly estimate the immense value of your national Union, to your collective and individual happiness; that you should cherish a cordial, habitual and immoveable attachment to it; accustoming yourselves to think and speak of it as of the Palladium of your political safety and prosperity; watching for its preservation with jealous anxiety; discountenancing whatever may suggest even a suspicion that it can in any event be abandoned; and indignantly frowning upon the first dawning of every attempt to alienate any portion of our Country from the rest, or to enfeeble the sacred ties which now link together the various parts.—

For this you have every inducement of sympathy and interest. Citizens by birth or choice, of a Common Country, that Country has a right to concentrate your affections.—The name of American, which belongs to you, in your national capacity, must always exalt the just pride of Patriotism, more than any appellation

appellation derived from local discriminations. —
With slight shades of difference, you have the same
religion, manners, habits, and political principles. —
You have in a common cause fought and triumphed
together; the Independence and Liberty you
possess are the work of joint councils, and joint
efforts, of common dangers, sufferings & successes. —

But these considerations, however pow-
erfully they address themselves to your sensibility,
are greatly outweighed by those which apply more
immediately to your interest. — Here every portion
of our Country finds the most commanding motives
for carefully guarding and preserving the Union
of the whole! —

The North, in an unrestrained intercourse with the South, protected by the equal laws
of a common Government, finds in the productions of
the latter, great additional resources of maritime and
commercial enterprise and precious materials of
manufacturing industry. — The South in the same
intercourse benefitting by the Agency of the North,
sees its agriculture grow and its commerce expand.
Turning partly into its own channels the seamen
of the North, it finds its particular navigation invi-
gorated; — and while it contributes, in different ways,
to nourish and increase the General mass of the
national navigation, it looks forward to the protection
of a maritime strength, to which itself is unequally
adapted. — The South, in a like intercourse with the
West, already finds; and in the progressive improvement
of interior communications, by land and water, will
more

more and more find a valuable vent for the commodities which it brings from abroad, or manufactures at home.—The West derives from the East, supplies requisite to its growth and comfort— and what is perhaps of still greater conse= quence, it must of necessity owe the secure enjoyment of indispensable outlets for its own productions to the weight, influence, and the future maritime strength of the Atlantic side of the Union, directed by an indissoluble community of interest as one nation.— Any other tenure by which the West can hold this essential advantage, whether derived from its own seperate strength, or from an apostate and unnatural connection with any foreign power, must be intrinsically precarious.—

            While then every part of our country thus feels an immediate and particular interest in Union, all the parts combined cannot fail to find in the united mass of means and efforts greater strength, greater resource, proportionably greater security from external danger, a less frequent interruption of their peace by foreign nations; and what is of inestimable value! they must derive from Union an exemption from those broils and wars between themselves, which so frequently afflict neighbouring coun= tries, not tied together by the same Government; which their own rivalships alone would be sufficient to produce; but which opposite foreign alliances, attachments and intrigues would stimulate and imbitter:— Hence likewise they will avoid the necessity of those overgrown military establishments, which, under any form of Govern= ment are inauspicious to Liberty, and which are to be regarded as particularly hostile to Republican Liberty; In this sense it is, that your Union ought to be
                                                considered

considered as a main prop of your liberty, and that the love of the one ought to endear to you the preservation of the other.—

These considerations speak a persuasive language to every reflecting and virtuous mind, and exhibit the continuance of the Union as a primary object of Patriotic desire.— Is there a doubt, whether a common government can embrace so large a sphere? — Let experience solve it. To listen to mere speculation in such a case were criminal. We are authorised to hope that a proper organization of the whole, with the auxiliary agency of governments for the respective subdivisions, will afford a happy issue to the experiment. 'Tis well worth a fair and full experiment. With such powerful and obvious motives to Union, affecting all parts of our country, while experience shall not have demonstrated its impracticability, there will always be reason to distrust the patriotism of those, who in any quarter may endeavour to weaken its bands.

In contemplating the causes which may disturb our Union, it occurs as matter of serious concern, that any ground should have been furnished for characterising parties by Geographical discriminations — Northern and Southern — Atlantic and Western; whence designing men may endeavour to excite a belief that there is a real difference of local interests and views. One of the expedients of party to acquire influence, within particular districts, is to misrepresent the opinions and aims of other districts. You cannot shield yourselves too much against the jealousies and heart burnings which spring from these.

these misrepresentations: they tend to render alien to each other those who ought to be bound together by fraternal affection. The inhabitants of our western country have lately had a useful lesson on this head: they have seen, in the negociation by the Executive, and in the unanimous ratification by the Senate, of the Treaty with Spain, and in the universal satisfaction at the event, throughout the United States, a decisive proof how unfounded were the suspicions propagated among them of a policy in the Genral Government and in the Atlantic States unfriendly to their interests in regard to the Mississippi: they have been witnesses to the formation of two treaties, that with great Britain and that with Spain, which secure to them every thing they could desire, in respect to our foreign relations, towards confirming their prosperity. Will it not be their wisdom to rely for the preservation of these advantages on the Union by which they were procured? Will they not henceforth be deaf to those advisers, if such there are, who would sever them from their Brethren and connect them with aliens?

In the efficacy and permanency of your Union a Government for the whole is indispensible — No alliances however strict, between the parts can be an adequate substitute; they must inevitably experience the infractions and interruptions which all alliances in all times have experienced. — Sensible of this momentous truth, you have improved upon your first essay, by the adoption of a Constitution of Government better calculated than your former for an intimate Union, and for the efficacious management of your common concerns. This Government, the offspring of our own choice, uninfluenced and unawed, adopted upon full investigation and mature deliberation, completely free in its

its principles, in the distribution of its powers, uniting security with energy, and containing within itself a provision for its own amendment, has a just claim to your confidence and your support. – Respect for its authority, compliance with its laws, acquiescence in its measures, are duties enjoined by the fundamental maxims of true Liberty. The basis of our political systems is the right of the people to make and to alter their Constitutions of Government – But, the Constitution which at any time exists, 'till changed by an explicit and authentic act of the whole people, is sacredly obligatory upon all. The very idea of the power and the right of the people to establish Government presupposes the duty of every individual to obey the established Government. –

.All obstructions to the execution of the Laws, all combinations and associations, under whatever plausible character, with the real design to direct, controul, counteract, or awe the regular deliberation and action of the constituted authorities, are destructive of this fundamental principle, and of fatal tendency – They serve to organize faction, to give it an artificial and extraordinary force – to put in the place of the delegated will of the nation, the will of party, often a small but artful and enterprising minority of the community; and according to the alternate triumphs of different parties, to make the public administration the mirror of the ill concerted and incongruous projects of faction, rather than the organ of consistent and wholesome plans digested by common councils, and modified by mutual interests. –

However

However combinations or associations of the above description may now and then answer popular ends, they are likely in the course of time and things to become potent engines, by which cunning, ambitious and unprincipled men will be enabled to subvert the power of the people, and to usurp for themselves the reigns of Government; destroying afterwards the very engines which have lifted them to unjust dominion.

Towards the preservation of your Government, and the permanency of your present happy state, it is requisite, not only that you steadily discountenance irregular oppositions to its acknowledged authority, but also that you resist with care the spirit of innovation upon its principles however specious the pretexts. — One method of assault may be to effect in the forms of the constitution alterations, which will impair the energy of the system, and thus to undermine what cannot be directly overthrown. In all the changes to which you may be invited, remember that time and habit are at least as necessary to fix the true character of Governments, as of other human institutions — that experience is the surest standard, by which to test the real tendency of the existing constitution of a country — that facility in changes upon the credit of mere hypothesis and opinion, exposes to perpetual change, from the endless variety of hypothesis and opinion; and remember especially, that for the efficient management of your common interests, in a country so extensive as ours, a Government of as much vigour as is consistent with the perfect security of liberty, is indispensable. Liberty itself, will find in such

a

a government, with powers properly distributed and adjusted, its surest guardian. It is, indeed, little else than a name, where the government is too feble to withstand the enterprises of faction, to confine each member of the Society within the limits prescribed by the laws, and to maintain all in the secure and tranquil enjoyment of the rights of person and property. —

I have already intimated to you, the danger of parties in the state, with particular reference to the founding them on geographical discriminations. Let me now take a more comprehensive view, and warn you in the most solemn manner against the baneful effects of the spirit of party, generally. —

This spirit, unfortunately, is inseperable from our nature, having its root in the strongest passions of the human mind. It exists under different shapes in all governments, more or less stifled, controuled, or repressed; but in those of the popular form, it is seen in its greatest rankness and is truly their worst enemy.

The alternate domination of one faction over another, sharpened by the spirit of revenge, natural to party dissention, which in different ages and countries has perpetrated the most horrid enormities, is itself a frightful despotism. But this leads at length to a more formal and permanent despotism. The disorders and miseries, which result, gradually incline the minds of men to seek security and repose in the absolute power of an individual: and sooner or later the chief of some prevailing faction, more able or more fortunate than his competitors,

turns

turns this disposition to the purposes of his own elevation, on the ruins of Public Liberty.

Without looking forward to an extremity of this kind (which nevertheless ought not to be entirely out of sight) the common and continual mischiefs of the spirit of party are sufficient, to make it the interest and duty of a wise People to discourage and restrain it.

It serves always to distract the public councils and enfeeble the public Administration. It agitates the Community with ill founded jealousies and false alarms; kindles the animosity of one part against another, foments occasionally riot and insurrection. It opens the door to foreign influence and corruption, which finds a facilitated access to the government itself; through the channels of party passions. Thus the policy and the will of one country are subjected to the policy and will of another. —

There is an opinion that parties in free countries are useful checks upon the administration of the Government, and serve to keep alive the spirit of Liberty. — This within certain limits is probably true; and in Governments of a Monarchical cast, Patriotism may look with indulgence, if not with favour upon the spirit of party. But in those of the popular character, in Governments purely elective, it is a spirit not to be encouraged. From their natural tendency, it is certain there will always be enough of that spirit for every salutary purpose. And there being constant danger of excess, the effort ought to be, by force of public opinion, to mitigate and assuage it. A fire not to be quenched; it demands a uniform vigilance to prevent its bursting into a flame, lest, instead of warming it should consume. —

It

It is important likewise, that the habits of thinking in a free country, should inspire caution in those entrusted with its administration, to confine themselves within their respective constitutional spheres, avoiding in the exercise of the powers of one department to encroach upon another. The spirit of encroachment tends to consolidate the powers of all the departments in one, and thus to create, whatever the form of Government, a real despotism. A just estimate of that love of power, and proneness to abuse it, which predominates in the human heart, is sufficient to satisfy us of the truth of this position. The necessity of reciprocal checks, in the exercise of political power; by dividing and distributing it into different depositories, and constituting each the guardian of the public weal against invasions by the others, has been evinced by experiments ancient and modern; some of them in our country and under our own eyes.— To preserve them must be as necessary as to institute them. If, in the opinion of the People, the distribution or modification of the constitutional powers be in any particular wrong, let it be corrected by an amendment in the way which the constitution designates.— But let there be no change by usurpation; for tho' this, in one instance, may be the instrument of good, it is the customary weapon by which free Governments are destroyed.— The precedent must always greatly overbalance in permanent evil any partial or transient benefit which the use can at any time yield.—

Of all the dispositions and habits which lead to political prosperity, Religion and Morality are indispensable supports.— In vain would that

Man

man claim the tribute of patriotism, who should labour to subvert these great pillars of human happiness, these firmest props of the duties of Men and Citizens. — The mere Politician, equally with the pious man ought to respect and to cherish them — A volume could not trace all their connections with private and public felicity. Let it simply be asked where is the security for property, for reputation, for Life, if the sense of religious obligation _desert_ the oaths, which are the instruments of investigation in Courts of justice? And let us with caution indulge the supposition, that morality can be maintained without religion. Whatever may be conceded to the influence of refined education on minds of peculiar structure; reason and experience both forbid us to expect that national morality can prevail in exclusion of religious principle. —

   Tis substantially true, that virtue or morality is a necessary spring of popular government. The rule indeed extends with more or less force to every species of free government. Who that is a sincere friend to it can look with indifference upon attempts to shake the foundation of the fabric?

   (Promote, then, as an object of primary importance, institutions for the general diffusion of knowledge. — In proportion as the structure of a Government gives force to public opinion, it is essential that public opinion should be enlightened. —

   As a very important source of strength and security cherish public credit. One method of preserving it is to use it as sparingly as possible; avoiding occasions of expense by cultivating peace, but remembering also that timely disbursements to prepare for danger frequently

       prevent

prevent much greater disbursements to repel it; avoid=
ing likewise the accumulation of debt, not only by shun=
ning occasions of expense, but by vigorous exertions in
time of peace to discharge the debts which unavoid=
able wars may have occasioned, not ungenerously throw=
ing upon posterity the burthen which we ourselves
ought to bear. — The execution of these maxims belongs
to your representatives, but it is necessary that public
opinion should cooperate. — To facilitate to them the
performance of their duty, it is essential that you should
practically bear in mind, that towards the payment
of debts there must be Revenue: that to have Revenue
there must be taxes; that no taxes can be devised which
are not more or less inconvenient and unpleasant;
that the intrinsic embarrassment, inseparable
from the selection of the proper objects (which is
always a choice of difficulties) ought to be a decisive
motive for a candid construction of the conduct of the
government in making it; and for a spirit of acqui=
escence in the measures for obtaining Revenue which
the public exigencies may at any time dictate. —

    Observe good faith and justice towards all
Nations, cultivate peace and harmony with all; Reli=
gion and Morality enjoin this conduct; and can it be
that good policy does not equally enjoin it? It will be
worthy of a free, enlightened, and, at no distant period,
a great Nation, to give to mankind the magnani=
mous and too novel example of a people always guided
by an exalted justice and benevolence. Who can doubt
that in the course of time & things the fruits of such a plan
would richly repay any temporary advantages which
might be lost by a steady adherence to it? can it be,
that

that Providence has not connected the permanent felicity of a nation with its virtue? The experiment, at least, is recommended by every sentiment which ennobles human nature. Alas! is it rendered impossible by its vices?

In the execution of such a plan, nothing is more essential than that permanent, inveterate antipathies against particular Nations, and passionate attachments for others should be excluded; and that in place of them just and amicable feelings towards all should be cultivated. The Nation, which indulges towards another an habitual hatred, or an habitual fondness, is in some degree a slave. It is a slave to its animosity or to its affection, either of which is sufficient to lead it astray from its duty & its interest. Antipathy in one nation against another disposes each more readily to offer insult and injury, to lay hold of slight causes of umbrage, and to be haughty and intractable, when accidental or trifling occasions of dispute occur. Hence frequent collisions, obstinate, envenomed, and bloody contests. The Nation, prompted by ill will and resentment, sometimes impels to war the Government, contrary to the best calculations of policy. The Government sometimes participates in the national propensity, and adopts through passion what reason would reject; at other times, it makes the animosity of the nation subservient to projects of hostility, instigated by pride, ambition and other sinister and pernicious motives. — The peace, often, sometimes perhaps the liberty, of Nations has been the victim. —

So likewise, a passionate attachment of one Nation for another produces a variety of evils. Sympathy for the favourite Nation, facilitating the illusion of an

imaginary

imaginary common interest, in cases where, no real common interest exists, and infusing into one the enmities of the other, betrays the former into a participation in the quarrels and wars of the latter, without adequate inducement or justification. It leads also to concessions to the favourite Nation of privileges denied to others, which is apt doubly to injure the nation making the concessions; by unnecessarily parting with what ought to have been retained; and by exciting jealousy ill will, and a disposition to retaliate, in the parties from whom equal privileges are withheld: And it gives to ambitious, corrupted, or deluded citizens (who devote themselves to the favorite nation) facility to betray, or sacrifice the interests of their own country, without odium, sometimes even without popularity; gilding with the appearances of a virtuous sense of obligation a commendable deference for public opinion, or a laudable zeal for public good, the base or foolish compliances of ambition, corruption or infatuation. —

As avenues to foreign influence in innumerable ways, such attachments are particularly alarming to the truly enlightened and independent patriot. How many opportunities do they afford to tamper with domestic factions, to practice the arts of seduction, to mislead public opinion, to influence or awe the public Councils! Such an attachment of a small or weak, towards a great and powerful nation, dooms the former to be the satellite of the latter. —

Against the insidious wiles of foreign influence (I conjure you to believe me, fellow-citizens) the jealousy of a free people ought to be <u>constantly awake</u>;

since

since history and experience prove that foreign influence is one of the most baneful foes of Republican Government. — But that jealousy to be useful must be impartial; else it becomes the instrument of the very influence to be avoided, instead of a defence against it. — Excessive partiality for one foreign nation, and excessive dislike of another, cause those whom they actuate to see danger only on one side, and serve to veil and even second the arts of influence on the other. — Real patriots, who may resist the intrigues of the favourite, are liable to become suspected and odious; while its tools and dupes usurp the applause and confidence of the people, to surrender their interests. —

The great rule of conduct for us, in regard to foreign Nations, is in extending our commercial relations, to have with them as little _political_ connection as possible. — So far as we have already formed engagements let them be fulfilled with perfect good faith. — Here let us stop. —

Europe, has a set of primary interests, which to us have none, or a very remote relation. Hence she must be engaged in frequent controversies the causes of which are essentially foreign to our concerns. Hence, therefore, it must be unwise in us to implicate ourselves, by artificial ties, in the ordinary vicissitudes of her politicks, or the ordinary combinations and collisions of her friendships, or enmities. —

Our detached and distant situation invites and enables us to pursue a different course. If we remain one people, under an efficient government, the period is not far off, when we may defy material injury from external annoyance; when we may take such an attitude as will cause the neutrality, we may at any time resolve upon, to be scrupulously respected; when belligerent Nations, under the impossibility of making acquisitions upon us, will not lightly hazard

hazard the giving us provocation; when we may choose peace or war, as our interest, guided by justice, shall counsel. —

Why forego the advantages of so peculiar a situation? Why quit our own to stand upon foreign ground? Why, by interweaving our destiny with that of any part of Europe, entangle our peace and prosperity in the toils of European ambition, rivalship, interest, humour or caprice?

'Tis our true policy to steer clear of permanent alliances, with any portion of the foreign world; so far, I mean, as we are now at liberty to do it; for let me not be understood as capable of patronising infidelity to existing engagements. I hold the maxim no less applicable to public than to private affairs, that honesty is always the best policy. I repeat it, therefore, let those engagements be observed in their genuine sense. But in my opinion, it is unnecessary and would be unwise to extend them. —

Taking care always to keep ourselves, by suitable establishments, on a respectable defensive posture, we may safely trust to temporary alliances for extraordinary emergencies.

Harmony, liberal intercourse with all nations, are recommended by policy, humanity, and interest. But even our commercial policy should hold an equal and impartial hand; neither seeking nor granting exclusive favours or preferences; consulting the natural course of things*; establishing, with powers so disposed, in order to give trade a stable course, to define the rights of our Merchants, and

to

*; diffusing and diversifying by gentle means the stream of commerce, but forcing nothing;

to enable the government to support them; conventional rules of intercourse, the best that present circumstances and mutual opinion will permit, but temporary, and liable to be, from time to time abandoned or varied, as experience and circumstances shall dictate; constantly keeping in view, that 'tis folly in one nation to look for disinterested favours from another; that it must pay with a portion of its independence for whatever it may accept under that character; that by such acceptance, it may place itself in the condition of having given equivalents for nominal favours, and yet of being reproached with ingratitude for not giving more. There can be no greater error than to expect, or calculate upon real favours from nation to nation. 'Tis an illusion which experience must cure, which a just pride ought to discard. —

In offering to you, my Countrymen, these counsels of an old and affectionate friend, I dare not hope they will make the strong and lasting impression I could wish; that they will controul the usual current of the passions, or prevent our nation from running the course which has hitherto marked the destiny of nations: But if I may even flatter myself, that they may be productive of some partial benefit, some occasional good; that they may now and then, recur to moderate the fury of party spirit, to warn against the mischiefs of foreign intrigue, to guard against the impostures of pretended patriotism; this hope will be a full recompence for the solicitude for your welfare, by which they have been dictated. —

How far, in the discharge of my official duties, I have been guided by the principles, which have

been

been delineated, the public records and other evidences of my conduct must witness to you and to the world. To myself, the assurance of my own conscience is, that I have at least believed myself to be guided by them.

In relation to the still subsisting War in Europe, my proclamation of the 22d. of April 1793 is the index to my plan. Sanctioned by your approving voice and by that of your Representatives in both Houses of Congress, the spirit of that measure has continually governed me; uninfluenced by any attempts to deter or divert me from it. —

After deliberate examination, with the aid of the best lights I could obtain, I was well satisfied that our country, under all the circumstances of the case, had a right to take, and was bound in duty and interest, to take a neutral position; — Having taken it, I determined, as far as should depend upon me, to maintain it, with moderation, perseverance and firmness. —

The considerations which respect the right to hold this conduct, it is not necessary on this occasion to detail. — I will only observe, that according to my understanding of the matter, that right, so far from being denied by any of the Belligerent powers, has been virtually admitted by all.

The duty of holding a neutral conduct may be inferred, without any thing more, from the obligation which justice and humanity impose on every nation, in cases in which it is free to act, to maintain inviolate the relations of peace and amity towards other nations. —

The

322

The inducements of interest for observing that conduct will best be referred to your own reflections and experience. With me, a predominant motive has been to endeavour to gain time to our country to settle & mature its yet recent institutions, and to progress without interruption, to that degree of strength and consistency, which is necessary to give it, humanly speaking, the command of its own fortunes. —

Though in reviewing the incidents of my administration, I am unconscious of intentional error: I am nevertheless too sensible of my defects not to think it probable that I may have committed many errors. whatever they may be I fervently beseech the Almighty to avert or mitigate the evils to which they may tend. I shall also carry with me the hope that my Country will never cease to view them with indulgence; and that after forty five years of my life dedicated to its service, with an upright zeal, the faults of incompetent abilities will be consigned to oblivion, as myself must soon be to the mansions of rest. —

Relying on its kindness in this as in other things, and actuated by that fervent love towards it, which is so natural to a man who views in it the native soil of himself and his progenitors for several generations; I anticipate with pleasing expectation that retreat in which I promise myself to realize, without alloy, the sweet enjoyment of partaking, in the midst of my fellow citizens, the benign influence of good laws under a free government—the ever favourite object of my heart, and the happy reward, as I trust, of our mutual cares, labours and dangers. —

United States,
17th September, 1796.⎬   G. Washington.

HIGH FLIGHT FOUNDATION

202 E. Cheyenne Mountain Blvd. • P.O. Box 1387 • Colorado Springs, Colorado 80901-9958

(303) 576-7700

December 21, 1988

Catherine Millard
Christian Heritage Tours, Inc.
6597 Forest Dew Court
Springfield, VA   22152

Dear Catherine,

Thank you for your letter and the invitation to serve on your Board of Reference. If you think the use of my name would be helpful to your work, you may use my name.

You probably know that our efforts have been to discover Ark of Noah, Ark of Covenant, Mt. Horeb, Pharoah's Chariots, ect. So our efforts have been far removed from our country.

We did establish a Christian site on the moon at Hadley Base in 1971. We left a memorial placque of all astronauts and cosmonauts giving their lives up to that time, a "fallen astronaut" and a Bible on the Rover I. We extended our Christian Heritage to another world, the moon.

Your grateful brother from the moon,

James B. Irwin
President

JBI/ji

"Man's flight through life is sustained by the power of *His* knowledge."

FOOTPRINTS ON
THE MOON
Astronaut James Irwin

I felt very special when I looked down at my footprints on the moon. The scientists said that they would be there for a million years. Looking up I could see the earth the size of a marble. It was so beautiful and so far away, and yet, I felt strangely at home on the moon.

When we left the earth, we carried a microfilmed copy of a prayer covenant. It was signed by those in my church.

After returning to earth, people around the world told me, "I prayed for you."

I was aware of that power on the moon. The days I spent on the moon were very exciting. Not because I was there but because God was there. I could feel His presence. There were difficult times when I prayed and the answer was immediate. "He was there because of your prayers," I have told so many.

God guided us to the discovery of the white rock, "The Genesis Rock." It was a modern day revelation. The rock was sitting on another rock almost free from dust. It was lifted up and gleaming in the sunlight. It seemed to be saying "Here am I, take me!" God works in mysterious and wonderful ways. This was a mountaintop experience.

The 1969 Commemorative Stamp, "Earthrise."

My valley experience was in 1961. I had just graduated from test pilot school and considered myself one of the "hottest" pilots in the sky. One morning as I was flying with a student in a light aircraft, we crashed. The plane did not burn, but we were seriously injured – broken legs, broken jaw, many teeth gone, concussion, multiple lacerations. When I awakened in the hospital, doctors told me I probably would not fly again. You can imagine my despair.

I called out to God, "Why did this happen to me?" As I lay in the hospital, I had much time to pray. I prayed for understanding and healing. I knew God loved me. I had invited Jesus Christ to be my Lord and Savior when I was 11 years old. God made it possible for me to fly again.

My love for going fast and high led me to the space program. I prepared for five years for that one flight. It was preparation of body, mind, and spirit. In 1971, ten years after the near tragic accident, I was ready to go to the moon.

When our mission returned, I thanked the men who designed and built our spacecraft, those who helped us operate the systems during the flight, those fellow Americans who payed for our trip, those dear friends around the world who had prayed for our success, and I thanked God for allowing us to leave the earth and explore a portion of His heavens.

The flight medallions carried by Apollo 15 have the following inscription, "Man's flight thru life is sustained by the power of his knowledge." Now I know my flight through life has been sustained by the power of my knowledge of Jesus Christ.

When I was on the moon, I was inspired to quote from Psalm 121, "I will lift up mine eyes unto the hills, from whence cometh my help?" I knew my help was coming from the Lord who made the heavens and the earth. He made the moon and made it possible for Jim Irwin to place his footprints there.

I believe Jesus Christ walking on the earth is more important than man walking on the moon. Just as surely as He walked 2000 years ago, He wants to walk today into your life. All you have to do is call upon Him. He wants you to have life and have it more abundantly. John 10:10. You do this by acknowledging your need of a Savior. Your first prayer must be, "Lord, help me a sinner," and then invite Him into your life by faith. Jesus said, "I am the way, the truth, and the life. No man cometh unto the Father but by me." John 4:6.

I will pray that as you read this you will yield your life to the Master and let Him guide your footprints.

Jim Irwin
APollo 15

APPENDIX I

The Jubilee of the Constitution[1]
John Quincy Adams

In his 1839 discourse entitled, *The Jubilee of the Constitution*, John Quincy Adams, sixth U.S. President, stated:

". . . Resistance, instantaneous, unconcerted, sympathetic, inflexible resistance like an electric shock startled and roused the people of all English colonies on this Continent. This was the first signal of the North American Union. The struggle was for the chartered rights - for English liberties - for the cause of Algernon Sidney and John Hambden – for trial by jury – the Habeas Corpus and Magna Charta.

But the English lawyers had decided that parliament was omnipotent, and Parliament in their omnipotence, instead of trial by jury and the Habeas Corpus, enacted admiralty courts in England to try Americans for offences charged against them as committed in America – instead of the privileges of Magna Charta, nullified the charter itself of Massachusetts Bay, shut up the port of Boston; sent armies and navies to keep the peace, and teach the colonies that John Hambden was a rebel, and Algernon Sidney a traitor. English liberties had failed them. From the omnipotence of Parliament, the colonists appealed to the rights of man and the omnipotence of the God of battles. Union! Union! was the instinctive and simultaneous cry throughout the land. Their Congress assembled at Philadelphia, once – twice had petitioned the king; had remonstrated to Parliament; had addressed the people of Britain, for rights of Englishmen – in vain. Fleets and armies, the blood of Lexington, and the fires of Charlestown and Falmouth, had been the answer to petition, remonstrance and address.

Independence was declared. The colonies were transformed into states. Their inhabitants were proclaimed one people, renouncing all allegiance to the British Crown, all co-patriotism with the British nation; all claims to chartered rights as Englishmen. Thenceforth their charter was the *Declaration of Independence*. Their rights, the natural rights of mankind. Their government, such as should be instituted by themselves, under the solemn mutual pledges of perpetual union, founded on the self-evident truths proclaimed in the Declaration. *The Declaration of Independence* was issued, in the excruciating agonies of a civil war, and by that war independence was to be maintained. Six long years it raged with unabated fury, and the Union was yet no more than a mutual pledge of faith, and a mutual participation of common sufferings and common dangers. The omnipotence of the British Parliament was vanquished. The Independence of the United States of America was not granted, but recognized. The nation had "assumed among the powers of the earth, the separate and equal station, to which the laws of nature and nature's God, entitled it," – but the one, united people had yet NO GOVERNMENT . . .

In these events there had been much controversy upon the platform of English liberties – upon the customs of the ancient Britons; the laws of Alfred, the Witena gamote of the Anglo-Saxons, and the Great Charter of Runnymeade with all its numberless confirmations. But the actors of those times had never ascended to the first foundation of civil society among men, nor had any revolutionary system of government been restored upon them. The motive for the *Declaration of Independence* was on its face avowed to be "a decent respect for the opinions of mankind." Its purpose to declare the causes which impelled the people of the English Colonies on the Continent of North America to separate themselves from the political community of the British Nation.

They declare *only the causes* of their separation, but they announce at the same time their assumption of the separate and equal station to which the laws of nature and nature's God entitle them, among the powers of the earth. Thus their first movement is to recognize and appeal to the laws of nature and to nature's God, for their right to assume the attributes of sovereign power as an independent nation.

The causes of their *necessary* separation, for they begin and end by declaring it necessary, alleged in the Declaration are all founded on the same laws of nature, and nature's God – and hence as prelminary to the enumeration of the causes of separation, they set forth as self-evident truths, the rights of individual man, by the laws of nature and nature's God, to life, to liberty, to the pursuit of happiness. That all men are created *equal.* That to *secure* the rights of life, liberty and the pursuit of happiness, governments are instituted among men, deriving their just powers from the *consent* of the governed. All this, is by the laws of nature and of nature's God, and of course presupposes the existence of a God, the moral ruler of the universe, and a rule of right and wrong, of just and unjust, binding upon man, preceding all institutions of human society and of government. It avers, also, that governments are instituted to *secure* these rights of nature and of nature's God, and that *whenever* any form of government becomes destructive of those ends, it is the right of THE PEOPLE to alter, or to abolish it, and to institute a new government - to throw off a government degenerating into despotism, and to provide new guards for their future security. They proceed then to say that such was then the situation of the colonies, and such the necessity which constrained them to alter their former systems of government.

Then follows the enumeration of the acts of tyranny by which the king, parliament, and the people of Great Britain, had perverted the powers to the destruction of the ends of government, over the Colonies, and the consequent necessity constraining the Colonies to the separation.

In conclusion, the Representatives of the United States of America, in General Congress assembled, appealing to the Supreme Judge of the world for the rectitude of their intentions, do, *in the name and by the authority of the good people of these colonies*, solemnly publish and declare that these United Colonies, are, and of right ought to be, free and independent States; that they are absolved from all allegiance to the British crown; and that all political connection between them and the States of Great Britain, is, and ought to be totally dissolved; and that as free and independent States, they have full power to levy war, conclude peace, contract alliances, establish commerce, and to do all other acts and things which independent States may of *right* do. The appeal to the Supreme Judge of the world, and the rule of right and wrong as paramount events to the power of independent States, are here again repeated in the very act of constituting a new sovereign community.

It is not immaterial to remark, that the signers of the Declaration, though qualifying themselves as the Representatives of the United States of America, in General Congress assembled, yet issue the Declaration, *in the name and by the authority of the good people of the Colonies* - and that they declare, not each of the separate Colonies, but the *United Colonies*, free and independent States. The whole people declared the Colonies in their *united condition*, of RIGHT, free and independent States.

The dissolution of allegiance to the British Crown, the severance of the Colonies from the British Empire, and their actual existence as Independent States, thus declared of *right*, were definitively established *in fact*, by war and peace. The independence of each separate State had never been declared of *right*. It never existed in fact. Upon the principles of the Declaration of Independence, the dissolution of the ties of allegiance, the assumption of sovereign power, and the institution of civil government are all acts of transcendent authority, which the people *alone* are competent to perform – and accordingly, it is in the name and by the authority of the people, that two of these acts – the dissolution of allegiance, with the severance from the British Empire, and the declaration of the United Colonies, as free and independent states, were performed by that instrument.

But there still remained the last and crowning act, which *the people* of the Union, alone were competent to perform – the institution of civil government, for that compound nation, the United States of America . . .

That Committee reported on the 12th of July, eight days after the *Declaration of Independence* had been issued, a draught of Articles of Confederation between the Colonies. This draught was prepared by John Dickinson, then a delegate from Pennsylvania, who voted against the *Declaration of Independence*, and never signed it - having been superceded by a new election of delegates from that State, eight days after his draught was reported.

There was thus no congeniality of principle between the *Declaration of Independence* and the *Articles of Confederation*. The foundation of the former were a superintending Providence – the rights of man, and the Constituent Revolutionary power of the people. That of the latter was the sovereignty of organized power, and the independence of the separate or disunited States. The fabric of the Declaration and that of the Confederation, were each consistent with its own foundation, but they could not form one consistent symmetrical edifice. They were the productions of different minds and of adverse passions – one, ascending for the foundation of human government to the laws of nature and of God, written upon the heart of man – the other, resting upon the basis of human institutions, and prescriptive law and colonial charters. The cornerstone of the one was *right* – that of the other was *power*.

The work of the founders of our Independence was thus but half done. Absorbed in that more than Herculean task of maintaining that independence and its principles, by one of the most cruel wars that ever glutted the furies with human woe, they marched undaunted and steadfast through the fiery ordeal, and consistent in their principles to the end, concluded, as an acknowledged sovereignty of the United States, proclaimed by their people in 1776, a peace with that same monarch, whose sovereignty over them they had abjured in obedience to the laws of nature and nature's God. But for these United States, they had formed no *Constitution*. Instead of resorting to the source of all constituted power, they had wasted their time, their talents, and their persevering, untiring toils, in erecting and roofing and buttressing a frail and temporary shed to shelter the nation from the storm, or rather a more baseless scaffolding on which to stand, when they should raise the marble palace of the people, to stand the test of time.

Five years were consumed by Congress and the State legislatures, in debating and altercating and adjusting the *Articles of Confederation*. The first of which was:

> Each State *retains* its sovereignty, freedom and independence, and every power, jurisdiction and right, which is not by this Confederation expressly delegated to the United States in Congress assembled.

Observe the departure from the language, and the consequent contrast of principles, with those of the *Declaration of Independence*. Each State RETAINS its sovereignty, &c. – where did each State get the sovereignty which it *retains*?

In the *Declaration of Independence*, the delegates of the Colonies in Congress assembled, *in the name and by the authority of the good people of the Colonies*, declare, not each Colony, but the *united* Colonies, in fact, and of right, not *sovereign*, but free and independent States. And why did they make this declaration in the name and by the authority of the one people of all the Colonies? Because by the principles before laid down in the Declaration, the people, and the people alone, as the rightful source of all legitimate government, were competent to dissolve the bands of subjection of all the Colonies to the nation of Great Britain, and to constitute them free and independent States. Now the people of the Colonies, speaking by their delegates in Congress, had not declared *each* Colony a sovereign, free and independent State – nor had the people of each Colony so declared the Colony itself, nor could they so declare it, because each was already bound in union with all the rest; a union formed de facto, by the spontaneous revolutionary movement of the whole people, and organized by the meeting of the first Congress, in 1774, a year and ten months before the *Declaration of Independence*.

Where, then, did *each* State get the sovereignty, freedom and independence, which the *Articles of Confederation* declare it *retains*? Not from the whole people of the whole nation – not from the *Declaration of Independence* – not from the people of the State itself. It was assumed by agreement between the legislatures of the several States, and their delegates in Congress, without authority from or consultation of the people at all.

In the *Declaration of Independence*, the enacting and constituent party dispensing and delegating sovereign power, is the whole people of the United Colonies. The recipient party, invested with power, is the United Colonies, declared United States.

In the *Articles of Confederation*, this order of agency is unmerited. Each State is the constituent and enacting party, and the United States in Congress assembled, the recipient of delegated power – and that power, delegated with such a penurious and carking hand, that it had more the aspect of a revocation of the *Declaration of Independence* than an instrument to carry it into effect.

It well deserves the judicious inquiry of an American statesman, at this time, how this involuntary and unconscious usurpation upon the rights of the people of the United States, originated and was pursued to its consummation.

In July, 1775, soon after the meeting of the Second Revolutionary Congress, and a year before the *Declaration of Independence*, Dr. Franklin had submitted to their consideration, a sketch of the *Articles of Confederation* between the Colonies, to continue until their reconciliation with Great Britain, and in failure of that event, to be perpetual.

The third article of that project provided "that each Colony shall enjoy and retain as much as it may think fit, of its own present laws, customs, rights, privileges, and peculiar jurisdictions *within its own limits*; and may amend its own constitution, as shall seem best to its own assembly or convention." Here was and could be no assertion of sovereignty . . .

Washington, though in retirement, was brooding over the cruel injustice suffered by his associates in arms, the warriors of the Revolution; over the prostration of the public credit and the faith of the nation, in the neglect to provide for the payment even of the interest upon the public debt; over the disappointed hopes of the friends of freedom; in the address from Congress to the States of the 18th of April, 1783 - "the pride and boast of America, that the rights for which she contended were the rights of human nature."

At his residence of Mount Vernon, in March, 1785, the first idea was started of a revisal of the *Articles of Confederation*, by an organization of means differing from that of a compact between the State Legislatures and their own delegates in Congress. A Convention of delegates from the State Legislatures, independent of Congress itself, was the expedient which presented itself for effecting the purpose, and an augmentation of the powers of Congress for the regulation of commerce, as the object for which this assembly was to be convened.

In January, 1786, the proposal was made and adopted in the Legislature of Virginia, and communicated to the other State Legislatures.

The Convention was held at Annapolis, in September of that year. It was attended by the delegates from only five of the central States, who, on comparing their restricted powers, with the glaring and universally acknowledged defects of the Confederation, reported only a recommendation for the assemblage of another Convention of delegates to meet in Philadelphia, in May, 1787, from all the States and with enlarged powers.

The Constitution of the United States was the work of this Convention. But in its construction the Convention immediately perceived that they must retrace their steps, and fall back from a league of friendship between the sovereign States, to the constituent sovereignty of *the people*; from *power* to *right* – from the irresponsible despotism of State sovereignty, to the self-evident truths of the *Declaration of Independence*. In that instrument, the right to institute and alter governments among men was ascribed exclusively to *the people* – the ends of government were declared to be to *secure* the natural rights of man; and that *when* the government degenerates from the promotion to the destruction of that end, the right and the duty accrues to the people, to dissolve this degenerate government and to institute another . . .

A Constitution for the people, and the distribution of the legislative, executive and judicial powers was prepared. It announced itself as the work of the people themselves; . . ."

APPENDIX II

Statuary Hall - The National Hall of Fame

In 1857, the new wing of the U.S. House of Representatives was constructed.

On April 19, 1864, the following proposition came from the Honorable Justin S. Morrell of the U.S. House of Representatives:

> To what end more useful or grand, and at the same time simple and inexpensive, can we devote it (the Old House Chamber) than to ordain that it shall be set apart for the reception of such statuary as each State shall elect to be deserving of this lasting commemoration?

The creation of a *National Statuary Hall (Hall of Fame)* became law on July 2, 1864 (Sec. 1814 of the Revised Statutes), as follows:

> And the President is hereby authorized to invite each and all of the States to provide and furnish statues, in marble or bronze, not exceeding two in number for each State, of deceased persons who have been citizens thereof, and illustrious for their historic renown or for distinguished civic or military services such as each State may deem to be worth of this national commemoration; and when so furnished the same shall be placed in the Old Hall of the House of Representatives, in the Capitol of the United States, which is set apart, or so much thereof as may be necessary, as a National Statuary Hall for the purpose herein indicated.

By 1933, 65 statues had been accepted into *Statuary Hall (The National Hall of Fame)*. Each one had to be voted upon for acceptance by the United States Congress. However, it became apparent that the chamber could not handle the number of statues initially planned for. Furthermore, the Chamber structure could not accomodate their excessive weight.

On February 24, 1933, by House Concurrent Resolution No. 47, the following Act of Congress became law:

> Resolved by the House of Representatives (The Senate concurring), That the Architect of the Capitol, upon the approval of the Joint Committee on the Library, with the advice of the Commission of Fine Arts, is hereby authorized and directed to relocate within the Capitol any of the statues already received and placed in Statuary Hall, and to provide for the reception and location of the statues received hereafter from the States.

As a result, it was decided that only one statue from each State should be included in Statuary Hall, and that the others would be assigned to prominent locations within the U.S. Capitol.

Below is a list of the 96 statues that have been contributed by our 50 United States. Four States - Nevada, New Mexico, North Dakota, and Wyoming, have sent just one statue to represent them in the U.S. Capitol's Hall of Fame:

THE NATIONAL HALL OF FAME

Statue	State	Sculptor	Medium	Location
Adams, Samuel	Massachusetts	Anne Whitney	Marble	Statuary Hall
Allen, Ethan	Vermont	Larkin G. Mead	Marble	Statuary Hall
Allen, William	Ohio	Charles H. Niehaus	Marble	Statuary Hall
Austin, Stephen F.	Texas	Elisabet Ney	Marble	Small House Rotunda
Aycock, Charles Brantley	North Carolina	Charles Keck	Bronze	Hall of Columns
Bartlett, E. L. "Bob"	Alaska	Felix W. de Weldon	Bronze	House connecting corridor
Beadle, William H.	South Dakota	H. Daniel Webster	Bronze	Statuary Hall
Benton, Thomas H.	Missouri	Alexander Doyle	Marble	Statuary Hall
Blair, Francis P., Jr.	Missouri	Alexander Doyle	Marble	Hall of Columns
Borah, William E.	Idaho	Bryant Baker	Bronze	Senate connecting corridor
Bryan, William Jennings	Nebraska	Rudulph Evans	Bronze	Statuary Hall
Burke, John	North Dakota	Avard Fairbanks	Bronze	Statuary Hall
Calhoun, John C.	South Carolina	Frederic W. Ruckstull	Marble	Statuary Hall
Carroll, Charles, of Carrollton	Maryland	Richard E. Brooks	Bronze	Statuary Hall
Cass, Lewis	Michigan	Daniel Chester French	Marble	Statuary Hall
Chandler, Zachariah	Michigan	Charles H. Niehaus	Marble	Hall of Columns
Chavez, Dennis	New Mexico	Felix W. de Weldon	Bronze	Vestibule north of Rotunda
Clarke, James P.	Arkansas	Pompeo Coppini	Marble	Hall of Columns
Clay, Henry	Kentucky	Charles H. Niehaus	Bronze	Statuary Hall
Clayton, John M.	Delaware	Bryant Baker	Marble	Senate connecting corridor
Clinton, George	New York	Henry Kirke Brown	Bronze	Small House Rotunda
Collamer, Jacob	Vermont	Preston Powers	Marble	Hall of Columns
Curry, Jabez Lamar Monroe	Alabama	Dante Sodini	Marble	Hall of Columns
Damien, Father	Hawaii	Marisol Escobar	Bronze	Hall of Columns
Davis, Jefferson	Mississippi	Augustus Lukeman	Bronze	Statuary Hall
Farnsworth, Philo T.	Utah	James R. Avati	Bronze	House connecting corridor
Fulton, Robert	Pennsylvania	Howard Roberts	Marble	Statuary Hall
Garfield, James A.	Ohio	Charles H. Niehaus	Marble	Rotunda
George, James Z.	Mississippi	Augustus Lukeman	Bronze	Hall of Columns
Glick, George W.	Kansas	Charles H. Niehaus	Marble	Hall of Columns
Gorrie, John, M.D.	Florida	C. A. Pillars	Marble	Statuary Hall
Greene, Nathanael	Rhode Island	Henry Kirke Brown	Marble	Vestibule north of Rotunda
Greenway, John C.	Arizona	Gutzon Borglum	Bronze	Statuary Hall
Gruening, Ernest	Alaska	George Anthonison	Bronze	Hall of Columns
Hamlin, Hannibal	Maine	Charles E. Tefft	Bronze	Statuary Hall
Hampton, Wade	South Carolina	Frederic W. Ruckstull	Marble	House connecting corridor
Hanson, John	Maryland	Richard E. Brooks	Bronze	Senate connecting corridor

Statue	State	Sculptor	Medium	Location
Harlan, James	Iowa	Nellie V. Walker	Bronze	Hall of Columns
Houston, Samuel	Texas	Elisabet Ney	Marble	Statuary Hall
Ingalls, John J.	Kansas	Charles H. Niehaus	Marble	Statuary Hall
Jackson, Andrew	Tennessee	Belle K. Scholz & Leopold Scholz	Bronze	Rotunda
Joseph, Mother	Washington	Felix de Weldon	Bronze	Hall of Columns
Kamehameha I	Hawaii	Thomas R. Gould	Bronze	Statuary Hall
Kearny, Philip	New Jersey	Henry Kirke Brown	Bronze	Hall of Columns
Kenna, John E.	West Virginia	Alexander Doyle	Marble	Hall of Columns
King, Thomas Starr	California	Haig Patigian	Bronze	Hall of Columns
King, William	Maine	Franklin Simmons	Marble	House connecting corridor
Kino, Eusebio F.	Arizona	Suzanne Silvercruys	Bronze	Hall of Columns
Kirkwood, Samuel J.	Iowa	Vinnie Ream	Bronze	Statuary Hall
La Follette, Robert M., Sr.	Wisconsin	Jo Davidson	Marble	Statuary Hall
Lee, Rev. Jason	Oregon	Gifford Proctor	Bronze	Statuary Hall
Lee, Robert E.	Virginia	Edward V. Valentine	Bronze	Statuary Hall
Livingston, Robert R.	New York	Erastus Dow Palmer	Bronze	Statuary Hall
Long, Dr. Crawford W.	Georgia	J. Massey Rhind	Marble	Senate connecting corridor
Long, Huey P.	Louisiana	Charles Keck	Bronze	Statuary Hall
Marquette, Pere Jacques	Wisconsin	Gaetano Trentanove	Marble	House connecting corridor
McCarran, Patrick A.	Nevada	Yolande Jacobson	Bronze	Statuary Hall vestibule north
McDowell, Dr. Ephraim	Kentucky	Charles H. Niehaus	Bronze	Senate connecting corridor
McLoughlin, Dr. John	Oregon	Gifford Proctor	Bronze	House connecting corridor
Morris, Esther H.	Wyoming	Avard Fairbanks	Bronze	Statuary Hall vestibule north
Morton, J. Sterling	Nebraska	Rudulph Evans	Bronze	Hall of Columns
Morton, Oliver P.	Indiana	Charles H. Niehaus	Marble	Hall of Columns
Muhlenberg, John Peter G.	Pennsylvania	Blanche Nevin	Marble	Small House Rotunda
Pierpont, Francis H.	West Virginia	Franklin Simmons	Marble	Statuary Hall
Rankin, Jeanette	Montana	Terry Minmaugh	Bronze	House connecting corridor
Rice, Henry Mower	Minnesota	Frederick E. Triebel	Marble	Statuary Hall
Rodney, Caeser	Delaware	Bryant Baker	Marble	Statuary Hall
Rogers, Will	Oklahoma	Jo Davidson	Bronze	House connecting corridor
Rose, Uriah M.	Arkansas	Frederic W. Ruckstull	Marble	Statuary Hall
Sabin, Dr. Florence	Colorado	Joy Buba	Bronze	Statuary Hall
Sanford, Maria L.	Minnesota	Evelyn Raymond	Bronze	Senate connecting corridor

Statue	State	Sculptor	Medium	Location
Sequoyah (Sequoya)	Oklahoma	Vinnie Ream (completed by G. Julian Zolnay)	Bronze	Statuary Hall
Serra, Junipero	California	Ettore Cadorin	Bronze	Statuary Hall
Sevier, John	Tennessee	Belle K. Scholz & Leopold Scholz	Bronze	Statuary Hall
Sherman, Roger	Connecticut	Chauncey B. Ives	Marble	Statuary Hall
Shields, Gen. James	Illinois	Leonard W. Volk	Bronze	Hall of Columns
Shoup, George L.	Idaho	Frederick E. Triebel	Marble	Statuary Hall
Smith, Gen. E. Kirby	Florida	C. Adrian Pillars	Bronze	Hall of Columns
Stark, John	New Hampshire	Carl Conrads	Marble	Vestibule north of Rotunda
Stephens, Alexander H.	Georgia	Gutzon Borglum	Marble	Statuary Hall
Stockton, Richard	New Jersey	Henry Kirke Brown	Marble	Statuary Hall
Swigert, Jack	Colorado	George and Mark Lundeen	Bronze	Rotunda
Trumbull, Jonathan	Connecticut	Chauncey B. Ives	Marble	House connecting corridor
Vance, Zebulon Baird	North Carolina	Gutzon Borglum	Bronze	Statuary Hall
Wallace, General Lew	Indiana	Andrew O'Connor	Marble	Statuary Hall
Ward, Joseph	South Dakota	Bruno Beghe´	Marble	Hall of Columns
Washington, George	Virginia	Jean Antoine Houdon	Bronze	Rotunda
Webster, Daniel	New Hampshire	Carl Conrads (after Thomas Ball)	Marble	Statuary Hall
Wheeler, General Joseph	Alabama	Berthold Nebel	Bronze	Statuary Hall
White, Edward Douglass	Louisiana	Arthur C. Morgan	Bronze	Senate connecting corridor
Whitman, Marcus	Washington	Avard Fairbanks	Bronze	Statuary Hall
Willard, Frances E.	Illinois	Helen Farnsworth Mears	Marble	Statuary Hall
Williams, Roger	Rhode Island	Franklin Simmons	Marble	Statuary Hall
Winthrop, John	Massachusetts	Richard S. Greenough	Marble	Hall of Columns
Young, Brigham	Utah	Mahonri Young	Marble	Statuary Hall

INDEX

A

B

C

D

E

F

G

H

ACKNOWLEDGMENTS

Gratitude is expressed to the following officers, organizations and historic associations, for their invaluable help and assistance in formulating this book:

The Delaware Public Archives, Hall of Records
John Y. Brown III, Secretary of State, Commonwealth of Kentucky
Wayne R. Douglas, Chief Counsel, State of Maine
Frank Keating, Governor of Oklahoma
Rebecca Vigil-Giron, Secretary of State, New Mexico
The Minnesota Historical Society Library
Alvin A. Jaeger, Secretary of State, North Dakota
Miren E. Artiach, Deputy Secretary of State, Idaho
Susan Bysiewicz, Secretary of State, Connecticut
Fran Ulmer, Lieutenant Governor of Alaska
Bill Jones, Secretary of State, California
R. Gwenn Stearn, State Archivist, Rhode Island and
    Providence Plantations

About the Author

Catherine Millard, B.A., M.A., D.Min. in Christian Education, is the founder and president of Christian Heritage Tours, Inc. and Christian Heritage Ministries. She has spent seventeen years as a scholar at the Library of Congress, researching the authentic Christian history and heritage of the United States. In 1995, she was elected to "Who's Who among students in American Universities and Colleges" for outstanding academic achievement in the realm of Christian education. Dr. Millard is also the recipient of the 1990 George Washington Honor Medal and the 1992 Faith and Freedom Religious Heritage of America Award, for significant contributions in affirming and strengthening the Biblical principles in American life.

She is the author of eight books on America's original history, *God's Signature Over the Nation's Capital, The Rewriting of America's History, A Children's Companion Guide to America's History, Great American Statesmen and Heroes, The Christian Heritage of Our Nation History Curricula - National Landmarks; National Memorials,* and *U.S. Presidents and Their Churches*; as well as six video documentaries on the subject. Dr. Millard has lectured and taught the original Christian heritage and history of America extensively in colleges, universities and schools throughout the nation.

If you or your group is going to be in the Washington, D.C. area; Philadelphia, Valley Forge or Gettysburg, Pennsylvania; or Jamestown, Williamsburg, Yorktown, Virginia and would like to take part in an exciting tour that points out the true history of our country, complete with references to the Biblical foundations of our land, contact Christian Heritage Tours, Inc., 6597 Forest Dew Court, Springfield, Virginia 22152, or call (703) 455-0333.

Catherine Millard is also available to provide teaching seminars, lectures, and multi-media presentations to your school or organization, on the subject of America's Christian heritage and history. You may contact her through the above address.

FOR ADDITIONAL COPIES OF
The Christian Heritage of the 50 United States of America
call or write Christian Heritage Ministries
or contact your local Christian bookstore.
www.christianheritagetours.com
www.christianheritagemins.org
(703) 455-0333